STATES, THE LAW AND ACCESS TO REFUGEE PROTECTION

This timely volume seeks to examine two of the most pertinent current challenges faced by asylum seekers in gaining access to international refugee protection: first, the obstacles to physical access to territory and, second, the barriers to accessing a quality asylum procedure—which the editors have termed 'access to asylum justice'. To address these aims, the book brings together leading commentators from a range of backgrounds, including law, sociology and political science. It also includes contributions from NGO practitioners. This allows the collection to offer interdisciplinary analysis and to incorporate both theoretical and practical perspectives on questions of immense contemporary significance. While the examination offers a strong focus on European legal and policy developments, the book also addresses the issues in different regions (Europe, North America, the Middle East, Africa and Australia). Given the currency of the questions under debate, this book will be essential reading for all scholars in the field of asylum law.

Volume 65 in the series Studies in International Law

Studies in International Law

Recent titles in this series

Democratic Statehood in International Law: The Emergence of New States in Post-Cold War Practice
Jure Vidmar

International Law and the Construction of the Liberal Peace
Russell Buchan

The OIC, the UN, and Counter-Terrorism Law-Making: Conflicting or Cooperative Legal Orders?
Katja Samuel

Statelessness: The Enigma of the International Community
William E Conklin

The Reception of Asylum Seekers under International Law: Between Sovereignty and Equality
Lieneke Slingenberg

International Law and Child Soldiers
Gus Waschefort

The Contractual Nature of the Optional Clause
Gunnar Törber

Non-State Actors in International Law
Edited by Math Noortmann, August Reinisch and Cedric Ryngaert

The Rule of Law at the National and International Levels: Contestations and Deference
Edited by Machiko Kanetake and André Nollkaemper

Human Rights Obligations of Non-State Armed Groups
Daragh Murray

Security and International Law
Edited by Mary E Footer, Julia Schmidt and Nigel D White

Complicity and its Limits in the Law of International Responsibility
Vladyslav Lanovoy

Complicity in International Criminal Law
Marina Aksenova

For the complete list of titles in this series, see 'Studies in International Law' link at www.hartpub.co.uk/books/series.asp

States, the Law and Access to Refugee Protection

Fortresses and Fairness

Edited by
Maria O'Sullivan and Dallal Stevens

·HART·
PUBLISHING
OXFORD AND PORTLAND, OREGON
2017

Hart Publishing
An imprint of Bloomsbury Publishing Plc

Hart Publishing Ltd
Kemp House
Chawley Park
Cumnor Hill
Oxford OX2 9PH
UK

Bloomsbury Publishing Plc
50 Bedford Square
London
WC1B 3DP
UK

www.hartpub.co.uk
www.bloomsbury.com

Published in North America (US and Canada) by
Hart Publishing
c/o International Specialized Book Services
920 NE 58th Avenue, Suite 300
Portland, OR 97213-3786
USA

www.isbs.com

First published 2017

British Library Cataloguing-in-Publication Data
A catalogue record for this book is available from the British Library.

ISBN: HB: 978-1-50990-128-9
ePDF: 978-1-50990-129-6
ePub: 978-1-50990-130-2

A catalogue record for this book is available from the Library of Congress.

Series: Studies in International Law, volume 65

Typeset by Compuscript Ltd, Shannon
Printed and bound in Great Britain by TJ International Ltd, Padstow, Cornwall

Preface

This book brings together a number of commissioned contributions by leading commentators in the field of asylum law, including a selection of the best papers presented at an international conference organised by Maria O'Sullivan and Susan Kneebone on refugee law and policy at the Monash Prato Centre in Italy in 2014 entitled 'Access to Asylum: Current Challenges and Future Directions'. The volume examines what we consider to be two of the most pertinent current challenges faced by asylum seekers in gaining access to international refugee protection: first, the obstacles to physical access to territory and, second, the barriers to accessing a fair and effective asylum procedure—which we have termed 'access to asylum justice'. In doing so, we have attempted to give readers a broad perspective on these issues. Thus, we chose contributors from a range of backgrounds, including academics from the fields of law, sociology and political science. We also sought the invaluable practical insight of non-governmental organisation (NGO) practitioners. Furthermore, while there is analysis of European legal and policy developments, the book also addresses law and practice in different regions including South Africa, the Middle East (Lebanon), Australia and the United States (US). Within Europe, we have included practical insights from the important border states of Hungary, Bosnia and Herzegovina and Croatia.

Refugee law and policy is a fast-moving area of law. We have made every attempt to provide an up-to-date analysis of the issues. To that end, the book deals with recent jurisprudence and developments that have not yet been analysed to any significant extent in the literature, such as the new asylum legislation in Turkey (the Law on Foreigners and International Protection 2014); the decision of the UK Supreme Court on fast track procedures (*Detention Action v Secretary of State for the Home Department* 2014); the decision of the High Court of Australia on the applicability of procedural fairness to the detention of asylum seekers at sea (*CPCF v Minister for Immigration and Border Protection* 2015), and the fluctuating legal approach to asylum seekers in the Levant countries of the Middle East. The information contained herein is accurate as of 30 June 2016.

We take this opportunity to thank a number of people for their contribution. We are grateful to Hart Publishing for commissioning the book and to Hart editorial staff: Bill Asquith, Sinead Moloney and Emily Braggins for their valued work on the volume. We acknowledge the contributors for their excellent chapters in this book. Particular recognition is given to those working in small NGOs who devoted their personal time to this endeavour when, in some cases, confronting extremely difficult circumstances of increased migration to Europe in 2015–16. We also thank Susan Kneebone for her role in organising the conference, which was the springboard to this volume, and Natalie Kyneswood, who worked closely with us for several months undertaking the final formatting and style guide checks. Her assistance was invaluable.

Finally, we express our gratitude to our institutions—Faculty of Law, Monash University and the School of Law, University of Warwick—for their ongoing support of our research and work in the areas of asylum and refugee law and policy.

Maria O'Sullivan
Faculty of Law, Monash University
Melbourne, Australia

Dallal Stevens
School of Law, University of Warwick
Coventry, United Kingdom
July 2016

Contents

Part II: Access to Territory

List of Editors and Contributors

The Editors

Dr Maria O'Sullivan is a Senior Lecturer in the Faculty of Law and an Associate of the Castan Centre for Human Rights Law at Monash University, Australia. She teaches Administrative Law, International Refugee Law and the Law of Armed Conflict. Prior to commencing her academic career, Maria worked as a Legal Adviser to the Australian Refugee Review Tribunal and is an Associate Member of the International Association for Refugee Law Judges. Her research focuses on a comparative analysis of Australian and European refugee law and practice. Maria's publications include 'The Ethics of Resettlement: Australia and the Asia-Pacific Region' (2016) 20(2) *International Journal of Human Rights* and 'Non-state Actors of Protection in Refugee law' (2012) 24(1) *International Journal of Refugee Law*. Her work has been cited by the High Court of Australia and in various reports of the Australian Parliament on refugee legislation. She is also a regular contributor to media commentary and community debate on asylum in Australia.

Dr Dallal Stevens is a Reader and Director of Research at the School of Law, University of Warwick. Her research interests focus on refugee and asylum law and policy. She has published numerous books, peer reviewed journal articles, book chapters and reports, including *UK Asylum Law and Policy: Historical and Contemporary Perspectives* (Sweet & Maxwell, 2004) and *Refugee Protection and the Role of Law: Conflicting Identities* (Routledge, 2014) edited with Susan Kneebone and Loretta Baldassar. Recently, she has been considering the impact of globalisation on asylum and her current research is concerned with the protection of refugees and forced migrants in the Middle East, and the movement of people across the Mediterranean to Europe. Stevens' work has been supported by external grants from the British Academy, the Arts and Humanities Research Board, and the ESRC. She has acted as an adviser to a number of national bodies, including the Home Office and Parliament and has served as a trustee for the former immigration law advisory agency in the UK—the Immigration Advisory Service—and for the Electronic Immigration Network. Stevens is on the editorial board of the *Journal of Immigration, Asylum and Nationality Law* and *Law and Humanities*.

The Contributors

Deborah Anker is Clinical Professor of Law and Director of the Harvard Law School Immigration and Refugee Clinical Program (HIRC). She has taught law students at Harvard for over 25 years. Author of a leading treatise, *Law of Asylum in the United States*, Anker has co-drafted groundbreaking gender asylum guidelines and *amicus curiae* briefs. Professor Anker is one of the most widely known asylum scholars and practitioners in the United States; she is cited frequently by international and domestic courts and tribunals, including the United States Supreme Court. Deborah Anker is a pioneer in the development of clinical legal education in the immigration field, training students in direct representation of refugees and creating a foundation for clinics at law schools around the country.

Sergio Carciotto has been the Director of the Scalabrini Institute for Human Mobility in Africa (SIHMA), a research centre based in Cape Town, since its establishment in April 2014. Sergio previously worked in South Africa for local NGOs and in Italy for the United Nations High Commissioner for Refugees. He holds an MA Degree in Development Studies from the University of the Western Cape in South Africa and an MA Degree in Refugee Rights and Migration Studies from La Sapienza University in Rome.

Nadine El-Enany is Senior Lecturer at Birkbeck School of Law, University of London, where she co-directs the Centre for Research on Law and Race. Nadine teaches and researches in the fields of migration law, European Union law and criminal justice. She has published widely in the field of EU asylum and immigration law. Her current research focuses on questions of race and criminal and social justice in migration, protest and death in custody cases. Nadine is Chair of the Runnymede Trust Emerging Scholars Race Forum. She has written for Media Diversified, the Guardian, London Review of Books, Truthout, Left Foot Forward and Critical Legal Thinking.

Nula Frei is working as a research associate at the Centre for Migration Law and the Swiss Centre of Expertise in Human Rights at the University of Bern, Switzerland. She has studied law and political science at the Universities of Bern, Fribourg, Zurich and Lille and is currently working on a PhD thesis on Identification and Protection of Victims of Human Trafficking in Asylum Procedures from a Human Rights Perspective.

Constantin Hruschka studied law, history and philosophy in Würzburg, Poitiers and Paris. Subsequently he worked as a scientific researcher at the Universities of Würzburg and Munich. After his bar exam in 2002, he also started working as a lawyer in Munich. Constantin is currently on special leave from the UNHCR where he worked as Associate Protection Officer in the UNHCR Office in Nuremberg (2004–09) and thereafter as Legal Officer in the Office for Switzerland and Liechtenstein prior to joining the Policy Development and Evaluation Service (PDES) of UNHCR in Geneva (2013–14). Currently he works as the Head of the Protection department at the Swiss Refugee Council (OSAR) and is a Member of the Swiss Federal Commission on Migration (FCM). He is also a lecturer for European Law and European Asylum Law at the Universities of Fribourg (Switzerland) and Bielefeld (Germany).

Júlia Iván holds a Masters in Law and Political Sciences in 2006 at the Eötvös Lóránd University in Budapest. She worked at the Hungarian Helsinki Committee (HHC) for nine years (2007–16) as a legal officer in the refugee programme. She was in charge of co-ordinating the lawyers' network of the HHC, which deals with several hundreds of asylum applicants each year. As a co-ordinator she was responsible for providing strategic guidance and updates on international legal developments for practitioners. Her main areas of work were drafting human rights reports on Hungary, on access to protection in the UNHCR-funded border monitoring programme and the protection of unaccompanied minor refugees. Besides individual case management and project co-ordination she also regularly delivered training to border guards, lawyers and judges with the HHC. She continues to work as an independent legal expert and researcher on migration.

Corey R Johnson holds a BSc in Political Science from the University of Wyoming, an MA in International Policy from La Trobe University and an LLM in Human Rights Law from Monash University. He currently works in the Advocacy Programme at the Scalabrini Centre of Cape Town and has worked with refugees and migrants in Australia and South Africa.

Linda Kirk is the Deputy Director and Sub-Dean of the Migration Law Program at the ANU College of Law, Australian National University, and a Visiting Fellow of the Refugee Law Initiative, School of Advanced Study, University of London. She was a Senior Member of the Australian Migration Review Tribunal and the Refugee Review Tribunal from 2009–14. From 2002–08 she was a Senator for South Australia and the Deputy Chair of the Joint Standing Committee on Migration of the Australian Parliament. Linda was the Chair of the Australasian Chapter of the International Association of Refugee Law Judges (IARLJ) from October 2011 to July 2016, and is now a member of the Committee of the Asia-Pacific Chapter of the IARLJ. She is currently enrolled on the Doctor of Juridical Science degree at Monash University, and is writing her dissertation on consistency in refugee status determination.

Maggie Morgan is the Albert M Sacks Clinical & Advocacy Fellow at the Harvard Immigration and Refugee Clinic (HIRC). She previously worked as a Clinical Fellow in the Health Law & Policy Clinic at Harvard Law School and clerked for the Honourable Nanette K Laughrey of the Western District of Missouri. She is a 2011 graduate of Harvard Law School, where she was a clinical student in HIRC and the Human Rights Clinic and interned at several international organisations including Asylum Access in Tanzania and the Supreme Court of Rwanda. Before law school, she earned an MA in International Relations at the University of Chicago, conducted research on the plight of migrant labourers in Jalisco, Mexico, and taught in Korea and Spain. She earned her AB from Harvard College, specialising in Government.

Kris Pollet is a senior legal and policy officer at the European Council on Refugees and Exiles (ECRE); a pan-European network of 82 organisations assisting asylum seekers and refugees in 37 European countries. Before joining ECRE he worked as a legal officer at Amnesty International's EU Office and the Flemish Refugee Council and as a research assistant at the European Institute, Faculty of Law, University of Gent. He is currently coordinating ECRE's legal and policy work on the Common European Asylum System as well as with regard to the activities of EASO and Frontex.

Selma Porobić holds a double MD and a PhD degree in Migration Studies focusing on forced migration from Lund University, Sweden, and is a Director of Centre for Refugee and IDP studies at the Faculty of Political Sciences, University of Sarajevo, Bosnia and Herzegovina. She has over 10 years' academic experience in the field and has produced a number of papers, books and educational events focusing on refugee experiences, psychological impacts of forced migration, forced migration research methods and refugee protection. Her current research interests range from return migration to Bosnia and other post-conflict areas, to asylum and refugee integration policies and practices in the Western Balkans region.

Cavidan Soykan works in the Faculty of Political Science Human Rights Centre at Ankara University. She has completed a PhD in Sociology at the University of Essex and holds a Bachelor and a Master's degree in Politics from Ankara University as well as certificates in International Human Rights Law from the European University Institute and the International Institute of Human Rights. The focus of her doctoral research is on Turkey's asylum system, exploring how it works and how asylum applicants experience it. Through the in-depth interviews with asylum applicants mainly from Iran, Iraq, Afghanistan, Somalia and Sudan, her study aims to explore people's asylum trajectories and the lived experiences of asylum and migration law in Turkey.

Drago Župarić-Iljić holds an MA degree in Sociology and Social Anthropology from the Central European University in Budapest, Hungary. He is currently a PhD candidate in Sociology at the Faculty of Humanities and

Social Sciences, University of Zagreb (Croatia). He works at the Institute for Migration and Ethnic Studies in Zagreb as a junior research assistant. He has published articles, books and reports in the field of forced migration, asylum and refugee studies, as well as on the topics of ethno-national minorities and foreigners' integration policies and implemented practices in Croatia.

Abbreviations

AAT	Administrative Appeal Tribunal (Australia)
AATA	Administrative Appeals Tribunal Act 1975 (Australia)
AIDA	Asylum Information Database
AITP	Act on International and Temporary Protection (Croatia)
ANC	African National Congress
BiH	Bosnia and Herzegovina
CAT	Convention Against Torture and Other Cruel Inhuman or Degrading Treatment or Punishment
CBP	Customs and Border Patrol (US)
CEAS	Common European Asylum System
CEDAW	Convention on the Elimination of all Forms of Discrimination Against Women
CJ	Chief Justice
CJEU	Court of Justice of the European Union
COI	Country of Origin Information
CoE	Council of Europe
CPT	Council of Europe's Committee for the Prevention of Torture and Inhuman or Degrading Treatment or Punishment
CRC	Convention on the Rights of the Child
CTRRO	Cape Town Refugee Reception Office
DFT	Detained Fast Track (UK)
DFID	Department for International Development (UK)
DGMM	Directorate General of Migration Management (Turkey)
DIBP	Department of Immigration and Border Protection (Australia)
DNSA	Detained Non-Suspensive Appeals (UK)
DPA	Dayton Peace Accords
EASO	European Asylum Support Office
ECHR	European Convention on Human Rights
ECRE	European Council on Refugees and Exiles
ECtHR	European Court of Human Rights
EMN	European Migration Network

EPIM	European Program for Integration and Migration
EU	European Union
Ex Comm	Executive Committee of the High Commissioner's Programme
FCC	Federal Circuit Court (Australia)
FRA	Fundamental Rights Agency
FTP	Fast Track Procedure (Australia)
FTR	Asylum and Immigration Tribunal Fast Track Procedure Rules 2005 (UK)
FTT	First Tier Tribunal (Immigration and Asylum Chamber) (UK)
GDP	Gross Domestic Product
GPS	Global Positioning System
HCA	High Court of Australia
HHC	Hungarian Helsinki Committee
IAA	Immigration Assessment Authority (Australia)
IAAAS	Immigration Advice and Application Assistance Scheme (Australia)
ICCPR	International Covenant on Civil and Political Rights
IDP	Internally Displaced Persons
ILO	International Labour Office
IMF	International Monetary Fund
IOM	International Organisation for Migration
NAAU	National Asylum Allocation Unit (UK)
NIA	Nationality Immigration and Asylum Act 2002 (UK)
NGO	Non-Governmental Organisation
MA	Migration Act 1958 (Australia)
MHRR	Ministry of Human Rights and Refugees (BiH)
MoI	Ministry of Interior (Croatia)
MoS	Ministry of Security (BiH)
MP	Member of Parliament
MPA	Maritime Powers Act 2013 (Australia)
MRD	Migration and Refugee Division of the AAT (Australia)
MSAAA	Movement and Stay of Aliens and Asylum Act (BiH)
OAU	Organisation of African Unity
ODIHR	Office for Democratic Institutions and Human Rights (OSCE)
OFPRA	*L'Office français de protection des réfugiés et apatrides*

OHCHR	Office of the United Nations High Commissioner for Human Rights
OIN	Office of Immigration and Nationality (Hungary)
OSCE	Organisation for Security and Cooperation in Europe
PAIG	Protection Application Information and Guides (Australia)
PJCHR	Parliamentary Joint Committee on Human Rights (Australia)
PSO	Protection Screening Officer (US)
RMA	Registered Migration Agent (Australia)
RRO	Refugee Reception Offices (South Africa)
RRT	Refugee Review Tribunal (Australia)
RRO	Refugee Reception Offices (South Africa)
RSD	Refugee Status Determination
RSDO	Refugee Status Determination Officer (South Africa)
SCA	Supreme Court of Appeal (South Africa)
SSHD	Secretary of State for the Home Department (UK)
TEU	Treaty on European Union
TFEU	Treaty on the Functioning of the European Union
TPC	Tribunal Procedure Committee
UDHR	Universal Declaration of Human Rights
UK	United Kingdom
UMAs	Unlawful Maritime Arrivals (Australia)
UNODC	United Nations Office on Drugs and Crime
UNCLOS	United Nations Convention on the Law of the Sea
UNHCR	United Nations High Commissioner for Refugees
US	United States
USAID	United States Agency for International Development
WB	Western Balkans

Part I

Conceptual Background

1

Access to Refugee Protection

Key Concepts and Contemporary Challenges

MARIA O'SULLIVAN AND DALLAL STEVENS

I. INTRODUCTION

THIS VOLUME SEEKS to address two of the most pertinent current challenges faced by asylum seekers in gaining access to international refugee protection: the obstacles to *physical* access to territory and the barriers to accessing a quality asylum *procedure* (which we have termed 'access to asylum justice')—'Fortresses and Fairness'.

Current figures show that there are 21.3 million refugees worldwide.[1] However, there is a reluctance on the part of many industrialised states to provide protection to such refugees with an increasing tendency of those states to deflect refugee flows. As is widely recognised, developing countries and those neighbouring refugee-producing states bear an unfair share of hosting refugees.[2] Contemporary practices of deflection include physical deterrence such as the erection of border fences, push-backs at sea and offshore processing, as well as procedural deterrence such as limitations on procedural fairness, accelerated procedures, at-sea screening and reductions in legal assistance. In Europe, the various deterrent policies utilised by some countries, such as the erection of fences and the 'push-back' of asylum seekers crossing by sea clearly restrict access to territory.[3] This problem has become particularly acute in recent years due to the Syrian refugee crisis with over 4 million people now displaced

[1] UNHCR, 'Global Trends: Forced Displacement in 2015' (Geneva, UNHCR 2016), 2 www.unhcr.org/statistics/unhcrstats/576408cd7/unhcr-global-trends-2015.html.

[2] ibid.

[3] eg Amnesty International, 'Refugees Endangered and Dying Due to EU's Reliance on Fences and Gatekeepers' (News, Amnesty International, 17 November 2015) www.amnesty.org.au/news/comments/38426/.

outside Syria,[4] but with many European states now maintaining a largely 'closed door' policy.[5] In 2015 there was a fracturing of the European Union (EU) Common European Asylum System (CEAS), with Germany seemingly willing to accept large numbers of Syrian refugees while key European border states such as Bulgaria and Hungary elected instead to erect border fences and introduce criminal sanctions for irregular entry to stop the arrival of asylum seekers.[6] In the Middle East, by contrast, the 'fortress' mentality is arguably less pronounced and refugees are able to enter neighbouring countries, but they often have fewer rights and face numerous challenges including lack of security of status and residence.[7] Similarly in South Africa, whilst large numbers of asylum seekers have been able to cross the border and claim asylum in the past,[8] they face long delays in the processing of claims. Recent policy changes have now also established institutional barriers to asylum, including restrictions limiting physical access at the border and at refugee processing centres.[9] In South-East Asia, the United Nations High Commissioner for Refugees (UNHCR) has also reported that some states have introduced increasingly restrictive policies, such as denying safe disembarkation, and have narrowed protection space and access to asylum.[10]

[4] UNHCR, 'Syria Regional Refugee Response—Inter-agency Information Sharing Portal' (UNHCR, 2016) www.data.unhcr.org/syrianrefugees/regional.php. This records the number of registered Syrian refugees as 4.8 million, comprised of 2.1 million Syrians registered by UNHCR in Egypt, Iraq, Jordan and Lebanon; 2.7 million Syrians registered by the Government of Turkey; as well as more than 29,000 Syrian refugees registered in North Africa (figures current as at 2 June 2016).

[5] See A Brasseur, President of the Parliamentary Assembly of the Council of Europe, 'Europe Slamming Its Doors on Refugees: Is This Really What Europe is About?' (Press Release, Council of Europe, 22 January 2016); J Dempsey, 'Merkel's Open-Door Refugee Policy Leaves Her Isolated' (Newsweek, 22 January 2016) www.newsweek.com/merkels-open-door-refugee-policy-leaves-her-isolated-418446.

[6] Bulgaria has erected a fence along its border with Turkey: see C Mortimer, 'Bulgaria Builds Final Part of Razor Wire Fence to Keep Out Refugees' (London, The Independent, 4 August 2015) www.independent.co.uk/news/world/europe/bulgaria-builds-final-part-of-razor-wire-fence-to-keep-out-refugees-10437962.html. See discussion of Hungary's practice in Iván, ch 3. Slovenia has also begun construction of a border fence: see The Guardian, 'Slovenia Starts Building Fence to Control Flow of Refugees' (London, The Guardian, 11 November 2015) www.theguardian.com/world/2015/nov/11/slovenia-fence-refugees-veliki-obrez.

[7] See further discussion of the Middle East in Stevens, ch 10. See also D Stevens, 'Shifting Conceptions of Refugee Identity and Protection: European and Middle Eastern Approaches' in S Kneebone, D Stevens and L Baldassar (eds), *Refugee Protection and the Role of Law* (Cambridge, Cambridge University Press, 2014) ch 5; D Stevens, 'Legal Status, Labelling and Protection: the Case of Iraqi "Refugees" in Jordan' (2013) 25 *International Journal of Refugee Law* 1, 1–38.

[8] The numbers of asylum seekers and refugees residing in South Africa is high. As at June 2015, UNHCR reports there were 114,512 recognised refugees and 798,080 asylum seekers: UNHCR, 'Mid Year Trends 2015' (Geneva, UNHCR, 2015) www.unhcr.org/statistics/unhcrstats/56701b969/mid-year-trends-june-2015.html.

[9] The position in South Africa is discussed in further detail by Johnson and Carciotto, ch 8.

[10] UNHCR, 'UNHCR Global Appeal 2015 Update—South-East Asia', 2015, www.unhcr.org/5461e60a558.pdf.

Access to territory is, of course, no guarantee of fairness or of justice. Many states seek to reduce both the time and costs of refugee status determination, with potentially serious implications for decision-making.[11] For instance, accelerated screening procedures operate in a number of EU countries and have recently been introduced into Australian law. Questions have been raised by the United Kingdom (UK) courts as to the appropriateness of fast tracking applicants and whether they can be afforded a fair opportunity to make an asylum claim.[12] Similarly, concerns arise in relation to the operation of the expedited removal process by United States (US) immigration authorities which is based on an assessment as to whether the person has a 'credible fear' of persecution.[13]

Asylum seekers consequently face two main challenges in the current international environment—difficulties in obtaining physical access to state territory to claim asylum and a significant reduction in rights and access to justice upon entry into a state's territory. These challenges raise the following questions: how can states be persuaded to open their borders to asylum applicants? What are the components of a quality asylum procedure? Is legal advice a prerequisite for asylum access to justice? Can accelerated 'screening' procedures suffice? What has been the impact of law on the implementation of refugee protection in practice?

The purpose of this chapter is to outline some of the key concepts analysed in this volume and to bring together the themes discussed by contributors. Section II considers the broad concepts central to the concept of asylum: 'asylum' and 'refugee protection'. Section III then discusses in greater detail the concepts and challenges relating to access to territory, such as 'states' and 'borders'. A focus of this analysis will be on the force of law in defining borders and the right of entry. This is followed by an analysis in Section IV of the concepts of asylum justice and contemporary due process challenges, including discussion of legal assistance, procedural fairness and the implications of the introduction in key asylum states of accelerated procedures.

II. BACKGROUND: 'ASYLUM' AND 'REFUGEE PROTECTION'

We acknowledge that many of the concepts within the asylum debate are contested—for instance, what does 'asylum' now mean and what is the level and quality of protection required to be granted to asylum seekers and refugees? It is generally agreed that 'asylum' is a broad term with a

[11] eg the reforms introduced in Australian legislation via the Migration and Maritime Powers (Resolving the Asylum Caseload) Act 2014, discussed by Kirk, ch 11.

[12] Discussed by Kirk, ch 11.

[13] Discussed by Morgan and Anker, ch 6.

number of definitions.[14] At a minimum, it may be interpreted as a state of refuge that gives protection from immediate harm.[15] Likewise, the term 'protection' is interpreted differently across jurisdictions and varies according to context.[16] At one end of the spectrum, asylum comprises full protection pursuant to the obligations set out in the the 1951 United Nations Convention relating to the Status of Refugees[17] (Refugee Convention), including *non-refoulement* and refugee associated rights such as the right to work and social security.[18] At the other end, it can also mean lesser forms of protection such as temporary protection and 'tolerated' stay or forms of temporary humanitarian sanctuary which offer little more than a right of 'non-return'.[19] This raises the question as to whether non-return is becoming the cornerstone of asylum and at what stage it requires additional rights such as some form of integration into the host state. On this issue, Alexander Betts has pointed out that:

> [A]n important element of protection is the access of refugees to a timely resolution (durable solution) to their predicament; that is, rather than refugees remaining indefinitely in a state of limbo without citizenship or residency, they should be fully reintegrated into a state.[20]

Whether states are willing to meet such obligations is addressed in this collection.

[14] 'The term "asylum" has no clear or agreed meaning': A Grahl-Madsen, *Territorial Asylum* (Stockholm, Almqvist and Wiksell International, 1980) 50. See for a discussion of asylum in international law, M-T Gil-Bazo, 'Asylum as a General Principle of International Law' (2015) 27 *International Journal of Refugee Law* 1, 3–28. For an ethical analysis of asylum, see J-F Durieux, 'Three Asylum Paradigms' (2013) 20 *International Journal on Minority and Group Rights* 147.

[15] As Roman Boed notes, 'Historically, asylum has been regarded as a place of refuge where one could be free from the reach of a pursuer': R Boed, 'The State of The Right of Asylum In International Law' (1994) 5(1) *Duke Journal of Comparative and International Law* 1, 2.

[16] See for discussion of the concept of 'protection', D Stevens, 'What Do We Mean by Protection?' (2013) 20 *International Journal on Minority and Group Rights* 233.

[17] 189 United Nations Treaty Series 150, supplemented by the 1967 Protocol relating to the Status of Refugees, 606 United Nations Treaty Series 267 (Refugee Convention). Art 39(2)–(3) provides that signature and accession to the Convention is open only to states (specifically, those states who participated in the Convention drafting process or who are Member States of the UN).

[18] Refugee Convention, above n 17, Arts 17, 24. Some states offer temporary residence permits which have restricted work rights, eg Finland where temporary residence is granted for a period of one year at a time and holders of such permits have a restricted right to employment pursuant to the Aliens Act: European Migration Network (EMN), 'Ad-hoc Query on Implementing Tolerated-Stay Requested by EE EMN NCP on 8th April 2014' (EMN, 3 July 2014) www.ec.europa.eu/dgs/home-affairs/what-we-do/networks/european_migration_network/reports/docs/ad-hoc-queries/illegal-immigration/549_emn_ahq_on_implementing_tolerated_stay_03072014_en.pdf.

[19] See I Máximo Pestana, '"Tolerated Stay": What Protection Does It Give?' (2012) 40 *Forced Migration Review* 38, www.fmreview.org/en/young-and-out-of-place/pestana.pdf; EMN (2014) above n 18.

[20] A Betts, *Protection by Persuasion* (Ithaca, Cornell University Press, 2009) 6.

A. Meaning of Asylum

A number of writers have sought to explain the meaning and contours of asylum. In 1950, the Institute of International Law defined asylum as 'the protection that a State grants on its territory or in some other place under the control of its organs to a person who comes to seek it'.[21] Guy Goodwin-Gill and Jane McAdam describe asylum as the 'protection granted to foreign national against the exercise of jurisdiction by another state' but also recognise that a more contemporary interpretation regards asylum as 'protection against harm, specifically violations of fundamental human rights'.[22] Matthew Price, in his book *Rethinking Asylum: History, Purpose and Limits*, traces the development of the concept of asylum from the early Grecian period to the present day, thereby providing a critical historical perspective to sanctuary seeking. He concludes that 'asylum should be reserved for those exposed to serious harm because they *lack political membership*' (emphasis in original),[23] and distinguishes temporary protection from asylum by noting that '[a]sylum confers a *political* good—*membership*' whereas recipients of temporary protection are simply given permission to remain in the country for a period of time.[24] This is of interest given the increasing use of temporary protection, temporary residence permits and 'humanitarian protection/right to remain' by asylum host states which may give only limited rights of protection. For instance, as Dallal Stevens discusses in Chapter 10, in the Middle East refugees are able to enter neighbouring countries, but they often have fewer rights and face numerous challenges including lack of security of status and residence due, in part, to the fact that many countries in the region have resisted signing the Refugee Convention.[25] Turkey has sought to address the Syrian refugee influx (at 2.7 million as at mid-2016)[26] by introducing a temporary protection regime, but its effectiveness is questionable.[27]

In discussing the concept of asylum, one must also consider the confluence made by states between immigration and asylum. As Nadine

[21] Institute of International Law, 'Asylum in Public International Law' (Bath Session, 5th Commission, September 1950) art 1.

[22] GS Goodwin-Gill and J McAdam, *The Refugee in International Law* (Oxford, Oxford University Press, 2007) 356.

[23] ibid 431.

[24] ME Price, 'Persecution Complex: Justifying Asylum Law's Preference for Persecuted People' (2006) 47 *Harvard International Law Journal* 413, 431.

[25] Note that Turkey is an exception and is party to the Refugee Convention but applies the geographical limitation to Europe. However, Turkey has recently introduced a new law—Law on Foreigners and International Protection, Law No 6458, 4 April 2013 and Regulation 29153 on Temporary Protection—which spell out a new approach and rights for Syrian refugees in Turkey. This is discussed further by Soykan in ch 4.

[26] UNHCR (2016) above n 4.

[27] See Soykan, ch 4.

El-Enany discusses in Chapter 2, the emergence of administrative immigration regimes, both in the UK and at the EU level, has led to asylum becoming imbricated in immigration law. Restrictive immigration and border control, both in the UK and at the EU level, has grown in strength and substance over recent decades. As El-Enany notes, the result has been the gradual attenuation, even subversion, of the protective potential of asylum. This is a problem recognised also by writers in other texts. For instance, in the US, Rebecca Hamlin notes that 'asylum is eclipsed by the much larger and politically contentious issue of undocumented migration, mostly from Mexico'.[28]

B. Right to Seek Asylum

In terms of access to asylum, there are questions about a right to seek asylum, the protections provided by the principle of *non-refoulement* and the right to seek asylum in a country of one's own choosing. Under international human rights principles, asylum seekers have the right to seek asylum: Article 14 of the Universal Declaration of Human Rights (UDHR) provides that '[e]veryone has the right to seek and to enjoy asylum from persecution in other countries'.[29] However, the UDHR is generally regarded as a non-binding instrument. Thus, many commentators acknowledge that there is no recognised right under international refugee law to seek and obtain asylum.[30] The Refugee Convention also obliges states not to return refugees back to a place of harm under the *non-refoulement* principle.[31] Due to these provisions, it is arguable that asylum seekers have a right to seek asylum. However, the notion that there is a right to seek asylum in a country of one's *choosing* is contested.[32]

[28] R Hamlin, *Let Me Be a Refugee: Administrative Justice and the Politics of Asylum in the United States, Canada and Australia* (Oxford, Oxford University Press, 2014) 8.

[29] UDHR, art 14 provides that '[e]veryone has the right to seek and to enjoy asylum from persecution in other countries': UNGA Res 217A (III), 10 December 1948.

[30] The Refugee Convention does not contain a specific right to seek asylum. As Goodwin-Gill notes: 'The principle of *non-refoulement*—the obligation on states not to send individuals to territories in which they may be persecuted, or in which they are at risk of torture or other serious harm—may not immediately correlate with the right of every one to seek asylum, but it does clearly place limits on what states may lawfully do': G Goodwin-Gill, 'The Right to Seek Asylum: Interception at Sea and the Principle of Non-Refoulement' (2011) 23 *International Journal of Refugee Law* 443, 444. See also R Boed, 'The State of the Right of Asylum in International Law' (1994) 5(1) *Duke Journal of Comparative and International Law* 1, 8–9.

[31] Refugee Convention, above n 17, art 33.

[32] S Kneebone, 'The Legal and Ethical Implications of Extra-territorial Processing of Asylum Seekers: the Safe Third Country Concept' in J McAdam (ed), *Moving On: Forced Migration and Human Rights* (Oxford, Hart Publishing, 2008) 139–40; M Gibney, 'Forced Migration, Engineered Regionalism and Justice Between States' in S Kneebone and F Rawlings-Sanaei (eds), *New Regionalism and Asylum Seekers: Challenges Ahead* (New York, Berghahn, 2007) 71–72.

As Kneebone notes, the right to seek asylum has tended to be interpreted by states as 'conferring an obligation to do so in the first "safe" place of asylum'.[33] Interestingly, a recent study commissioned by the EU Parliamentary Committee on Civil Liberties, Justice and Home Affairs notes that whilst asylum seekers may not necessarily choose their preferred country of destination, they should be given due process rights to explain *why* they have chosen that particular country for asylum:

> In making explicit the principled commitment to avoid unnecessary coercion, we do not endorse the notion that asylum seekers should have 'free choice' as to their country of destination in all instances. But rather, the law, properly interpreted, requires that *they should be heard* as regards the reasons for their choice of destination, and if there are strong reasons, such as kin or connections, access to that country of asylum should be facilitated [emphasis added].[34]

C. 'Refugee Protection'

Interestingly, despite its centrality to the refugee law framework and its widespread usage, the concept of 'protection' has received relatively academic analysis.[35] As Stevens discusses elsewhere, 'protection' can have different meanings for the individual, the state, UNHCR or humanitarian organisations. And the duty of protection owed by a state to its citizens can vary between states.[36] At times, there is an overlap with 'asylum'.[37] Protection can have active and passive qualities—that is actively protecting from harm or avoiding an action which leads to harm. For many refugee lawyers, though, the Refugee Convention is the source of obligations owed by the state to the refugee, broadly regarded as 'rights' or 'protection'. The granting of 'protection' by a state can range from integration and the full set of acquired rights set out in Articles 2–34 of the Refugee Convention to only basic protection from return (Article 33 prohibition of *refoulement*) with none of the associated rights given to refugees formally recognised as such under the Refugee Convention. In terms of temporality, we also note the trend away from permanent forms of refugee protection to the increasing use by some states of temporary protection in situations of mass influx, humanitarian/subsidiary/complementary protection for

[33] Kneebone, above n 32, 141.

[34] EU Directorate General for Internal Policies, *New Approaches, Alternative Avenues and Means of Access to Asylum Procedures for Persons Seeking International Protection* (Doc no PE509.989, Study for the LIBE Committee, European Parliament, Publications Office, 2014) www.europarl.europa.eu/RegData/etudes/STUD/2014/509989/IPOL_STU(2014)509989_EN.pdf,17.

[35] See Stevens, above n 16.

[36] J Hathaway, *The Law of Refugee Status* (Toronto, Butterworths, 1991) 105–06.

[37] See discussion above at Section II(A).

those not seen as falling within the strict definition of 'refugee', and time-limited visas/temporary residence permits for recognised refugees. For the purposes of this volume, we understand 'protection' as encompassing these various forms of protection, whilst noting that they vary in quality and durability.

III. STATES, ACCESS TO TERRITORY AND THE LAW

A. 'The State' (or States) and 'Borders'

As this volume argues, there are two fundamental principles underlying asylum: access to territory and, once within territory, access to asylum justice in relation to refugee status determination.[38] The title of this volume refers to 'States' and 'the Law' in the context of refugee protection. This is because, despite the importance of non-state organisations in providing humanitarian assistance to refugees, the act of granting refugee status and refugee protection remains dependent on the acts of *states*: states are parties to international treaties such as the Refugee Convention, and are defined as having special attributes and responsibilities, including the responsibility to protect their citizens.[39] In particular, the existence of state protection is a key element of the definition of refugee status under Article 1A(2) of the Refugee Convention.[40] State responsibility is also a key legal concept which has been used in litigation to attempt to render states accountable for their actions in relation to asylum seekers, even when that occurs outside national boundaries. We will analyse these key concepts in this section.

(i) Territory, Borders and the Law

The notions of *'territory'* and *'border'* have particular significance in the refugee law context. Article 1A(2) requires that a forced migrant must have crossed a state border (either that of his country of nationality or country of former habitual residence for those without nationality).

[38] Robert Thomas has noted, 'this right to seek asylum cuts across one of the defining features of the modern state: its ability to control entry into its physical territory': R Thomas, *Administrative Justice and Asylum Appeals: A Study of Tribunal Adjudication* (Oxford, Hart Publishing, 2011) 16.

[39] See eg the UK House of Lords in *Horvath v SSHD* [2000] UKHL 37, [2001] 1 AC 489, 499–500 (per Hope LJ); M Gibney, 'Liberal Democratic States and Responsibilities to Refugees' (1999) 93 *American Political Science Review* 169, 175; A Shacknove, 'Who is a Refugee?'(1985) 95 *Ethics* 274, 275.

[40] Refugee Convention, Art 1A(2) refers to an applicant's willingness to avail himself of the protection of the 'country of his nationality'.

However, many people who flee persecution, armed conflict and other harm are unable to cross a state border, but instead seek refuge within their own country. This volume is not focused on such 'internally displaced people' (IDP), but rather on those that leave their country of origin to seek asylum elsewhere.[41]

The concepts of 'territory' and 'border' are contested and may be understood differently under international as opposed to regional or domestic law of some asylum-host countries.[42] The relaxation of border controls within the EU Schengen area has facilitated the ability to travel across the EU territory but has resulted in increased fortification of external borders of the EU. Recent events in the Mediterranean and in Eastern Europe with burgeoning numbers of people seeking entry to Europe through irregular means and by boat are testing the EU's ability to manage its external frontiers and raising difficult legal and practical questions, many of which are related to access.

The Dublin Regulation III, which allows for return to the first country of arrival in the EU, has been intermittently suspended by a number of EU states during 2015. Member States in the Schengen area (in which there is passport-free movement between participating countries) also started to reintroduce border controls as a reaction to the rising inward migration and apparent ease of inter-state travel. Finally, in December 2015, the EU Commission proposed major amendments to the Schengen Borders Code.[43]

Challenges to gaining *access to asylum territory* are, arguably, not new: there is a general reluctance by the major asylum host states in the developed north to be deemed 'soft' on asylum seekers ('pull factor') and the creation of mechanisms to deter asylum flows (strict visa requirements; airline liaison officers; carrier sanctions; criminalisation of irregular entry;

[41] That is not to dilute/ignore the humanitarian need of such persons, which is significant. Many commentators have emphasised the complex humanitarian and protection needs of IDPs eg R Cohen: 'Often [the internally displaced] are caught up in internal conflicts between their governments and opposing forces. Some of the highest mortality rates ever recorded during humanitarian emergencies have come from situations involving internally displaced persons.' R Cohen, 'Refugee and Internally Displaced Women: A Development Perspective '(1995) cited in J Mertus, The State and The Post-Cold War Refugee Regime: New Models, New Questions' (1998–1999) 20 *Michigan Journal of International Law* 59, 67.

[42] For instance, excision of certain territory in Australia from the migration zone means that for the purposes of international law, such territory is part of Australia, but under domestic law, it is not part of the migration zone. In practice, this means asylum seekers who reach Australian territory by boat are not permitted to make a valid application for a protection visa under the Migration Act 1958 (Cth) (MA) unless the Minister for Immigration permits them to do so (MA, s 46A).

[43] European Commission, 'Proposal for a Regulation of the European Parliament and of the Council Amending Regulation No 562/2006 (EC) as Regards the Reinforcement of Checks Against Relevant Databases at External Borders (Strasbourg, COM(2015) 670 final, 15 December 2015).

externalisation of immigration control). EU Member States have long been guilty of adopting such mechanisms to deter entry. While these might be described as somewhat subtler preventive measures, events in 2015 clearly indicated that some Member States were prepared to adopt much more aggressive strategies for excluding access to territory:

— The erection of fences across borders: for instance, Bulgaria has constructed a 33 km long fence at its south-eastern border with Turkey;[44] Hungary hurriedly built fences on its borders with Serbia and Croatia;[45] Slovenia started its razor-wire fence in mid-November 2015,[46] while Macedonia commenced the erection of a metal fence on its southern border with Greece in late November 2015.[47]

— 'Push backs' by border guards (some of whom do not let asylum seekers cross borders).[48]

— Push backs by states: those between Libya and Italy have halted as a consequence of case law of the European Court of Human Rights (ECtHR)[49] but they are still being practised elsewhere, particularly in Australia and SE Asia.[50]

— Policies of containment: this includes the granting of large sums of aid/funding by developed countries to developing countries neighbouring the source of refugee flows in substitution for physical and legal refugee protection (see Stevens, Chapter 10). For instance, in response to calls by the UNHCR for states to offer more resettlement

[44] A Krasimirov, 'Bulgaria may Extend Turkish Border Fence to Bar Syrian, Iraqi Refugees' (Reuters, 20 August 2014) www.uk.reuters.com/article/2014/08/20/uk-bulgaria-turkey-fence-idUKKBN0GK1IK20140820.

[45] M Feher, 'Hungary Completes Croatia Border Fence to Keep Migrants Out' (The Wall Street Journal, 15 October 2015) www.wsj.com/articles/hungary-completes-croatia-border-fence-to-keep-migrants-out-1444927774.

[46] M Feher, 'Slovenia Erects Razor-Wire Fence to Control Migrant Flow' (The Wall Street Journal, 11 November 2015) www.wsj.com/articles/slovenia-starts-building-border-fence-to-control-migrant-flow-1447237240.

[47] Y Behrakis and K Casule, 'FYROM Army Starts Building Fence on Greek Border' (Ekathimerini, 28 November 2015) www.ekathimerini.com/203874/article/ekathimerini/news/fyrom-army-starts-building-fence-on-greek-border.

[48] On this, Maryellen Fullerton notes that the 'snap decisions of border guards and airline personnel are virtually unreviewable'. She raises due process concerns notes: 'the lack of an adequate record of the initial decision, the inability to obtain legal assistance, and the time pressures that prevent gathering evidence to support further the asylum seeker's claim ensure that any appeal that is permitted fails to provide a meaningful opportunity for review… Such inadequate and unfair procedures necessarily will result in a number of erroneous decisions': M Fullerton, 'Restricting the Flow of Asylum Seekers in Belgium, Denmark, the Federal Republic of Germany, and the Netherlands: New Challenges to the Geneva Convention Relating to the Status of Refugees and the European Convention on Human Rights' (1988) 29 *Virginia Journal of International Law* 33, 113–14.

[49] See Iván, ch 3 and Pollet, ch 7.

[50] See O'Sullivan, ch 5.

places, the UK allocated further funding to the UNHCR and implementing partners to assist with the needs of refugees forced from Syria to neighbouring countries, bringing the total committed by the UK to the Syrian crisis to £1.1 billion.[51] In contrast, the UK Government has been criticised for being slow to offer resettlement places to Syrian refugees. For instance, although it established a 'Syrian Vulnerable Person Resettlement (VPR) Programme' in January 2014, it had only offered 187 people places in this scheme by March 2015, and had resettled only 252 by September 2015 (of the 20,000 resettlement places offered from September 2015–20).[52] Although more recent statistics show that this number has risen, with a total of 1,602 people having now been resettled in the UK,[53] its response to the refugee crisis has been criticised.[54]

Access to territory by sea raises particular legal and humanitarian issues. We note here that the maritime environment involves complex questions of territory which are not applicable to land: for instance, defining jurisdiction requires consideration of the international law of the sea,[55] and demarcation of rescue zones under the Search and Rescue Convention.[56] Thus, access to territory via the sea requires special considerations of key concepts such as (a) jurisdiction; (b) state responsibility for search and rescue; and (c) the meaning of 'safe disembarkation' that are not required in relation to land borders/territory. Similarly, due to the shared

[51] UK Department for International Development (DFID), 'Syria Crisis Response Summary' (DFID, 4 January 2016) www.gov.uk/government/uploads/system/uploads/attachment_data/file/489691/DFID_Syria_Crisis_Response_Summary__2016.01.04_.pdf.

[52] See M Gower and B Politowski, 'Syrian Refugees and the UK Response' (House of Commons Library Briefing Paper No 06805, 10 June 2015).

[53] M Gower and B Politowski, 'Syrian Refugees and the UK Response' (House of Commons Library Briefing Paper No 06805, 10 June 2016).

[54] H Lambert, 'The Government's Shameful Response to the Refugee Crisis in Four Charts', The Independent, 19 January 2016, www.independent.co.uk/news/world/politics/the-government-s-shameful-response-to-the-refugee-crisis-in-four-charts-a6814391.html.

[55] eg under the International Law of the Sea, no state has 'jurisdiction' on the high seas. Art 87(1) of the UN Convention on the Law of the Sea (opened for signature 10 December 1982, 1833 United Nations Treaty Series 3) (UNCLOS), states that the high seas shall not be subjected to the sovereignty of any state: 'The high seas are open to all States, whether coastal or land-locked. Freedom of the high seas … comprises, inter alia, both for coastal and land-locked States: (a) freedom of navigation'. See also UNCLOS, art 89: 'No State may validly purport to subject any part of the high seas to its sovereignty' and art 92(1): 'Ships shall sail under the flag of one State only and, save in exceptional cases expressly provided for in international treaties or in this Convention, shall be subject to its exclusive jurisdiction on the high seas': UNCLOS, 1833 United Nations Treaty Series 3 (entered into force 16 November 1994).

[56] UNCLOS, above n 55, art 98(1)(a) provides that every state shall require the master of a ship flying its flag to render assistance to any person found at sea in danger of being lost. The International Convention on Maritime Search and Rescue also requires the responsible state party to ensure that rescued persons are delivered to a place of safety: International Convention on Maritime Search and Rescue, 1405 United Nations Treaty Series 119 (entered into force 22 June 1985).

responsibility of search and rescue, there tends to be greater sharing of border control and a blurring of state responsibility, as illustrated by the operation of Frontex in the context of the EU.[57]

The act of fleeing across the sea poses particular dangers to the lives of asylum seekers, as the significant fatalities in the Mediterranean starkly illustrate.[58] Some states have exploited these events to support restrictions on acceptance of boat arrivals and criminalisation of 'people smugglers'. This is best demonstrated by the policies of Australia which has prosecuted a significant number of persons under domestic people smuggling provisions. In some circumstances, domestic law may erect 'borders' for exclusion purposes. Australia again provides a salient example: the 'migration borders' of Australia have been defined under Australian migration legislation in such a way that asylum seekers arriving by boat into Australian territory are not seen as arriving in the Australian 'migration zone' and are therefore denied important legal rights.[59] Thus, Australian law assigns separate identities to different asylum seekers depending on their mode of arrival and excludes and penalises those that are compelled to come to Australia by boat to seek protection.

The significant dangers of sea crossings also means that states dealing with asylum flows via the sea are inclined to classify assistance as humanitarian in nature, rather than as responding to a refugee situation—so the response is one of aid rather than necessarily channelling persons into a refugee status determination procedure.

[57] For instance, Guy Goodwin-Gill, writing on interception in Europe, has commented that 'it helps to think about the geographical context in which interception operations by the EU and Member States take place. Here we find states operating, nominally in the management of the EU's external borders, but actually in a physical domain where borders, as we commonly understand them, simply do not exist—at sea, on the high seas, or even in the contiguous zone or territorial waters of other states, in fact, at notional or virtual borders reconstituted on the basis of national and regional interest': Goodwin-Gill, above n 30, 446–47.

[58] eg UNHCR estimate that 2,500 refugees and migrants died or went missing trying to reach Europe via the Mediterranean Sea during 2015: UNHCR, 'Crossings of Mediterranean Sea Exceed 300,000, Including 200,000 to Greece' (Press Release, 28 August 2015) www.unhcr.org/55e06a5b6.html.

[59] In 2001, all outlying territories belonging to Australia were 'excised' from the Australian migration zone. This had the effect that asylum seekers intercepted and held on these territories (eg Christmas Island) were not permitted to lodge a protection visa application under mainstream Australian law but were processed separately: Migration Amendment (Excision from Migration Zone) Act 2001 (Cth); Migration Amendment (Excision from Migration Zone) (Consequential Provisions) Act 2001 (Cth). In May 2013, the MA was again amended which effectively excises the Australian mainland from the Australian migration zone. Following this amendment, all those who arrive by boat, including those who actually land on Australia's shores, are now barred from lodging a valid application for a visa. See further O'Sullivan, ch 5.

Finally, in addition to the above differences, the laws and practices pertaining to access to territory via land and sea also have similarities. In both situations, access is often dependent on the discretion of border personnel. In the land environment, border guards may not permit entry of asylum seekers or subject them to a cursory screening process. In the maritime environment, naval personnel may be instructed to turn boats back to their place of embarkation or may also subject asylum seekers to a screening process.[60]

Linked to the importance of states is the operation of *the law* in defining state responsibility and the contours of borders and territory. The force of law is important to consider in this context because, increasingly, there is a tendency by major industrialised countries to subvert key aspects of the Refugee Convention[61] or to fail to accord fully with judicial rulings such as those of the ECtHR.[62] The 'law' also refers to the existence of an independent judiciary, willing and capable of reviewing executive power in relation to asylum decisions, and the lawful functioning of administrative agencies which undertake refugee status determinations—key components of asylum justice.[63] The operation of the law by these institutions can sometimes be limited due to cost and efficiency rationalisations (which may, for instance, lead to limitations on procedural justice).[64]

The force of law in defining borders and the right of entry is particularly strong in preventing both access to territory and access to justice. In Australia, for instance, the notion of lawful arrival is defined in such a way that boat arrivals are deemed to be 'illegal' and processed extraterritorially (in Nauru and Papua New Guinea). Serious concerns have been raised about the quality of refugee status determination in these extraterritorial locations.[65] This has the effect that the legal definition of asylum seekers leads to both territorial exclusion and due process limitations. This is of significant contemporary relevance internationally, given that

[60] See O'Sullivan, ch 5.

[61] eg via 'push backs' at sea by Australia on the basis that this does not represent *non-refoulement*. See also the erection of fences at key EU borders, eg Greece has erected a 12.5 km wall at a critical section of the Greece–Turkish border near the town of Orestiada; Bulgaria has constructed a 33 km long fence at its south-eastern border with Turkey.

[62] See ch 3 on the application of the *Hirsi Jamaa and Others v Italy* App no 27765/09 (ECtHR, 23 February 2012) in Hungary.

[63] See Hamlin, above n 28, 10 who discusses the differing levels of insulation of bodies from the 'exclusionary politics of deterrence': 'When administrative agencies are insulated, they can weather political storms more easily, and policy is more stable over time. However, when RSD tends to be driven by administrative concerns for efficiency and cost saving, there is less room for drawn out vetting of individual cases.'

[64] eg the introduction of accelerated procedures discussed by Kirk, ch 11.

[65] UNHCR, 'UNHCR Monitoring Visit to the Republic of Nauru 7 to 9 October 2013' (UNHCR Regional Representation Canberra, 26 November 2013) 7–10.

the EU Commission may be willing to reconsider the introduction of similar 'offshore' reception centres in Africa.[66]

The interpretation of 'border' by states is heavily influenced by notions of security. For instance, Australian discourse of asylum is largely connected to 'border security', to the extent that boat arrivals have been classified as a 'national emergency'. There is a similar 'crisis' occurring in the EU in terms of the Mediterranean crossings and with regard to 'the jungle'—where an estimated 5,000 refugees and migrants have gathered at Sangatte near Calais and attempt to get into the tunnel on a nightly basis. More recently, the outflow of Syrian asylum seekers to Europe has illustrated the polarised nature of EU Member States' refugee policies, with Germany opening its borders and accepting a significant number of Syrian asylum seekers,[67] while others refused to participate in a mandatory relocation scheme or closed their borders, despite the very serious consequences for other EU states and for refugees and asylum seekers. Attempts to adopt a harmonised approach to the issue, which occupied the EU throughout 2015, appeared to flounder in November 2015, when the German Chancellor, Angela Merkel, held a mini-summit of nine EU states prepared to accept the majority of refugees from the Middle East—named 'the coalition of the willing'—thereby acknowledging a fundamental split in the EU.[68] The 2015 Syrian 'crisis' illustrates starkly the key themes of 'fortresses' and 'fairness' of this collection: state attempts to create a fortress through the physical erection of fences and closure of borders, together with several aspects of fairness in the asylum system—the fair provision of access to territory for the claiming of refugee protection and due process for asylum claims (individual fairness) and the 'fair' allocation of protection places across asylum host states (communal fairness).

We now turn to consider these notions of state responsibility in relation to the fairness of so-called 'burden sharing'.

(ii) State 'Responsibility'

State responsibility is an important concept for addressing access to territory for asylum seekers and refugees. As a result, a number of chapters

[66] I Traynor, 'Brussels Plans Migration Centres Outside EU to Process Asylum Applications' (London, The Guardian, 5 March 2015) www.theguardian.com/world/2015/mar/05/european-commission-third-country-immigrant-processing-centres.

[67] eg in the third quarter of 2015, Germany made 54,335 first instance decisions and granted refugee status to 18,135 Syrians: Eurostat, 'First Time Asylum Applicants and First Instance Decisions on Asylum Applications: Third Quarter 2015' (Eurostat Asylum Quarterly Report, 3 March 2016). www.ec.europa.eu/eurostat/documents/6049358/7005580/Asylum+quarterly+report+-+Q3+2015.pdf/b265b920-3027-4e69-95cf-63f8fb8c80ed.

[68] I Traynor, 'Europe Split Over Refugee Deal as Germany Leads Breakaway Coalition' (London, The Guardian, 30 November 2015) www.theguardian.com/world/2015/nov/29/germanys-plan-to-strike-eu-wide-refugee-sharing-deal-stalls.

in this volume consider the responsibility of states towards refugees. This concept is particularly relevant given the increasing trend by key asylum host states to 'outsource' or 'contain' asylum flows to certain regions in exchange for funding. This has been done for many years by Australia via its 'Pacific Solution',[69] and more recently by the EU via its controversial asylum agreement with Turkey.[70]

State responsibility under international and regional human rights law is particularly important for asylum seekers who are not yet recognised as refugees (or who may be excluded from refugee status) and who may be able to argue that states are responsible for harm that may occur to them if returned to their country of origin or another country where they may face relevant harm.[71] The concept of state responsibility means that the existence of adequate refugee status determination procedures, including asylum claim recognition at the border, is an important part of access to justice for refugees. As Júlia Iván notes in Chapter 3 and Cavidan Soykan in Chapter 4, in practice, the access of an asylum seeker to territory is often dependent on a border guard understanding and properly registering an asylum claim. In discussing Hungary, Iván analyses the findings of the border monitoring programme of the Hungarian Helsinki Committee and concludes that, despite the favourable ruling of the ECtHR in *Hirsi Jamaa and Others v Italy*[72] (which emphasised the positive obligation on the state to identify asylum seekers and to offer them a fair and individual status determination procedure), it is impossible to utilise the judgment to protect the rights of asylum seekers unless individual border procedures are properly conducted prior to removing a particular refugee. Similarly, in Chapter 4 on Turkey, Soykan considers returns and raises concerns that untrained police officers and gendarmerie hold significant discretionary power in deterring asylum seekers at the borders.

[69] See S Taylor, 'Australia's Pacific Solution Mark II: The Lessons to be Learned' (2007) 9 *UTS Law Review* 106.

[70] European Council, 'EU–Turkey Statement 18 March 2016' (Press Release, 18 March 2016) www.consilium.europa.eu/en/press/press-releases/2016/03/18-eu-turkey-statement/.

[71] Note that the principle of *non-refoulement* in art 33 of the Refugee Convention not only prohibits states from returning asylum seekers to the country in which they fear persecution, but also any other country where they may face relevant harm or which might return them to such harm; see discussion in 'UNHCR Written Submission by the Office of the United Nations High Commissioner for Refugees in the Case of Sharifi and Ors v Italy and Greece (Application No 16643/09)' (UNHCR, October 2009) [2.1]. Relevant harm includes that referred to in art 33, as well as certain provisions of the International Covenant on Civil and Political Rights (ICCPR), Convention Against Torture and Other Cruel Inhuman or Degrading Treatment or Punishment (CAT) and the ECHR; see discussion in E Lauterpacht and D Bethlehem, 'The Scope and Content of the Principle of Non-Refoulement: Opinion' in E Feller, V Türk and F Nicholson (eds), *Refugee Protection in International Law: UNHCR's Global Consultations on International Protection* (Cambridge, Cambridge University Press, UNHCR 2003) 121–28.

[72] *Hirsi Jamaa and Others v Italy*, above n 62.

'Burden' or 'Responsibility' Sharing

The idea of co-operation or sharing responsibility for refugees has a long history and is a key recommendation of the Refugee Convention.[73] The term 'responsibility' is often invoked by the UNHCR and some states to encourage a fairer distribution of the 'burden' of dealing with refugee flows, that is, 'responsibility sharing'. The UNHCR refers to state responsibility and co-operation to persuade states to take refugees directly from source areas via resettlement or directly. In this way, international institutions are attempting to hold states 'responsible' under international law—that is, through either the spirit or the 'force of law'—for two types of refugees: (a) those in source areas (eg Syria, or neighbouring countries), whom asylum host states have a humanitarian obligation to assist, and (b) those who enter asylum host state territory (thereby raising legal responsibility pursuant to the Refugee Convention or other domestic/regional laws).

In theory, the notion of responsibility-sharing is designed to counteract the 'fortress' mentality assumed by many states in the industrialised world (which has been assumed despite the commitment to co-operation expressed by the Conference of Plenipotentiaries convened to draft the Refugee Convention). As Hathaway and Gammeltoft-Hansen have recently suggested:

> Contemporary understandings of jurisdiction, shared responsibility, and aiding or assisting—taken together—can and should be invoked in aid of the dismantling of the non-entrée regime.[74]

In the EU, during the migration events of 2015, the discussion on responsibility-sharing was articulated in terms of 'solidarity', a relatively long standing principle of EU law and policy and widely employed in discussions on asylum and migration.[75] However, as clearly evidenced in recent times, even this 'thicker' notion of mutual support provided by the *rule* of

[73] UN General Assembly, 'Final Act of the UN Conference of Plenipotentiaries on the Status of Refugees and Stateless Persons' (Geneva, 28 July 1951) Recommendation D: 'THE CONFERENCE, CONSIDERING that many persons still leave their country of origin for reasons of persecution and are entitled to special protection on account of their position, RECOMMENDS that Governments continue to receive refugees in their territories and that the concert true spirit of international cooperation in order that these refugees may find asylum and the possibility of resettlement.'

[74] JC Hathaway and T Gammeltoft-Hansen, 'Non-Refoulement in a World of Cooperative Deterrence' (University of Michigan Law School, Law & Economics Working Papers, 2014) 8.

[75] Treaty on the Functioning of the European Union (TFEU), art 80 states: 'The policies of the Union set out in this Chapter and their implementation shall be governed by the principle of solidarity and fair sharing of responsibility, including its financial implications, between the Member States. Whenever necessary, the Union acts adopted pursuant to this Chapter shall contain appropriate measures to give effect to this principle.'

'solidarity' has failed to deliver in the context of asylum. Furthermore, as Noll has noted, 'article 80 TFEU concerns solidarity … between Member States only, and not solidarity between Member States and refugees, or Member States and other recipient states in crisis regions'.[76] The failure to share responsibility in a truly meaningful way is revealed in Chapters 4 and 10, in which Soykan and Stevens explore the consequences and pressures on Turkey and Lebanon of mass influx.

Extraterritorial Responsibility

This issue is complicated by the application of state responsibility to situations of 'outsourcing' or 'contracting out' of protection, detention and refugee status determination (RSD) services to other countries—for example, Australia's use of companies such as G4S/Transfield to operate detention facilities both in Australia and in the Pacific (Nauru, Papua New Guinea). Although nominally these companies are 'responsible' for providing services in each centre under the terms of their contracts with the Australian Government, we would argue that state responsibility lies with the Australian Government under international law.[77] In the EU, the 2014 Regulation on Maritime Border Surveillance in the Framework of Frontex-led Joint Operations at Sea prohibits Member States from handing over any third country national to the authorities of a country where there is a serious risk of persecution, torture or ill-treatment or from where there is a serious risk of an expulsion, removal or extradition to another country in contravention of the principle of *non-refoulement*. Though this might suggest a heightened level of protection which, together with the Charter of Fundamental Rights and the European Convention on Human Rights (ECHR), should ensure that asylum seekers have an opportunity to access refugee determination procedures, many states or state agents are ignoring or side-stepping their *non-refoulement* responsibilities which the contributions in this volume highlight (see eg Iván, Chapter 3; Soykan, Chapter 4; Pollet, Chapter 7; Stevens, Chapter 10).

[76] G Noll, 'Why the EU Gets in the Way of Refugee Solidarity' (London School of Economics Blog, 16 October 2015) www.blogs.lse.ac.uk/eurocrisispress/2015/10/16/why-the-eu-gets-in-the-way-of-refugee-solidarity/.

[77] Indeed, the exercise of effective control via such contacts was recognised by one of the judges of the Australian High Court in a recent landmark judgment on the legality of the Nauruan Regional Processing Centre. In this case, Bell J recognised that Australia exercised 'effective control' over the detention of the transferees through the contractual obligations it imposed on Transfield (*Plaintiff M68/2015 v Minister for Immigration and Border Protection & Ors* [2016] HCA 1, 3 February 2016, [93] Bell J.

IV. 'ASYLUM JUSTICE' AND CONTEMPORARY DUE PROCESS CHALLENGES

A. The Concept of Access to Justice

Part II of this volume seeks to analyse the provision by states to access to justice, by which we mean access to due process. This topic has obvious links to the material addressed in Part I (Access to Territory) in that access to a state's refugee status determination process requires first that the asylum seeker is able to cross a border. The contributions in Part II of the volume will examine issues arising from reductions in legal assistance, and limitations on procedural fairness posed by screening and accelerated procedures.

What then does access to justice mean in an asylum context? The notion of access to justice may be interpreted as including the ability to seek redress for wrongdoing, procedural protections, access to both judicial and non-judicial procedures (eg a tribunal hearing and judicial review), and the provision of legal assistance. As non-citizens/non-residents, asylum seekers tend to face significant obstacles in gaining access to justice. This is particularly so for those excluded from the territories of states. This includes, for instance, those interdicted by states on the high seas and returned to their country of disembarkation, and those removed under accelerated procedures without being afforded an opportunity to apply for asylum.

One of the problems which many commentators have noted is that there is no agreed mechanism for determination of refugee status.[78] Certainly, there is nothing in the Refugee Convention which *requires* a certain procedure to be followed in assessing refugee claims. Despite this, many states have developed sophisticated RSD processes comprising protections of natural justice and review mechanisms which suggest there is some agreement amongst State Parties to the Convention as to a minimum notion of 'asylum justice'.

Certain due process rights are set out in the Refugee Convention and international human rights treaties. For instance, the Refugee Convention provides in Article 16 a right to free access to courts on the territory of all Contracting States. A State Party is not permitted to make a reservation to Article 16(1). However, this provision has rarely been utilised in litigation and is often overlooked in academic commentary.[79] Article 14 of the International Covenant on Civil and Political Rights (ICCPR) also

[78] eg JC Hathaway and RA Neve, 'Fundamental Justice and the Deflection of Refugees from Canada' (1996) 34(2) *Osgoode Hall Law Journal* 213, 215.

[79] For a brief commentary, see JC Hathaway, *The Rights of Refugees under International Law* (Cambridge, Cambridge University Press, 2005) 643–47.

includes access to justice provisions in the context of criminal charges. For instance, Article 14(1) states that:

> In the determination of any criminal charge against him, or of his rights and obligations in a suit at law, everyone shall be entitled to a fair and public hearing by a competent, independent and impartial tribunal established by law.

However, the case law on this has largely focused on its application to criminal law rather than refugee law—as is reflected in the emphasis given to criminal law issues in the UN Human Rights Committee General Comment on Article 14.[80]

In the ECtHR judgment of *Hirsi*, Judge Albuquerque (in his separate opinion) set out a useful summary of the basic requirements for fairness in refugee status determination procedures:

> For the refugee-status determination procedure to be individual, fair and effective, it must necessarily have at least the following features: (1) a reasonable time-limit in which to submit the asylum application; (2) a personal interview with the asylum applicant before the decision on the application is taken; (3) the opportunity to submit evidence in support of the application and dispute evidence submitted against the application; (4) a fully reasoned written decision by an independent first-instance body, based on the asylum-seeker's individual situation and not solely on a general evaluation of his or her country of origin, the asylum-seeker having the right to rebut the presumption of safety of any country in his or her regard; (5) a reasonable time-limit in which to appeal against the decision and automatic suspensive effect of an appeal against the first-instance decision; (6) full and speedy judicial review of both the factual and legal grounds of the first-instance decision and (7) free legal advice and representation and, if necessary, free linguistic assistance at both first and second instance, and unrestricted access to UNHCR or any other organisation working on behalf of UNHCR.[81]

When discussing administrative justice in the asylum context, Robert Thomas has stated that:

> Administrative justice concerns the overall system by which administrative decisions affecting individuals are taken, including the procedures and law governing such decisions and the processes for resolving disputes and airing grievances in relation to them.[82]… At its irreducible core, the quality of an administrative-legal process is informed by four values: its propensity to produce accurate decisions; the fairness of the procedures by which decisions are

[80] UN Human Rights Committee, 'General Comment No 13: Article 14 (Administration of Justice)' (Twenty-First Session 1984) in *Compilation of General Comments and General Recommendations Adopted by Human Rights Treaty Bodies* (UN Doc HRI/GEN/1/Rev.1 Vol 1, 27 May 2008) 187 [14].

[81] *Hirsi Jamaa and Others v Italy*, above n 62, 72 (citations omitted).

[82] R Thomas, *Administrative Justice and Asylum Appeals: A Study of Tribunal Adjudication* (Oxford, Hart Publishing, 2011) 1.

made; the resources needed to fund the decision process; and the timeliness of decision-making.[83]

Reference can also be made to a 2013 decision of the Inter-American Court of Human Rights, which formulated important guidance concerning due process in asylum proceedings. The Court's contribution is significant since it drew on the Inter-American human rights instruments and jurisprudence, in addition to the Refugee Convention and UNHCR position statements. According to the Court, essential due process elements in RSD include:

— 'necessary facilities' for submission of the claim for asylum (this includes an interpreter and may include legal representation);
— objective consideration of the claim by a 'competent and clearly identified authority', including a personal interview;
— respect for the principles of privacy and confidentiality;
— an appeal (including provisions of a reasonable period to appeal, and information on how to appeal); and
— the suspensive effect of any appeal.[84]

A number of these principles have been recognised by EU law and incorporated in the separate Directives on Procedures and Reception Conditions, both of which have now been recast.[85] As Pollet notes in Chapter 7, some improvements have been made in this process, for instance the recast Procedures Directive establishes a number of safeguards for the proper conduct of a personal interview. However, aspects of these directives also raise problems for effective access to the asylum procedure, due to the vague and unclear wording of some articles or lack of guidance as to the content of key rights.

(i) State Interpretation and Implementation of Due Process

Some positive values of due process are reflected in the EU Procedures Directive.[86] However, these are problematic. However, aspects of the EU asylum directives are problematic, as discussed by Pollet of the European Council on Refugees and Exiles (ECRE) in Chapter 7. In that chapter Pollet examines the obstacles that asylum seekers face in accessing the asylum

[83] ibid 12–13.

[84] *Case of the Pacheco Tineo Family v Plurinational State of Bolivia* (25 November 2013) Inter-American Court of Human Rights [159] www.corteidh.or.cr/docs/casos/articulos/seriec_272_ing.pdf.

[85] Council Directive 2013/32/EU of 26 June 2013 on common procedures for granting and withdrawing international protection (recast) [2013] OJ L180/60 (Recast Procedures Directive); and Council Directive 2013/33/EU of 26 June 2013 laying down standards for the reception of applicants for international protection (recast) [2013] OJ L180/96 (Recast Receptions Directive).

[86] Recast Procedures Directive, ibid.

procedure and protection in a host EU Member State. In the EU, there are issues related to registration of asylum applications, the organisation of personal interviews at the first instance, the impact of the use of accelerated and admissibility procedures on asylum seekers' access to protection in the EU and access to an effective remedy. He also highlights the obstacles that detention creates in terms of access to information, interpretation and free legal assistance. More generally, the EU situation highlights the pros and cons of practical co-operation between EU Member States within the framework of the European Asylum Support Office (EASO), including new thinking on 'joint' or 'supported processing' from a protection perspective.

In South Africa, by contrast, different access issues arise. In Chapter 8, Corey Johnson and Sergio Carciotto discuss problems arising from the operation of Refugee Reception Offices (RRO) established in urban centres throughout South Africa. They note that access to these facilities is a critical component of the refugee protection framework. They discuss the implications of the closure of urban RROs and their relocation to sparsely populated towns on international land borders.

An interesting development has been changing practices regarding access and the promulgation of asylum laws in emerging asylum host states. One such example is Turkey, which has faced a significant surge in asylum seeker numbers in recent years, particularly from nearby Syria and Iraq.[87] When the first flows of refugees from Syria began arriving in Turkey in 2011, it practised an open border policy and established camps to house the asylum seekers. It also granted the asylum seekers 'temporary protection', since Turkey applies the geographical limitation of the Refugee Convention and defines 'refugees' as only those coming from Europe. However, in the face of rising numbers, and a strain on resources, in the second half of 2012, Turkish authorities began to attempt to limit flows from Syria.[88] In addition, Turkey passed its first piece of legislation on asylum—the Law on Foreigners and International Protection—which

[87] eg between 19–25 September 2014 more than 144,000 Syrian refugees, mainly Kurds, sought refuge in southern Turkey's Sanilurfa province. These people were fleeing conflict and ISIS advances on towns and villages near Kobani (or Ayn al-Arab) in northern Syria: F Markus, 'UNHCR Airlifts Urgent Aid into Turkey to Help Refugees Fleeing ISIS' (UNHCR News, 25 September 2014) www.unhcr.org/turkey/uploads/root/unhcr_airlifts_urgent_aid_into_turkey_to_help_refugees_fleeing_isis_25_september_2014.pdf.

[88] O Bahadır Dinçer, V Federici, E Ferris, S Karaca, K Kirişci and E Özmenek Çarmikli, 'Turkey and Syrian Refugees: The Limits of Hospitality' (Washington, Brookings, November 2013) www.brookings.edu/~/media/research/files/reports/2013/11/18-syria-turkey-refugees/turkey-and-syrian-refugees_the-limits-of-hospitality-(2014).pdf. See also K Kirişci, 'Syrian Refugees and Turkey's Challenges: Going Beyond Hospitality' (Washington, Brookings, May 2014) www.brookings.edu/~/media/research/files/reports/2014/05/12-turkey-syrian-refugees-kirisci/syrian-refugees-and-turkeys-challenges-may-14-2014.pdf.

became operative in 2014.[89] (The implementation of this law is one of the topics discussed by Soykan in Chapter 4 of this volume.) The intertwining of access to territory, access to protection processes and legal developments is very clear in the Turkish case.

Similar arguments can be made in the case of Lebanon. While not party to the Refugee Convention, it too has had a generous approach to Syrians seeking entry to its territory, until 2015, when it introduced new regulations and made specific demands on the UNHCR, clearly with the intent of stopping the flow. Lebanon provides an example of a state under increasing pressure which has avoided international refugee law, preferring a mixed regime of immigration law, UNHCR involvement, ad hoc policy, humanitarian aid and international diplomacy. The consequences, though, for both state and refugees are depressing (see Stevens, Chapter 10).

Other exemplars of the emerging refugee protection frameworks are those being established in Bosnia-Herzegovina (BiH), Croatia and Serbia. In Chapter 9, Selma Porobić and Drago Župarić-Iljić note that the countries of the Western Balkans (WB) have traditionally been emigration and refugee-producing countries. However, in the last decade the WB has also transformed into a transit route for out-of-regional flows of migrants and asylum seekers attempting to reach Western Europe. Some progress has been made in the development of refugee procedures in the region, largely propelled by EU harmonisation process. For instance, Croatia committed to introducing a new International Protection Act in 2015, which will further align Croatian law with the new EU Reception and Procedure Directives. Yet, as Porobić and Župarić-Iljić note, in practice many refugees remain excluded from society, higher education and the labour market in that country. For instance, there is a lack of integration programmes and sufficient support services in both Bosnia-Herzegovina and Croatia. This illustrates once more one of the broader themes running throughout this book: the provision of national legislation and systems of asylum and refugee protection on the one hand, and the practical limitations faced by asylum seekers and refugees in accessing and benefiting from the rights/provisions of those systems.

(ii) Fair Hearing/Procedural Fairness

One component of access to asylum justice which is provided in many states is the administrative law concept of 'procedural fairness'.[90]

[89] www.refworld.org/docid/5167fbb20.html. See also Regulation No 29153 on Temporary Protection of October 2014.

[90] eg the principle is recognised in the UK, Australia and Canada.

This typically requires a decision-maker to assess an application for asylum individually and inform the applicant of any adverse information or allegations they intend to make on the case—therefore giving the applicant a right to have 'procedural fairness' accorded in the decision. Another core component of fairness is the right to appeal any negative decision. However, due to state concerns with efficiency and delays in RSD, some of these procedural guarantees are being reduced in countries such in Europe, Australia and Canada. Furthermore, in Australia, key components of procedural fairness are denied to those facing interdiction at sea or transferred to offshore processing locations in the Pacific.

(iii) Legal Assistance

The importance of legal assistance in due process is important in the context of RSD where applicants face particular challenges to comprehension of their rights: they are usually unaware of how the national legal system operates and may not speak the national language. Many commentators have highlighted the difference which legal assistance makes in this area. For instance, in the Canadian context, Rehaag conducted empirical work which demonstrated that competent legal counsel was a key factor in driving successful outcomes in refugee claims,[91] while McAdam has argued that:

> Legal aid assistance is a crucial element of a fair and efficient justice system founded on the rule of law. It helps to ensure fairness, public confidence in the way that justice is administered, and to eliminate barriers that impair access to justice for those otherwise unable to afford legal representation. The evidence shows that we get better decisions when asylum seekers have early access to properly resourced legal services by specialist lawyers. Refugee lawyers provide an important 'triage' service and help to prevent the courts from being flooded with unmeritorious claims. The bottom line is that, without legal assistance, there is a real risk that refugees will be sent back to persecution and other serious forms of harm, such as torture and death.[92]

In the EU, the recast 2013 EU Asylum Procedures Directive[93] does not include an obligation for Member States to provide free legal assistance and representation at the first instance of the asylum procedure. At the

[91] S Rehaag, 'The Role of Counsel in Canada's Refugee Determination System: An Empirical Assessment' (2011) 49 *Osgoode Hall Law Journal* 71.

[92] J McAdam, 'Australia and Asylum Seekers' (2013) 25 *International Journal of Refugee Law* 435, 441–42 (citations omitted).

[93] Council Directive 2013/32/EU of 26 June 2013 on common procedures for granting and withdrawing international protection (recast) [2013] OJ L180/60 (Asylum Procedures Directive (recast)).

appeal stage, although there is an obligation to provide free legal assistance and representation on request, this can be made conditional on the appeal having a tangible prospect of success.[94] Interestingly, Turkey's New Law grants important procedural rights to asylum seekers, including certain entitlements to legal aid, discussed in Chapter 4.

(iv) Fast Track/Accelerated Procedures

Accelerated procedures are perhaps best exemplified by the 'detained fast track' (DFT) process introduced in the UK. These are used for those cases assessed as being 'straightforward' and able to be decided quickly. Significantly, applicants subject to this procedure are detained throughout the review of the asylum application. The DFT rules lay down a short timescale for the procedure, requiring that decisions be taken within three days of detention (although in practice it appears this timescale is not adhered to). Fast track detainees are entitled to have a publicly funded legal adviser present at their initial interview. However, legal representation in appeals from the DFT is problematic: for instance, research in 2011 revealed that 60 per cent of asylum seekers were unrepresented at their DFT appeal.[95] There is a very high refusal rate.

In Chapter 11, Linda Kirk addresses the problems associated with the DFT and examines recent ground-breaking judgments of the High Court and Court of Appeal.[96] This chapter also analyses the concept of a 'risk of unfairness' as it relates to both the UK and Australian accelerated procedures, and reflects on some key questions: Do these systems provide a fair opportunity to asylum seekers to put their case? How can any risk of unfairness be mitigated and what role does legal representation need to play in providing that fairness (for instance, is it necessary for legal representation to be provided at both interview and appeal stages)? In addressing these questions, this chapter will interrogate the term 'fairness' to determine how it should be defined in accelerated or screening procedures.

The importance of due process in screening procedures has also been underlined by the practices at the border. For example, at the US–Mexico border, in mid-2014, a 'crisis' emerged due to a large flow of asylum seekers from Central America fleeing what are termed 'third generation'

[94] Asylum Procedures Directive (recast), arts 20 and 20(3).

[95] T Alger and J Phelps (on behalf of Detention Action), *Fast Track to Despair: The Unnecessary Detention of Asylum-seekers*, Detention Action, May 2011, 4.

[96] *Detention Action v SSHD* [2014] EWHC 2245; *Detention Action v SSHD* [2014] EWHC 2525 (Admin); *R (Detention Action) v SSHD* [2014] EWCA Civ 1634; *R (Detention Action) v FTT (Immigration and Asylum Chamber)* [2015] EWHC 1689 (Admin); *R (Detention Action) v FTT (Immigration and Asylum Chamber)* [2015] EWCA Civ 840; [2015] 1 WLR 5341.

gangs. Those seeking refuge included thousands of women and children. In 2014, the US Government built detention facilities to deal with this situation, including the Artesia Federal Training Centre in New Mexico. The object of this centre is to detain persons whilst they are quickly processed for removal. Due process protections have been minimal as many asylum seekers in these facilities have been subject to inadequate screening processes while at or near the US border, preventing their access to rights and protections under the Refugee Convention. Chapter 6 by Maggie Morgan and Deborah Anker deals with this important contemporary issue. They argue that this urgent situation calls for a re-examination of the US asylum system.

(v) Vulnerable Applicants

Due to the reason for asylum flows, many asylum seekers are vulnerable in some way—either due to past trauma, disability, age or gender. One problem is whether these vulnerabilities are identified by refugee status decision-makers and taken into account in any RSD. For instance, in assessing credibility, it is important to take into account past trauma and its psychological aspect, and its effect on the ability of applicants to clearly tell their 'story'. This issue is addressed by Nula Frei and Constantin Hruschka in Chapter 12 which focuses on the way in which asylum determination procedures adequately identify and deal with victims of trafficking. Some of the most common problems they identify are that trafficking is seen as a purely criminal law issue rather than a human rights problem, that in asylum procedures self-identification and a coherent account seem to be expected from the victims and that there is no clear distinction between trafficking and smuggling. They also focus on the particular problems raised for dealing properly with trafficking issues in the EU Dublin Procedure. Using a human rights perspective, they argue that Dublin transfers of victims of trafficking should not take place to countries of exploitation, and in other cases only if protection is guaranteed.

V. CONCLUSION

This volume shows that access to territory and justice are intertwined.[97] For asylum to be meaningful, states must grant both admission to territory and certain 'rights' to asylum seekers and refugees once in an asylum host

[97] eg in Australia the ability of the state to interdict asylum seekers at sea not only allows it to deny access to its physical territory but also permits the state to deny the application of the normal protections of the law to those persons, including the right to procedural fairness, see O'Sullivan, ch 5.

country. In many countries, there are developed asylum laws and procedures but significant restrictions on access to the territory of a state in order to avail themselves of that system. In other parts of the world, access to territory is relatively straightforward but there are limited procedural safeguards or opportunities to claim asylum. The contemporary challenge is to ensure both access to territory and to justice.

More broadly, the chapters in this volume illustrate the overriding power of state sovereignty in controlling asylum seekers' access to territory and access to law. A common theme is the increasing tendency for asylum seekers to be placed outside the law's protection. Despite the fact that many courts have handed down strong jurisprudence upholding the rights of asylum seekers, significant problems still exist in the practical implementation of these protections. Another theme across the contributions in this collection is the lack of political will in many industrialised states to adopt a truly equitable concept of burden sharing and a reluctance by states to recognise that the meaning of a 'state' and the responsibility for its actions goes beyond its borders. What follows in this volume is a deeper analysis of these issues as they arise in Europe, Australia, the US, the Middle East and South Africa.

2

Asylum in the Context of Immigration Control

Exclusion by Default or Design?

NADINE EL-ENANY

I. INTRODUCTION

ACCESS TO PROTECTION is made increasingly difficult for refugees due to controls on their movement. In spite of laws such as the United Nations Convention Relating to the Status of Refugees[1] (Refugee Convention), many refugees cannot reach places of safety. This chapter argues that migration controls and asylum law are out of sync. It outlines the practical difficulties for refugees in finding protection as a result of the impact of immigration and border control in the United Kingdom (UK) and the European Union (EU). For refugees to access territorial protection in Europe, they are frequently forced to make hazardous journeys. Due to strict immigration controls combined with the absence of legal routes into Europe for the vast majority of refugees, people are forced to travel irregularly. The chapter highlights the political and ethical implications of the bifurcated asylum and immigration regimes. The roots of the distinction made between asylum and immigration control regimes lie in the origins of the Refugee Convention, which was drafted in an era in which migration faced relatively few legal restrictions. The problem of limited access to protection was compounded by the narrow terms of the Convention as well as the historical contingency of its provisions and their applicability. With the emergence of administrative immigration regimes at the EU level, asylum has become imbricated in immigration law. Restrictive immigration and border control at the EU level has grown in strength and substance over recent decades. The upshot has

[1] 189 United Nations Treaty Series 150, supplemented by the 1967 Protocol relating to the Status of Refugees, 606 United Nations Treaty Series 267 (Refugee Convention).

been the gradual attenuation, even subversion, of the protective potential of asylum.

By examining the discourse of the 'migrant' and the 'refugee', this chapter seeks in particular to contextualise legally the way in which the media has portrayed people seeking entry into Europe as well as popular understandings of the distinction between migrants and refugees. While law makes a claim to neutrality, in fact legal categories are artificial and historically contingent. They do not represent natural or predefined groups of people, but instead construct them. The terms 'refugee', 'asylum seeker' and 'migrant' are arbitrary categories, some of which are given meaning and consequence through the force of the law, whilst others are not. Nevertheless, so long as the law draws a distinction between one group and another, for lawyers working with the law, there is necessary instrumental justification not to conflate categories. However, there is much to be gained from conflation if we are trying to understand not only what these categories signify in actuality, but also their effects. All people moving are migrants: people moving out of a desire to better their existence, whether in flight from extreme poverty or from persecution. It is merely that the law grants some people rights, at least in theory, and others not. This chapter argues that the distinction drawn between migrants and refugees is both false and dangerous in reinforcing the idea that some migrants are worthy of humanisation, while others are not.

II. THE LIMITS OF THE REFUGEE CONVENTION

The Refugee Convention definition of a refugee is narrowly constructed, meaning many refugees do not fall within its scope. According to Patricia Tuitt, '[w]hat distinguishes the Geneva Convention definition from other legal definitions of the refugee is its position of dominance—formal at least over other definitions—and its continued dominance in Europe in spite of the fact that few refugees seeking asylum in Europe fall within the Article 1A(2) definition'.[2] The Convention refugee definition is as follows:

> [O]wing to well-founded fear of being persecuted for reasons of race, religion, nationality, membership of a particular social group or political opinion, is outside the country of his nationality and is unable, or owing to such fear, is unwilling to avail himself of the protection of that country; or who, not having a nationality and being outside the country of his former habitual residence as a result of such events, is unable or, owing to such fear is unwilling to return to it …[3]

[2] P Tuitt, *False Images: The Law's Construction of the Refugee* (London, Pluto Press, 1996) 42.
[3] Refugee Convention, above n 1, art 1A(2).

At the time the Refugee Convention was drafted, states attempted to capture in the definition the idea of the refugee they were willing to protect. This idea was of an individual who has had to flee political persecution of an individualised nature in her country of origin.[4] As we can see from the definition above, by the end of the Second World War, it was understood that a person could be persecuted for reasons beyond her political opinion. Thus the definition of a refugee was drafted so as to include various grounds of discrimination such as race and religion. To be recognised as a refugee, a person must cross an international border after having suffered a discriminatory human rights breach, or must be in fear of persecution. Along with proof of persecution or threat of persecution, according to the definition, a person must show that the threat she faces is as a result of discrimination on the basis of her 'race, religion, nationality, membership of a social group or political opinion'. Persecution is left undefined in the Convention. It is clear that certain harms have traditionally been seen as falling within its scope of meaning for Convention purposes whilst others not. In this regard, persons fleeing poverty or environmental degradation are not considered deserving of refugee protection. Instead, the practice is to regard '[t]he solution to their problem, if any, [as lying]… within the province of international aid and development, rather than in the institution of asylum'.[5] According to Patricia Tuitt, the system becomes a 'lottery of state humanitarian protection'.[6] Having developed an historically informed understanding of the Refugee Convention definition, we can see that it is reflective of the threat Western states perceived in the Eastern bloc. According to Tuitt, 'it demonstrates the political goals of Western states who were largely instrumental in the drafting of the Geneva Convention'.[7]

Despite the narrow and arguably self-serving terms in which the Convention is framed, the demand has often been made of states that they 'fulfil their legal obligations', along with the allegation that states are 'in breach of legal obligations' they have signed up to in regards to refugee protection. These statements are made by activists, the United Nations High Commissioner for Refugees (UNHCR), NGOs, academics and legal practitioners alike. As I have argued previously, the difficulty with these demands is that the legal obligations set out in the Convention are so limited that they can be respected by states in an inhumane manner.[8]

[4] JH Simpson, *Refugees Preliminary Report of a Survey* (London, Royal Institute of International Affairs, 1938) 1.

[5] GS Goodwin-Gill and J McAdam, *The Refugee in International Law* (Oxford, Oxford University Press, 2007) 15.

[6] Tuitt, above n 2, 47.

[7] ibid 42.

[8] See N El-Enany, 'On Pragmatism and Legal Idolatry: Fortress Europe and the Desertion of the Refugee' (2015) 22 *International Journal on Minority and Group Rights* 7.

The severely restrictive effects of immigration law in limiting access to protection for refugees are not necessarily in violation of the law. EU Member States can argue that they are in compliance with their legal obligations towards refugees and that restrictive migration control measures are legitimate. Restrictive immigration controls, even those which hinder refugees' access to territorial protection, are argued by states to fall within their prerogative to protect national state sovereignty. In terms of procedural and practical measures which have the effect of deflecting or accelerating claims or deterrence measures, states insist that these are justified in protecting against abuse of the asylum process.[9]

Traditionally the principle of *non-refoulement* has been considered to be the most important obligation in the Refugee Convention. Goodwin-Gill has observed that 'the international legal status of a refugee necessarily imports certain legal consequences, the most important of which is the obligation of States to respect the principle of *non-refoulement* through time'.[10] According to Article 33(1) of the Refugee Convention:

> No Contracting State shall expel or return ('refouler') a refugee in any manner whatsoever to the frontiers of territories where his life or freedom would be threatened on account of his race, religion, nationality, membership of a particular social group or political opinion.

Legal scholars have in general argued that the principle of *non-refoulement* is applicable to all individuals claiming protection whether or not they have yet been recognised as a refugee. The UNHCR has explained that the rationale behind this is that recognition of a refugee's status does not 'make him a refugee', but merely 'declares him to be one'.[11] Complying with the principle of *non-refoulement* therefore requires the receiving state to process each application before an individual can be removed. According to this position, all asylum applicants benefit from 'presumptive refugee status' whereby 'an applicant has the same [Article 33] rights as a refugee unless and until his or her non-refugee status has been established'.[12] The response from states has been to limit access to territory in order to ensure that the principle of *non-refoulement* applies to as limited a number of persons as possible. One tool that has been used to limit asylum applications on EU territory is the 'safe country' concept. This is a procedural measure designed to reduce the number of asylum claims to be

[9] ibid 15.

[10] Goodwin-Gill and Mc Adam, above n 5, v.

[11] UNHCR, 'Handbook and Guidelines on Procedures and Criteria for Determining Refugee Status' (Geneva, reissued December 2011) para 28.

[12] J Vedsted-Hansen, 'Non-Admission Policies and the Right to Protection: Refugees' Choice Versus States' Exclusion?' in F Nicholson and P Twomey (eds), *Refugee Rights and Realities: Evolving International Concepts and Regimes* (Cambridge, Cambridge University Press, 1999) 275, 276.

processed. It does so by determining that individuals lodging asylum claims in destination states who originate from or pass through a so-called 'safe country' can have their claims left unheard or accelerated and can be returned to that 'safe country'. The criteria used to designate countries as safe are precarious, including human rights records and prevailing political situations, leading to a concern that presumptions of safety are misplaced.

Most scholars in the field insist that the principle of *non-refoulement* ensures that individuals cannot be deported to countries in which they would be exposed to a risk of persecution, including countries which might be labelled safe, but which are not in fact safe. The reason for this interpretation of the principle of *non-refoulement* is that it avoids a reading that would weaken the effectiveness of the Convention by allowing states to deny recognition of refugee status to those falling within the definition.[13] While it is the case that on alternative interpretations the effectiveness of the Convention would be hindered, as I have argued elsewhere, the flaw in this otherwise logical, principled and morally defensible argument is that the Convention is not necessarily breached on other interpretations. States only risk breaching the Convention where they turn away or apply accelerated procedures to individuals who have not yet entered their territory.[14]

In this case, the question policy-makers face is whether the risk of *refoulement* is worth assuming. It is clear that the existence of the principle of *non-refoulement* in the Convention has not led to a situation whereby states ensure that those seeking protection necessarily have access to their territories and asylum procedures.

The Refugee Convention does not have an inbuilt enforcement mechanism as do some international treaties, such as the European Convention on Human Rights (ECHR) with its Court that rules on states' compliance with the Convention. In the absence of a court finding against a state, one with material consequences and costs, either financial or political, it is likely that the state's restrictive interpretation of the law will continue to prevail. Even in cases where a court finds in favour of a migrant or a group of migrants, law-makers have at times responded by legislating so as to 'to close the protective "gap" in the law, ensuring that future like cases will not be treated alike'.[15] The 1996 Conservative Government in Britain passed the Social Security (Persons from Abroad) Miscellaneous

[13] E Lauterpacht and D Bethlehem, 'The Scope and Content of the Principle of *Non-refoulement*' in E Feller, V Turk and F Nicholson (eds), *Refugee Protection in International Law: UNHCR's Global Consultations on International Protection* (Cambridge, Cambridge University Press, 2003) 32.

[14] El-Enany, above n 8, 16.

[15] ibid 17.

Amendment Regulations 1996, which excluded asylum seekers from welfare benefits where they did not apply for asylum at the border and also persons whose first instance claim had failed.[16] In the course of legal challenge to the legislation, Lord Justice Simon Brown held:

> Parliament cannot have intended a significant number of genuine asylum seekers to be impaled on the horns of so intolerable a dilemma: the need either to abandon their claims to refugee status, or to maintain them as best they can but in a state of utter destitution.[17]

The response of the Government was to pass the Asylum and Immigration Act 1996, which effectively reversed the Court of Appeal's ruling.[18]

As I have argued previously, the pattern we see developing is that states seek to offset the narrow legal protections they have signed up to, such as those set out in the Refugee Convention, elsewhere—often at the border—where strict controls on entry of all irregular migrants persist.[19] The absence of legal routes into European countries forces those in need of protection to travel via irregular routes, which are frequently dangerous. The imposition of visa requirements on countries from which refugees originate, for instance, 'place[s] refugees in a position whereby, if they are to seek any form of territorial protection in Western European states, they are forced to comply with the image of the fraudulent refugee which Western states have constructed'.[20]

III. THE IMPACT OF 'FORTRESS EUROPE' ON PROTECTION

The project of enforcing the EU's external border can be described as one of the greatest exclusionary projects of today. The coming together of European countries has not created a challenge to the worst aspects of the nation state. In the words of Rogers Brubaker, in spite of the promise of a 'post-national' re-invention of itself, 'the future displayed recently by Europe to the world looks depressingly like the past'.[21] While the 1985 Schengen Agreement meant a liberation of movement within the internal borders of some Member States, the idea of a borderless Europe has not encompassed the Union's external borders. Indeed, in the name of this

[16] T Hayter, *Open Borders: The Case Against Immigration Control* (London, Pluto Press, 2000) 106.

[17] *R* v *Secretary of State for Social Security ex parte Joint Council for the Welfare of Immigrants* [1996] 4 All ER 385 (Eng CA, 21 June 1996).

[18] See Hayter, above n 15, 107.

[19] El-Enany, above n 7, 18.

[20] Tuitt, above n 2, 73.

[21] R Brubaker, *Nationalism Reframed: Nationhood and the National Question in the New Europe* (Cambridge, Cambridge University Press, 1996) 2.

new imagining of Europe, there was a strengthening of the outer borders of the Union.[22]

Notwithstanding the arbitrariness of legal categories, people who would be considered refugees according to states' legislation find themselves excluded along with other people whose motives for moving are not considered legitimate. Measures deployed to limit access to all migrants have proliferated over the years and include the imposition of visa requirements, carrier sanctions, the use of 'safe country' concepts, juxtaposed border controls, and the activities of Frontex, the EU Borders Agency. Common EU visa rules are applicable to nationals of 128 countries, including the majority of African countries, Asia and significant parts of Central America. Consular officials are instructed to be 'particularly vigilant when dealing with … unemployed persons or those with irregular income'.[23]

Immigration controls impact heavily on countries in regions of origin, which are primarily located in the south. These countries host the vast majority of people fleeing conflict and persecution. Most Syrians, for instance, remain in neighbouring countries in the region, with only 10 per cent seeking protection in Europe. This is not an incidental result of the reduction in access routes to the north. Northern countries have made concerted efforts to contain people in southern countries and have sought to facilitate the return of individuals found to have no legal right to be on European territory, both through European law in the form of the Return Directive,[24] as well as through the conclusion of readmission agreements, Action Plans and Mobility Partnerships with non-European countries.[25]

While it may be that policy-makers are relatively unsuccessful in reducing overall numbers of entrants, their efforts to control borders are not

[22] See N El-Enany, 'The "New Europe" and the "New European Refugee": The Subversion of the European Union's Refugee Law by its Migration Policy' in S Juss (ed), *The Ashgate Research Companion to Migration Theory and Policy* (London and New York, Ashgate, 2011).

[23] T Gammeltoft-Hansen, *Access to Asylum: International Refugee Law and the Globalisation of Migration Control* (Cambridge, Cambridge University Press, 2011) 133.

[24] Council Directive 2008/115/EC of 16 December 2008 on common standards and procedures in Member States for returning illegally staying third country nationals [2008] OJ L348/98.

[25] Under the 1999 Treaty of Amsterdam, the EU has the authority to conclude readmission agreements with non-EU states. Although the first multilateral readmission agreement was the 1991 Readmission Agreement between Poland and the Schengen countries, the EU has concluded further accords with countries such as Hong Kong, Sri Lanka, Macao, Albania, Russia and Ukraine. Member States may also conclude bilateral accords of their own. For example, together with its constitutional reforms implementing the 'safe third country' concept, Germany negotiated agreements with both European and non-European States, including Romania, Poland, the Czech Republic, Bulgaria, Croatia, the Federal Republic of Yugoslavia, Bosnia, Vietnam, Pakistan and Algeria. The rapid increase in the use of readmission agreements can be seen in Poland's conclusion of similar instruments with the Czech Republic in 1993, four days after that with Germany, and with Slovakia, Ukraine, Romania and Bulgaria in the same year. See S Lavenex, '"Passing the Buck": European Union Refugee Policies towards Central and Eastern Europe' (1998) 11(2) *Journal of International Law* 139.

altogether without implication.[26] Thomas Spijkerboer has found that the impact of intensified border control is an increase in the number of deaths.[27] Following intensification of border controls at departure points, migrants travelling to Europe have shifted their departure points further south, to Libya, Tunisia, Guinea-Bissau, Ivory Coast, as well as Mauritania and Senegal. Thus, while the number of migrants entering at particular points of the Union can be reduced, this merely has a 'displacement' effect whereby migrants move their departure points further away, making more dangerous journeys. Between 1993 and 2006, 7,182 deaths at the European border were documented by the non-governmental organisation (NGO), United. Since then, the number has leapt to 22,394.[28]

IV. THE MIGRANT AND THE REFUGEE: A COSTLY DISTINCTION

The UNHCR has previously been accused of not sufficiently taking into consideration the position of southern states in its work. In 2001, Chimni proposed that a dialogue on refugee protection take place between the UNHCR and southern states 'to be conducted on a continuous and institutionalised basis'.[29] Chimni highlighted the importance of the principle of deliberative democracy for the purposes of any reform of the international refugee protection regime that would account for the interests of the international community as a whole rather than merely those of northern states. Chimni argued that northern states' persistent implementation of restrictive measures on entry effectively meant they had unilaterally determined the shape of the current regime.[30] In Chimni's view, it is not the movement of people that is indicative of crisis in refugee protection, rather it is the prevalence of restrictive border regimes in northern countries.[31]

In September 2015, following the rise in the number of Syrian people arriving at the borders of Europe, the UNHCR commissioned a number of high profile actors and celebrities including Cate Blanchett, Colin Firth and Patrick Stewart to take part in a promotional video explaining the

[26] See N El-Enany, 'The EU Asylum, Immigration and Border Control Regime: Including and Excluding the "Deserving Migrant"' (2013) 15(2) *European Journal of Social Security* 171.

[27] T Spijkerboer, 'The Human Cost of Border Control' (2007) 9 *European Journal of Migration and Law* 127.

[28] See UNITED, 'The Fatal Policies of Fortress Europe' (Amsterdam, UNITED for Intercultural Action, 19 June 2015) www.unitedagainstracism.org/campaigns/refugee-campaign/fortress-europe/.

[29] BS Chimni, 'Reforming the International Refugee Regime: A Dialogue Model' (2001) 14 *Journal of Refugee Studies* 2, 152.

[30] ibid.

[31] ibid 151–52.

difference between a 'refugee' and a 'migrant'.[32] The video, released under the hashtag #WordsMatter, entails clips of each of the celebrities looking sincerely into the camera while making urgent statements about the difference between migrants and refugees. It begins with the line: 'A migrant chooses to move country, often to improve their life … They are free to return home and if they return home they still have the protection of their government.' Underlying this understanding of a migrant is an assumption that people risking their lives to cross the Mediterranean, leaving lives of desperate poverty behind have a real capacity for choice in the matter of their movement. The statement is also inaccurate in its presumption that migrants necessarily 'have the protection of their governments'. An illustrative example is that of Egypt, a key political ally of northern countries. While people arriving in Europe from Egypt are unlikely to be considered refugees in legal terms, the political and economic situation in the country means citizens do not in fact 'have the protection of their government', but are instead at risk of being harassed and beaten in the street by police and even disappeared, the fate of more than 160 Egyptians since April 2015. Yet their leader, Sisi, has been given a warm welcome in a number of European counties.[33]

The video continues with another collage of actors and models popping up to tell viewers that: 'A refugee is running for their life … they often undertake traumatic and treacherous journeys of escape in order to find sanctuary, by land, by sea.' This is of course true, but the same goes for all irregular migrants, who are often fleeing life-threatening levels of poverty. Although the video contains the statement 'we need to treat all human beings—refugee or migrant—with respect and dignity', the objective of the message is to highlight that refugees are more deserving of protection and sympathy. The video ends with the words: 'but meanings matter. Words matter. Your words matter'. Of course, by delivering this message from the UNHCR though the mouths of celebrity messengers, the organisation hopes it will hold sway with a star-struck public. The UNHCR is well aware of its mandate and the definition of a Convention refugee. By communicating the distinction between those deserving of protection and those not according to the law, the UNHCR is saying that the meanings which matter are those with legal force behind them, even if these are ethically narrow or problematic in other ways.

[32] See H Saul, 'Patrick Stewart Joins Actors Explaining Difference Between "Refugee" and "Migrant" for UNCHR Words Matter Campaign' (The Independent 28 September 2015) www.independent.co.uk/news/people/patrick-stewart-and-cat-blanchett-join-actors-explaining-difference-between-refugee-and-migrant-for-a6670481.html.

[33] See A Accorsi, 'Without a Trace, More than 100 Egyptians Disappear from Homes, Streets: Report' (Cairo, Middle East Eye, 13 June 2015) www.middleeasteye.net/news/egypts-disappeared-191078261.

Individuals fleeing extreme poverty or environmental degradation are not considered deserving of protection according to the law. This is despite the fact that both poverty and environmental degradation can be conceived of as subtle but grindingly powerful forms of persecution if we consider that they are frequently the consequences of power relations at the global level. Patricia Tuitt has noted, 'Inevitably once a demand is made to prove that persecution was for a specified and recognised reason, then one introduces judgements which crudely are about when it is and is not justifiable or acceptable to persecute someone'.[34] For the UNHCR to valorise refugees and minimise the condition of suffering of migrants in the interests of its more immediate goals, is ethically problematic, but it is also ineffective and counter-productive as a solution to the problem the organisation is trying to tackle with this promotional video for refugees in the first place—that is, that refugees and migrants alike are struggling to access territorial protection across Europe.

In the face of the increasing number of deaths of people trying to reach Europe last autumn, various media outlets pondered the terminology they used. Al Jazeera announced it would be jettisoning the word 'migrant' because of its dehumanising implications for the people behind the word. If, as one online editor at Al Jazeera wrote in the course of explaining the news outlet's switch to 'refugee', 'migrant is a word that strips suffering people of voice', where does that leave migrants?[35] Surely the question that begs is why the term 'migrant' strips suffering people of voice? It is not the word 'migrant' in and of itself that is the problem, the problem is that migrants are not humanised. The contemporary official discourse on migration, along with Europe's history of imperial conquest and colonialism has contributed to the entrenchment of racism in northern societies. The former UK Prime Minister, David Cameron's reference to the Calais migrants trying to reach Britain as 'a swarm' was criticised for its dehumanising effect. In the wake of the Paris attacks, the British Daily Mail newspaper published a cartoon depicting racialised images of Muslims crossing Europe's borders along with rats.[36] While Poland[37] reneged on

[34] Tuitt, above n 2, 43.

[35] See B Malone, 'Why Al Jazeera Will Not Say Mediterranean "Migrants"' (Al Jazeera Blog, 20 August 2015) www.aljazeera.com/blogs/editors-blog/2015/08/al-jazeera-mediterranean-migrants-150820082226309.html.

[36] See B McKernan, 'The Daily Mail Has Been Accused of Xenophobia After Publishing a Cartoon that Depicts Refugees as Rats' (Indy 100, The Independent, 2015) www.i100.independent.co.uk/article/the-daily-mail-has-been-accused-of-xenophobia-after-publishing-a-cartoon-that-depicts-refugees-as-rats--bkJRYorPYe.

[37] See H Austin, 'Paris Attacks: Poland Slams Door to Syrian Refugees Following Massacres in France's Capital' (International Business Times, 14 November 2015) www.ibtimes.co.uk/paris-attacks-poland-slams-door-syrian-refugees-following-massacres-frances-capital-1528766.

its refugee quota agreement following the attacks, more than half of all US state governors refused to accept Syrian refugees.[38] Meanwhile, Australia declared its official policy was to focus its protection efforts on Christian Syrians.[39] Each of these decisions is reproductive of Islamophobia in buying into the idea that Muslims are associated with terror by virtue of being Muslim.

Hamid Dabashi has described the racism against Muslims in North America and Europe as 'unabated and growing',[40] a statement borne out in the statistics of hate crime targeted against Muslims.[41] London's Muslims, for instance, faced a 70 per cent increase in hate crimes in 2015, with the Met Police recording a total of 816 offences between July and September of last year. According to Theresa Hayter,

> Immigration controls embody, legitimate and institutionalise racism. They have both been caused by and caused a racism which has become deeply embedded and widely manifest in the rich nation states of the West, and especially so in their apparatus of control, including the police, the immigration authorities and private security guards.[42]

Migrants are a useful political scapegoat that no government since the introduction of immigration controls has resisted manipulating for populist goals. Although restrictive border control regimes have been presented as the norm by northern governments, the movement of people has throughout time been a part of the human experience. In view of this, rejecting the normality of the movement of people is 'to deny part of the social nature of human beings'.[43] Or rather, of certain human beings, because, as we know, those who are privileged enough to be able to move regularly go by any name but migrant, whether expat, tourist, international student or ambassador. Those who travel irregularly are for the most part people of colour from poor southern countries with histories of colonisation, neoliberal exploitation in the form of debt, land-grabbing, the calamitous effects of International Monetary Fund (IMF) and World Bank-imposed structural adjustment programmes and the catastrophic effects of military intervention by northern countries.

[38] See S Frostenson and D Lind, 'Here's a Map of Every State Refusing to Accept Syrian Refugees' (Vox Policy and Politics, 18 November 2015) www.vox.com/2015/11/16/9746456/map-syrian-refugees-governors.

[39] See S McNeill, 'Government Set to Focus Syrian Refugee Program on Christians in Wake of Paris Attacks: Scott Morrison (ABC News, 18 November 2015) www.abc.net.au/news/2015-11-18/morrison-expects-christians-to-be-focus-of-refugee-program/6952854.

[40] H Dabashi, *Brown Skin White Masks* (London, Pluto Press, 2011) 114.

[41] See J Githens-Mazer and R Lambert, 'Islamophobia and Anti-Muslim Hate Crime: A London Case Study' (European Muslim Research Centre, University of Exeter, 2010) www.counterextremism.org/resources/details/id/107/islamophobia-and-anti-muslim-hate-crime-a-london-case-study.

[42] Hayter, above n 16, 21.

[43] ibid 8.

The conception of race that I am drawing upon here builds on racial formation theory which understands race as a socially constructed identity.[44] Drawing on Foucault, Renisa Mawani understands race as 'a regime of power that cannot be reduced to ideology, corporeality, or exclusion alone' and further that 'it is through the production of racial regimes of power that subjection and subjectification are made possible, occurring and unfolding as mutable and mobile forces, responding to various social relations and occurrences, and assuming different manifestations and meanings'.[45] Ruth Wilson Gilmore puts forward a conception of racism as 'the state-sanctioned and/or extra-legal production and exploitation of group-differentiated vulnerability to premature death'.[46] Immigration law exists as a regime of power that categorises people into groups. The division of people into groups—those with and those without rights of entry and stay—makes the latter vulnerable to premature death. Those people without a right of entry or stay are rendered vulnerable to premature death in being forced to undertake treacherous journeys in search of safety. Having accessed northern countries, the absence of a right to stay can mean homelessness, lack of access to healthcare, and confinement to a camp or detention centre. Migrants in these conditions are at risk of being subjected to physical and mental violence and abuse and even death, whether as a result of violent abuse[47] or suicide.[48]

Gilmore's definition of racism, as Dean Spade has noted, can be 'useful for thinking about how various systems of meaning and control distribute chances at life and death'.[49] We can see this in operation in the way in which the valorisation of the refugee is enabled by means of the law's differentiation between the migrant and the refugee. While the refugee is deemed deserving, the position of the migrant is deemed undeserving. Words matter therefore precisely because the law, as expressed through legal language, is productive of categories—it differentiates between

[44] M Omi and H Winant, *Racial Formation in the United States: From the 1960s to the 1990s* (New York, Routledge, 1994); DM HoSang, O LaBennett and L Pulido (eds), *Racial Formation in the Twenty-First Century* (California, University of California Press, 2012).

[45] R Mawani, 'Law as Temporality: Colonial Politics and Indian Settlers' (2014) 4 *UC Irvine Law Review* 65, 68.

[46] RW Gilmore, *Golden Gulag: Prisons, Surplus, Crisis, and Opposition in Globalizing California* (California, University of California Press, 2006) 28.

[47] eg on the case of Jimmy Mubenga: N El-Enany, 'The Violence of Deportation and the Exclusion of Evidence of Racism in the Case of Jimmy Mubenga' in N El-Enany and E Bruce-Jones (eds), *Justice, Resistance and Solidarity: Race and Policing in England and Wales* (Runnymede Trust, 2015) 14.

[48] See nodeportations.org.uk, 'No Deportations: Residence Papers for All' (24 March 2016) www.no-deportations.org.uk/Media-6-4-2011/DeathInRemovalCentres.html on the details of deaths in UK detention centres and statistics of those on suicide watch.

[49] D Spade, *Normal Life: Administrative Violence, Critical Trans Politics and the Limits of the Law* (New York, South End Press, 2011) 46.

groups. While these categories may appear to be pre-existing, it is in fact the law that is creating them, determining them and what is available to each, apportioning life chances between them accordingly. Gilmore's definition of racism as being structurally produced is helpful 'because traditional legal definitions of discrimination focus on finding an individual discriminator who can be proven to have intended to discriminate' meaning 'harmful conditions that are faced by populations targeted for abandonment and imprisonment cannot be addressed'.[50] According to Dean Spade, 'thinking about the distribution of vulnerability to premature death across the population allows us to see the significance of administration and let go of the focus on individual wrongdoers and intent'.[51] If we are concerned to end deaths at sea and the suffering of those affected by immigration and border control, shifting the terminology of choice to 'refugee' in order to bypass the dehumanisation effect of the word 'migrant' is not an effective long-term strategy. It is not the word migrant that is the problem—the problem is the dehumanisation of migrants. Placing the emphasis on a narrowly contrived legal definition is not only ineffective, but is also counterproductive in reinforcing the arbitrary and discriminatory effects of the law.

With this in mind, I now turn to consider the case of Alan Kurdi. While the public outpouring of grief and solidarity with refugees following the emergence of the photograph of this young boy who drowned in some ways challenges the narrative presented thus far, in other important ways it is illustrative of it.

V. ALAN KURDI: THE HUMAN REFUGEE

Rather than acknowledge the racism endemic in European societies, some scholars have understood anti-migrant sentiment in the context of the recent movement of Syrians towards Europe as being an expression of different values, or viewpoints in what is presented as a debate on migration.[52] For example, Slavoj Zizek has described the demands of anti-migrant populists as being about the 'protection of our way of life' and insisted that the assertion that Europeans lack empathy for the pain of others is 'merely the obverse of … anti-immigrant brutality'.[53] In a move

[50] ibid.
[51] ibid.
[52] eg M Everson, 'The Continuing Relevance of the Convention?' (2015) 27(1) *Law & Critique* 9; S Zizek, 'Slavoj Zizek: We Can't Address the EU Refugee Crisis Without Confronting Global Capitalism' (In These Times, 9 September 2015) inthesetimes.com/article/18385/slavoj-zizek-european-refugee-crisis-and-global-capitalism.
[53] Zizek, above n 52.

that is arguably demonstrative of negative stereotyping of people seeking entry to Europe, Zizek demands that it be 'made clear' to them that they are to 'respect the laws and social norms of European states' which entails 'No tolerance of religious, sexist or ethnic violence', as though such forms of violence were not fundamental aspects of European life.[54]

According to the International Organisation for Migration, an estimated 700,000 people arrived at Europe's borders between January and October 2015. In the same period in 2014, the number was 280,000.[55] Although many have died trying to reach Europe through irregular means, the European public were galvanised over the question of refugee protection following the emergence of the photograph of Alan Kurdi, a toddler who drowned en route to Europe along with his elder brother and mother in September 2015.[56] Since Alan Kurdi's death, more than 70 children have lost their lives off the Greek coast.[57] Social and other media suggests that when some white Europeans looked at the photo of Alan Kurdi they saw their own[58] sons[59] and nephews. This was perhaps illustrated in the emergence of #CouldBeMyChild, which was trending on Twitter after the discovery of Kurdi's body.[60] It is clear that much of the potency of the image came from the fact that it depicted the death of a very young child. Susan Sontag has observed how 'Photographs lay down routes of reference, and serve as totems of causes: sentiment is more likely to crystallize around a photograph than around a verbal slogan'.[61] Indeed, the power of an image to transform public opinion is well-established and not without precedent,[62] but the question remains as to the specificity of the image in question and the reaction that it elicits or does not elicit. It is perhaps notable that this particular image was of a light-skinned child. The question this begs is whether this feature enabled his humanisation and the public support for refugees which ensued, an effect which previous border deaths had not

[54] European Union Agency for Fundamental Rights (FRA), 'Hate Crime in the European Union' (Factsheet, Vienna, FRA, 2012) fra.europa.eu/sites/default/files/fra-factsheet_hate-crime_en_final_0.pdf.

[55] See BBC News, 'Migrant Crisis: Migration to Europe Explained in Seven Charts' (Europe, BBC, 4 March 2016) www.bbc.co.uk/news/world-europe-34131911.

[56] See N El-Enany, 'Who Remembers Aylan Kurdi Now?' (Media Diversified, 4 February 2016) mediadiversified.org/2016/01/04/who-remembers-aylan-kurdi-now/.

[57] See Save the Children, 'More Than 70 Children Have Drowned Trying to get to Greece Since Aylan Kurdi' (Media, Save the Children, March 2016) www.savethechildren.org.uk/2015-10/more-70-children-have-drowned-trying-get-greece-aylan-kurdi.

[58] See @Costa Constanti, 'Don't forget #refugees & #AylanKurdi -#DenXehnw #Could BeMyChild #Cyprus #Syria #RefugeesWelcome #Iraq #Daesh #Europe' (Tweet to Twitter Account, Twitter, 28 October 2015) twitter.com/CostaConstanti/status/659433327611346948.

[59] See Blackwell, 'Aylan Kurdi's Picture' (Post to Blackwell's Mark Blog, 4 September 2015) blackwellsmark.blogspot.co.uk/2015/09/aylan-kurdis-picture.html.

[60] See Twitter, '#CouldBeMyChild' (Hashtag, Twitter) twitter.com/hashtag/Could BeMyChild?src=hash.

[61] S Sontag, *Regarding the Pain of Others* (New York, Penguin, 2003).

[62] See S Sliwinski, *Human Rights in Camera* (Chicago, University of Chicago Press, 2011).

elicited.[63] Migrants are so often presented and understood in popular discourse as 'wanting something of us' rather than 'being of us'. The image of the foreigner as a 'taking foreigner',[64] in Bonnie Honig's words, has become ubiquitous. Perhaps there was something distinctive about the photograph of Alan Kurdi that allowed him to be seen as 'one of us' rather than 'one of them'. Research has demonstrated that the extent to which white people feel empathy and humanise others correlates with implicit racial biases. White people tend to engage in negative stereotyping of those with darker skin and this corresponds to a lower level of empathy shown for them.[65] Co-operation and assistance between people is known to follow feelings of empathy. However, in cases where people do not identify with the pain of others, violence and abuse can ensue,[66] both characteristics of Europe's militarised border regime.[67] It is indeed the case that, unlike the photograph of Alan Kurdi, the images of black African bodies washed up on the shores of Europe's Mediterranean beaches last spring did not elicit an outpouring of public grief and action.[68] Further, the Islamophobia that is prevalent in European societies today means that coded images of Muslims—the bearded Muslim, the woman in the hijab or burka—inhibit their humanisation and means that rather than compassion, they are likely to elicit feelings of apprehension and fear.

Although it might be that Alan Kurdi's light skin colour helped along his humanisation by some white Europeans, despite the use of the #Could Be My Child hashtag, their children could not have met Alan Kurdi's end. As I have argued previously, the hashtag is demonstrative of a lack of 'understanding of the specificity of colonial histories and present imperial wars and the way in which these structurally determine positions of power and privilege as between white people and people of colour'.[69] To paraphrase Sivanandan, refugees are here, their bodies washing up on European beaches, because white Europeans were, and continue to be, there.[70]

[63] See J Grierson, A Bonomolo and A Travis, 'Migrant Deaths: Funerals Held as EU Leaders Meet for Crisis Summit' (The Guardian, 23 April 2015) www.theguardian.com/world/2015/apr/23/migrant-deaths-funerals-held-after-mediterranean-disaster.

[64] B Honig, *Democracy and the Foreigner* (Princeton-Oxford, Princeton University Press, 2001) 8.

[65] See M Forgiarini, M Gallucci and A Maravita, 'Racism and the Empathy for Pain on Our Skin' (2011) 2 *Frontiers in Psychology* 108.

[66] ibid.

[67] See M Carr, *Fortress Europe: Inside the War against Immigration* (London, Hurst, 2015).

[68] See D Sim, 'Mediterranean Migrant Crisis: The Drowned and the Saved—A Photo Report' (International Business Times, 20 April 2015) www.ibtimes.co.uk/mediterranean-migrant-crisis-drowned-saved-photo-report-1497412.

[69] El-Enany, above n 55.

[70] A Sivanandan, 'Catching History on a Wing' (Speech to Institute of Race Relations 50th Anniversary Conference, 1 November 2008) www.irr.org.uk/news/catching-history-on-the-wing/.

VI. CONCLUSION: RACISM, EXCLUSION AND BLAMING THE VICTIM

In the aftermath of the recent racially motivated attacks at the Trollhättan school in Sweden, a Guardian journalist reported that the killings had 'forced Swedes to ask if the traditional openness of their society may be putting pupils and teachers at risk' and that 'the revelation that the government would attempt to stem the flow of refugees to Sweden marks an official recognition that the country is finding it hard to cope.'[71] Shortly afterwards, the Swedish Government did indeed introduce border controls to limit the entry of refugees.[72] Here is an instance of Europeans, on being confronted by the true horror of racism, responding with a call for closure, blaming the victims of racism for being present, for inviting fascism in. Yet, it is racism that is the cause of the violence, not the presence of the victim. Eradicating the presence of the victim will not solve the problem, just as switching the terminology from migrant to refugee will not stem the suffering of either.

In his book, *Illegality Inc*, Ruben Andersson includes an excerpt from an interview with a border guard in the Spanish enclave, Melilla (claimed by Morocco to be occupied territory), in which the guard, 'pointing to the pristine coves across the [fortified border] fence', says, 'There I used to go swimming as a child … We caught fish with our bare hands … Migration has closed this city a lot'.[73] Yet, just as it is not the presence of people of colour that is the cause of racist violence, it is not migration that closes spaces off. This is the effect of borders.

[71] See D Crouch, 'Swedish Police Say School Attack was Racist, as Refugee Rules Tightened' (The Guardian, 23 October 2015) www.theguardian.com/world/2015/oct/23/swedish-police-treat-school-attack-as-racist-as-government-plans-to-stem-refugees.

[72] See P Kingsley in M Weaverin and A Kassam, 'Sweden Introduces Border Checks as Refugee Crisis Grows' (The Guardian, 12 November 2015) www.theguardian.com/world/2015/nov/12/refugee-crisis-sweden-introduces-border-checks.

[73] R Andersson, *Illegality Inc* (California, University of California Press, 2014) 165.

Part II

Access to Territory

3

Where Do State Responsibilities Begin and End?

Border Exclusions and State Responsibility

JÚLIA IVÁN

I. INTRODUCTION

THIS CHAPTER ANALYSES the border practices of Hungarian state authorities in line with principles of European human rights and international law to establish whether there are gaps in the provision of access to refugee protection. The analysis draws upon the practical experiences of the Hungarian Helsinki Committee (HHC) which has engaged in the systematic monitoring of border management activities carried out at Hungary's borders with Ukraine, Serbia and at the international airport in Budapest.[1] This study has found that, despite the general understanding that human rights protect all individuals whether residing or on the move, there is a reluctance by Hungarian border guards to facilitate access to protection and territory for those in need. The experience of lawyers working with the HHC shows that even the most vulnerable asylum seekers struggle to gain access to procedures to obtain international protection. An examination of border control practices reveals that authorities can disregard basic principles of international human rights and refugee law instruments, such as non-discrimination, *non-refoulement* and the non-criminalisation of irregular entry by refugees.

Hungary is a party to the United Nations Convention Relating to the Status of Refugees (Refugee Convention)[2] and has broadly transposed

[1] For more information on the UN High Commissioner for Refugees (UNHCR) Border Management and Protection of Refugees Programme in Central Europe, see www.unhcr-centraleurope.org/pdf/what-we-do/monitoring-the-border/border-management/border-monitoring-who-does-what.html.

[2] 189 United Nations Treaty Series 150, supplemented by the 1967 Protocol relating to the Status of Refugees, 606 United Nations Treaty Series 267 (Refugee Convention).

the relevant European Union (EU) asylum-related directives into national legislation.[3] However, the 'fortress' mechanisms enacted by Hungary in recent years create significant difficulties for asylum seekers to obtain access to territory, particularly the erection of physical border restrictions such as the fence on the Serbian border.[4] This is problematic as the submission of a protection application requires the physical presence of the applicant in the requested state. That is, access to refugee protection is often dependent on access to the territory of a state which is able and willing to provide protection.

However, problems also arise for asylum seekers obtaining access to procedures once in Hungarian territory.[5] Asylum seekers may state to border authorities that they are fleeing harm due to conflict, but this is not interpreted as a claim for asylum. Hungarian state authorities often inform practitioners that deported migrants did not formally seek asylum or that the border police were not obliged to respect their right to asylum and that *non-refoulement* does not apply in such situations. This is the case despite compelling case law from the European Court of Human Rights (ECtHR) about refugee protection. For instance, in the landmark case of *Hirsi Jamaa and Others v Italy*,[6] the ECtHR made a significant advance by broadening the interpretation of the state's obligation to protect refugees, and even undocumented migrants. The Court stated clearly that 'Italy is not exempt from complying with its obligations under Article 3 of the Convention because the applicants failed to ask for asylum or to describe the risks faced as a result of the lack of an asylum system in Libya.'[7]

A second important statement of the *Hirsi* judgment from the practitioner's point of view is that the size of the group concerned does not matter. The Court ruled that '[t]he fact that a large number of irregular immigrants in Libya found themselves in the same situation as the applicants does not make the risk concerned any less individual where it is sufficiently real and probable.'[8]

[3] UNHCR, 'Hungary as a Country of Asylum' (April 2012) www.refworld.org/pdfid/4f9167db2.pdf, 4. Although the EC instituted an infringement notice against Hungary in December 2015: European Commission, 'Commission Opens Infringement Procedure Against Hungary Concerning Its Asylum Law' (Press release, Brussels, 10 December 2015) www.europa.eu/rapid/press-release_IP-15-6228_en.htm.

[4] See A Smale, 'Migrants Race North as Hungary Builds a Border Fence' New York Times (24 August 2015) www.nytimes.com/2015/08/25/world/europe/migrants-push-toward-hungary-as-a-border-fence-rises.html?_r=0; M Dunai, 'Hungary to Fence off Border With Serbia to Stop Migrants' Reuters (17 June 2015) www.reuters.com/article/2015/06/17/us-hungary-immigration-idUSKBN0OX17I20150617.

[5] For instance, as of 1 August 2015, persons who transited Serbia are not entitled to have their asylum claim examined on the merits (see discussion below at Pt V).

[6] *Hirsi Jamaa and Others v Italy* App no 27765/09 (ECtHR, 23 February 2012).

[7] ibid para 157.

[8] *Hirsi Jamaa and Others v Italy*, above n 6, para 136.

This chapter will analyse the border management practices at the EU's external land borders in Central Eastern Europe, with a particular focus on the consequences of the *Hirsi* judgment and the extent to which that judgment assists the asylum seeker in gaining access to justice. Whilst it is the case that the *Hirsi* decision dealt with interception at sea, the principles espoused are also applicable to land borders, particularly the statements of Judge Albuquerque on access to a fair procedure. Indeed, the events of summer 2015 have clearly shown that asylum seekers continue to encounter problems in accessing a fair procedure.

This chapter will begin by examining the application of refugee law and human rights principles to border zones (section II), before continuing to address access issues at the border in practice in sections III and IV. This analysis discusses the differences in regimes between 2007 and 2013, and then from 2013 onwards when there was a change in procedure. As Hungary became one of the main entry points of asylum seekers heading to the EU during the summer of 2015, the events and legal measures adopted in August and September 2015 will be presented separately in section V of this chapter, offering insight into what is an increasingly restrictive asylum policy within the heart of Central Europe. This will be followed by an analysis in section VI of the ability of practitioners in Hungary to litigate to address *refoulement* in the courts.

II. THE APPLICATION OF HUMAN RIGHTS LAW TO BORDERS

It is generally understood that human rights are not limited to certain parts of the state's territory and thus international human rights obligations must be fulfilled at border zones as well. States are obliged to carry out their border management duties under their jurisdiction with respect to general human rights and refugee law obligations. The Office of the High Commissioner for Human Rights (OHCHR) has collected a set of recommendations to translate general human rights obligations into practical border management measures to ensure that the human rights of persons on the move are equally respected (OHCHR Guidelines).[9] The OHCHR Guidelines are clear in emphasising that besides protecting their borders as sovereign states, state authorities are first and foremost obliged to protect the lives of all human beings, including those in an irregular situation (most typically irregular migrants and asylum seekers). It is not yet known what impact these Guidelines will have on state practices in border control and governance. They appear on their face to be clear: they

[9] The Office of the High Commissioner for Human Rights (OHCHR), 'Recommended Principles and Guidelines' (23 July 2014) www.ohchr.org/Documents/Issues/Migration/A-69-CRP-1_en.pdf, 3.

reiterate that border control has to respect the principle of *non-refoulement*, a cornerstone of refugee protection in international law.

In the *Hirsi case*, the ECtHR attempted to end the practice whereby European states make continuous attempts to prevent irregular migrants from arriving at their borders; in order to comply with international protection obligations these attempts may often be in the form of readmission agreements[10] or other forms of international (bilateral) co-operation agreements, such as the Italian–Libyan Friendship Treaty of 2008[11] and associated agreements.[12] Under the framework of this agreement, the Libyan authorities supported their Italian counterparts in fighting against irregular migration in exchange for financial support from Italy.[13] This form of transferring state responsibility and exporting border control reportedly led to many refugees being detained in Libya and prevented from establishing the capacity to seek protection where they wished.[14]

Other reports have also underlined the challenges faced by asylum seekers in obtaining access to EU territory to lodge a protection application and the significance of *Hirsi*. For instance, a 2014 report by the European Programme for Integration and Migration (EPIM) notes that:

> Access to protection and to asylum procedures has become increasingly difficult in European Union countries due to a combination of policies and measures that hamper regular and safe arrival of asylum seekers. In this context, the Hirsi case is of fundamental importance as it delineates clear standards that EU Member States must respect when conducting border controls.[15]

Based on statistics from the EU's border agency, FRONTEX,[16] Human Rights Watch reported that '[i]rregular boat migrants to Sicily (including

[10] Readmission defines a procedure which does not allow individuals to stay at the territory of a given country and results in their physical removal: see JP Cassarino (ed), 'Special Edition Viewpoints: Unbalanced Reciprocities: Cooperation on Readmission in the Euro-Mediterranean Area' (Middle Eastern Institute, Washington DC, 2010) i.

[11] See N Ronzitti, 'The Treaty on Friendship, Partnership and Cooperation between Italy and Libya: New Prospects for Cooperation in the Mediterranean?' (2009) 1 *Bulletin of Italian Politics*, 125.

[12] Italy–Libya Co-operation Protocol, 29 December 2007 and its implementing protocol of 4 February 2009, discussed in *Hirsi Jamaa and Others v Italy*, above n 6, para 19. See also UNHCR, 'Submission by the Office of the United Nations High Commissioner for Refugees in the Case of *Hirsi and Others v Italy* (Application No. 27765/09)' (March 2010) 2.

[13] The Italian Minister of Interior reported to the Senate that 471 irregular migrants were transferred back to Libya in 2009: Strasbourg Observers, 'Interception-At-Sea: Illegal as Currently Practiced—Hirsi and Others v Italy' (Blog, 1 March 2012) www.strasbourgobservers.com/2012/03/01/interception-at-sea-illegal-as-currently-practiced-hirsi-and-others-v-italy/. See also Human Rights Watch, *Pushed Back, Pushed Around: Italy's Forced Return of Boat Migrants and Asylum Seekers, Libya's Mistreatment of Migrants and Asylum Seekers* (United States of America, HRW, 21 September 2009) 23.

[14] *Hirsi Jamaa and Others v Italy*, above n 6, paras 38–41.

[15] European Programme for Integration and Migration (EPIM), 'Access to Protection: Bridges not Walls' (Inprinting SRL—Roma, October 2014) www.cir-onlus.org/images/pdf/ACCESS%20TO%20PROTECION-%20BRIDGES%20NOT%20WALLS_REPORT.pdf, 15.

[16] See http://frontex.europa.eu/trends-and-routes/central-mediterranean-route/.

Lampedusa) and Sardinia fell by 55 per cent in the first six months of 2009 compared to the same period the previous year.'[17] This sharp decrease in irregular migrants arriving in Italy could be a consequence of executing the treaty with Libya by returning migrants there. This practice violated Italy's obligations under the Refugee Convention which prohibits the return of refugees to places (both transit countries and countries of origin) where their lives of freedom would be threatened, and which was ruled unlawful by the ECtHR. In *Hirsi*, along with the interpretation of the Court, the UNHCR stated that the coastguard's boats were under Italy's jurisdiction on the high seas and therefore the prohibition of *non-refoulement* was applicable in that situation.[18] The number of migrants affected by this practice was significant, as the ECtHR noted: 'during 2009 Italy had carried out nine operations on the high seas, returning 834 Somali, Eritrean and Nigerian nationals to Libya.'[19]

The UNHCR argued in its Note on International Protection that the principle of *non-refoulement* laid down in Article 33 of the Refugee Convention was a cardinal protection principle enshrined in the Convention, to which no reservations are permitted. In many ways, the principle is the logical complement to the right to seek asylum recognised in the Universal Declaration of Human Rights. It has come to be considered a rule of customary international law binding on all States. In addition, international human rights law has established non-refoulement as a fundamental component of the absolute prohibition of torture and cruel, inhuman or degrading treatment or punishment. The duty not to refoule is also recognised as applying to refugees irrespective of their formal recognition, thus obviously including asylum seekers whose status has not yet been determined.[20]

In light of the ECtHR's jurisprudence, the UNHCR's statements, and the views of many academics and human rights NGOs, we may conclude that state authorities have to respect the fundamental principle of *non-refoulement* when carrying out border controls.[21] In the *Hirsi* case the Grand Chamber unanimously found a violation of Article 3 of the ECHR prohibiting inhuman and degrading treatment for two reasons: first, the risk of ill-treatment in Libya and, second, the risk of repatriation from Libya to the applicants' countries of origin.[22] In addition, the Court found

[17] Human Rights Watch, above n 13, 24.

[18] UNHCR, above n 12, 12, 14. See also UNHCR statement on *refoulement* in UNHCR, 'Note on International Protection' (A/AC.96/951, 13 September 2001) 16.

[19] *Hirsi Jamaa and Others v Italy*, above n 6, para 101.

[20] UNHCR, above n 18, 16.

[21] See UNHCR, above n 12, 12: 'the principle of non-refoulement applies whenever a state exercises jurisdiction'.

[22] *Hirsi Jamaa and Others v Italy*, above n 6, paras 156–58.

a violation of Article 4 of Protocol No 4 prohibiting collective expulsion and Article 13 of the ECHR providing for a right to an effective remedy.[23]

The decision in *Hirsi* has been the subject of substantial academic commentary.[24] In this chapter I focus on the finding of the Court that the principle of protection applies irrespective of a migrant's status or the number of migrants involved. That is, '[t]he fact that a large number of irregular immigrants in Libya found themselves in the same situation as the applicants does not make the risk concerned any less individual where it is sufficiently real and probable.'[25] This is a conclusion that may be extremely useful for practitioners dealing with expulsion cases.

In his concurring opinion, Judge Albuquerque—in my opinion correctly—goes further when he argues that the prohibition of *refoulement* has two procedural consequences in the light of the collective expulsion of the applicants: the duty to provide advice on the migrant's right to seek international protection and the state's duty to provide for a fair, effective and individual refugee-status determination procedure. Judge Albuquerque's remarkable opinion is a promising direction towards a more proactive interpretation of the state's duties to protect the rights of refugees when stating that 'the Italian Government also have a positive obligation to provide the applicants with practical and effective access to an asylum procedure in Italy.'[26] This interpretation rebuts the typical defence of state authorities—including the Italian Government in the *Hirsi* case[27]—which denies responsibility for the removal of those migrants who did not formally lodge an asylum application even though those migrants are in a situation which may suggest that they are in need of international protection (either by genuinely identifying their country of origin by valid travel documents or clearly demonstrating their individual vulnerabilities to the authorities).

The HHC has been monitoring border control practices since 2007.[28] The Hungarian practice shows similarities to the facts of the *Hirsi* case despite the obvious difference that Hungary does not have sea borders therefore the argument of the lack of jurisdiction in high seas cannot be applied. There are, however, similarities between the two situations. For instance,

[23] ibid 186 and 207.

[24] See V Moreno-Lax, 'Hirsi Jamaa and Others v Italy or the Strasbourg Court Versus Extraterritorial Migration Control?' (2012) 12(3) *Human Rights Law Review* 574; C Costello, 'Courting Access to Asylum in Europe: Recent Supranational Jurisprudence Explored' (2012) 12(2) *Human Rights Law Review* 287.

[25] *Hirsi Jamaa and Others v Italy*, above n 6, para 136.

[26] ibid. Cathryn Costello has also noted, 'The powerful Concurring Opinion of Judge Pinto de Albuquerque in Hirsi urges a decisive move to a broad, more encompassing construction of State jurisdiction. Under his approach, jurisdiction would embrace all official border control-related activities, irrespective of where they were carried out': Costello, above n 24, 305.

[27] Discussed in *Hirsi Jamaa and Others v Italy*, above n 6, para 132.

[28] See http://helsinki.hu/en/border-monitoring-2007.

there have been situations where Hungarian border police have deported migrants who had a prima facie case for protection. In one example documented by HHC, an Iraqi man intercepted at the Serbian–Hungarian land border in May 2011 claimed that he left Iraq as a result of the war and for economic reasons. However, this was not considered as a request for protection as it was not explicit enough for the border police to refer the case to the asylum authority. Although his statement during the interview was not an explicit application for asylum, according to the viewpoint of the HHC, the clear reference to the war raises a claim for international protection.[29]

As noted above, Judge Albuquerque in *Hirsi* underlined the importance of state obligations to provide advice on the migrant's right to seek international protection and to provide for a fair, effective and individual refugee-status determination procedure. However, the HHC has analysed the practice as part of the border monitoring programme of the HHC, it remains the case that success in submitting an asylum application depends on several subjective factors, including:

> which representative of the authorities the foreign applicant meets, how sensitive that particular police officer is to hearing the asylum claim, and that individual's professional experience in recognizing the desire to seek asylum, as well as the skills and ability of the asylum seeker in expressing his/her desire to request asylum.[30]

Using the example discussed earlier in relation to the Iraqi asylum seeker claiming to be fleeing from conflict, one can conclude that the Hungarian border police was not acting consistently with its international duties.

I will now turn to examine the practice of border access as reflected in the HHC's border monitoring experience between 2007 and 2013 (section III) and 2013 and 2014 (section IV).

III. THE BORDER MONITORING EXPERIENCE IN HUNGARY 2007–13: DIFFICULTIES IN ACCESSING PROTECTION

In 2006 the Hungarian Border Guard (which was merged with the police in 2008), the UNHCR Regional Representation for Central Europe and the HHC concluded a tripartite agreement, which allows for the systematic monitoring of border management activities carried out at Hungary's borders with Ukraine, Serbia and at the international airport in Budapest

[29] J Iván, L Balázs, and K Varga-Szabó, *Access to Territory and Asylum Procedure in Hungary (2011)* (Hungary, HHC, National Police Headquarters, UNHCR, 2012) 9.

[30] ibid 10.

(Liszt Ferenc Airport).[31] The HHC contracted three independent attorneys to visit border areas including border crossing checkpoints, short-term holding facilities at the border and the transit zone of the airport with the aim to interview intercepted foreigners, to provide them with information on access to asylum in Hungary and to consult the anonymised case files of those persons who had already been removed from Hungarian territory. These visits usually take place twice a month, and due to the arrangements with the Border Guard all visits require a two-day notice period before each visit.[32]

In terms of practical implementation, it is important to note that since Hungary's accession to the Schengen Area in December 2007, external border management activities are carried out under the Schengen Borders Code, which foresees a unified set of rules for all participating Member States.[33] Border control became stricter at the Serbian, Ukrainian and Romanian borders, while internal border control was abolished with other neighbouring EU Member States such as Slovenia, Austria and Slovakia. Testimonies of the clients of the HHC confirm that this may be considered as a pull factor because refugees and migrants hope to arrive in their Western European destination countries faster, and once they have avoided Hungarian border police control they are free to move on towards the west.

For many years, the HHC identified border management practices that prevented refugees from submitting their asylum claims by not 'hearing' the applicant's own words. This trend and the attitude of Hungarian police officers serving at the Serbian–Hungarian border, however, significantly changed in 2013–14, which will be explained below.[34]

Until 2013, it was typical that some groups of apprehended migrants at the Hungarian border chose not to express their wish to seek asylum in the hope of being able to continue their journey. The Hungarian police claimed that many of the intercepted migrants did not wish to apply for asylum since Hungary was never their destination and it was 'still not typical for third country nationals who arrive in the country illegally to present themselves voluntary to the police and express their claim for protection'.[35]

[31] See the UNHRC Border Management and Protection of Refugees Programme, above n 1.

[32] See http://helsinki.hu/en/border-monitoring-2007.

[33] Council Regulation 562/2006 of 15 March 2006 establishing a Community Code on the rules governing the movement of persons across borders (Schengen Borders Code) [2006] OJ L105/1.

[34] 'In 2013, the number of asylum applications submitted by third-country nationals increased significantly, which was an important change as compared to previous years. The attorney carrying out the border monitoring experienced that the identification of the intention to seek asylum as well as the lodging of applications was carried out much swifter than in previous years': Iván, Balázs and Varga-Szabó, above n 29, 5.

[35] ibid 9.

While admitting that there is a large number of (potential) asylum seekers who do not wish to stay in Hungary, it is difficult to accept the above explanation from the police since testimonies from asylum seekers conducted by HHC confirmed that besides the original plans regarding their destination country, asylum seekers may be in fact be discouraged from seeking asylum due to communication barriers and the hostile attitude of the police officer they meet with.[36] The HHC assisted a Somali refugee who specifically told the police on their interception at the Hungarian–Ukrainian land border that he would like to go to a refugee camp and his life was in danger in his country of origin.[37] In my view these statements can be considered as an implicit asylum claim and should have been sufficient for the police to ask the person directly about his willingness to submit an asylum application. However, the police refused to do so, claiming that their tasks do not cover the information and identification of asylum seekers since they are not the asylum authority carrying out refugee status determination procedures.

In case no 7.B.VIII.20.776/2013/34, the Pest Central District Court delivered an important ruling on access to protection and territory regarding another Somali refugee, SAB, who attempted to enter Hungary from Ukraine twice. After successfully entering Hungary on the third occasion, he was charged with continued felony forgery of official documents committed on two counts and for the misdemeanour of violating the restriction of entry and stay. The case concerns the application of the Refugee Convention, Article 31(1), on the non-criminalisation of refugees for irregular border crossing.[38] The Somali applicant was first held in pretrial detention and was later found guilty of using fake names in official proceedings and re-entering the country irregularly. This was so despite the position of the Attorney-General confirming that those foreigners who receive refugee status or subsidiary protection cannot be held responsible for irregular border crossing and the use of forged travel documents if they fulfil the criteria set forth in Article 31 of the Refugee Convention

[36] The importance of police and border guards as those with whom asylum seekers are likely to first come into contact and the key responsibilities they hold in ensuring respect for *non-refoulement* are discussed in Pollet, ch 7.

[37] As recorded in case no 16.B.VIII.33.149/2010/7, Pest Central District Court, 3 December 2013 (unpublished). At the Pest Central District Court, the accused Somali national expressed his clear intention to seek asylum in Hungary to the police officers in Szabolcs-Szatmár-Bereg County (bordering Ukraine) twice, still he was deported to Ukraine twice before finally submitting his third asylum application successfully.

[38] Case no 7.B.VIII.20.776/2013/34, Pest Central District Court. The Refugee Convention, art 31 provides: '1. The Contracting States shall not impose penalties, on account of their illegal entry or presence, on refugees who, coming directly from a territory where their life or freedom was threatened in the sense of Article 1, enter or are present in their territory without authorization, provided they present themselves without delay to the authorities and show good cause for their illegal entry or presence.'

(namely that the refugee comes directly from a territory where his/her life or freedom would be threatened, he/she presents him/herself without delay and shows a good cause for the illegal entry or presence). The Somali refugee was finally acquitted in a repeated criminal procedure[39] and in its judgment the court interpreted the constitutive elements of an asylum application and the police officers' failure to identify the accused as an asylum seeker.[40]

The failure of the police to identify the accused as an asylum seeker arose from actions taken in response to the two first attempts by the applicant to gain access to Hungary. It was argued that the accused had made a request during interrogation by the police which could be construed by its content as a claim for asylum (whilst also presenting false personal data to the police because of his fear of persecution). During his interrogation on 23 April 2008, the accused represented that he had left his home country due to tribal wars as he was persecuted, threatened, insulted and discriminated for reasons of his origin of a minority background. When interrogated on 19 August 2008, he repeatedly mentioned (together with some statements irrelevant for the case) that he had been seriously insulted for belonging to a clan of a lower class and that he had to be hospitalised. The Court ruled:

> [The] Szabolcs Szatmár-Bereg County Police Headquarters failed to construe the request of the accused by its actual content, and by way of Decision No 1-7/1460-17/2008, the police authority imposed on the accused a ban of entry and stay for 4 years and ordered the expulsion of the accused into the territory of the Ukraine, which does not qualify as a safe country.[41]

In relation to the second attempt by the Somali refugee attempted to enter Hungary, again the Court found that:

> the Szabolcs-Szatmár-Bereg County Police Headquarters failed to construe the request of the accused by its actual content, and by way of Decision No 1-7/2882-17/2008, the authority imposed on the accused a ban of entry and stay for 3 years and repeatedly ordered his expulsion into the territory of Ukraine, which does not qualify as a safe country.[42]

The Court further concluded that:

> By his behaviour described before, the accused did contribute to the registration of false data as regards his personal particulars into interview records No I-7/1460/7/2008 and 1-7/2882-12/2008 as well as into the reports on his arrest.

[39] The first judgment of the Pest District Court was quashed by the Supreme Court who ordered that the case be reopened. The procedure had to be repeated due to certain legal errors (for instance, failure to consider whether Greece was an option for safe transit).

[40] Case no 7.B.VIII.20.776/2013/34, above n 38.

[41] ibid.

[42] ibid.

> However, bearing in mind the fact that he had arrived directly from a territory where his life and freedom were threatened and, on the occasion of his first contact with the authorities in the presence of an interpreter, he made a request for asylum, showing a good cause for his illegal entry, and the Office of Immigration and Nationality did recognise him as beneficiary of subsidiary protection by way of its Decision 106-2-3.455/8/2010-M, taking effect on 19 May 2010, the conduct of the accused shall not be regarded as a criminal act.[43]

The Court elaborated its position on how to interpret an asylum application and what sort of statements may be considered as an asylum application. It held that 'the qualification of a legal statement as a claim for asylum depends on not whether the claimant articulates the word "refugee" but whether he/she makes reference to facts falling under Section 6 (1) of the Asylum Act'[44] (that is, facts relating to a well-founded fear of persecution for a Convention reason).[45] The above ruling may be considered as a milestone regarding the identification of statements that construe an asylum application. Thus it may orientate the police on how to handle such situations and how to register asylum claims, a practice which should eventually contribute to asylum seekers' better access to protection.

IV. THE CHANGE OF PRACTICE IN 2013–14: TOWARDS A MORE COMPREHENSIVE BORDER CONTROL PRACTICE

According to statistics provided by the Hungarian National Police Headquarters, migratory trends increased markedly in 2013 and 2014. Besides the dramatic increase of intercepted migrants arriving from the Balkans, the number of asylum application registered by the police increased simultaneously: according to the data shared with the HHC by the Hungarian National Police, 42,894 foreigners were apprehended by the police at the Serbian–Hungarian external Schengen border[46] of the EU, out of which 30,398 sought asylum. Migrants interviewed by the HHC reported that their strategy was to look for the police officers at the green border and when they were intercepted they immediately expressed their wish to seek asylum.

[43] ibid.

[44] ibid.

[45] Asylum Act, art 6(1) provides that Hungary shall recognise as a refugee a foreigner who, owing to a well-founded fear of being persecuted for reasons of race, religion, nationality, membership of a particular social group, or political opinion, is outside of the country of his/her origin and is unable or, owing to such fear, unwilling to avail himself/herself of the protection of that country.

[46] European Commission, Migration and Home Affairs, 'Schengen Area' (29 January 2016) www.ec.europa.eu/dgs/home-affairs/what-we-do/policies/borders-and-visas/schengen/index_en.htm.

It appears that those refugees and migrants that managed to express their wish to seek asylum were not expelled to Serbia. Due to swift co-operation between Serbian and Hungarian border guard officials, a majority (73 per cent)[47] of the expelled foreigners (those perceived as not presenting a wish to seek asylum) were returned to Serbia under the framework of the readmission agreement between the EU and Serbia.[48]

According to police, the majority of the migrants intercepted in Hungary were aware that due to changes in the legal framework on detention after 1 January 2013, if they submitted an asylum application they would not be detained and expelled to Serbia, but could continue their journey within the Schengen Area towards Western European Member States of the EU. Until 1 January 2013, the Hungarian police systematically and automatically detained intercepted migrants, including those that sought asylum in Hungary, which resulted in most migrants deciding not to seek asylum in Hungary but instead accepting deportation to Serbia which would allow them to immediately re-attempt entry into a Western European country. To illustrate the increase, in 2012, 4,476 foreigners were intercepted but only 696 asylum applications were registered by the police at Hungary's external Schengen borders.[49] By contrast, the figures for 2014 show that whilst 42,894 persons were apprehended, a total of 30,398 asylum applications were registered.[50]

The significance of 'understanding' and properly registering an asylum claim lies in the fact that the police are only entitled to remove those migrants who do not submit an asylum application, as deportation is supposed to be suspended if the migrant claims asylum.[51] There is also a category of migrants, whose cases are decided upon without a personal

[47] Representing 2,767 out of a total of 3,758 persons expelled.

[48] Government Decree 53/2010, III (11) on the Protocol between the Government of the Republic of Hungary and the Government of the Republic of Serbia on the Implementation of the Agreement between the European Community and the Republic of Serbia on the Readmission of Persons Residing Without Authorisation, Brussels, 18 September 2007. For the agreement between the European Community and the Republic of Serbia see [2007] OJ L334/46.

[49] According to the 2012 statistics of the National Police Headquarters, the police ordered expulsion in 4,476 cases and return in 7,508 cases at the airport and the borders. At the border sections monitored by the programme, the police registered a total of 696 asylum applications during 2012: Iván, Balázs and Varga-Szabó, above n 30, 8.

[50] ibid 9. See also ibid 6: 'In 2014 30,398 foreigners declared before the Police during the alien policing procedure at the Hungarian-Serbian border section that they needed international protection based on the information provided by the Police or the information they had received before their arrival.'

[51] Hungary: Act II of 2007 on the Admission and Right of Residence of Third-Country Nationals and the Government Decree 114/2007(24) on the Implementation of Act II of 2007 on the Admission and Right of Residence of Third-Country Nationals, 1 July 2007, www.refworld.org/docid/4979cae12.html, s 48(4).

hearing being conducted by the Hungarian police—those that may be readmitted almost immediately to Serbia. This situation is similar to that in the *Hirsi* case, that is, the police effect removal without assessing the individual circumstances of the case.

There are therefore concerns arising from the procedures utilised by police in returning certain persons at the border. Return may be ordered if the person presents him or herself to the police to enter the country at a border crossing checkpoint and not in situations where the migrants cross the green border in an irregular manner trying to avoid police control. The current regulation of return is viewed as serving the purpose of removal by providing a rapid measure to the state from where these persons crossed the external Schengen borders to Hungary without meeting the conditions for entry.[52] Hungarian police have taken the view that there was no need to hold hearings for substantial numbers of persons subjected to return procedures.[53] This approach has been heavily criticised by both the UNHCR and the HHC.[54]

The increasing number of asylum applications registered by the police may also be explained by the ability of the migrants to express their intention to seek asylum and the willingness of the police to 'hear' these claims by ensuring better communication with the foreigners. The submission of the asylum claim is typically carried out by using the words asylum (*asil*) or refugee, but at this stage of the procedure the police do not register the application yet. Practice shows that:

It is difficult to deduce the exact circumstances of how an asylum application was made from the case files. The border guards' remarks are inconsistent in this regard, the content and length of the notes in the files varies,

[52] TCN Act, s 40, provides that the authority carrying out border checks shall refuse entry to third country nationals seeking admission for stays not exceeding three months according to the provisions of the Schengen Borders Code, and shall return such persons—in due observance of its interests: a) to the country of origin of the third country national in question; b) to the country that is liable to accept the third country national in question; c) to the country where the customary residence of the third country national in question is located; d) to any third country prepared to accept the third country national in question.

[53] According to the Hungarian National Police, there was no need to hold hearings for 11,632 persons under the return procedure in 2010, 11,819 persons returned in 2011 and 9,316 persons returned in 2012: Iván, Balázs and Varga-Szabó, above n 30, 5.

[54] Both the UNHCR and the HHC have criticised the practice of not interviewing irregular migrants en masse, ibid 5: 'However, as previous reports on border monitoring activities have pointed out, return is generally a measure that is enforced within a relatively short period of time, and due to its special procedural characteristics, it is not preceded by a substantive interview. Both the UNHCR and the HHC support the idea of introducing such an interview requirement in the Hungarian alien policing legislation, as through such an interview it would be possible for the Police to gain more information about the reasons why the foreigner left his/her country of origin. In the absence of this substantive interview the assessment of *non-refoulement* carried out by the authorities in the course of the return procedure remains a mere formality.'

and the official records often do not accurately reflect what had happened when the asylum application was submitted.[55]

It was reported to the HHC through its border monitoring programme that the police changed their practice at the end of 2014 when a short written form was introduced in which migrants can tick if they wish to seek asylum (*asil* or *no asil* are the two options), which is already a more proactive approach enabling migrants not to have to rely only on their own words and ability (or pure luck) when trying to seek protection.

V. BUILDING A PHYSICAL AND LEGAL FENCE: CLOSURE OF HUNGARY'S SOUTHERN BORDERS

The year 2015 brought significant changes in the border management practices of Hungarian authorities.[56] Due to the sudden increase in the number of irregular border crossings and asylum applications registered throughout 2015, the Hungarian Government decided to adopt extremely harsh measures to deter asylum seekers (and genuine refugees amongst them) from Hungary and change their route to Europe.

In 2015, the Hungarian–Serbian border section has become one of the three main entry points for irregular migrants and asylum seekers into the EU. By mid-September, Hungary registered over 170,000 asylum claims, while the total number of registered applicants remained slightly above 176,000 as of mid-December. Two-thirds of the applicants had fled from Syria, Afghanistan and Iraq. However, most of them moved onwards to Western Europe in a couple of days.[57] What has happened in Hungary with regard to asylum is a crucial challenge to the Common European Asylum System (CEAS), and therefore has a direct impact on the EU as a whole and all its Member States.

[55] HHC, *Asylum Seekers' Access to Territory and to the Asylum Procedure in the Republic of Hungary: Report on the Border Monitoring Program's First Year in 2007* (Hungary, HHC, December 2008), 12 www.unhcr.org/4aa0d5139.pdf (HHC Access to Territory).

[56] This section is based on HHC, 'No Country for Refugees: New Asylum Rules Deny Protection to Refugees and Lead to Unprecedented Human Rights Violations in Hungary' (Information Note, Budapest, 18 September 2015) www.helsinki.hu/wp-content/uploads/HHC_Hungary_Info_Note_Sept_2015_No_country_for_refugees.pdf (HHC No Country for Refugees).

[57] General practice shows that the vast majority of the asylum seekers did not consider Hungary as their destination country. Based on several interviews by the HHC with the persons concerned, we can conclude that there are various reasons for this: Hungary is not a typical immigration country in the sense that the majority of the applicants are not aware of its existence, there are significant language barriers and the overall economic situation of the country indicates that refugees would have a better life elsewhere. After the German chancellor Angela Merkel announced that Syrians could lodge their asylum applications in Germany this phenomenon was even more visible amongst asylum seekers.

During the summer of 2015, Hungary constructed a fence on the 175 km-long border with Serbia, with the explicit aim of diverting refugee and migration flows from this border section elsewhere. The fence, which was completed on 15 September 2015, consists of two lines of fences: a smaller barbed wire fence and a 3 m-tall fence next to each other.

In July 2015, Hungary made various amendments to its asylum legislation (including the Hungarian Asylum Act,[58] its implementing Asylum Government Decree), and adopted a National List of Safe Countries of Origin and Safe Third Countries.[59] Unlike any other EU Member State, Hungary considers all the countries that are situated in the Balkans safe (EU candidate countries and Bosnia-Herzegovina, Kosovo, Switzerland, Canada, Australia and New Zealand are considered safe countries of origin and transit). These changes, which came into force on 1 August 2015, have already started an extremely worrying trend, with the clear purpose of dismantling the entire Hungarian asylum system. The most problematic amendments are discussed below.

Considering Serbia is considered to be a safe third country for asylum seekers (in contradiction to the clear position of both the UNHCR[60] and the Hungarian Supreme Court),[61] resulting in the quasi-automatic rejection at first glance of over 99 per cent of asylum claims (as 99 per cent of asylum seekers enter Hungary from Serbia), without any consideration of protection needs. Despite the lack of available official statistics from the Office of Immigration and Nationality (OIN), by mid-December 2015, it was obvious that this change had led to the rejection of practically all asylum applications in a very fast procedure declaring Serbia a safe third country and ordering the applicant's deportation. As the Director General of the OIN, Ms Zsuzsanna Végh stated on national television on 25 November 2015, Serbia is reluctant to readmit those third country nationals to its territory who originate from war torn countries like Syria, Iraq or Afghanistan (despite the acceptance by the EU that many are entitled to protection).[62] This means that all rejected asylum applicants find

[58] The unofficial English translation of the modified asylum legislation as of 15 September 2015 is available at www.helsinki.hu/en/latest-text-of-asylum-law-and-related-rules-august-2015.

[59] Government Decree 191/2015, VII, (21), on the national list of safe countries of origin and safe third countries, available in Hungarian at www.njt.hu/cgi_bin/njt_doc.cgi?docid=176824.296526.

[60] UNHCR, 'Serbia as a Country of Asylum: Observations on the Situation of Asylum-Seekers and Beneficiaries of International Protection in Serbia' (August 2012) www.refworld.org/docid/50471f7e2.htm.

[61] Opinion 2/2012, XII (10) KMK of the Supreme Court of Hungary (Kúria) on Certain Questions Related to the Application of the Safe Third Country Concept, 10 December 2012, www.helsinki.hu/wp-content/uploads/HU-Supreme-Court-on-S3C-Dec-2012.pdf.

[62] For footage of this interview see www.rtl.hu/rtl2/magyarul/hivatal-a-menekultvalsag-kozepen (in Hungarian).

themselves in a limbo situation—they have no legal channels to international protection in Hungary and they cannot lawfully submit their asylum applications in Serbia either. It is also important to note that the vast majority of these asylum seekers wish to continue their journeys towards Western European EU Member States.

Extremely accelerated asylum proceedings are provided, which essentially refer all asylum claims to a fast track procedure. Prior to the amendments of the asylum laws in 2015 the Hungarian asylum procedure was already among the fastest within the EU. However, from 1 August 2015 the generally applicable procedural deadline dropped to 15 days since almost all applications are examined in the fast track procedure or inadmissibility procedure due to the widespread application of the safe third country concept.[63]

The one-instance judicial review[64] of asylum cases is rendered ineffective, with unreasonably short deadlines for submitting an appeal (seven days) and for the judge to make a decision (eight days), with no automatic suspensive effect on most removal measures and no personal interview in the judicial review phase.[65] The courts lost their reformatory power in the judicial review phase[66] and therefore the only option remains to quash the decisions of the OIN which will reopen the files and reassess the cases—according to the HHC's lawyers, practice shows that the repeated procedures often lead to the same results by declaring Serbia a safe third country disregarding the courts' guidance.

Legal grounds have been created to officially tolerate overcrowding in 'asylum jails' through the introduction of a provision on the physical requirements of an asylum jail that has already been quashed as unlawful by the Constitutional Court in another context.[67] The new text only obliges the authorities to observe the provision preventing overcrowding 'if possible'.

Irregular entry into Hungarian territory has been made a criminal offence.[68] As the HHC notes:

> The Government recently introduced three new crimes related to crossing the border, tightened criminal rules relating to smuggling in human beings, and

[63] Act no LXXX of 2007 on Asylum, s 47(2).

[64] There is only one judicial instance involved, and its decision is not subject to appeal.

[65] Act no LXXX of 2007 on Asylum, s 53.

[66] Reformatory power in this context means that the court is empowered to change the original administrative decision on the merits, mostly to grant refugee status, even if it was rejected at the administrative level of the proceedings.

[67] Government Decree 301/2007, XI (9), s 36/D on the implementation of the Asylum Act.

[68] For instance, unauthorised entry into the territory 'protected by the border closure' has now become a criminal act, which can be punished with up to three years in prison. See Asylum Information Database (AIDA), 'Crossing Boundaries: The New Asylum Procedure at the Border and Restrictions to Accessing Protection in Hungary' (Belgium, ECRE, 27 October 2015) www.ecre.org/component/downloads/downloads/1056, 21–24.

> introduced special rules expediting criminal procedures for those illegally crossing the fence. Several elements of these new rules are in direct violation of international legal obligations, and they are practically impossible to implement, the expected case load will produce an enormous pressure on the whole of the Hungarian criminal justice system. Hungary has already been condemned to pay compensation by the European Court of Human Rights several times due to the lengthiness of criminal procedures, and recently lost a strategic case before the Court due to overcrowding in criminal detention. It is easy to predict that the handling of these new cases, 'with priority over all other cases' according to the new rules, will further delay the procedure in other criminal cases and further increase the overcrowding of detention facilities.[69]

The amended rules also allow for the construction of so-called transit zones at a maximum distance of 60 metres from the frontier. The transit zone is a new legal construction in Hungarian asylum law, where immigration and asylum procedures are conducted and where buildings required for conducting such procedures and housing migrants and asylum seekers are located. As the HHC reported in its 2015 report, 'No Country for Refugees', there are serious problems associated with these transit zones:

At the time when these rules were adopted (on 4 September), it was foreseen that the transit zones would actually be massive prison camps, where asylum seekers could be held for a maximum period of 4 weeks. With thousands of asylum seekers arriving in Hungary each day during the summer, such facilities should have had the capacity to detain up to 10,000 or more asylum seekers at any point in time. Only two days after the entry into force of the law allowing for the construction of transit zones, the government announced that 'there will be no transit zones'. A few days later, it turned out that this information was also misleading, as two transit zones started to operate on 15 September [2015]: one in Röszke and another in Tompa, the two main border crossing points between Hungary and Serbia. In parallel, around 00.30 AM at night on 15 September, the border was closed between the two countries for asylum seekers, who until then had been allowed to enter Hungary in large numbers on preceding days (and transported close to the Austrian border). As a consequence, hundreds of asylum seekers got stranded on the Serbian side of the border.[70]

It is symbolic that, despite the various co-operation agreements, both the UNHCR and the HHC were denied access in the first few days after the transit zone in Röszke started to operate. As a result of the very limited access to the transit zone the HHC had difficulties in maintaining

[69] See HHC's analyses on the modification of the criminal code: HHC, 'The Hungarian Helsinki Committee's Opinion on the Governments Amendments to Criminal Law Related to the Sealed Border (Budapest)' www.helsinki.hu/wp-content/uploads/modification-of-criminal-laws-16092015.pdf.

[70] HCC, above n 56, 2.

attorney–client communications with two Bangladeshi asylum seekers who were detained within the transit zone for more than three weeks. Hungarian authorities did not consider the 'placement' of the two Bangladeshis as a form of detention, which in the view of the HHC and the European Council for Refugees and Exiles (ECRE) clearly falls under Article 5 of the ECHR.[71]

Even if all the above measures seem to fulfil their aim by dramatically hindering refugees' access to protection in Hungary, the Government launched a second anti-refugee campaign in December 2015, again linking terrorism to refugees and immigrants. In response to this, the UNHCR, the Council of Europe and the Office for Democratic Institutions and Human Rights (ODHIR) have urged Hungary to refrain from policies and practices that promote intolerance and fear, and fuel xenophobia against refugees and migrants.[72]

VI. LITIGATION AND FOLLOW-UP OF THE CASES OF REMOVED REFUGEES AND MIGRANTS

Despite the relatively large number of expelled and deported migrants in the past few years, the HHC has not yet been successful in pursuing individual cases in the courts. Indeed, one application was struck out from the list of pending cases of the ECtHR for loss of communication between the legal representative and the applicant after the client was deported and disappeared in Serbia.[73]

The *Hirsi* judgment gives valuable clues to practitioners on how to successfully litigate a case where the *refoulement* of a refugee is at stake. According to the conclusions of the Court in that case, successful litigation depends on extended co-operation between various actors from international monitoring bodies and the applicants and their legal representatives. The Court attributed importance to the fact that extensive international reports were available that documented the human rights situation in Libya and the consequences of the push backs from Italy.[74] It is still relatively rare that either international or nationals human rights organisations are able to provide such detailed information. In successfully substantiating the claims it is evident that the proactive role of the UNHCR, the Council of Europe's Committee for the Prevention of Torture and Inhuman or Degrading treatment or Punishment (CPT), Human

[71] AIDA, above n 68, 15.

[72] UNHCR, 'Hungary Urged to Refrain from Policies and Practices that Promote Intolerance and Hatred' (Press Release, 21 December 2015) www.unhcr.org/5677cf666.html.

[73] ECtHR unpublished decision.

[74] *Hirsi Jamaa and Others v Italy*, above n 6, para 123.

Rights Watch and Amnesty International was a key factor. Unfortunately, such a wide collaboration and such a level of detail are not usually available to human rights advocates or practitioners. Consequently there is still room for improvement to better document major human rights violations in non-accessible areas (such as transit zones, border areas or high seas). As a lawyer working with a human rights NGO and given the fact that denied access to protection may have irreparable consequences on human lives, I would encourage all international human rights actors to take the lead in systematically documenting incidents or situations where refugees may be *refouled*. These efforts are essential to successfully bring future cases before the ECtHR where the *non-refoulement* principle may have been violated.

These incidents are difficult to monitor and document as independent observers rarely have access to transit zones and detention facilities in all instances, both in Hungary and in Serbia. Given the fact that the Serbian asylum system is dysfunctional and unable to deal with the tens of thousands of asylum seekers transiting its territory, *refouled* persons are rarely offered adequate assistance, shelter and legal advice, all of which are essential for there to be any chance of following their progress. Most of these people end up being homeless somewhere in Serbia and disappear quite soon after attempting to reach Western Europe once again.

Another factor that renders the follow-up of these cases difficult is the traditional mistrust of state authorities towards civil society and, in some cases, international organisations. Therefore access to data related to the whereabouts of the persons of concern is often impossible without a signed original power of attorney from the asylum seekers.

Currently, it remains a challenge for many practitioners to be able to track the fate of the individuals removed due to capacity constraints and the general lack of transparency and openness in border procedures. Legal representatives have very little access to any documents related to the removal of the migrant concerned without a valid power of attorney. However, due to the extremely short timeframe—at land borders removals often take place within a few hours—the 'potential asylum seeker' may not have any contact with individual experts or legal representatives at all to seek assistance, and is thus unlikely to be able to give such a power of attorney.

Hungarian authorities are obliged to report on their activities to the public or comply with the provisions of the Freedom of Information Act.[75] This does not, however, cover individual measures or decisions taken, only the regular publication of statistical data, which by its nature does not allow human rights organisation to follow individual cases of interest.

[75] Act no CXII of 2011 on the Right to Informational Self-Determination and Freedom of Information.

Individual freedom of information requests may be submitted to the police related to deportation practices, but the information will only be provided in an anonymised manner, lacking all personal data of the foreigners.

VII. CONCLUSIONS

Despite the favourable ruling of the Court in the *Hirsi case*, which emphasised the positive obligation on the state to identify asylum seekers and offer them a fair and individual status determination procedure, it is impossible to utilise the judgment to protect the rights of asylum seekers unless individual border procedures are properly conducted prior to deporting the particular refugee. In other words, in the absence of a fair removal procedure, an informed decision and the opportunity to intervene on behalf of the migrant, it is impossible to give effect to the protection-oriented interpretation of the state's duties at border areas in practice, as suggested by the *Hirsi* judgment.[76]

I would argue strongly that, following the *Hirsi* judgment, the above practice of direct identification of asylum seekers is the only means by which police can act in compliance with its international human rights obligations and achieve a balance between efficient border management and protecting those in need of international protection.[77] A lack of qualitative research as yet means it remains to be seen to what extent the *Hirsi* judgment contributed to the shift of practice towards a more proactive approach followed by the police at the Hungarian–Serbian border.

Based on a close examination of the events in 2015 with the refugee crisis we can, however, conclude that the *Hirsi* judgment has yet to exert a positive impact on the practice of border agencies in the region. It was documented that the police or border guards failed to register thousands of potential asylum seekers from Greece to Austria, including the Hungarian police which organised the daily transfer of thousands of migrants from the Hungarian–Croatian border to Austria by trains and buses without ever properly registering them. One may argue that this was an exceptional situation in which it is understandable that the general rules did not

[76] This also illustrates the broader point made by some academic commentators about the chasm between EU legal standards and the reality for asylum seekers in many EU Member States: eg Costello, above n 24, 339.

[77] See also ibid 338: 'Screening migrants and providing information about asylum procedures is required in order to avoid findings that states have engaged in collective expulsion, and to demonstrate compliance with the right to an effective remedy. We may speculate that the EU right to asylum, if read together with the evolving ECHR jurisdictional scope (or an autonomous EU functional criterion), has potentially dramatic implications for access to protection. After Hirsi, the need to formalise screening processes for migrants intercepted at sea, and indeed encountered in other scenarios triggering extra-territorial jurisdiction, is urgent.'

apply, yet it remains the case that such an approach could easily lead to the neglect of basic human rights principles protecting refugees.

Thus, in addressing the specific issue of a state's responsibilities at the border, I argue that the most protection-oriented approach should be accepted: that a state's responsibilities begin when a government agent first interacts with a potential asylum seeker or refugee. If this is not accepted as the relevant principle, it leaves open the possibility that refugees will be *refouled* as occurred in the *Hirsi* case or in the case of the Somali refugee SAB from Hungary to Ukraine.

4

Access to International Protection

Border Issues in Turkey

CAVIDAN SOYKAN

I. BACKGROUND AND CONTEXT

TURKEY'S FIRST ASYLUM law, the Law on Foreigners and International Protection (New Law), fully entered into force in April 2014.[1] This law was prepared in accordance with Turkey's European Union (EU) accession process. Although the European Council suspended the negotiations on eight chapters in 2006 due to Turkey's restrictions regarding the Republic of Cyprus,[2] the Turkish Government adopted its renewed National Programme in 2008 and continued its reform efforts in the field of migration and asylum for full membership.[3] However, the New Law adopted the current system as it stands in a number of ways, notably with regards to the geographical limitation. Turkey ratified the 1951 United Nations Convention Relating to the Status of Refugees and the 1967 Protocol (Refugee Convention)[4] with the optional geographical limitation

[1] The law was accepted in parliament on 4 April 2013 and entered into force on 11 April 2014. For the English version see www.goc.gov.tr/files/files/YUKK_I%CC%87NGI%CC%87LI%CC%87ZCE_BASKI(1)(1).pdf.

[2] According to the 2006 European Council conclusions, negotiations will not be opened on chapters with regards to free movement of goods, right of establishment and freedom to provide services, financial services, agriculture and rural development, fisheries, transport policy, customs union, and external relations until Turkey normalises its bilateral relations with the Republic of Cyprus and the Commission confirms that Turkey has fully implemented the Additional Protocol to the Association Agreement. European Commission, 'Turkey 2015 Report' (SWD (2015) 216 final, Commission Staff Working Document, Brussels, 10 November 2015) 6.

[3] Turkey was accepted as a candidate country for the EU membership in 1999. However, the negotiations did not start until 2005. After signing the Accession Partnership Document in 2001, the Government announced its National Programme and Action Plan in the same year to adopt the EU *Acquis*. Republic of Turkey, the Ministry of Interior, 'Turkey's Action Plan for Asylum and Migration' (17 January 2005).

[4] 189 United Nations Treaty Series 150, supplemented by the 1967 Protocol relating to the Status of Refugees, 606 United Nations Treaty Series 267 (Refugee Convention).

pursuant to Article 1B of the Convention.[5] As a result, the application of the Refugee Convention for Turkey has been limited to 'persons who have become refugees as a result of events occurring in Europe'. Under the new system, it remains the case that only European asylum seekers from the Council of Europe Member States can benefit from refugee protection in Turkey.

Given this geographical limitation, Turkey created its own temporary protection mechanism in 1994 with the introduction of an Asylum Regulation.[6] Under this mechanism, both non-European and European asylum seekers had to apply for a residence permit to the General Directorate of Security under the Ministry of Interior. The non-European applicants then had to register with the local foreigners' police and comply with reporting obligations in order to be eligible for resettlement in a third country with the help of the UN High Commissioner for Refugees (UNHCR). This temporary protection mechanism used to run in parallel with a UNHCR procedure. According to this parallel procedure, both the Turkish state and the UNHCR conducted refugee status determination (RSD) interviews with the registered non-European asylum applicants. When the non-European applicants were recognised as refugees by both, then they were potentially eligible for resettlement in a third country. However, there was no standard procedure that ensured the UNHCR's involvement with all cases from the outset, in particular with regard to cases from removal centres (where foreigners with an irregular status are held for deportation purposes).

Today, most asylum seekers have to travel to their destinations in an irregular manner because of the restrictive immigration and visa policies of nation states. Gaining access to international protection has also become problematic for potential applicants in Turkey. This chapter will argue that access to international protection in Turkey is a challenge faced by asylum seekers, who enter or exit the country in an irregular manner. Based on applicants' real experiences, this chapter defends the thesis that even after the adoption of the New Law, the Turkish asylum system still tries to minimise the number of applications due to the limited chances of resettlement in third countries for non-European asylum seekers. The system deters applications, especially from those who were initially en route to Western Europe by irregular means. The asylum system works at two levels: deferring or deterring asylum seekers through both informal and formal (lawful) mechanisms. At the informal level, 'unlawful forcible

[5] Turkey ratified the 1967 Protocol on 31 July 1968. Apart from Turkey, only two other states opted for this geographical limitation, namely Congo and Madagascar.

[6] The 1994 Regulation on Procedures and Principles related to Mass Influx and Foreigners Arriving in Turkey either as Individuals or in Groups wishing to Seek Asylum either from Turkey or Requesting Residence Permits with the Intention of Seeking Asylum from a Third Country, 30 November 1994, 94/6169, the Official Gazette 22127.

returns' defer the arrival of asylum seekers on to Turkish territory, while administrative detention works as a formal deterrent and, together with degrading conditions in detention, creates, in turn, an informal deterrent effect on potential applicants. Hence, informal (unlawful) mechanisms minimise the number of arrivals into Turkey, whereas formal (lawful) mechanisms discourage potential applicants from seeking asylum in removal centres.

Notwithstanding these concerns, the New Law provides, for the first time, certain procedural guarantees for asylum seekers during the application process. In order to understand whether these guarantees will work in practice, this chapter will focus on the experiences of registered asylum seekers, who faced both informal and formal deterrent mechanisms before accessing asylum justice in Turkey. It will first review the current situation and the general framework of the New Law and will address the changes, which have filled some of the legal gaps regarding gaining access to international protection in Turkey. After considering past practice, the chapter will reflect upon the possible implementation of the new rules. Finally, the chapter will claim that the New Law may end up simply replicating past practice since it maintains the geographical limitation to the Refugee Convention.

II. THE CURRENT SITUATION AND THE NEW LAW

The active caseload—all nationalities except Syrians—of UNHCR Turkey is 246,280, as at November 2015.[7] The majority of these asylum applications within the parallel procedure originate from Iraq, Afghanistan, Iran and Somalia.[8] In order to be resettled in a third country asylum seekers have to register with both the UNHCR and the new Directorate General of Migration Management (DGMM) and then, they must be recognised as conditional refugees by the DGMM according to the New Law. There are also 10,050 Syrians who are registered with the UNHCR and are under consideration for resettlement.[9] Since the Temporary Protection Regulation[10] came into force in late 2014, Syrians cannot apply for international protection (conditional refugee status) in Turkey. Under this Regulation, the international protection applications of those who came from the

[7] UNHCR, 'External Update: Turkey' (30 November 2015) 7, www.unhcr.org.tr/uploads/root/november_-_external_update_2015.pdf.

[8] ibid.

[9] UNHCR, 'External Update: Turkey' (30 June 2015), 7 www.unhcr.org.tr/uploads/root/unhcr_turkey_external_update_-_june_2015.pdf.

[10] 22 October 2014, 2014/6883, the Official Gazette 29153. The Regulation was issued three years after the open border policy was initiated in 2011. Until 2014, the Turkish Prime Ministry defined Syrian asylum seekers as 'guests'.

Syrian Arab Republic to Turkey after 28 April 2011 will not be processed and they will all be placed under temporary protection for an indefinite period of time.[11] It is estimated that around 3 million Syrians are currently living under temporary protection in Turkey.[12] Of this number, 264,169 people have been held in 24 camps in the south-eastern part of the country.[13] The Temporary Protection Regulation creates another track for Syrians separate from that which is set for non-European asylum applicants in the New Law. The main authority responsible for the implementation of this Regulation is the Disaster and Emergency Management Presidency under the Prime Ministry.

There is no guarantee that every non-European applicant will be resettled in a third country after recognition. Canada, the US, Australia, Sweden, Finland and Norway accept small numbers of non-European conditional refugees from Turkey.[14] Due to the growing number of asylum applications, the chance of resettlement has become increasingly elusive. For instance, since 2005, only 44,349 out of 167,515 non-European applicants have been resettled in other countries.[15] Whether Syrian or Iraqi, the uncertainty of the wait and the quality of protection in Turkey makes all asylum applicants vulnerable to human smugglers with the hope of seeking protection elsewhere in Western Europe. The waiting period for resettlement could take up to five years depending on the country of origin of the applicant. The majority of the would-be refugees intercepted at sea between Greece and Turkey are now Syrians.[16] In the absence of an integration/naturalisation option in the New Law due to the geographical limitation, non-European applicants are still expected to leave the country in the long term. The New Law does not allow international status holders—European refugees, non-European conditional refugees, subsidiary protection, humanitarian leave and temporary protection holders—to apply for a permanent resident status, which is the closest status to Turkish citizenship (Article 42). In this respect, the work of UNHCR Turkey remains very important, even after the adoption of the New Law.

The New Law established a new civil institution, the DGMM under the Ministry of Interior (Article 103). The DGMM has taken over the responsibility of processing asylum applications from the foreigners' police across the country from May 2015 onwards. The junior migration specialists were assigned to their provincial directorates in early 2015 and started to receive asylum applications in each city.[17] The biggest problem in the

[11] ibid Temporary Provisions, art 1.
[12] DGMM Update (5 May 2016) www.goc.gov.tr/icerik3/gecici-koruma_363_378_4713.
[13] ibid.
[14] UNHCR, above n 7, 8.
[15] Personal communication from the DGMM to the author (5 June 2015).
[16] UNHCR, above n 7, 5.
[17] Personal communication from the DGMM to the author (5 June 2015).

field was the ad hoc implementation of different practices towards asylum applicants by the foreigners' police at an informal level. With this new civil institution, it is expected that there will be greater co-ordination and harmonisation in the field.

The most important aspect of the New Law is that it will grant certain procedural guarantees to asylum applicants during the process. Under the New Law, asylum applicants: are entitled to free legal aid by bar associations and to counselling services by non-governmental organisations (NGOs) (Article 81); have access to interpretation services (Article 70); and are able to stay at reception and accommodation centres during the asylum process (Article 95). The UNHCR's access to asylum seekers, even in the border areas, is guaranteed by law (Article 92). According to Article 65(2) where an application is lodged with law enforcement units or at the border, it will immediately be reported to the relevant governorship. Unaccompanied minors and persons with special needs seeking international protection—for example, disabled people, single women, single mothers and the victims of torture or sexual harassment—will also have special assistance and priority during the asylum process (Articles 66 and 67). The law also grants access to personal documents in the files for applicants and their legal representatives (Article 94).

The incorporation of the EU *Acquis* through this New Law into the domestic legislation points to a policy transfer for Turkey. This policy transfer to candidate countries is called the 'externalisation' of migration control.[18] After the elimination of internal borders, all EU Member States defended the idea of externalising migration control tools and restrictive asylum policies to neighbouring countries in order to raise the borders of the EU against irregular migration.[19] In fact, the EU *Acquis* on asylum and migration was the delineation of a wide range of European practices—both bilateral and sub-regional—that seeks to deter and deflect the arrival of asylum seekers and guarantee only minimum standards for those claimants, who could enter Western Europe.[20] These practices include the acceleration of asylum procedures by the concepts of 'manifestly unfounded' claims and of 'safe countries of origin', the exclusion of certain categories of persons from access to asylum (safe third country rule) and tightening of visa requirements, which are developed as measures to limit generous refugee regimes in Member States. In addition to migration control measures, readmission agreements made with countries of origin and transit serve as part of this policy. This way, Member States and/or the EU itself

[18] C Boswell, 'The "External Dimension" of EU Cooperation in Immigration and Asylum' (2003) 73(3) *International Affairs* 622.

[19] ibid 623.

[20] R Byrne, G Noll and J Vedsted-Hansen, 'Understanding Refugee Law in an Enlarged European Union' (2004) 15(2) *European Journal of International Law* 363.

commit candidate countries to readmit irregular migrants who passed through their border into the EU territory.[21]

The New Law adopts this externalisation policy by including concepts such as 'first country of asylum' (Article 73) and 'safe third country' (Article 74) alongside accelerated procedures. Article 72 states that the applications of persons coming from a first country of asylum or a safe third country will be *ipso facto* refused. The concept of 'safe country'—either as safe first country of asylum or safe third country—helps states to avoid the responsibility of examining the merits of an asylum claim by shuttling asylum seekers to other states where they could have received effective protection.[22] Article 79 of the New Law asserts that the applications of persons who, inter alia, used forged documents or identities, are in detention awaiting removal or who are allegedly applying for asylum to delay or stop their removal will be fast-tracked within five days. Article 80 completes this picture by reducing the right to appeal to judicial review alone of any decisions made under Articles 72 and 79, thereby eliminating administrative review from the procedure. Under normal circumstances, administrative review is permitted by appealing to the International Protection Assessment Commission within 10 days of refusal notification (Article 80(1)(a)). Accordingly, the courts reach a decision regarding an appeal against a fast track procedure or a manifestly unfounded application within 15 days.[23] This time limit calls the effectiveness of the judicial review into question since there are no courts specialising in refugee law in Turkey.

In addition to these so-called safe country mechanisms, detention for unauthorised entries has also been incorporated into the New Law. The law introduces administrative detention for an asylum applicant who has used forged documents; whose identity or nationality needs to be verified; who has entered the country in an unauthorised way; or who constitutes a threat to public order and security or the assessment of the grounds of whose application is otherwise not possible (Article 68). The detention is limited to 30 days and its necessity can be reviewed by a magistrates' court at any time upon appeal (Article 68(5) and (7)). However, there is another type of administrative detention for irregular entrants under the section on removal. Article 54 requires the removal of those who entered or exited the country in an irregular manner or without legal documents

[21] As part of the externalisation policy, Turkey also signed bilateral readmission agreements with Bosnia-Herzegovina in 2012, Kyrgyzstan in 2003, Moldova in 2012, Nigeria in 2011, Pakistan in 2010, Romania in 2004, Russia in 2011, Syria in 2001, Ukraine in 2005, Yemen in 2011 and Greece in 2001. See the Ministry of Foreign Affairs' website, www.mfa.gov.tr/turkiye_nin-yasadisi-gocle-mucadelesi-.tr.mfa.

[22] G Goodwin-Gill and J McAdam, *The Refugee in International Law* (Oxford, Oxford University Press, 2007) 392.

[23] Article 80(1)(d).

and of those who overstayed their visas for more than 10 days or worked in the country illegally. When this group of people is caught by security forces, they can be detained for up to a year in removal centres. There are procedural guarantees provided in the law such as prohibition on the return of individuals who would need humanitarian leave to remain or subsidiary protection. Article 59 also grants the UNHCR access to the removal centres. Article 57 authorises governorships to review the need to continue the detention every 30 days. Moreover, detainees are provided with the right to appeal to the magistrates' court. Notwithstanding these apparent protections, the effect of such guarantees provided to irregular entrants, who might be potential refugees, still depends on the interpretation of the rules by the authorities.

Access to asylum justice in Turkey is a challenge facing those applicants who enter the country in an irregular manner, rather than those who travel with their passports and approach the authorities as soon as possible with the intention of seeking international protection. In the next section, which is based on an empirical legal study conducted into the Turkish asylum system in five different cities between 2008 and 2012, this chapter will illustrate the types of formal and informal impediments at work in access to physical territory and, thus, to asylum justice in Turkey.[24] With the help of in-depth interviews with non-European applicants, who were once pushed back at the borders or detained, it will seek to anticipate potential problems that may arise in the implementation of the new rules.

III. ACCESS TO PHYSICAL TERRITORY: PROBLEMS AT THE TURKISH BORDERS

In the early 2000s, Turkey started to face increasing flows of asylum migration due to its proximity to conflict-torn countries such as Iraq and Afghanistan.[25] Most of these asylum seekers travelled to Turkey with the help of human smugglers.[26] Until 2003, 88 per cent of all new asylum applicants were either Iranian or Iraqi; in 2009, Afghan asylum seekers became the third biggest group within the caseload of the UNHCR.[27] The most interesting point about the Afghans is that they do not come from

[24] See C Soykan, 'Refuge or Limbo? A Sociological Analysis of the Turkish Asylum System' (PhD thesis, University of Essex 2015).

[25] D Danis, C Taraghi and J Perpouse 'Integration in Limbo: Iraqi, Afghan, Maghrebi and Iranian Migrants in Istanbul' in A Icduygu and K Kirisci (eds), *Land of Diverse Migrations, Challenges of Emigration and Immigration in Turkey* (Istanbul, Bilgi University Publications, 2000) 465.

[26] See A Icduygu and S Toktas, 'How Do Smuggling and Trafficking Operate via Irregular Border Crossings in the Middle East?'(2002) 40(6) *International Migration* 25.

[27] UNHCR, *UNHCR in Turkey, Facts and Figures* (Ankara, Anil Publishing House, 2010) 12.

a country that has a common border with Turkey, unlike Iraqi and Iranian applicants. The empirical legal study undertaken by the author has revealed that Afghan asylum migration to Turkey is based on unplanned journeys, which often harbour the intentions of going further to the West, dependent on sufficient financial resources. Consequently, Afghans often could not continue their journeys and sought international protection at their first entry point in Turkey.

> When the gendarmerie caught us, they took us back to the Iranian border. We begged to them and cried a lot. We begged them to let us stay in Turkey. There were many children among us. We were 25 people. We told them we cannot go back to Iran. Then, they pitied us and said OK. They said 'you can follow us but we did not see you before'. We said fine and started to follow them in the night towards Turkey.[28]

Gulnaz was 10 years old when she left Bamyan, her hometown in Afghanistan, for Iran.[29] Before she came to Turkey with her husband and two sons, she lived in Iran for nearly 25 years. Three years before their arrival in Turkey, they were forced to go back to Afghanistan from Iran as a result of the repatriation programme.[30] She said they did not have any legal status or even a short-term residency in Iran but what they experienced in Afghanistan in a year was even worse compared to Iran. Therefore, they decided to go to Turkey. After saving money for three years to pay the smugglers, they finally reached the Turkish border at night but they were caught and pushed back towards Iran by the Turkish gendarmerie. These kinds of informal impediments of access to the physical territory had already been reported and documented by human rights NGOs in Turkey. According to one report by Amnesty International, an informal agreement existed between Turkish and Iranian authorities to return any irregular migrant thought to have entered Turkey from Iran and caught within 50 km of the border in 2009.[31]

A. Forced Returns and Illegal Removals: Getting into Turkey from Iran

Gulnaz and her family were not forced to go all the way back to the nearest town in Iran like the other respondents in the author's research and

[28] Interview with an Afghan female asylum applicant (City of Van, 4 June 2010).

[29] Fictitious names are used throughout to protect the interviewees.

[30] Between 2002–14, the UNHCR assisted nearly 1 million Afghans in voluntarily returning home from the Islamic Republic of Iran. See UNHCR, 'Country Operations Profile—Islamic Republic of Iran' (2015) www.unhcr.org/pages/49e486f96.html.

[31] Amnesty International, *Stranded: Refugees in Turkey Denied Protection* (London, Amnesty International Publications, 2009) 20.

they were able to access to the asylum system in the end. In their case, they were taken to the UNHCR office in Van by the same gendarmerie officers. However, not every asylum seeker has the same experience as Gulnaz in terms of access to asylum justice. The human rights NGOs reported that there were cases of illegal removals and deportations and forced returns conducted by the Turkish security forces.

Such acts of *refoulement* have been found to be unlawful by the European Court of Human Rights (ECtHR). The Court has recently found a violation of Article 3 of the European Convention on Human Rights (ECHR) in a case where 25 Uzbek recognised refugees were forcibly removed from Turkey to Iran in 2008.[32] Here, the refugees, including 12 minors, were invited to the police headquarters for distribution of food rations and school stationery and, without notice, were removed to Iran on the same day. The refugees re-entered Turkey a week later in an irregular manner but were removed to Iran once again without a removal decision. This illegal removal was not even recorded by the Turkish authorities. The Court stated that the applicants' suffering was amount to inhuman treatment within the meaning of Article 3. In another case, four asylum seekers, including a UNHCR mandate refugee, drowned in 2008 at the Habur border, whilst being returned to Iraq by the Turkish authorities as part of a group of Iraqis and Syrians. Eigh asylum seekers were forced to swim across the Tigris river dividing Turkey and Iraq after the Iraqi authorities refused to accept them back into their territory through legal means.[33] A recent Amnesty International study showed that the Turkish authorities deported more than 100 people at the risk of serious human rights violations in Iraq and Syria in 2015.[34] In these cases, the security forces conducted illegal deportations and returns outside the official border posts.[35] These practices not only constitute breach of the principle of *non-refoulement* but also put the lives of asylum applicants in great danger.

In contrast to Gulnaz, some of the Afghan asylum applicants among the interview subjects were detained and two of them were forcibly returned back to Iran during their first attempt to cross into the Turkish territory. In one of these cases, the detained asylum seeker was sent back to Kabul by air with the help of the Afghanistan Embassy and in the other case, the asylum applicant—with her family and children—was illegally removed by being forced to walk across the border separating Iran and Turkey after midnight. In both cases, the interviewees claimed that they were not given any information either about their rights or how to access

[32] *Ghorbanov and Others v Turkey* App no 28127/09 (ECtHR, 3 March 2014) paras 28–35.

[33] T Hammarberg, 'The Report on Human Rights of Asylum Seekers and Refugees by the Commissioner for Human Rights of the Council of Europe' (The Council of Europe, 2009) 17.

[34] Amnesty International, *Europe's Gatekeeper: Unlawful Detention and Deportation of Refugees from Turkey* (London, Amnesty International Publications, 2015) 10.

[35] ibid 10 and Amnesty International, above n 31, 27.

the asylum procedure while they were in detention. According to a report published by the Human Rights Inquiry Commission under the Grand National Assembly of Turkey, 41 per cent of interviewees from three different removal centres claimed that they faced serious impediments to claiming international protection in Turkey and 61 per cent of them stated that no information was given about the asylum procedure while they were detained.[36] As was noted earlier, the New Law requires the administrative detention of those who enter the country in an irregular manner or without the necessary legal documents (Article 54(1)(c), (h)). Although NGOs have access to the removal centres, there is no guarantee that the requests of those detained asylum seekers will be forwarded to one of them by the authorities. Visits from human rights NGOs require the permission of the DGMM. Therefore, the informal impediments in relation to accessing to asylum justice look set to continue even after the adoption of the New Law.

B. Transiting Turkey: Push Backs and Detention

Greece has become the major entrance point for migrants and asylum seekers into the EU.[37] In 2015, the irregular migrants were mainly Syrians and Afghans.[38] Between 1 January and 18 December 2015, 801,919 migrants entered Greece, mostly via Turkey.[39] Since migration routes shifted in the Mediterranean in reaction to the border patrolling activities of FRONTEX[40] against the crossing through Italy and Spain in 2008, irregular migration to Greece increased threefold.[41] This development made Turkey the last stop for irregular migrants and asylum seekers en route to Western Europe before their final journey to Greece.[42]

In response to the increased numbers, the Greek authorities deployed a range of abusive border control practices, foremost among which is pushing intercepted migrants and asylum seekers back across the border to

[36] The Human Rights Inquiry Commission, 'The Report on the Problems of Asylum Seekers, Refugees and Illegal Migrants in Turkey' (The Grand National Assembly of Turkey, 2010) 197.

[37] IOM, 'Mediterranean Update: Missing Migrants Project' (18 December 2015) www.iom.int/sites/default/files/infographic/Mediterranean_Update_18_December.pdf.

[38] ibid.

[39] ibid.

[40] The European Agency for the Management of Operational Cooperation at the External Borders of the Member States of the European Union.

[41] Human Rights Watch, *Stuck in a Revolving Door, Iraqis and Other Asylum Seekers and Migrants at the Greece/Turkey Entrance to the European Union* (New York, Human Right Watch Publications, 2008) 19.

[42] M Østergaard, 'Europe's 'Boat People': Mixed Migration Flows by Sea into Southern Europe by the Rapporteur to the Committee on Migration, Refugees, and Population' (Council of Europe, 2008) 27.

Turkey.[43] Push backs (informal forced returns), as explained, point to a systematic and collective practice carried out by the Greek authorities. Asylum seekers and migrants are pushed back either from the Greek territorial waters to Turkey or in Evros area at the land border after their arrival on to the Greek territory.[44] The recent NGO reports indicate that those migrants, who are intercepted at sea, are mostly Syrians and they try to enter the EU to seek international protection and reunite with their families living in different European countries. The same reports also state that once pushed back to Turkey, asylum seekers and migrants are caught and detained under degrading conditions without being offered the opportunity to seek international protection.[45]

Among the respondents, those (including two Iranian sisters) who were planning to go to Greece had the experience of being detained before they could exit the country.[46] These asylum seekers were recognised refugees by the UNHCR Ankara office when they were interviewed by the author in Kayseri in 2010, despite being first caught by the security forces as irregular migrants. Four of these migrants contacted the UNHCR office in Ankara by phone either with the help of other detainees or the NGO Helsinki Citizens' Assembly, as in the case of Rashid, who called the UNHCR from detention after being caught in an unsuccessful attempt to exit the country, bound for Greece.

> I came to Izmir from Istanbul. I was going to be smuggled to Greece but the police caught me in a hotel on my first day here. Then they took us to the hospital and there, the doctors examined us. Later I was put in prison with others and I stayed there for around ninety days… One day I met a guy in my cell and he gave me his mobile phone with a phone number when I told him my story. It was for UNHCR. I called them and the UNHCR officers told the police that they should not send me back to Afghanistan. Three weeks later I was released.[47]

Rashid was about to leave for a Greek island when he was caught by the security forces in Izmir. An irregular minor, he did not have any identification documents with him. In cases such as these, removals and detentions

[43] Amnesty International has been documenting push back practices and accompanying human rights abuses by the Greek police since 2012. See Amnesty International, *Fear and Fences: Europe's Approach to Keeping Refugees at Bay* (London, Amnesty International Publications, 2015) 58.

[44] Amnesty International, *Greece: Frontier of Hope and Fear, Migrants and Refugees Pushed Backed at Europe's Borders* (London, Amnesty International Publications, 2014) 21; ProAsyl, *Pushed Back: Systematic Human Rights Violations Against Refugees in the Aegean Sea and at the Greek–Turkish Land Border* (Frankfurt, Pro Asyl Publications, 2013) 10; FIDH-Migreurop-Remdh, 'Frontex Between Greece and Turkey' (May 2014) 35.

[45] Pro Asyl, above n 44, 11.

[46] Interview with Iranian recognised female refugees (Kayseri, 20 May 2010).

[47] Interview with an Afghan recognised male refugee (Izmir, 1 September 2009).

were carried out in compliance with the rules of the Passport Law and the Law on Sojourn and Movement of Foreigners in Turkey, until 2013.[48] In terms of Articles 34 and 35 of the Passport Law, foreigners who somehow entered Turkey without passports or travel documents were subject to administrative fines as well as a prison sentence of up to six months prior to their removal until 2011.[49] Illegal entry, exit or presence in the country constituted a violation of Article 4 of the Passport Law and required detention for the purpose of removal. Article 23 of the Law on Sojourn and Movement of Foreigners in Turkey was used as the legal basis for the practice of detention. According to this Article:

> Persons who are to be deported but cannot leave Turkey due to their inability to obtain a passport or for other reasons are obliged to reside at places designated by the Ministry of Interior.

Asylum seekers in transit, like Rashid, who are caught by the security forces just before their exit or during their irregular movement through the country, are first detained in custody at police or gendarmerie stations and then transferred to removal centres.[50] Although the relevant regulation stated that the stay in these places was temporary for asylum seekers and refugees,[51] there was no mention of a time limit for the duration of detention anywhere in the legislation before the adoption of the New Law. According to a report of the Helsinki Citizens' Assembly, the length of detention ranged from less than a week to more than a year depending on when the families or relatives of the detainees could afford to travel back to their countries.[52] In its report, the Human Rights Inquiry Commission found that in Edirne removal centre irregular migrants were detained up to a maximum of 35 days while in the Kırklareli centre the detention period was about three months in 2012.[53] Before the New Law, those who were to be removed or deported had to pay for their own travel expenses,[54] which partly explained the somewhat lengthy detention periods in some cases.

[48] With the adoption of the New Law on 11 April 2013, the Law on Sojourn and Movement of Foreigners in Turkey is abolished and the Passport Law largely became invalidated.

[49] Prior to the adoption of the New Law an amendment was made to the Passport Law on 31 March 2011 by Law 6217 and the criminal sanctions in this section were removed (arts 33–38).

[50] These centres were called Foreigners' Guesthouses until 2010.

[51] Article 16 of the Regulation on Guesthouses, 29 April 1983, the Official Gazette 18032.

[52] The Helsinki Citizens' Assembly, 'Unwelcome Guests: the Detention of Refugees in Turkey's Foreigners' Guesthouses' (Istanbul, 2007) 33.

[53] The Human Rights Inquiry Commission, 'A Report about the Return Centres in Edirne, Kirklareli and Istanbul' (The Grand National Assembly of Turkey, 2012) 11.

[54] In practice, the IOM helped the Turkish state to pay for aeroplane tickets. In an interview with a security official in Ankara the author was told that 2,983 people were sent back to their countries in 2008 with the help of the IOM (Interview in Ankara, 13 August 2009).

When Greece tightened controls at its sea and land borders,[55] the number of migrants entering the EU through the Turkish–Bulgarian border increased. A number of asylum seekers and migrants interviewed by Amnesty International in 2014 stated that their fear of ill-treatment and push backs at the Greek borders forced them to choose to cross to Bulgaria instead.[56] Among those interviewed by the author, the case of Hamid, a political refugee from Iran, proved rather interesting in this regard. Hamid's case was unique in the sense that he managed to travel all the way from the Iranian border to Istanbul by himself with his brother's passport and then succeeded in exiting the country and reaching the Bulgarian territory without any help from human smugglers. He said he bought a map, identified the nearest village to the border and took a bus to get there. However, his successful escape story from Iran ended up in a Bulgarian removal centre after he crossed the Turkish side of the border but was caught after he cut through a second barbed wire fence on the Bulgarian side.

After being caught, Hamid was transferred to a removal centre where he spent an entire month without having a proper meal. He said it was not as bad as the Turkish removal centre in terms of the number of people kept in one room, but there were still 20 to 30 people held together over the course of his stay. He contacted his refugee friend in Canada at some point by using a secret mobile phone in his cell and that friend called the Bulgarian UNHCR office to send help to him. The UNHCR officer proved unhelpful since she brought an interpreter for Arabic instead of Farsi. At the end of the month, Hamid found himself sitting in a car directed back towards the Turkish border, whilst all the others in his cell were being transferred to Sofia.

IV. BARRIERS TO ACCESSING ASYLUM JUSTICE: THE ROLE OF THE UNHCR IN TURKEY

Hamid's story continues:

> Turkish police came to the Bulgarian border to take me back. They asked me if I wanted to go back to Turkey and I actually said no. However, they took me from the Bulgarian police and drove me to Edirne, the Tunca removal centre. The officers in the centre told me that I should get in contact with my embassy

[55] Up until 2010, the main migration route was by sea. In 2012 the Greek–Turkish land border along the Evros River saw the largest number of irregular entries to the EU along the EU's external borders. Most of those arriving were migrants from either Syria or Afghanistan. However, in that year, the construction of a 10.5 km fence along the northern section of this border meant that the migration route shifted back to the Aegean Sea once more. See Frontex, *Annual Risk Analysis* (Risk Analysis Unit, Warsaw, April 2013) 21.

[56] Amnesty International, above n 44, 24.

> as soon as possible so that they can issue me a new passport. I did not know any Turkish. I could not explain my situation... I wrote a letter to express my wish to seek asylum and gave it to the police officers three times after talking to the UNHCR people on the phone but the police rejected it... Three months later after I entered the centre, a UNHCR officer finally came to visit me.[57]

Hamid was not able to lodge an asylum application either in Bulgaria or in Turkey by himself. After a one-month stay in the Bulgarian centre, he was sent back to Turkey and put in the Edirne-Tunca removal centre at the beginning of 2008. When he was finally released after his asylum application was accepted in detention, he had already been detained for 10 months. Hamid was initially told to get in contact with his embassy in order to be issued with a new passport by the Turkish officers so that he could be returned to Iran. Due to the lack of interpreters, Hamid was not able to tell the officers for a long time that he was wanted as a political criminal in Iran. He called the same friend in Canada from a public phone in the centre and the friend advised him to get in contact with UNHCR Turkey this time. He wrote three letters to express his intention of seeking asylum in Turkey but the officers in the removal centre refused to accept them.[58] When he could submit an application and finally have an interview with the UNHCR, he had already been in the removal centre for three months, and only after the Helsinki Citizens' Assembly got involved in his case was he able to apply. As in the Christian sisters' case, which is considered later in the chapter, Hamid could access the UNHCR only with the help of a human rights NGO in Istanbul, which runs a refugee advocacy and support programme offering advice to asylum seekers over the phone or by intervening directly in detention cases.

Based on the data collected for this research, it is argued here that there were two unwritten administrative decisions from the Ministry of Interior before the adoption of the New Law, which were informal understandings of the policy and allowed the Turkish security officers not to accept asylum applications in detention.[59] The first unwritten decision said if those migrants (especially those from a non-neighbouring country), who were caught by the security forces while attempting to exit the country, want to seek asylum while in detention, their claims should be ignored. This was because the authorities believed that most of the migrants make asylum claims in detention in order not to be removed or deported from the country and that their sole aim is to abuse the system. On the other hand, according to the second unwritten decision, irregular migrants who had Document 23 (see below) were not able to make an asylum application if they were first apprehended for being in the country illegally.

[57] Interview with an Iranian recognised male refugee (Kayseri, 21 May 2010).
[58] Similar cases were reported at the same border. See Amnesty International, above n 31.
[59] Interview with an NGO coordinator (Izmir, 2 February 2012).

Under Article 23 of the Law on Sojourn and Movement of Foreigners in Turkey,[60] persons who were to be deported but could not leave the country due to their inability to obtain a passport could be obliged to reside at certain places designated by the Ministry of Interior. Although these 'certain places' often referred to removal centres, there were occasions on which irregular migrants were released from custody with a piece of paper called 'Document 23'. Document 23 basically meant that since the Turkish state could not remove the irregular migrant to his or her country of nationality due to the cost of doing so, there was no point in transferring him or her from custody to a removal centre. Therefore, the migrant was usually released on the condition that he or she would leave the country within two months.[61] What usually happened was that since these migrants could not leave the country through legal ways, they were instead arrested again for being there illegally, and this practice turned into a repeat cycle. However, despite the unwritten instruction, if they were able or chose to register with the UNHCR, they would be within the system and presumably protected against possible deportation.[62]

Article 79 of the New Law asserts that if the arrested migrant without ID or with a fake passport seeks asylum, the application should be fast-tracked. The time limit for the case to be concluded is five days and there is no administrative review for these RSD decisions (as discussed earlier). Although it is possible to apply for judicial review to an administrative court of a fast track decision, the 15-day time limit for the court to make a decision calls the effectiveness of this mechanism into question. Since the New Law came into effect in April 2014, the main issue for those representing claimants has been the rising number of fast track cases. Almost every international protection application from detention has to be fast-tracked. Since the administrative courts are not specialised in international

[60] The Law on Sojourn and Movement of Foreigners in Turkey, 15 July 1950, 5683, the Official Gazette 7564, 24 July 1950.

[61] The Human Rights Inquiry Commission, above n 53, 5.

[62] One of the respondents had Document 23. She was an Eritrean asylum seeker and prior to her application to the UNHCR, she had tried to go to a Greek island from Izmir. However, she was caught by the Greek coastguards, detained for a while and sent back to Izmir in accordance with the rules of a readmission agreement signed in 2001 between Turkey and Greece. When the author met her in the Basmane neighbourhood in 2009, she had just had her interview with the UNHCR in Ankara. A few days later after the first meeting it came to light that she did have Document 23 and, because of this, she was taken into custody when she went to the Department of Foreigners, Borders and Asylum for her asylum interview appointment. Her fingerprints were found in the database of apprehended irregular migrants and at the time of her apprehension she had lied to the Turkish authorities stating that she was from Somalia (Izmir, 22 July 2009). During fieldwork in Izmir, it was also discovered that African irregular migrants often lie that they are from Somalia when they are apprehended by the security forces in order not to be deported since they think that Somalia does not have an official representation in Turkey. In 2014, there was no progress with regard to this readmission agreement between Turkey and Greece. See European Commission, 'Turkey 2014 Progress Report' (SWD (2014) 307, Brussels, 8 October 2014) 64.

protection cases, it is nearly impossible to reach a decision within this time limit. Neither the administrative courts nor the lawyers have been well prepared for the implementation of the new rules. As mentioned, Article 65(2) states that when an application is lodged at the border or with law enforcement units, it will be immediately reported to the relevant governorship. Although the management of removal centres was transferred to the DGMM at the end of 2015, the same personnel, that is, police officers still work at these centres. This means the same practice of rejecting applications in detention may well continue despite the procedural guarantees provided by the New Law.[63] Thus, the UNHCR continues to play an important role in access to asylum justice in Turkey.

V. UNHCR'S LIMITED ACCESS TO REMOVAL CENTRES

> The police officers shouted at us many times and forced us to tell who we know in Turkey. They treated us like criminals. They already caught the smuggler so we did not understand why we were questioned. We were just crying during those interrogations. First they did not believe what we said but later a policeman helped us. He gave us a paper so we could write down our problem in Farsi. We also called the Helsinki Citizens' Assembly from custody. We got a card from them once when two women came to help a Palestinian guy into our prison… UNHCR people came to interview us and then two weeks later we were finally released from the Kırklareli camp.[64]

Shirin and Banu were able to speak a little Turkish. When they said they had converted to Christianity in Iran, a police officer at the police station where they were kept for 40 days, after an unsuccessful attempt to cross to Greece, gave them a piece of paper so that they could explain their situation in Farsi. They were later able to make an asylum application in a police station in Ayvalik, Balikesir, before being transferred to a removal centre in Kırklareli. However, even though the police officers accepted their applications, the sisters were detained in the removal centre for another three months. Two weeks after the UNHCR officers came to the removal centre to conduct their RSD interviews, the sisters were finally released. Among the respondents who had experienced detention in Turkey, only four were able to seek asylum from detention and none of these four, now recognised as refugees, knew how to lodge an application. However, they did know how to ask for help from the Helsinki Citizens' Assembly by telephone, and were able to find the phone number

[63] Similar cases are still being reported by human rights NGOs. See the observations of Mülteci-Der on the refugee situation in Turkey (22 April 2016) www.multeci.org.tr/haberdetay.aspx?Id=141.

[64] Interview with Iranian recognised female refugees (Kayseri, 20 May 2010).

of the UNHCR. In all cases the UNHCR had to intervene and contact the authorities of the removal centres to stop the deportations.

It is not possible for the UNHCR to inform all detained migrants about its existence or about the asylum procedure in Turkey. For the UNHCR, the only way to reach the detained migrants in removal centres, if any of them wants to make an application, is to wait until they call for help. There was no formal Host Country agreement between the Turkish state and the UNHCR until 2016, although the office started working in Turkey in 1960.[65] This lack of co-operation made the supervising duty defined in Article 35 of the Refugee Convention impossible for the Office to fulfil.[66] A related problem was that the Turkish authorities did not recognise the refugees whose statuses were given by the UNHCR outside of Turkey. The refugees recognised in other countries, specifically from Iraq in the post-2003 period, were required once more to go through the same RSD procedure in Turkey.[67]

As a result of the lack of official co-operation, the Ministry of Interior does not share any information with the UNHCR about the situation of detained migrants in removal centres. As the author's research has shown, prior to implementation of the New Law, the Helsinki Citizens' Assembly managed to contact removal centres by phone and then urged the UNHCR to intervene in specific cases. If the UNHCR officers were able to talk directly to the migrant on the phone, they advised her or him to write a petition and give it to a security officer under the Department of Foreigners, Borders and Asylum. Sometimes giving this petition to the correct officer would take far too long simply because nobody in the facility where the migrant was kept knew what the term 'refugee' meant. Most of the officers at the police and the gendarmerie stations[68] in the remote parts of the country are not trained in the field of human rights and refugee protection in Turkey. However, under the New Law, even if an application

[65] UNHCR, 'Latest News' (1 September 2016) www.unhcr.org/news/latest/2016/9/57c856484/unhcr-chief-pledges-support-turkey-refugee-response.html.

[66] '[T]he Contracting States undertake to provide them in the appropriate form within formation and statistical data requested concerning: (a) The condition of refugees, (b) The implementation of this Convention, and; (c) Laws, regulations and decrees which are, or may hereafter be, in force relating to refugees': Refugee Convention, art 35(2).

[67] For instance, in the case of *Abdolkhani and Karimnia v Turkey Abdolkhani and Karimnia v Turkey* App no 30471/08 (ECtHR, 22 September 2009) 4, the applicants were recognised Iranian refugees from Iraq, who had crossed the border 'illegally' to seek resettlement via Turkey after the UNHCR office in Northern Iraq was blown up. The Turkish state, instead of providing protection for them, preferred to put them into detention and refused to accept their applications. When the ECtHR decision was handed down in late 2009, ruling that the applicants had been arbitrarily detained in violation of ECHR, art 5, they were still in detention.

[68] While both the police and the gendarmerie answer to the Ministry of Interior, the gendarmerie is an armed military security and law enforcement organisation and is responsible for maintaining public security and order outside the official borders of city centres.

is received by the correct officer, it will still need to be translated into Turkish and sent to the governorship. Only if the governorship agrees will the police officers then register the asylum application and refer it to the relevant provincial directorate of the DGMM.

In the past, UNHCR officers were allowed to enter the removal centre to meet with the asylum seeker for an interview with the permission of the Ministry of Interior. According to the report of the Commissioner for the Human Rights of Council of Europe, in 2008, for instance, the UNHCR only intervened in 393 incidents out of a total of 3,351 irregular migrants, many of whom wished to seek asylum in Turkey. In fact, the UNHCR was given permission to see only 72 individuals and access to all others was denied by the Turkish authorities.[69] Furthermore, according to the report of Mülteci-Der, between 2004 and 2008, 258,590 out of 300,666 apprehended irregular migrants were deported from Turkey. The state officials acknowledged that 548 people out of this total made an asylum application in detention, but only 67 applications out of this 548 were accepted and processed.[70]

Article 31 of the Refugee Convention protects refugees from penalties for their irregular entry to a country as long as they present themselves to the authorities to claim asylum without delay and show good cause for their illegal entry and presence. The 1994 Asylum Regulation stated that asylum seekers who entered Turkey 'illegally' should approach the authorities as soon as possible to make a claim at their point of entry to the country (Article 4). However in practice, asylum seekers, especially those irregular entrants who did not know anything about the parallel procedure in Turkey and were intent on seeking protection in Western Europe, were usually treated as 'illegal migrants' and detained by the security forces in accordance with Article 23 of the Law on Sojourn and Movements of Foreigners in Turkey. The physical conditions of the removal centres together with the indefinite character of detention, often forced potential claimants to make a decision to return voluntarily, which was then encouraged by the security officers in the detention centres.

Human rights organisations have challenged this attitude of the Turkish state at the international level since the mid-2000s. During the course of this author's research, the Helsinki Citizens' Assembly together with Mülteci-Der stopped deportations in numerous cases at the very last minute, in particular at the airports, where it was not possible to claim asylum in Turkey, by requesting an interim measure from the ECtHR. The Court finally issued a watershed decision in 2009 stating that the practice of detention in Turkey did not have a sufficient legal basis, and was therefore unlawful.

[69] Hammarberg, above n 33, 11.

[70] Mülteci-Der, 'A General Overview of the Developments in the Field of Asylum and Migration' (Izmir, 2010) 25.

This meant that asylum seekers were arbitrarily detained in the removal centres in violation of Article 5 of the ECHR.[71] Article 23 of the Law on Sojourn and Movement of Foreigners in Turkey was being used by the Government as the legal basis of the detention in the context of deportation proceedings. However, the Court stated that this provision pertained to the residence of certain groups of foreigners, not about their detention. The provision neither provided any details as to the conditions for ordering detention with a view of deportation, nor set a time limit as such.[72] In a number of cases, the Court also reiterated that detained migrants were not informed of the grounds for their detention and the Turkish legal system did not provide the applicants with a remedy whereby they could obtain a judicial review of the lawfulness of their detention, within the meaning of Article 5(4).[73] Later in 2010, the Court ruled that the conditions in two detention facilities (one of them was the Edirne-Tunca removal centre) amounted to inhuman or degrading treatment or punishment in violation of Article 3 of the Convention.[74] The excessive overcrowding and a lack of orderliness and hygiene in the Edirne-Tunca removal centre, even for a period as short as two hours, meant that the centre was considered unfit for human habitation.[75]

Since the New Law came into force, there has been a legal basis for detention in the Turkish legislation. Under Article 54, migrants who enter or exit the country in an irregular manner or without legal documents, and who then overstay their visas for more than ten days, can be detained for up to a year for deportation purposes. Article 55 regulates the exemptions from removal decisions. If there are serious indications that migrants may be subjected to the death penalty, torture, inhuman or degrading treatment or punishment in the country to which they will be returned, a removal decision must not be issued. In addition to this general protection, there is also Article 4, which incorporates the *non-refoulement* principle of the Refugee Convention directly into the New Law.[76] Article 59 states that the detained migrant must be given the opportunity to meet with UNHCR officials. Conversely, as is shown in the accounts of detained asylum seekers, the main problem regarding access to asylum justice in Turkey is the attitude of police or gendarmerie officers. These officers in removal

[71] *Abdolkhani and Karimnia v Turkey* App no 30471/08 (ECtHR, 22 September 2009).

[72] ibid para 133.

[73] ibid para 142. See also *Yarashonen v Turkey* App no 72710/11 (ECtHR, 24 September 2014); *Aliev v Turkey* App no 30518/11 (ECtHR, 21 January 2015).

[74] *Tehrani and Others v Turkey* App nos 32940/08, 41626/08, 43616/08 (ECtHR, 13 April 2010) and *Charahili v Turkey* App no 46605/07 (ECtHR, 13 April 2010).

[75] *Tehrani and Others v Turkey*, above n 74, para 93.

[76] 'No Contracting State shall expel or return ("refouler") a refugee in any manner whatsoever to the frontiers of territories where his life or freedom would be threatened on account of his race, religion, nationality, membership of a particular social group or political opinion': Refugee Convention, art 33(1).

centres cannot speak the languages of migrants; they treat them as criminals and refuse to accept their international protection applications. One innovation of the New Law is that applicants are now entitled to free legal aid by bar associations. Article 81 directly refers to the Attorneyship Law and states that in cases where the applicant is unable to afford the attorney's fee for his or her judicial appeals, legal assistance must be provided. It may be assumed that this provision is applicable throughout the whole procedure. In most of the ECtHR cases, the applicants were able to stop their deportations only with the help of legal representation. This indicates the importance of training all the personnel working for the DGMM in human rights and refugee law. Otherwise, the old practice might easily prevail despite the changes.

VI. CONCLUSION

Due to the adoption of the Refugee Convention with the optional geographical limitation, the protection provided by the Turkish state has been limited and temporary for non-Europeans. The Turkish asylum system works towards minimising the number of applications, especially from those who were initially en route to Western Europe via Turkey. Similar to its European counterparts, the system first defers the arrival of asylum seekers onto Turkish territory through push backs and illegal deportations at the borders; and then deters international protection applications via a detention mechanism by creating disincentives for the potential applicants with degrading detention conditions. The system therefore first stops and then detains the asylum seeker by turning him or her into 'an illegal migrant' through its legal framework, and then refuses access to asylum justice. Against this backdrop, the UNHCR plays an important role both as a resettlement unit and a facilitator to access asylum justice. A third mechanism can be added to this framework after the long summer of migration in 2015.[77] The sudden peak in the number of arrivals to Western Europe through Greece indicated that the Turkish authorities let registered Syrians and other asylum seekers to leave the country via irregular sea crossings in order to minimise the number of international and temporary protection applicants within the system.[78]

[77] B Kasparek and M Speer, 'Of Hope. Hungary and the Long Summer of Migration' (9 September 2015) www.bordermonitoring.eu/ungarn/2015/09/of-hope-en/.

[78] The dire conditions for asylum seekers and Syrian temporary protection holders in Turkey contribute to their secondary irregular movement to the EU. The arrivals in the first ten months of the year represents 1300% more than during the same period in 2014. See Amnesty International, above n 34, 2.

The New Law was drafted as part of Turkey's EU accession process. Although the law contains, for the first time, important safeguards for the treatment of asylum seekers—such as procedural guarantees throughout the asylum process—the enactment of these adopted norms in less-developed asylum systems might cause legal shortfalls and protection problems. As a result of the EU externalisation policy, the candidate countries mimic the strategies of restriction.[79] In the case of Turkey, the untrained police and gendarmerie officers enjoying great discretionary power in deterring asylum seekers at the borders and the lack of an effective judicial review can easily lead to a more restrictive asylum policy. Although the UNHCR provides training on interviewing techniques, drafting legal analyses and country of origin information, the newly assigned junior migration specialists, who will conduct the RSD interviews at the provincial DGMM directorates, still lack experience in the field. Most importantly, it is unclear whether the parallel procedure, where the role of the UNHCR is significant, will continue in the future. Since the Syrian refugee issue appears to have no end in sight, some time will be needed to assess the real changes that the New Law brings to the migration and asylum field in Turkey.

The EU–Turkey migration deal that was signed on 18 March 2016 reinforces the arguments of this chapter. Under the terms of this deal, Turkey agreed to readmit all irregular migrants who crossed to the Greek islands from Turkey as of 20 March 2016.[80] The deal requires the resettlement of a Syrian refugee from Turkey to the EU for every Syrian being returned to Turkey from the Greek islands. Turkey agreed to take necessary measures to prevent opening of new sea or land routes for irregular migration from Turkey to the EU. In return, the EU agreed to provide an initial €3 billion for the further improvement of the socio-economic situation of Syrians living under the temporary protection in Turkey, as well as to lift the visa requirement for Turkish citizens in the Schengen area once the visa roadmap is implemented by Turkey.[81] The legal basis of returns according to this deal is the 2001 Greece–Turkey Readmission Agreement until the Readmission Agreement signed between Turkey and the EU in 2013 comes into force.[82]

[79] R Byrne, G Noll and J Vedsted-Hansen, *New Asylum Countries? Migration Control and Refugee Protection in an Enlarged European Union* (Netherlands, Kluwer Law International, 2002) 28.

[80] It should be noted that collective expulsion of aliens is prohibited according to the ECHR, Protocol No 4, art 4. In order to comply with this rule, the Greek authorities should examine the merits of every claim of international protection before that person's return to Turkey is effected.

[81] The European Commission, 'Factsheet on the EU-Turkey Agreement' (Press Release, Brussels, 19 March 2016) www.europa.eu/rapid/press-release_MEMO-16-963_en.htm.

[82] Agreement between the European Union and the Republic of Turkey on the readmission of persons residing without authorisation [2014] OJ L 134/3 (Readmission Agreement).

The first group of people readmitted by Turkey from Lesbos and Chios islands arrived at Dikili, Izmir on 4 April 2016.[83] Except the two Syrians who allegedly wished to return to Turkey, all non-Syrians were directly transferred to Pehlivankoy, Kirklareli Removal Centre. According to a statement from Mülteci-Der, there were people among these returnees who wished to seek international protection in Turkey. However, the authorities of a provincial unit of the DGMM denied the request for access to these potential applicants by Mülteci-Der.[84] Even if these applications were received with the help of this NGO, they would be assessed under the fast track procedure (since once these persons breach the terms and conditions for legal entry into or exit from Turkey according to Article 54 (1) (h) of the New Law, they are under administrative detention for deportation purposes). Turkey added a temporary provision into the Temporary Protection Regulation on 5 April 2016 for Syrian returnees.[85] Under this provision, after being readmitted, Syrians may be granted temporary protection upon request. However, this provision does not guarantee automatic access to the temporary protection mechanism for Syrians. Article 12(1) of the Temporary Protection Regulation states that if the beneficiaries of temporary protection leave Turkey for a third country—either in a regular or an irregular manner—they lose their status. There is no clarification as to what will happen to those Syrians who are not granted temporary protection after being readmitted from the Aegean islands.[86]

When the EU–Turkey Readmission Agreement starts to be implemented, there will be even more fast track cases and related access to asylum justice issues in Turkey. Although the Agreement refers to the responsibilities of the parties arising from international law and, in particular from the Refugee Convention, migrants with international protection needs will still be returned to Turkey without having the opportunity to seek asylum in the EU because they have travelled in an irregular manner and thus immediately fall into the category of irregular migrants.[87] The EU–Turkey

The European Commission, 'Factsheet: EU-Turkey Joint Action Plan' (MEMO/15/5860, Brussels, 15 October 2015) www.europa.eu/rapid/press-release_MEMO-15-5860_en.htm.

[83] According to the official statements, except the two Syrians, all 323 non-Syrians were taken to Pehlivankoy Removal Centre. The two readmitted Syrians were transferred to Duzici Camp which is the only camp in Turkey governed by the DGMM. See the observations of Mülteci-Der on the refugee situation in Turkey (22 April 2016) www.multeci.org.tr/haberdetay.aspx?Id=141.

[84] ibid.

[85] 7 April 2016, the Council of Ministers decision, No 2016/8722, the Official Gazette 29677.

[86] Mülteci-Der, above n 83.

[87] 'This agreement shall be without prejudice to the rights, obligations and responsibilities of the Union, its Member States and Turkey arising from international law including from international conventions to which they are party, in particular: the Convention of 28 July 1951 on the Status of Refugees as amended by the Protocol of 31 January 1967 on the Status of Refugees': Readmission Agreement, art 18.

deal now constitutes the last step for Turkey's incorporation into the EU externalisation policy. Turkey takes responsibility for protecting the EU's external borders by accepting the role of gatekeeper of those Syrians who might engage in a secondary movement towards Western Europe due to substandard living conditions in Turkey.

5

Interdiction and Screening of Asylum Seekers at Sea

Implications for Asylum Justice

MARIA O'SULLIVAN

I. INTRODUCTION

GLOBAL PRESSURES HAVE led to increasing numbers of asylum seekers travelling on overloaded and unseaworthy boats across the sea to access refugee protection.[1] In order to deter such arrivals, a number of states around the world interdict asylum seeker vessels and return them to their country of embarkation or a third state. Various legal issues arise from such interdictions, such as safety and rescue principles and the prohibition against *refoulement*.[2] This also raises an important access to justice issue in relation to the use of screening processes that may take place at sea prior to the transfer or return of those asylum seekers.

This chapter will examine a due process issue aspect of interdiction by focusing on the on-board screening procedures utilised by the Australian

[1] UNHCR and the International Organisation for Migration (IOM) statistics show that during 2015, there were just over 1,000,000 arrivals across the Mediterranean Sea, with 3,771 missing or dead: www.data.unhcr.org/mediterranean/regional.php; www.iom.int/news/iom-counts-3771-migrant-fatalities-mediterranean-2015. Many of these arrivals go on to seek asylum in Europe.

[2] These issues have been well-traversed in the academic literature, eg M Giuffré, 'State Responsibility Beyond Borders: What Legal Basis for Italy's Push-backs to Libya?' (2013) 24(4) *International Journal of Refugee Law* 692; M Den Heijer, 'Reflections on *Refoulement* and Collective Expulsion in the *Hirsi* Case' (2013) 25(2) *International Journal of Refugee Law* 265; G Goodwin-Gill, 'The Right to Seek Asylum: Interception at Sea and the Principle of Non-Refoulement' (2011) 23 *International Journal of Refugee Law* 443; S Trevisanut, 'The Principle of Non-Refoulement at Sea and the Effectiveness of Asylum Protection' (2008) 12 *Max Planck Yearbook of United Nations Law* 205.

Government as part of its policy to 'stop the boats'. This practice is part of the Australian Government's pledge to turn asylum seeker boats around 'when it is safe to do so' under its policy: Operation Sovereign Borders.[3] As part of this, asylum seekers intercepted on the high seas and held on naval vessels are subject to a short screening procedure comprised of four basic questions: name, country of origin, country of embarkation and the reason for leaving. There are no specific questions asked in relation to protection obligations under the United Nations Convention relating to the Status of Refugees (Refugee Convention)[4] and interdicted persons are not notified of their right to seek asylum. It is therefore not an assessment of a person's refugee claim, but a filter mechanism to screen asylum seekers 'in' or 'out' based upon whether the authorities perceive that person as presenting a valid refugee claim.

This screening procedure became the subject of a legal challenge in the High Court of Australia, which was handed down in January 2015: *CPCF v Minister for Immigration and Border Protection and Anor*.[5] One legal issue in that case is the extent to which the legal concept of procedural fairness can apply extraterritorially to screening procedures carried out at sea.

Practices such as those used by Australian authorities raise concerns about the impact of screening procedures on the ability of asylum seekers to access refugee protection. In particular, do asylum seekers in such a situation have an adequate opportunity to present their case and what are the implications of the absence of legal assistance and review mechanisms at sea? Such screening raises special legal issues as compared to those raised in refugee status determination (RSD) carried out on land because of the geographical isolation from mainland refugee status decision-making institutions and the difficulties with adequate provision of interpreters and legal assistance. In such circumstances, can such screening ever be considered 'fair'?[6] This chapter will begin by examining the relevant legal principles applicable to screening at sea, with a focus on UNHCR guidance and domestic procedural fairness principles (section II). Section III will then discuss Australian practice and recent jurisprudence on screening. Section IV will analyse this from an international law and procedural fairness perspective, after which section V will set out some conclusions about the use of screening at sea.

[3] Australian Liberal Party and National Party, 'The Coalition's Operation Sovereign Borders Policy' (Canberra ACT, Brian Loughnane, July 2013) www.rowanramsey.com.au/Portals/0/Operation-Sovereign-Borders-Policy-2.pdf

[4] 189 United Nations Treaty Series 150, supplemented by the 1967 Protocol relating to the Status of Refugees, 606 United Nations Treaty Series 267 (Refugee Convention).

[5] *CPCF v Minister for Immigration and Border Protection & Anor* [2015] HCA 1, 28 January 2015, www.refworld.org/docid/54c8be3c4.html.

[6] As that term is understood and set out in ch 1 of this volume.

II. RELEVANT LEGAL PRINCIPLES

A. International Standards

The Refugee Convention does not oblige State Parties to provide a particular processing regime for refugee status determination.[7] However, provision of a fair and effective form of processing is considered implicit in the *non-refoulement* principle set out in Article 33 of the Refugee Convention. That is, return of asylum seekers to their country of origin without properly ascertaining if they are refugees is considered to be contrary to Article 33. Both the UN High Commissioner for Refugees (UNHCR) Executive Committee (Ex Com) Conclusions[8] and refugee law scholars[9] have emphasised that there is a need for an adequate system of status determination to ensure refugees are not returned to harm pursuant to Article 33. In practice, this means asylum seekers must be given an effective opportunity to express their need for international protection and access to a fair and effective RSD process.

A number of UNHCR documents have set out guidance as to what constitutes a fair and accurate status determination procedure. For instance, in UNHCR Ex Com Conclusion Number 8, the Committee stated that basic requirements for status determination include the provision of guidance to an asylum seeker as to the procedure to be followed, necessary facilities (including the services of a competent interpreter) for submitting his or her case to the authorities concerned, the opportunity to contact a representative of the UNHCR and appeal rights.[10] The UNHCR has also set out specific principles on screening at sea, pointing to the significant challenges posed by individual examination of asylum claims in interdiction situations. It has taken the position that processing on board maritime

[7] eg UNHCR, 'Handbook and Guidelines on Procedures and Criteria for Determining Refugee Status Under the 1951 Convention and the 1967 Protocol Relating to the Status of Refugees' (HCR/1P/4/ENG/REV. 3, Geneva, December 2011) 37: 'the Convention does not indicate what type of procedures are to be adopted for the determination of refugee status. It is therefore left to each Contracting State to establish the procedure that it considers most appropriate, having regard to its particular constitutional and administrative structure.'

[8] eg UNHCR Ex Comm, 'Conclusion on Protection Safeguards in Interception Measures No 97 (LIV)—2003', (Executive Committee 54th Session, UN General Assembly Doc A/AC.96/987and 12A (A/58/12/Add.1) 10 October 2003) www.refworld.org/docid/3f93b2894.html [iv].

[9] M Pallis, 'Obligations of States Towards Asylum Seekers at Sea: Interactions and Conflicts Between Legal Regimes' (2002) 31 *International Journal of Refugee Law* 329, 342; G Goodwin-Gill and J McAdam, *The Refugee in International Law*, 3rd edn (Oxford, Oxford University Press, 2007) 528; J Hathaway, *The Rights of Refugees under International Law* (Cambridge, Cambridge University Press, 2005) 159–60.

[10] UNHCR ExCom, 'Conclusion No 8 (XXVIII) Determination of Refugee Status' (28th Session, UN Doc A/10012/Add.1, 14 October 1975).

vessels is generally not appropriate[11] and that protection screening and refugee status determination should not take place at sea.[12] It states: '[i]t is UNHCR's position that asylum seekers and refugees should ordinarily be processed in the territory of the State where they arrive, or which otherwise has jurisdiction over them'.[13] In the context of interdiction situations, UNHCR has recommended that 'requests for international protection should be considered within the territory of the intercepting state, consistent with fundamental refugee protection principles'.[14]

However, the UNHCR has also recognised that there may be exceptional circumstances in which pre-screening may be utilised as a means of profiling persons. However, it interprets screening as a means of filtering different caseloads to appropriate RSD avenues, rather than as a mechanism for turning back boats at sea. It states:

> Where extraterritorial processing is limited to initial profiling or pre-screening, this is understood to mean a process that precedes formal RSD and aims to identify and differentiate between categories of arrivals (eg persons who are seeking international protection, victims of trafficking, unaccompanied children, irregular economic migrants).[15]

If such profiling is utilised, the UNHCR has stated that those persons identified as having potential protection needs would need to be disembarked in the territory of the intercepting state to have their international protection claims considered in regular in-country RSD procedures.[16] If any RSD is carried out at sea, the UNHCR has indicated this would need to attract high level procedural standards, including access to legal assistance, the granting of sufficient time to prepare asylum claims, the provision of a reasoned decision in writing, and provision of an independent appeal of any negative decision with suspensive effect.[17] The UNHCR also emphasises that trained asylum experts would be required on-board, and that it is not appropriate for RSD to be carried out by border or coastguard officials. In addition, trained translators or interpreters may also be necessary.[18]

[11] UNHCR, 'Maritime Interception Operations and the Processing of International Protection Claims: Legal Standards and Policy Considerations with Respect to Extraterritorial Processing' (Protection Policy Paper, Division of International Protection, November 2010) 15 [55].

[12] UNHCR, 'High Commissioner's Dialogue on Protection Challenges: Protection at Sea—Background Paper' (11 November 2014) www.unhcr.org/5464c3dc9.pdf, 4 [17].

[13] UNHCR, 'Guidance Note on Bilateral and/or Multilateral Transfer Arrangements of Asylum Seekers' (Division of International Protection, May 2013).

[14] UNHCR Regional Representation Canberra, 'UNHCR Position: Interception and Turn Back of Boats Carrying Asylum Seekers' (23 July 2015) www.unhcr.org.au/wp-content/uploads/2015/05/unhcr-position-interception-and-turn-back-of-boats-carrying-asylum-seekers.pdf.

[15] UNHCR (2010) above n 11, 5 [15].

[16] ibid 15 [55].

[17] UNHCR (2010) above n 11, 15 [58].

[18] ibid.

B. Regional Standards

Other regional bodies have also highlighted the importance of procedural safeguards in relation to maritime enforcement mechanisms. For instance, the 2013 EU Procedures Directive (recast) sets out procedural protections to be met at maritime borders and in the territorial seas of Member States, including the right to a personal interview, legal representation and interpreters.[19] Significantly, Recital 26 of the Directive directs that '[w]here those persons are present in the territorial waters of a Member State, they should be disembarked on land and have their applications examined in accordance with this Directive'.[20] However, the Directive is stated to apply only to territorial waters. Thus, it would appear inapplicable to actions on the high seas. In contrast, Article 4(3) of the European Parliament's Regulation on Border Surveillance applies more broadly to 'sea operations' at the external sea borders of EU states, not merely actions within Member States' territorial waters. This Regulation requires participating units to grant certain procedural rights to persons intercepted or rescued during sea operations. It provides that before such persons are disembarked, forced to enter, conducted to or otherwise handed over to the authorities of a third country, the authorities must:

> assess their personal circumstances, inform them of their destination in a way that those persons understand or may reasonably be presumed to understand and *give them an opportunity to express any reasons for believing that disembarkation in the proposed place would be in violation of the principle of non-refoulement*. [Emphasis added.][21]

This provision is significant as such an opportunity was said *not* to apply to interdicted persons in the Australian High Court case of *CPCF*, which is examined in section III(B) of this chapter.

Further, as discussed by Iván in Chapter 3 of this volume, jurisprudence from the European Court of Human Rights (ECtHR) has also established that States Parties may breach provisions of the European Convention on

[19] Council Directive 2013/32/EU of 26 June 2013 on common procedures for granting and withdrawing international protection (recast) [2013] OJ L180/60, arts 12, 14–16, 22.

[20] ibid Recital 26. Recital 26 also provides that authorities carrying out border enforcement 'should be able to provide third-country nationals or stateless persons who are present in the territory, including at the border, in the territorial waters or in the transit zones of the Member States, and who make an application for international protection, with relevant information as to where and how applications for international protection may be lodged.'

[21] Council Regulation 656/2014 of 15 May 2014 establishing rules for the surveillance of the external sea borders in the context of operational cooperation coordinated by the European Agency for the Management of Operational Cooperation at the External Borders of the Member States of the European Union [2014] OJ L189/93, art 4(3). The Regulation also seeks to support that provision by stating that any operational plan for sea operations must set out details as to the availability of interpreters, legal advisers and other relevant experts of the host and participating Member States. The implications of this are discussed by Pollet in ch 7.

Human Rights (ECHR) via interception and transfer actions on the high seas. For instance, in *Hirsi Jamaa and Others v Italy*,[22] the ECtHR held, amongst other things, that Italy had violated Article 13 (right to an effective remedy) because the applicants were unable to lodge their complaint with a competent authority and 'obtain a thorough and rigorous assessment' of their protection claims before Italy transferred them to Libya.[23]

C. Domestic Procedural Fairness Principles

In addition to the above international and regional principles, many domestic jurisdictions have also developed procedural standards in case law and legislation. The due process concept which will be the focus of this chapter is that of 'procedural fairness', which is recognised in many common law jurisdictions, and is particularly well-developed in the United Kingdom (UK) and Australia.[24] This principle is regarded as a cornerstone of fairness and the rule of law, with the current Chief Justice of the Australian High Court, Chief Justice French, describing procedural fairness as 'indispensable to justice'.[25]

In Australia, the common law recognises a duty to accord a person procedural fairness when a decision is made that affects a person's rights, interests or legitimate expectations.[26] Such a duty gives the applicant an important entitlement: to know the case sought to be made against him or her and to be given an opportunity of responding to it.[27] This is a particularly significant entitlement in the context of push backs at sea given the possible risk of return of a person to harm. Once a person establishes this right, the content of fairness will differ according to individual circumstances, but can include a right to a hearing, to challenge adverse information, provision of legal assistance and an interpreter.

Australian legislation contains specific procedural fairness provision for RSD carried out in Australia. For instance, the Migration Act 1958 (Cth) (MA) requires decision-makers to notify applicants of certain adverse information personal to the applicant in writing and an opportunity to respond to that information.[28] Australian courts have tended to apply

[22] *Hirsi Jamaa and Others v Italy* App no 27765/09 (ECtHR, 23 February 2012).

[23] See Iván, ch 3.

[24] eg Bingham LJ in *SSHD v Thirukumar* [1989] Imm AR 402, 414: 'It is … plain that asylum decisions are of such moment that only the highest standards of fairness will suffice'.

[25] R French, 'Sir Anthony Mason Lecture: Procedural Fairness—Indispensable to Justice?' (University of Melbourne Law School, 7 October 2010) www.hcourt.gov.au/assets/publications/speeches/current-justices/frenchcj/frenchcj07oct10.pdf.

[26] *Kioa v West* (1985) 159 CLR 550, 582 (Mason J).

[27] ibid.

[28] MA, s 424A.

procedural fairness principles strictly to refugee cases—an approach which recognises the vulnerability of the applicants and the significance of the decision to refuse a refugee application (denial of liberty or possible return to harm).[29] This strong procedural fairness jurisprudence is supported by a sophisticated review framework for applications lodged by 'lawful' arrivals within Australian territory: a primary assessment by the Department of Immigration, a full *de novo* merits review by the Refugee Review Tribunal and access to judicial review to the Federal and High Court of Australia—with procedural fairness attaching to all levels.[30] No such framework is available to asylum seekers intercepted and returned on the high seas.

Despite the rich jurisprudence on procedural fairness in Australia, the courts have held that procedural fairness may be excluded or limited in some instances. Such a finding will depend on the nature of the decision under consideration, but is usually made due to the urgent nature of a decision or where provision of procedural fairness would defeat purposes of the decision.[31] In other instances the Government may justify exclusion of natural justice because it is considered inappropriate in certain circumstances.[32] Whilst factors such as urgency may contribute to a finding of exclusion in some circumstances, the High Court of Australia has stated that in asylum cases, matters of urgency must be weighed against other factors that may arise in an individual case, including whether the decision is preliminary or final; whether it was made in public or private; the formalities required for the original decision; the breadth of any appeal and the nature of the interest and subject matter at stake.[33] This is significant for procedural fairness rights at sea, as one of the arguments before the Australian High Court in the 2015 litigation was that the powers relating to interdiction are powers which maritime officers must be able to

[29] See the recent High Court of Australia case *Minister for Immigration and Border Protection v WZARH and Anor* [2015] HCA 40.

[30] However, as discussed by Kirk in ch 11, a 'fast track' RSD process for a defined group of asylum seekers was introduced into Australian law in 2014. As Kirk notes, the body set up to undertake merits review of these decisions, the Immigration Assessment Authority, has limited procedural fairness obligations. Further, certain 'excluded' applicants who are refused a protection visa by the Department of Immigration do not have access to review by the Immigration Assessment Authority, only internal review to the Department.

[31] *Twist v Randwick Municipal Council* [1976] HCA 58.

[32] eg MA, s 198AE provides that natural justice rules do not apply to a decision by the Minister that an unauthorised maritime arrival be taken to a regional processing centre (Nauru or Papua New Guinea).

[33] *Minister Immigration; ex parte Miah* (2001) 206 CLR 57, McHugh J. In this case the RSD officer did not give Mr Miah an opportunity to comment on country information reports upon which the Department had relied to reject his application. See also *Saeed v Minister for Immigration and Citizenship* (2010) 241 CLR, 252 where the High Court held that a provision in the MA was insufficient to exclude the common law principle of procedural fairness in relation to offshore refugee applicants.

exercise flexibly and quickly in the maritime environment, particularly in circumstances of urgency.[34]

This chapter now turns to discuss the Australian state practice of screening at sea and jurisprudence on the applicability of procedural standards to this practice.

III. SCREENING AT SEA AND FAIRNESS—STATE PRACTICE

A. Introduction

A number of countries practise interdiction and 'push back' on the high seas. However, it appears that only a small number of those carry out a form of screening prior to such returns. The focus of this chapter is the screening practice of Australia. But in order to understand this, it is necessary briefly to canvass the screening procedures carried out in the United States (US) and the concerns this screening has raised.

In the US, screening is carried out by US naval forces as part of its interdiction programme against Cuban and Haitian asylum seekers.[35] The nature of the screening carried out has varied over time according to the particular caseload interdicted and due to changes in policy. For instance, Azadeh Dastyari notes that the US differentiates between Cuban and non-Cuban nationals in relation to screening at sea. Those Cubans intercepted at sea generally undergo two steps: first, there is a pre-screening by a protection screening officer (PSO)—a trained representative of the Refugee Affairs Division of the US Citizenship and Immigration Services—to establish whether the person has a 'credible fear' of persecution. If a PSO is satisfied that a Cuban national has a credible fear of persecution or torture, that person is then transferred to Guantanamo Bay for further RSD procedures.[36] The position for those who are *not* Cuban nationals (such as Haitians) is quite different, particularly in relation to the involvement of government PSOs. When non-Cuban nationals are interdicted, they must first notify the coastguard that they fear *refoulement* before they will be given the opportunity to have a pre-screening interview with a PSO. This is of concern, because as Dastyari points out, it is very difficult in practice for non-Cuban asylum seekers to communicate their protection needs to coastguard personnel.[37]

Similar concerns about the US screening process at sea have been raised by the UNHCR and other commentators. The UNHCR has expressed its

[34] See discussion at section III(B).

[35] See an excellent discussion of this in A Dastyari, *United States Migrant Interdiction and the Detention of Refugees in Guantanamo Bay* (New York, Cambridge University Press, 2015).

[36] ibid 138–39.

[37] See Dastyari, above n 35, 139–41.

concern about the lack of individual screening procedures for Haitians intercepted at sea by the US in relation to interdictions in the Caribbean Sea.[38] Academic commentator, Suzanne Gluck, also argues that shipboard interviews are an inadequate screening device.[39] She notes that US immigration officials have admitted that the system is 'dysfunctional', with these officials describing the ships as 'the worst possible place to conduct an interview.'[40]

Despite these problems, litigation on these screening practices foundered due to the interpretation by US courts of jurisdictional requirements. For instance, in litigation relating to push backs of Haitian asylum seekers in the 1980s, the Government argued that US courts did not have jurisdiction to review the adequacy of the shipboard screening procedures 'because the interdiction and screening took place in international waters'.[41] In *Haitian Refugee Center v Gracey*,[42] a district court ruled that the relevant laws (the US Refugee Act and Immigration and Nationality Act) which establish due process rights such as a right to a hearing 'only establish procedures guaranteed to aliens *within* the United States'.[43] Because the interdicted Haitians never reached the US, the court held that these laws could provide no relief to the plaintiffs.[44] This has striking similarities to the Australian jurisprudence in *CPCF*, where the High Court held that procedural fairness does not apply to asylum seekers intercepted by Australian authorities outside Australian territorial waters (that is, in the contiguous zone or on the high seas). The approaches of both the US and Australian courts on this issue take a narrow interpretation of jurisdiction for the purpose of procedural safeguards and do not recognise the procedural implications of the exercise of effective control over these interdicted persons.

Australian practice and jurisprudence will now be discussed.

[38] UNHCR, 'UNHCR Urges Adequate Asylum Screening of Haitians Intercepted at Sea' (Washington DC, Press Release, 25 January 2013).

[39] S Gluck, 'Intercepting Refugees at Sea: An Analysis of the United States' Legal and Moral Obligations' (1993) 61 *Fordham Law Review* 865, 888.

[40] ibid 889 [footnotes omitted]. Officials pointed to the physical problems associated with conducting interviews at sea and the privacy problems raised by interviewing persons on sensitive matters in crowded conditions.

[41] See discussion in M Flynn, 'How and Why Immigration Detention Crossed the Globe' (Global Detention Project, Working Paper No 8, April 2014) 7–8.

[42] *Haitian Refugee Center v Gracey* 600 F Supp 1396 (DDC 1985) 1404 (United States District Court, District of Columbia Circuit).

[43] As Dastyari has argued, the two provisions of the US Constitution that may assist asylum seekers interdicted at sea—the First and Fifth Amendments to the US Constitution—do not apply to status determination under the US Migrant Interdiction Program: Dastyari, above n 35, 144. The First Amendment guarantees freedom of speech and association and the Fifth Amendment provides that no person shall be deprived of life liberty or property without due process of law.

[44] *Haitian Refugee Center v Gracey*, above n 42.

B. Australian Interdiction and Screening at Sea

Australian authorities have practised interdiction of asylum seekers at sea in various ways since 2001. This practice represents a development that began after the 2001 Tampa crisis,[45] when maritime operations changed from reactive measures to boat arrivals coming *within* Australian waters, to preventative actions *outside* Australian territory (in the contiguous zone and high seas).[46] More recently, there have been two developments which raise particular concerns for *non-refoulement* and procedural standards. First, this interdiction practice has generally involved intercepting boats carrying asylum seekers at sea and towing them or otherwise compelling their return to Indonesia from which they embarked (Indonesia being a transit country for asylum seekers coming from countries such as Afghanistan, Iran and Syria). As a result of the nationalities of those on board, previous practice has not involved the direct return of interdicted persons to their country of nationality or origin.[47] However, from 2014 onwards, interdiction has been expanded to include returns to the *country of nationality*. Examples include the screening and return of 41 Sri Lankan asylum seekers to Sri Lanka in 2014,[48] the screening and return of 46 Vietnamese asylum seekers to Vietnam in 2015 and the return (by plane) of an estimated 12 Sri Lankan asylum seekers to Sri Lanka in May 2016.[49]

A further development, which is the focus of this chapter, is the introduction of screening procedures at sea by Australian authorities since July 2014.

[45] This political and legal crisis occurred when the Norwegian cargo ship MV Tampa was refused entry to Australian waters after rescuing 438 people (mostly Afghan asylum seekers), from a distressed Indonesian fishing boat 140km northwest of Australian territory: see summary in *Ruddock v Vadarlis* (2001) 110 FCR 491.

[46] This deterrent strategy was actioned from 2001 onwards as part of 'Operation Relex'. As the 2002 Senate Committee report on Tampa—'A Certain Maritime Incident'—noted: 'As an operation aimed at preventing unauthorised vessels from crossing into Australia's so-called "contiguous zone", Relex was fundamentally a forward deterrence strategy. This marked a shift in border protection strategy and the nature of previous operations, away from the more reactive posture associated with Operation Cranberry that sought to detect and intercept unauthorised boats *inside* Australian waters and escort them to Australian ports': Senate Select Committee on a Certain Maritime Incident, *Report of the Senate Select Committee on a Certain Maritime Incident* (Canberra, Senate Printing Unit, Parliament House, 23 October 2002) 14 [2.7] www.aph.gov.au/Parliamentary_Business/Committees/Senate/Former_Committees/maritimeincident/report/index.

[47] eg by placing the asylum seekers in lifeboats and directing those vessels back to Indonesia: see ABC News, 'Asylum Seekers Towed Back in Lifeboat: New Video Emerges as Defence Minister Criticises ABC' (Sydney, ABC News, 18 Mar 2014) www.abc.net.au/news/2014-02-07/video-emerges-of-lifeboat-towback-operation/5245280.

[48] M Knott, 'Asylum seekers screened at sea returned to Sri Lanka' (Sydney, Sydney Morning Herald, 7 July 2014) www.smh.com.au/federal-politics/political-news/asylum-seekers-screened-at-sea-returned-to-sri-lanka-20140706-3bh3x.html. The Minister for Immigration reported that only one of the asylum seekers, who was Sinhalese, passed screening to seek asylum but chose to return to Sri Lanka with the other asylum seekers.

[49] B Hall, 'Labor Wants Answers After Asylum Seekers Flown Back to Sri Lanka from Cocos Islands' (Sydney, Sydney Morning Herald, 6 May 2016) www.smh.com.

This involves officials from the Department of Immigration who are stationed on the Australian mainland conducting an interview with interdicted persons at sea (on customs vessels) via Skype or teleconference. This interview comprises only four questions: name, country of origin, where they have come from and why they have left. There are no protection-focused questions asking whether the person fears persecution or wishes to claim asylum.[50] Further, there is no provision for independent legal advice prior to or during the screening process. Those who do not satisfy the screening process are then returned to their country of origin or place of embarkation.[51]

C. The High Court Decision in CPCF

The use of interdiction and screening at sea was litigated before Australia's highest court in 2015. This litigation was in response to the interception by Australian authorities of a boat from India that was carrying 157 Tamil asylum seekers (Sri Lankan nationals). This interdiction took place in the contiguous zone[52] and the asylum seekers were detained on an Australian naval ship for a period of 29 days.[53] The plaintiff in the case (named 'CPCF') was one of the 157 asylum seekers detained at sea: a Sri Lankan national of Tamil ethnicity who claimed to have a well-founded fear of persecution in Sri Lanka on grounds that would qualify him as a refugee under the Refugee Convention.[54] The fact that the interdictees were Sri Lankan nationals was of central importance as the evidence presented in the case was that the Australian authorities were attempting to return the interdictees back to India—their place of *embarkation* (where they had been living for some time). There was no attempt to return them to their

au/federal-politics/political-news/asylum-seekers-flown-back-to-sri-lanka-from-cocos-islands-20160506-gonsvx.html.

[50] See Special Case lodged as part of the litigation in *CPCF*, discussed in *CPCF v Minister for Immigration and Border Protection & Anor*, above n 5, [308] Kiefel J.

[51] S Whyte, 'Immigration Department Officials Screen Asylum Seekers at Sea "Via Teleconference"' (Sydney, Sydney Morning Herald, 2 July 2014) www.smh.com.au/federal-politics/political-news/immigration-department-officials-screen-asylum-seekers-at-sea-via-teleconference-20140702-3b837.html.

[52] The 'contiguous zone' is defined in the United Nations Convention on the Law of the Sea (UNCLOS), as the seas extending 24 nautical miles from a country's coastal baseline (that is, extending an additional 12 nautical miles beyond the territorial waters of a country): UNCLOS [1994] Australian Treaty Series 31.

[53] The defendant's chronology submitted by the Commonwealth Government as part of the High Court litigation indicates that a person on the asylum seeker vessel called the Australian Maritime Safety Authority and requested assistance on 26/27 June 2014. See Case S169/2014, '*CPCF v Minister for Immigration and Border Protection & Anor*: Chronology (Defendants)' (HCA, 30 September 2014) 1–2; Case S169/2014, '*CPCF v Minister for Immigration and Border Protection & Anor*: Written Submissions (Defendants)' (HCA, 30 September 2014) 1 [6].

[54] *CPCF v Minister for Immigration and Border Protection & Anor*, above n 5, [1].

country of origin (Sri Lanka). This was a pivotal issue in relation to arguments about *non-refoulement*.[55]

The legal arguments in *CPCF* centred on Australian domestic law, in particular, a statute called the Maritime Powers Act 2013 (Cth) (MPA) and were primarily focused on whether asylum seekers were and could be detained under that statute. Section 72(4) of the MPA (as it then stood)[56] provided that:

> A maritime officer may detain the person and take the person, or cause the person to be taken:
>
> (a) to a place in the migration zone; or
> (b) to a place outside the migration zone, including a place outside Australia.

This subsection has to be read with section 74 of the MPA, which refers to the safety of the place of transfer: '[a] maritime officer must not place or keep a person in a place, unless the officer is satisfied, on reasonable grounds, that it is *safe* for the person to be in that place' (emphasis added).[57]

The argument that the plaintiff was entitled to—but had not been given—procedural fairness, was linked to the primary argument about the power to detain and transfer the plaintiff. The plaintiff submitted that the power under the MPA to detain and take him to India was conditioned by an obligation to give him an opportunity to be heard about the exercise of that power.[58] The plaintiff's counsel directly addressed the issue of exclusion of natural justice, submitting that:

> even where matters of urgency attend a particular decision making process, that will generally be taken to affect the content of the obligation to provide procedural fairness, rather than indicating as a threshold matter that the principles of natural justice are excluded altogether.[59]

Counsel for the plaintiff noted that although certain biographical and identity questions were asked of the plaintiff, he was not asked protection-focused questions nor whether he claimed, in effect, to be a refugee.[60]

[55] ibid [219] Crennan J: 'If the s 72(4)(b) power had been invoked to return the plaintiff to Sri Lanka or to take the plaintiff to a place outside the migration zone which was not safe, questions might have arisen about an interpretation of s 72(4)(b) consistent with Australia's obligations under the Refugees Convention. However, no such issues arose on the facts in the special case.'

[56] The MPA was amended after the High Court hearings concluded in *CPCF* (but before judgment was delivered in January 2015): see Migration and Maritime Powers Legislation Amendment (Resolving the Asylum Legacy Caseload) Act 2014 (Cth).

[57] MPA, s 74.

[58] Case S169/2014, '*CPCF v Minister for Immigration and Border Protection & Anor*: Written Submissions (Plaintiff)' (HCA, 11 September 2014) www.hcourt.gov.au/cases/case_s169-2014, [6]–[30].

[59] ibid [11].

[60] See discussion of the Special Case lodged with the High Court, in *CPCF v Minister for Immigration and Border Protection*, above n 5, [308] Kiefel J.

Despite these strong arguments by the plaintiff, the Australian High Court ultimately found that procedural fairness did *not* apply to the decision by maritime officials to take the asylum seeker to another country.[61] The basis for this finding varied amongst the judges. Some judges held that a person on a detained vessel does not meet the preliminary test for procedural fairness, that is, such a person has no relevant right, interest or expectation that may be affected adversely by a decision about the exercise of powers under the MPA (to return and detain).[62] For instance Chief Justice (CJ) French held that:

> Plainly, the exercise of the power under s 72(4) will have an adverse effect upon the liberty of the persons affected by it and depending upon the destinations to which they are taken, may have the potential to affect their ultimate safety and wellbeing. However, given the nature and purposes of the power and the circumstances in which it is exercised, the plaintiff's submission cannot be accepted.[63]

Two of the judges, Chief Justice French and Justice Kiefel, placed weight on the fact that the power of detention and transfer at sea was exercised for the purpose of preventing a contravention of Australia's migration laws.[64] Such an approach reflects a much broader trend in Australian law involving the criminalisation of asylum and the tendency to prioritise such domestic criminalisation provisions over any recognition of an international right to seek and enjoy asylum.[65] The significance of the approach of some of the members of the High Court in *CPCF* is that this focus on criminalisation also infects the approach taken by the courts to limit the procedural entitlements of those persons wishing to seek asylum in Australia.

Several of the judges in *CPCF* also considered the practicalities of imposing an obligation of procedural fairness in the maritime environment.[66] French CJ placed reliance on the fact that the MPA contains no

[61] Ibid [51] French CJ.

[62] *CPCF v Minister for Immigration and Border Protection*, above n 5, [51]–[53] French CJ; [117]–[18] Hayne J and Bell J; [226]–[27] Crennan J (agreeing with Gageler J).

[63] ibid [51] French CJ.

[64] *CPCF v Minister for Immigration and Border Protection*, above n 5, [52] French CJ; [306] Kiefel J.

[65] MA, s 42(1) specifically provides that 'a non-citizen must not travel to Australia without a visa that is in effect' (note that the term used is 'travel to' not 'enter'). In *CPCF* the High Court identified contravention of s 42(1) as a sufficient basis for enlivening the detention powers under the MPA. Other provisions of the MA criminalise aspects of asylum. For instance, s 229(1)(a) provides that each of the 'master, owner, agent, charterer and operator of a vessel on which a non-citizen is brought into Australia' is guilty of an offence 'if the non-citizen, when entering Australia … is not in possession of evidence of a visa that is in effect and that permits him or her to travel to and enter Australia'. Furthermore, s 228B(1)(a) reiterates that 'a non-citizen has, at a particular time, no lawful right to come to Australia if, at that time … the non-citizen does not hold a visa that is in effect'.

[66] *CPCF v Minister for Immigration and Border Protection*, above n 5, French CJ, Kiefel J, Keane J and Gageler J.

'appropriate administrative framework' to afford asylum seekers a meaningful opportunity to be heard.[67] Like French CJ, Justice Kiefel underlined the particular framework of the legislation and the practicalities of the situation. However, in doing so, she also emphasised the security of those persons on board the vessel:

> No opportunity for him to comment upon these matters could arise. Further, there would be good reason, having regard to the security of the 56 maritime officers and crew aboard the Australian vessel, not to advise the 157 persons placed on board that they were not to be taken to Australia and instead were to be taken to the place from which they had come.[68]

Further, Justice Kiefel took a reductionist view of procedural fairness—appearing only to suggest that information about the plaintiff's ethnicity was relevant and such information would have been 'evident' to maritime officers on the boat:

> The fact that the plaintiff is a Tamil would itself be sufficient to alert maritime officers to the likelihood that he may claim to fear persecution in Sri Lanka. There was therefore no need to ask him directly as to these matters and whether he claimed to be a person in respect of whom Australia owes protection obligations. The omission of the maritime officers to make further enquiries of the plaintiff, therefore, did not constitute a breach of procedural fairness.[69]

Similarly, Justice Gageler put weight on the exigencies of the maritime situation and considered this weighed against any implication of procedural fairness, noting that 'maritime powers are powers which maritime officers must be able to exercise flexibly and quickly in the maritime environment, particularly in circumstances of urgency'.[70] His Honour held that it would be incongruous for the common law to imply a duty on a maritime officer to afford procedural fairness as a condition of the exercise of a maritime power.[71]

In reaching these conclusions, the court focused upon the interpretation of key provisions of the Australian Migration Act 1958 (Cth) and the MPA. There was very little reference to international law, despite the fact

[67] Keane J also stated that the maritime officers on the Commonwealth ship 'had no decision-making function in the circumstances of this case, and, even if they did, they had no authority to disobey the orders they had been given': ibid [502].

[68] ibid [306] Kiefel J.

[69] ibid [308]–[09] Kiefel J.

[70] ibid [368] Gageler J.

[71] ibid. Gageler J also placed weight on the requirement of safety under MPA, s 74 (see discussion at [369]–[72]). His Honour states: 'To be able to form that prerequisite satisfaction on reasonable grounds, a maritime officer might well need to give personal consideration to the individual circumstances of the person. But that will not necessarily be so in every case. Satisfaction might well be formed on reasonable grounds as a result of the maritime officer obtaining information in other ways, including through reasonable reliance on the opinion or assurance of other persons with apparent knowledge and authority.'

that both the UNHCR and the Australian Human Rights Commission lodged *amicus curiae* briefs with the court outlining these international law arguments.[72]

The reluctance to implement international law is not a new development in Australian jurisprudence and has been evident in many other decisions of the High Court.[73] In *CPCF* there was an opportunity for the court to consider *non-refoulement* due to the inclusion of the term 'safety' in section 74 of the MPA. As noted above, this section requires consideration of the *safety* of the place to which the asylum seekers are to be transferred. Thus, it is highly arguable that the concept of 'safety' referred to in the MPA implements the *non-refoulement* principle into Australian interdiction provisions and is the 'right' or 'interest' which attracts the domestic principle of procedural fairness. In the Australian High Court adjudication of interdiction and return in *CPCF*, Justice Keane recognised that some form of procedural fairness may arise from the requirement of 'safety' in section 74 of the MPA in a situation where the asylum seeker was to be returned to the territory of a third state.[74] However, other judges differed in their views as to whether this consideration attracted the principles of procedural fairness. Justices Hayne and Bell held that in deciding whether to detain and take to a place *in* Australia or to a place *outside* Australia, a maritime officer is not obliged to ask the person which of those courses should be taken.[75] French CJ recognised that the maritime officers exercising powers of detention and transfer may use their discretion to find out information about the ethnicity of the passengers and general information about the country of proposed return in determining whether it is safe to return them to that place. However, he held that this did not lead to application of procedural fairness.[76]

In contrast to the approach of the High Court in this case, I would argue that the reference to 'safety' in the MPA is the very type of consideration

[72] Case S169/2014, '*CPCF v Minister for Immigration and Border Protection & Anor*: Written Submissions (Australian Human Rights Commission Seeking Leave to Intervene)' (HCA, 11 September 2014) www.hcourt.gov.au/cases/case_s169-2014.

[73] See *Minister for Immigration, Multicultural and Indigenous Affairs v QAAH* [2006] HCA 53, 231 ALR 340, 348, 350, where the Court held that 'it is the law of Australia which prevails in case of any conflict between it and the [Refugee] Convention. It is the law of Australia which must first be identified' and despite the ways in which 'the Convention may be used in construing the Act, it is the words of the Act which govern'. For discussion, see M O'Sullivan, 'Withdrawing Protection under Article 1C(5) of the 1951 Convention: Lessons from Australia' (2008) 20(4) *International Journal of Refugee Law* 586.

[74] *CPCF v Minister for Immigration and Border Protection and Anor*, above n 5, [501] Keane J.

[75] ibid [118].

[76] ibid [53] French CJ: 'The ultimate safety of persons taken to a place under s 72(4) is a mandatory relevant consideration by reason of s 74. It does not follow from that that the power conferred under s 72(4) is conditioned by the requirements of procedural fairness… While the obtaining of basic information from the passengers may be a necessary incident of compliance with the requirement of s 74 in particular circumstances, it is not a matter which goes to power under the rubric of procedural fairness.'

which should attract the application of procedural fairness. Despite the fact that Australian authorities are acting outside Australian territory in interdicting and returning asylum seekers at sea, they are exercising jurisdiction over them. It is widely accepted in international law that a state's human rights obligations can apply extraterritorially where that state is exercising 'effective control' or jurisdiction.[77] Indeed, this principle was accepted by an Australian Parliamentary body—the Senate Legal and Constitutional Affairs References Committee—which stated in a 2014 report on offshore processing that:

> Australia's human rights obligations apply to all people subject to Australia's jurisdiction, regardless of whether they are Australian citizens. This means Australia owes human rights obligations to everyone in Australia, as well as to persons outside Australia over whom Australia is exercising 'effective control', or who are otherwise under Australia's jurisdiction.[78]

Once this is accepted, the application of procedural fairness principles becomes applicable and it is clear that the act of return at sea affects serious 'rights' or 'interests'.[79] These include: deprivation of liberty (by the act of interdiction and detention at sea) and considerations of safety (the principle of *non-refoulement* in addition to interests of physical safety in being turned back at sea in dangerous conditions).

D. Legislative Changes: 2014

As noted above, whilst the High Court of Australia was deliberating on the submissions made in *CPCF*, the Australian Parliament passed an amendment to the MPA in late 2014. This amendment clarified the Australian Government's position that interception and detention of vessels in Australian maritime waters does not attract the rules of natural justice.[80] The explanatory memorandum to that set of provisions referred to the need to recognise that the 'unique circumstances…in a maritime environment'

[77] eg Office of the United Nations High Commissioner for Human Rights (OHCHR), 'Human Rights Committee General Comment No 35: Article 9 (Liberty and Security of Person)' (112th Session, UN Doc CCPR/C/GC/35, 16 December 2014) 18 [63]; OHCHR, 'Committee Against Torture General Comment No 2: Implementation of Article 2 by States Parties' (UN Doc CAT/C/GC/2, 24 January 2008) [16]; *Al-Jedda v United Kingdom* App no 27021/08 (ECtHR, 7 July 2011); *Al-Skeini v United Kingdom* App no 55721/07 (ECtHR, 7 July 2011).

[78] Senate Legal and Constitutional Affairs References Committee, Parliament of Australia, *Incident at the Manus Island Detention Centre from 16 February to 18 February 2014* (Canberra, Senate Printing Unit, Parliament House, 2014) 131 [7.20] www.aph.gov.au/Parliamentary_Business/Committees/Senate/Legal_and_Constitutional_Affairs/Manus_Island/Report.

[79] This is the hinge upon which procedural fairness is applied under Australian law, see *Kioa v West*, above n 26.

[80] MPA, s 75B (as amended).

render the provision of natural justice in most circumstances impracticable.[81] This therefore echoes the reasoning of some of the judges in the High Court decision in *CPCF* who also relied quite heavily on the notion of impracticability in denying the application of procedural fairness to interdictions at sea.

IV. ANALYSIS

The screening practice of Australia raises significant due process concerns. Under international standards set out in various UNHCR documents (discussed in section II above), it appears that many of the UNHCR requirements are not being met under the current process. In particular, there is no opportunity to contact a representative of the UNHCR, no right to legal representation and no appeal rights. Whilst interdicted persons are asked why they left their country, they are not given information on how to lodge an asylum application. The legitimacy of the screening process as a valid means of profiling persons at sea is therefore dependent on interdictees knowing about refugee status and their ability to lodge a claim via an asylum process. In the absence of such information, it is argued that the Australian screening procedure fails to give interdicted persons an effective opportunity to express their need for international protection and access to a fair and effective RSD process. The use of screening as a profiling mechanism without undertaking a more robust status determination procedure also raises significant dangers that persons will be returned to their country of nationality or origin or transferred to a third state in breach of the *non-refoulement* principle.

The use of screening at sea as a profiling mechanism (to establish biographical details/identity), which does not also have sufficient measures in place to identify people that may have a protection need, is therefore highly problematic. The Kaldor Centre for International Refugee Law has also raised concerns about this, stating that if a country implements pre-screening procedures prior to full RSD, it must ensure that such an assessment does not replace full RSD, or become a de facto RSD procedure with limited procedural guarantees.[82] Given that the Australian screening procedure asks only four basic questions (which do not directly raise any protection issues), there are doubts that those persons with little knowledge of their rights or of the asylum procedure will be able spontaneously to ask for the opportunity to apply for refugee status.

[81] Explanatory Memorandum, Migration Amendment (Resolving the Asylum Legacy Caseload) Bill 2014 (Cth) 92.

[82] Kaldor Centre for International Refugee Law, 'Maritime Interception and Screening of Asylum Seekers at Sea' (Fact Sheet, University of New South Wales, 1 July 2015).

These concerns with on board screening are also echoed by non-governmental organisations (NGOs) and academics. For instance, the Law Council of Australia states that screening at sea of persons rescued or intercepted at sea is unlikely to meet the relevant minimum international standards.[83] Similarly, the Kaldor Centre for International Refugee Law notes that there are considerable logistical difficulties in ensuring that on-water reception arrangements and asylum procedures accord with minimum international standards. It has stated that '*[i]n exceptional circumstances*, initial screening at sea may be undertaken to proactively identify people with protection needs and expedite their access to a full RSD process. However, it should not be used as a routine policy measure' (emphasis in original).[84] It also specifically recommended that pre-screening should not take place if an asylum seeker's physical and/or mental state suggests that they are not able to express a need for protection effectively.[85]

The approach taken to screening at sea by the Australian High Court in *CPCF* also reveals a very limited interpretation of procedural fairness which contrasts strongly with strict principles applied to in-country refugee status determinations in Australia. Whilst interdiction on the high seas represents the exercise of Australian jurisdiction and extraterritorial application of domestic law, the High Court has not recognised a parallel application of procedural obligations. Instead, much of the Court's analysis focused on the impracticability of applying procedural fairness standards to interdictions at sea. Rather than focusing on *impracticability* as a reason for excluding procedural fairness, it is argued here that the inherent dangers of screening on naval vessels in fact *strengthens* the case for strict adherence to procedural standards. Navy vessels constitute a militarised environment lacking privacy and other physical conditions that are necessary for the effective processing of claims. The provision of a teleconference with immigration officials based in Australia, communicating with the asylum seeker whilst they are still at sea, is not a sufficient answer to these problems.

Placing the Australian example within the broader themes of access discussed in this book, it is clear that similar concerns raised by screening at sea are also evident in summary procedures carried out on land. For instance, in Chapter 11 of this volume, Kirk analyses the accelerated procedures used in the UK and Australia in certain detained cases, which have been criticised for lack of legal assistance and limited review procedures. Indeed, Chapter 11 identifies that a 'major flaw' with the UK detained fast

[83] Law Council of Australia, 'Asylum Seeker Policy' (Braddon ACT, 2014) 11 [24] www.lawcouncil.asn.au/lawcouncil/images/LCA-PDF/a-z-docs/AsylumSeeker_Policy_web.pdf.

[84] Kaldor Centre for International Refugee Law, above n 82.

[85] ibid.

track screening 'is that it assumes that the applicant is willing and able to present important information about their claims and their personal circumstances to the screening officer'.[86] These issues are also relevant to at sea screening. However, it is suggested that the consequences are more serious in relation to interdictions because of the geographical isolation and particular vulnerabilities of those asylum seekers interdicted and detained at sea.

V. CONCLUSION

The Australian practice of screening and the denial of the Australian courts to apply procedural fairness standards to such screening represent a significant danger to the rights of asylum seekers interdicted at sea. Asylum seekers on the high seas are particularly vulnerable in contrast to those at land borders, given that their ability to seek legal assistance is highly constrained. The approach of the High Court of Australia to deny procedural fairness to this cohort of asylum seekers does not appear to consider such vulnerability but instead focuses on the practical constraints of applying procedural fairness at sea. As other chapters in this volume have noted, asylum seekers require an appropriate environment in which to claim refugee status—to be given information on their right to seek asylum and an appropriate means of communicating their claim.[87] Asylum seekers interdicted and interviewed at sea are not in a situation in which they can properly exercise that right.

Screening practices also raise several broader issues about the way in which industrialised states around the world are seeking to prevent asylum seekers from gaining access to territory in order to claim asylum and limiting procedural safeguards. The Australian practice illustrates the ability of states to take deterrent measures contrary to normal domestic law constraints by conducting interdiction outside territorial waters. This is reflected in the decision of the Australian High Court in *CPCF*, which held that important procedural fairness protections did not apply to interdicted asylum seekers on the high seas, thus denying an extraterritorial application of domestic due process standards.

The Australian example also highlights the difficulty of utilising international procedural standards in domestic litigation. For instance, although the UNHCR has set out a list of comprehensive requirements for interdictions at sea, litigation in Australia has turned on domestic legal

[86] As noted by Kirk in ch 11, 'Vulnerable applicants in particular may not be willing to reveal the details of their vulnerability at this early stage of the process, particularly if they are not represented'.

[87] See Iván, ch 3 on the difficulties faced by asylum seekers at Hungarian borders.

requirements and very little attention is paid by Australian courts to international standards. This is part of a wider problem with the lack of domestic implementation and recognition of UNHCR position statements, which is a feature of many jurisdictions, not merely that of Australia.

This chapter also reflects the wider themes canvassed in this volume about the meaning of the state, law and borders and the impact of these concepts on access to refugee protection. The Australian example of screening represents the exercise of state jurisdiction outside national boundaries without the concomitant application of rule of law principles such as procedural fairness. A leading Australian judge, Allsop CJ, neatly summarises the key issue as follows:

> What is unfair will often be a matter of debate; it will often be affected by the terms of a statute or the content of a precedent; but in essence, it is an enduring human response rooted in democratic society's expectations of equal and fair treatment of individuals by organs of power.[88]

Finally, the Australian practice and jurisprudence examined in this chapter demonstrates the weakness of law in protecting asylum seekers at sea. The Australian approach leaves a legal vacuum in which asylum seekers can neither assert domestic procedural fairness provisions nor international law in asserting a right to seek asylum (or at least to be protected from *refoulement*). In this instance, the ability of the state to interdict asylum seekers at sea not only allows it to deny access to its physical territory but also permits the state to deny the application of the normal protections of the law to those persons. Thus, such asylum seekers are placed outside the law's protection—they become non-subjects before the law in a context in which the consequences of such a denial may be significant.[89] This chapter therefore illustrates the overriding power of state sovereignty in exercising border control and access to law.

[88] J Allsop, 'The James Spigelman Oration 2015: Values in Public Law' (27 October 2015) www.fedcourt.gov.au/publications/judges-speeches/chief-justice-allsop/allsop-cj-20151027.

[89] eg if they are 'screened out' and returned to their country of origin or another country where they face harm contrary to the *non-refoulement* principle, as discussed above in section III(A) and (B).

6

Detained at the Border

Obstacles to Entry for Central American Refugees in the United States

MAGGIE MORGAN AND DEBORAH ANKER

I. INTRODUCTION

SINCE THE 1970S, the south-western border[1] between the United States (US) and Mexico has been the site of significant migration from Central America.[2] Over one million Central American refugees crossed into the US from the late 1970s to the early 1990s to escape civil wars in Guatemala and El Salvador, while thousands more went to Canada, Mexico, Costa Rica and Belize.[3] While this growth in refugees slowed after these conflicts ended in the late 1990s, a second increase in migration began in 2012 and peaked in 2014. This migration included a dramatic increase in the number of women and children leaving Honduras, El Salvador and Guatemala (a region referred to as the 'Northern Triangle' of Central America) for the US.[4] Thousands fled, and continue

[1] The south-western border between the US and Mexico spans 1,989 miles. Many parts of the border are regarded as extremely harsh and inhospitable terrain, with hundreds of miles of open desert, rugged mountains, the Rio Grande River and coastal waters: US Customs and Border Protection, 'Southwest Border Region: Fact Sheet' (US Department of Homeland Security, 18 September 2013) www.nemo.cbp.gov/air_marine/FS_Southwest_Border_Region.pdf.

[2] Central America is defined as Honduras, Guatemala, El Salvador, Nicaragua, Costa Rica, Belize and Panama. Mexico is traditionally considered a part of North America.

[3] During the 1980s, asylum seekers from Central America faced significant hurdles in receiving asylum in the US due at least in part to US foreign policy. eg in 1984 asylum approval rates for Salvadorans and Guatemalans in the US were less than 3% compared to 32% approval rates for Poles and 60% for Iranians: J Zong and J Batalova, 'Central American Migrants in the United States' (Washington DC, Migration Information Source, Migration Policy Institute, 2 September 2015) www.migrationpolicy.org/article/central-american-immigrants-united-states; S Mahler, 'Central America: Crossroads of the Americas' (Washington DC, Migration Information Source, Migration Policy Institute, 1 April 2006) www.migrationpolicy.org/article/central-america-crossroads-americas.

[4] United States Border Patrol, 'US Border Patrol Apprehensions From Mexico and Other Than Mexico (FY 2000–FY 2015)' (Stat and Summaries, US Department of Homeland Security,

to flee, persecution from powerful 'third-generation'[5] gangs and other politically powerful criminal organisations[6] that had targeted them or their family members for rape, murder, extortion and other harms. Many are also escaping pervasive gender-based violence, including rape, femicide (gender-based homicide) and domestic violence. Both third-generation gangs and domestic abusers in these countries often operate with impunity due to the inability or unwillingness of state governments to protect victims from harm. It has been recognised that many of those individuals fleeing the Northern Triangle have grounds for asylum or related protection under domestic and international law.[7]

Having little choice but to flee their countries, these individuals face a number of life-threatening dangers when attempting to reach the US. Many refugees, particularly women and girls, face the ever-present risk of sexual and physical abuse at the hands of human and drug traffickers.[8] Refugees, including unaccompanied children and mothers carrying

2015) Table 3 Illegal Alien Apprehensions From Countries Other Than Mexico By Fiscal Year (Oct 1st through Sept 30th) www.cbp.gov/sites/default/files/documents/BP%20Total%20Apps%2C%20Mexico%2C%20OTM%20FY2000-FY2015.pdf; United States Border Patrol, 'Southwest Border Sections: Family Unit and Unaccompanied Alien Children (0–17) Apprehensions FY 14 compared to FY 13' (Stat and Summaries, US Department of Homeland Security, 2014) www.cbp.gov/sites/default/files/documents/BP%20Southwest%20Border%20Family%20Units%20and%20UAC%20Apps%20FY13%20-%20FY14.pdf.

5 Third-generation gangs are large-scale, armed criminal organisations which often function as de facto governments, controlling significant territory and competing with the state for power. The gangs, much more organised and formidable than ordinary street gangs, often use brutal tactics to fight for territorial and political power. One of the most powerful gangs in Central America, Mara Salvatrucha (MS-13), rules entire municipalities in countries such as El Salvador and thus can be classified as a third-generation gang. See DE Anker and P Lawrence, 'Third-Generation Gangs, Warfare in Central America, and Refugee Law's Political Opinion Ground' (2014) 14-10 *Immigration Briefings* 1.

6 When referring generically to 'gangs' or 'criminal organisations' throughout this chapter, the authors refer to the definition provided by the UNHCR: 'organized armed criminal actors (groups that are largely transnational and may work collaboratively within countries and across the region).' UNHCR Regional Office for the United States and the Caribbean, 'Children on the Run: Unaccompanied Children Leaving Central America and Mexico and the Need for International Protection' (Washington DC, UNHCR, July 2014) 26.

7 See 1951 United Nations Convention relating to the Status of Refugees, 189 United Nations Treaty Series 150, supplemented by the 1967 Protocol relating to the Status of Refugees, 606 United Nations Treaty Series 267 (Refugee Convention); Immigration and Nationality Act, 8 USCA § 1101(a)(42)(A); MR Rosenblum, 'Top 10 of 2014—Issue 5: New Era in Immigration Enforcement at the US Southwest Border' (Washington DC, Migration Information Source, Migration Policy Institute, 16 December 2014) www.migrationpolicy.org/article/top-10-2014-issue-5-new-era-immigration-enforcement-us-southwest-border: 'these recent Central American arrivals present a classic "mixed flow": many are deportable, but a large number (mostly women and children) have valid asylum or other humanitarian claims.'

8 Surveys have estimated that 60–80% of women and girls crossing the US–Mexico border are sexually assaulted. See Amnesty International, 'Invisible Victims: Migrants on the Move in Mexico' (London, Amnesty International Publications, 8 April 2010) 5; E Siegal McIntyre and D Bonello, 'Is Rape the Price to Pay for Migrant Women Chasing the American Dream?' (Fusion, 10 September 2014) www.fusion.net/story/17321/is-rape-the-price-to-pay-for-migrant-women-chasing-the-american-dream/.

young children, must navigate perilous desert terrain while managing to avoid detection by the many drones, advanced surveillance systems and border patrols along the 1989 mile-long border between the US and Mexico.[9] In addition, recent co-operation between the Mexican and US governments has led Mexico to step up efforts to intercept and deport individuals before they reach the US.[10] These developments have forced refugees to take more remote and dangerous routes that increase their risk of being robbed, sexually assaulted or even killed on their journeys.[11]

Those who manage to reach the US face barriers of a different sort. Many individuals, including thousands of women and children,[12] have been detained near the border in US-run detention facilities for months or even years without proper access to legal assistance.[13] Even those with valid refugee claims face the constant threat of deportation due to improper screening procedures.[14] If deported, refugees face the risk of severe harm or even death. From January 2014–October 2015, as many as 83 individuals deported from the US back to Guatemala, El Salvador and Honduras were killed upon their return, according to at least one report.[15]

Like others across the world fleeing conflict zones,[16] many fleeing Central Americans have international protection needs that may qualify them for

[9] See section II below for more discussion of the effects of US border militarisation on the journeys of Central American refugees.

[10] See S Nazario, 'The Refugees at Our Door' (New York Times, 15 October 2015) www.nytimes.com/2015/10/11/opinion/sunday/the-refugees-at-our-door.html?_r=0.

[11] See S Brodzinsky and E Pilkington, 'US Government Deporting Central American Migrants to their Deaths' (The Guardian, 12 October 2015) www.theguardian.com/us-news/2015/oct/12/obama-immigration-deportations-central-america.

[12] In August 2015, a US federal judge ruled that the US Government could not hold children in immigration detention facilities for more than 72 hours unless they represented a significant flight risk or constituted a danger to themselves or to others. At the time of writing of this article, this case is still working its way through appeals courts and thousands of children remain detained: *Flores v Johnson* [2015] CV 85–4544 DMG (AGRx).

[13] Attorneys and advocates from the American Civil Liberties Union (ACLU), the American Immigration Lawyers Association (AILA) and other groups have filed complaints on behalf of immigrants detained at detention facilities near the US–Mexico border, alleging, among other things, that immigrants have been deprived of their right to access counsel and to fully present their claims at initial screening interviews, known as 'credible fear' interviews. See section III below for more discussion of these screenings. See *MSPC v Jeh Johnson*, Complaint for Injunctive and Declaratory Relief, United States District Court for the District of Columbia, 22 August 2014 (on file with author).

[14] See section IV below for more discussion.

[15] Brodzinsky and Pilkington, above n 11.

[16] This large-scale refugee inflow from Central America to the US is hardly an isolated phenomenon. The number of refugees across the world is at its highest levels since the Second World War, at an estimated 19 million including 4.8 million Syrians fleeing largely to other Middle Eastern countries and Europe to escape the civil war currently decimating their country. See United Nations Office for the Coordination of Humanitarian Affairs (OCHA), 'Syrian Arab Republic: Key Figures' www.unocha.org/syria; P Boehler and S Pecanhla, 'The Global Refugee Crisis, Region by Region' (The New York Times, 26 August 2015) www.nytimes.com/interactive/2015/06/09/world/migrants-global-refugee-crisis-mediterranean-ukraine-syria-rohingya-malaysia-iraq.html.

asylum or other legal relief under the United Nations Convention Relating to the Status of Refugees (Refugee Convention)[17] and US domestic asylum law.[18] However, the US has been slow in recognising the validity of the refugee claims of these new arrivals. Instead, US policy prescriptions have tended to focus either on deporting these individuals,[19] or on finding ways to prevent them from arriving in the first place,[20] such as through increasing deportations of Central Americans as they attempt to traverse Mexico or through expanding border militarisation efforts.[21] These obstacles have created a tremendous humanitarian tragedy at the south-western US border.

This chapter provides an overview of the recent migration and flight of Central Americans to the US, from the primary causes of the massive flight from the region, to the obstacles to entry that refugees face while attempting to seek asylum and related protections in the US. In particular, the chapter focuses on women and children entrants, given the sudden increase in migration of these groups in recent years. Section II of the chapter provides background information, including statistical data, to illuminate the scale and scope of the recent refugee inflow from Central America. Section III details the major reasons, primarily persecution by third-generation gangs and gender-based violence, which have compelled many Central Americans, including large numbers of women and children, to flee their homes. Section IV outlines some of the major obstacles to entry that Central American refugees face after fleeing their countries for the US. In particular, this section focuses on the impact of major US policy developments, including border militarisation, expedited removal and screening processes, and restrictive detention policies, on Central Americans' access to international protection. The persecution that Central American refugees face has historically been under-appreciated as a basis for protection under the international treaty regime. The acute problems Central Americans are facing—the

[17] Above n 7.

[18] Immigration and Nationality Act, 8 USCA § 1101(a)(42)(A).

[19] eg in 2015, the Obama administration asked Congress to amend a child anti-trafficking law so that deportations of undocumented children could be implemented faster. The law, known as the William Wilberforce Trafficking Victims Protection Reauthorization Act of 2008, remains unamended at the time of writing. See A Gomez, 'Obama Seeks Change to Law that Protects Immigrant Kids' (USA Today, 2 July 2014) www.usatoday.com/story/news/nation/2014/07/02/immigration-obama-deportation-children-border/11915723/.

[20] Many US politicians acknowledge that some recent Central American entrants might qualify for asylum, but appear to take it for granted that most do not. 2016 presidential candidate Hillary Clinton, mirroring the position of the Obama administration, has repeatedly emphasised that deportations send a message to Central Americans to not attempt to enter the US; at a press conference, she remarked that '[s]pecifically with respect to children on the border, if you remember, we had an emergency, and it was very important to send a message to families in Central America: Do not let your children take this very dangerous journey': R Planas, 'Hillary Clinton Defends Call To Deport Child Migrants' (Huffington Post, 19 August 2014) www.huffingtonpost.com/entry/hillary-clinton-child-migrants_55d4a5c5e4b055a6dab24c2f.

[21] See section IV on border militarisation for more information.

entrenched third-generation gang violence, high rates of femicide and domestic violence, and concomitant lack of state protection—all form the basis of legitimate, but under-recognised and under-appreciated, asylum claims.

II. OVERVIEW OF CENTRAL AMERICAN REFUGEE MIGRATION TO THE UNITED STATES

The number of Central Americans apprehended at the US border with Mexico has greatly increased in recent years, even as the number of apprehensions of Mexican nationals (historically very high) has declined. In 2014 alone, over 250,000 apprehensions of so-called 'non-Mexican' nationals, mostly Central Americans,[22] occurred at the south-western border, an increase of almost 70 per cent from 2013.[23]

Of the Central American refugees attempting to enter the US over the past several years, the number of women and children making the journey has grown most rapidly. Unaccompanied children under age 18 from Honduras, Guatemala and El Salvador represented almost a quarter of total 'non-Mexican' apprehensions in 2014.[24] Another quarter was made up of families from these countries; many were women travelling only with their children.[25] The actual number of entrants from Central America may be even higher, as the official government figures include only those individuals who were apprehended, not those who evaded detection.[26]

The following table documents the increased number of apprehensions of unaccompanied Central American children[27] at the south-western border in 2014.

[22] In fiscal year 2014, 90% of apprehensions of individuals traveling as part of a 'family unit' and 75% of unaccompanied children apprehended at the south-western border originated in one of three Central American countries: Guatemala, Honduras or El Salvador. United States Border Patrol (2014), above n 4.

[23] 148,988 non-Mexican nationals were apprehended at the US southwestern border in 2013, compared to 252,600 in 2014: United States Border Patrol (2015), above n 4.

[24] ibid.

[25] The US Border Patrol calculates apprehensions of families by measuring 'family units' which are defined as 'the number of individuals (either a child under 18 years old, parent or legal guardian) apprehended with a family member by the US Border Patrol.': United States Border Patrol (2014), above n 4.

[26] Though the number of apprehensions of Central American families and unaccompanied children fell significantly in FY 2015, these figures are still higher than those from 2012 and 3013: ibid.

[27] Unaccompanied children is a legal term defined by the US government as encompassing children under the age of 18 who are not in the custody of a parent or legal guardian upon entry, who remain unaccompanied after entry, and who lack a family member or legal guardian able or willing to care for them in the United States: Homeland Security Act of 2002 § 462(g); 6 USC § 276(g); adopted by TVPRA § 235(g).

Country	FY 2009	FY 2010	FY 2011	FY 2012	FY 2013	FY 2014	FY 2015
El Salvador	1,221	1,910	1,394	3,314	5,990	16,404	7,956
Guatemala	1,115	1,517	1,565	3,835	8,068	17,057	12,231
Honduras	968	1,017	974	2,997	6,747	18,244	4,680
Mexico	16,114	13,724	11,768	13,974	17,240	15,634	10,121

Figure 1: Unaccompanied Alien Children Encountered by Fiscal Year[28]
Fiscal years 2009–2014; Fiscal years 2015 to date (1 October 2014–31 August 2015)
Source: US Border Patrol (2015)

The figures show that in 2009, Mexican children accounted for the vast majority of unaccompanied children apprehended by the US Government on the south-western border. However, by 2014, a reversal had occurred, with most unaccompanied children coming from Honduras, Guatemala and El Salvador. A dramatic drop-off in apprehensions occurred in 2015, though the total number of apprehensions of non-Mexican children was still significantly higher than it had been only five years previously.

The next graph shows the changing national demographics of all immigrants (not just children) apprehended at the south-western border.

More Non-Mexicans than Mexicans Apprehended in '14
Border patrol apprehensions, 1970–2014

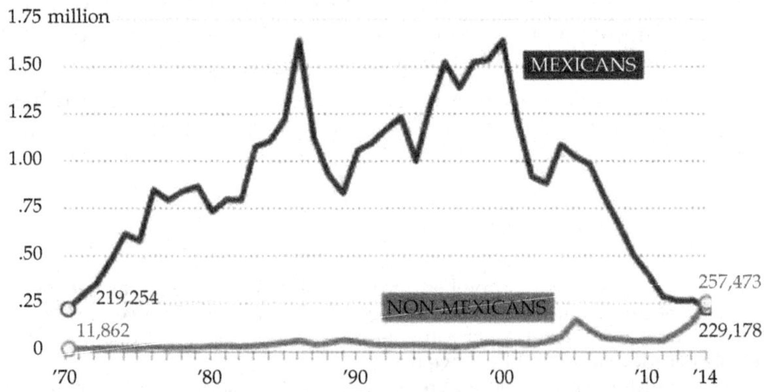

Note: 1976 covers 15 months due to change in fiscal year period.

Source: US Border Patrol apprehensions table. FY 2000–2014: Immigration and Naturalization Service statistical yearbooks. FY 1970–2000.

PEW RESEARCH CENTER

Figure 2: More Central Americans than Mexicans Apprehended[29]

[28] The fiscal year included in government statistics begins in October and ends in September of the following year. For example, FY 2013 spanned from 1 October 2013–30 September 2014.

[29] AG Barrera and JM Krogstad, 'What We Know about Illegal Immigration from Mexico' (Washington DC, Pew Research Center, 20 November 2015) www.pewresearch.org/fact-tank/2015/07/15/what-we-know-about-illegal-immigration-from-mexico.

As the graph shows, from the 1970s onwards, almost all immigrants apprehended at the US border originated from Mexico; however by the mid-2000s, the number of Mexican apprehensions dropped dramatically. In 2012, the number of non-Mexican apprehensions grew considerably, surpassing the number of Mexican apprehensions; almost all of the growth in the non-Mexican category stemmed from increased migration from El Salvador, Honduras and Guatemala, a sudden and substantial transformation in traditional migration patterns.[30]

III. PRIMARY CAUSES OF FLIGHT FROM CENTRAL AMERICA

What forces are compelling such large numbers of Central Americans, particularly women and children, to make the dangerous, 2,000-plus mile journey to the US?[31] Among the major factors of flight are the high rates of gang and gender-based violence in the Northern Triangle countries, related attacks on indigenous people, and states' unwillingness or inability to provide protection. The section below briefly examines both the nature of gang and gender-related violence within the region.

A. 'Third-generation' Gang Violence

The 'Northern Triangle' countries of El Salvador, Honduras and Guatemala have some of the highest murder rates in the world. El Salvador leads the world in homicide rates, with 103.1 murders per 100,000 people in 2015.[32] According to a US military expert, 'the so-called Northern Triangle of Guatemala, El Salvador and Honduras is the deadliest zone in the world

[30] See United States Border Patrol (2014) and United States Border Patrol (2015), above n 4.

[31] The number of Central Americans seeking asylum outside the US is increasing. The number of asylum applications filed in Costa Rica, eg, grew almost 500% from 2010, when there were 52 applications, to 2014, when there were 307. The growth in applications was largest among Hondurans and Salvadorans, though most refugees in Costa Rica currently come from Venezuela and Colombia. However, Costa Rica granted no asylum applications in the year prior to October 2014, with some officials citing fear of crime and concerns about overuse of the asylum system as the basis for the lack of approvals. The number of asylum seekers in Mexico more than doubled from 2013–14, with 1,196 applications. Many asylum seekers in Mexico are from nearby Guatemala, Honduras and El Salvador, as well as Venezuela and Colombia. Roughly a third of these applications are withdrawn before a decision is reached; of those which reach the final stage, 40% are granted. See Z Dyer, 'Costa Rica Sees Spike in Refugees Driven by Northern Triangle Violence' (El Tico Times, 17 June 2015) www.ticotimes.net/2015/06/17/costa-rica-sees-spike-refugees-driven-northern-triangle-violence; M Ureste, 'Asylum-Seekers are Pouring Into Mexico' (El Daily Post, 18 September 2015) www.eldailypost.com/news/2015/06/asylum-seekers-are-pouring-into-mexico/.

[32] US Passports and International Travel, 'El Salvador Travel Warning' (Bureau of Consular Affairs, US Department of State, 15 January 2016) www.travel.state.gov/content/passports/en/alertswarnings/el-salvador-travel-warning.html.

outside of active war zones.'[33] In recent years, El Salvador has had the highest rate of child homicide in the world, with Guatemala ranking second.[34] Approximately 70 per cent of killings are of young people between 15–30 years old.[35] Scholars also underscore the growing organisation and brutality of the gangs driving migration to the US.[36] The sheer size of the gangs (also known as 'maras') alone makes them a formidable threat. One 2012 study estimated that one gang, Mara Salvatrucha (MS-13), had 27,500 members in El Salvador alone.[37]

These extraordinarily high rates of violence can principally be attributed to the power and reach of large 'third-generation' gangs.[38] Third-generation gangs are not simple street gangs or criminal organisations operating in an apolitical space. Rather, they are organisations with a substantial degree of politicisation, sophistication and international reach.[39] Third-generation gangs often function as de facto governments, often competing with the state and controlling significant territory; the gangs often use brutal tactics to fight for such territorial and political power.[40] One of the most powerful gangs in Central America, Mara Salvatrucha (MS-13), rules

33 A Mulrine, 'Pentagon: Central America "Deadliest" Non-war Zone in the World' (The Christian Science Monitor, 11 April 2011) www.csmonitor.com/USA/Military/2011/0411/Pentagon-Central-America-deadliest-non-war-zone-in-the-world (describing conflict in Central America as tantamount to the wars in Afghanistan and Iraq in terms of scale, spending and weapons used).

34 United Nations Children's Fund (UNICEF), *Hidden in Plain Sight: A Statistical Analysis of Violence Against Children* (New York, UNICEF Division of Data, Research and Policy, September 2014) www.files.unicef.org/publications/files/Hidden_in_plain_sight_statistical_analysis_EN_3_Sept_2014.pdf; United Nations Office on Drugs and Crime (UNODC), *Global Study on Homicide 2013: Trends, Contexts, Data* (Vienna, United Nations Publication, March 2014) www.unodc.org/documents/gsh/pdfs/2014_GLOBAL_HOMICIDE_BOOK_web.pdf.

35 UNODC, above n 34.

36 See eg, D Cantor, 'Gangs: the Real "Humanitarian Crisis" Driving Central American Children to the US' (The Conversation UK, 22 August 2014) www.theconversation.com/gangs-the-real-humanitarian-crisis-driving-central-american-children-to-the-us-30672.

37 D Farah, 'Central American Gangs: Changing Nature and New Partners' (2012) 66 *Journal of International Affairs* 53, 58. By comparison, during the civil war in El Salvador, the guerrilla group, Farabundo Marti National Liberation Front (FMLN) had no more than 9,000–12,000 members at its peak yet was strong enough to negotiate an end to civil war without surrendering. LR Lerman and R Humphreys, 'Brief of Amici Curiae: Harvard Immigration and Refugee Clinical Program and Other Immigration Rights Advocates in Support of Petitioner' (Akin Gump Strauss Hauer & Feld LLP, Los Angeles, 19 November 2013) at 10, in *Fuentes-Colocho v Holder*, No 13–70470 (9th Cir. Aug 13, 2014) citing Farah, 59.

38 See International Human Rights Clinic, 'No Place to Hide: Gang, State, and Clandestine Violence in El Salvador' (Human Rights Programme Harvard Law School, February 2007) www.wola.org/sites/default/files/downloadable/Citizen%20Security/past/Harvard_Gangs_NoPlaceToHide.pdf, 20–29.

39 HL Gray, 'Gangs and Transnational Criminals Threaten Central American Stability' (Strategy Research Project, Pennsylvania, US Army War College, 10 March 2009) www.hsdl.org/?view&did=740050.

40 Gray, ibid 7–8 states: 'The third-generation gang poses a challenge to the legitimate state monopoly on the exercise of control and use of violence within a given political territory. This challenge elevates the leader of the gang to warlord or drug baron status. That

entire municipalities in countries such as El Salvador.[41] The US Agency for International Development (USAID) reports that these groups 'exercise… [their] own justice, demanding certain behaviour from… citizens and sanctioning those who do not obey.'[42] Like a government, the MS-13, for example, collects 'taxes' by extorting payments from bus drivers, cab drivers and local business owners, among others.[43] Those who resist paying are targeted for violent retribution.[44]

As Max Manwaring, Military Strategy Professor at the Strategic Studies Institute of the United States Army War College, wrote in his examination of gang violence in Central America:

> In describing the gang phenomenon as a simple mutation of a violent act we label as insurgency, we mischaracterize the activities of nonstate organizations that are attempting to take control of the state. We traditionally think of insurgency as primarily a military activity, and we think of gangs as a simple law-enforcement problem. Yet, insurgents and third-generation gangs are engaged in a highly complex political act—political war.[45]

The growth and increasing sophistication of these third-generation gangs has been fuelled largely by the deportation of large numbers of Central

status clearly takes the gang into intrastate war or nonstate war. Third-generation gangs have broad objectives that surpass petty criminal activities and work to erode the very core of national sovereignty. … [T]hird-generation gangs look to depose or replace the incumbent government, control parts or regions within a nation-state and work to change the values in a society to those of the gang.'

[41] International Human Rights Clinic, above n 38, 28–29; US Agency for International Development Bureau for Latin America; Caribbean Office of Regional Sustainable Development, 'Central America and Mexico Gang Assessment' (US Agency for International Development, April 2006) www.pdf.usaid.gov/pdf_docs/PNADG834.pdf, 51; Immigration and Refugee Board of Canada, 'Responses to Information Requests SLV101080.FE El Salvador: The Gang Called the Mara Salvatrucha (MS-13); Its Activities and Recruitment of Members; Protection Offered to Witnesses and Victims of Violent Acts Perpetrated by Gang Members (April 2006)' (Ottawa, Research Directorate, Immigration and Refugee Board of Canada, 7 April 2006) www.irb-cisr.gc.ca/Eng/ResRec/RirRdi/Pages/index.aspx?doc=450161; interview with Jose Miguel Cruz, specialist on violence in Central America, in San Salvador, El Salvador (2 February 2006) (on file with the author).

[42] US Agency for International Development Bureau for Latin America; Caribbean Office of Regional Sustainable Development, above n 42.

[43] International Human Rights Clinic, above n 38, 28–29; J Beaubien, 'Extortion, Gang Violence Terrorize El Salvador' (National Public Radio, 12 March 2009) www.npr.org/templates/story/story.php?storyId=101426190; C Ribando Seelke, 'Gangs in Central America' (Congressional Research Service Report RL34112, 20 February 2014) www.fas.org/sgp/crs/row/RL34112.pdf, 4; interview with Jose Miguel Cruz above n 42.

[44] 'In 2010, for example, after bus drivers banded together to resist paying "taxes" to MS-13, the gang attacked two crowded buses in the capital, San Salvador, spraying one bus with automatic weapons power and setting another on fire with the passengers inside'; Lerman and Humphreys, above n 37 citing Farah, above n 37, 60; see also International Human Rights Clinic, above n 38, 76–79.

[45] MG Manwaring, *Street Gangs: The New Urban Insurgency* (Carlisle, Strategic Studies Institute, US Army War College, March 2005) www.strategicstudiesinstitute.army.mil/pdffiles/pub597.pdf, vi.

American youth who joined gangs in the US in the mid-1990s.[46] In 1996, changes in US immigration law resulted in mass deportation of these gang youths and others on the basis of expanding categories of criminal conduct.[47] Between 1998 and 2005, more than 200,000 individuals were deported from the US to Central America, and fledging criminal justice systems in receiving countries were unable to cope with these en masse arrivals.[48] The gangs grew exponentially, aided substantially by the weakness of the governments in their primary countries of operation. Although several Central American governments have attempted to control gang violence with a 'firm hand' (or 'mano dura') policy, these attempts have been ineffective at best—if not actively contributing to the violence through corruption and collaboration with the gangs.[49] The gangs have often reacted to 'mano dura' policies with violent retaliation.[50]

The growth of third-generation gangs has been a major factor compelling large numbers of Central American women and children to flee their homelands. In a 2015 UNHCR survey of female detainees at the US border, over 60 per cent of the women from Guatemala, Honduras and El Salvador cited direct attacks and threats by gangs as a primary reason they had fled their countries.[51] Many women said that they, or their close family members, had been beaten, raped, robbed and/or extorted by gang members. Sixty-two per cent of the women had witnessed violent crimes in their neighbourhoods and the same percentage had seen dead bodies.[52] Some women were innocent bystanders caught in the middle of rival gang

[46] Many of these youths originally migrated to the US when their families fled the Central American wars of the 1980s: Washington Office on Latin America (WOLA), 'Central American Gang-Related Asylum: A Resource Guide' (Washington DC, WOLA, May 2008) www.wola.org/sites/default/files/downloadable/Central%20America/past/CA%20Gang-Related%20Asylum.pdf, 2; see UNHCR, 'Guidance Note on Refugee Claims Relating to Victims of Organized Gangs' (Geneva, UNHCR Division of International Protection 31 March 2010) www.unhcr.org/refworld/docid/4bb21fa02.html.

[47] International Human Rights Clinic, above n 38, 30–37; the Illegal Immigration and Reform and Immigration Responsibility Act of 1996 and the Anti-Terrorism and Effective Death Penalty Act of 1996 expanded the removability of legal and undocumented immigrants convicted of various crimes. See generally Illegal Immigration Reform and Immigrant Responsibility Act (IIRIRA), Pub L No 104–208, 110 Stat 3009 (30 September 1996); Antiterrorism and Effective Death Penalty Act of 1996, Pub L No 104–132, § 413(f), 110 Stat 1214 (24 April 1996). Over the years, the definition of a removable crime expanded greatly. See DE Anker, *Law of Asylum in the United States: A Guide to Administrative Practice and Case Law*, 5th edn (Thompson West, 2012) §§ 6:1 et seq.

[48] The World Bank, *World Development Report 2011: Conflict, Security and Development* (Washington DC, The International Bank for Reconstruction and Development/The World Bank, 2011) www.siteresources.worldbank.org/INTWDRS/Resources/WDR_Full_Text.pdf, 78. See also Blake, above n 39, 32

[49] US Agency for International Development Bureau for Latin America; Caribbean Office of Regional Sustainable Development, above n 42.

[50] ibid.

[51] UNHCR, 'Women On The Run: First-Hand Accounts of Refugees Fleeing El Salvador, Guatemala, Honduras, and Mexico' (Washington DC, UNHCR, October 2015) 4.

[52] ibid 19–32.

wars, some had been raped by gang members, and others were small shop owners or neighbourhood residents who had been threatened with death because they refused to give in to extortion attempts by gangs.[53]

A separate UNHCR survey, which questioned unaccompanied Central American children at the US border in 2014, found that 48 per cent of the children had been personally affected by violence at the hands of these armed organisations. The children described death threats against them and their families, sexual assault, beatings and homicide against family members and friends.[54]

B. Gender-based Violence

Gender-based violence, which includes rape, femicide (gender-based murder) and domestic violence,[55] is widespread in Honduras, El Salvador and Guatemala. Brutal femicides have skyrocketed over the last decade in the Northern Triangle region. El Salvador has the highest rate of femicide in the world, with Guatemala and Honduras not far behind.[56] Forced disappearances of women are also all-too-common in these three countries.[57]

In the UNHCR's 2015 study of Central American women detained at the US south-western border, many women cited 'prolonged instances of physical, sexual, and psychological domestic violence, for which authorities provided no meaningful help' as a major reason for their flight.[58] Over two-thirds of the women reported that they had tried to internally relocate within their country but that relocation did not protect them from the abuse.[59]

Service providers at non-governmental organisations (NGOs) that assist victims from these countries report that domestic violence has become more frequent in recent years.[60] Many women are killed by their

[53] ibid; *MSPC v Jeh Johnson*, Complaint for Injunctive and Declaratory Relief, United States District Court for the District of Columbia, 22 August 2014 (on file with author).

[54] UNHCR Regional Office for the United States and the Caribbean, above n 6, 31–48.

[55] Domestic violence is a form of gender-based violence defined for the purposes of this chapter as physical, sexual or psychological violence perpetrated by domestic partners, such as husbands or boyfriends, or relatives such as fathers or legal guardians.

[56] See UN Women, 'Femicide in Latin America' (News, 4 April 2013) www.unwomen.org/en/news/stories/2013/4/femicide-in-latin-america; H Stone, 'Violence Against Women Rises in El Salvador' (Christian Science Monitor, 24 May 2011) www.csmonitor.com/World/Americas/Latin-America-Monitor/2011/0524/Violence-against-women-rises-in-El-Salvador; Freedom House, 'Honduras: Countries at the Crossroads 2010' (Freedom House Report, 2010) www.freedomhouse.org/report/countries-crossroads/2010/honduras.

[57] See UN Women; Stone; Freedom House, all above n 57.

[58] UNHCR, above n 52, 4–5.

[59] ibid.

[60] See Immigration and Refugee Border of Canada, 'Responses to Information Requests HND104660.FE Honduras: Domestic Violence, Including Legislation and Protection Available to Victims (2010–November 2013)' (Ottawa, Research Directorate, Immigration and

husbands and partners, others by gang members; increasing numbers of women are forcibly disappeared.[61] In the Northern Triangle of Central America, many acts of domestic violence and rape against women are likely to go unreported in large part because of a lack of police protection and effective criminal sanctions for gender-related violence, as well as prevailing cultural attitudes that consider these forms of violence as the legitimate exercise of patriarchal authority within the household. The culture of *machismo* that runs deep within family and institutional structures often legitimises treating women as the personal property of their intimate partners or fathers. Neighbours or others who hear or witness the effects of domestic violence will often not intervene, believing that domestic abuse is a private family matter that must be resolved at home.[62] The UNHCR's 2015 survey found that 60 per cent of the women interviewed had attempted to seek protection from police against their abusers to no avail, while 40 per cent did not report their harm because they believed it was futile. Many women reported that their partners were affiliated with gangs which further discouraged police intervention.[63] Ten per cent of the women said that the police or other authorities were the direct source of harm perpetrated against them.[64]

IV. CROSSING THE BORDER: OBSTACLES TO ENTRY FOR CENTRAL AMERICAN REFUGEES

Widespread violence by third-generation gangs as well as epidemic levels of gender-based violence have left thousands of women and children from the Northern Triangle of Central America with little option other than to flee their homelands. Still, the decision to cross the border is a formidable one as these individuals face a new set of dangers in seeking safety in the US.

This section outlines some of the major obstacles to entry that Central American refugees, in particular women and children, face after fleeing their countries seeking safety and protection in the US. In particular, this section focuses on the impact of major US policy developments, including

Refugee Board of Canada, 10 December 2013) www.irb-cisr.gc.ca/Eng/ResRec/RirRdi/Pages/index.aspx?doc=455002&pls=1; Immigration and Refugee Board of Canada, 'Responses to Information Requests SLV105266.E El Salvador: Violence Against Women, Including Non-Domestic Sexual Violence, Legislation, State Protection and Support Services' (Ottawa, Research Directorate, Immigration and Refugee Board of Canada, 15 September 2015) www.justice.gov/eoir/file/798251/download.

[61] UNHCR, above n 52, 4–5.

[62] See R Manjoo, 'Special Rapporteur on Violence Against Women Finalizes Country Mission to Honduras and Calls for Urgent Action to Address the Culture of Impunity for Crimes Against Women and Girls' (Tegucigalpa, UNHCR, 7 July 2014) www.ohchr.org/EN/NewsEvents/Pages/DisplayNews.aspx?NewsID=14833&LangID=E.

[63] UNHCR, above n 52.

[64] ibid.

border militarisation, screening and removal procedures (known as expedited removal), and detention policies, on the ability of Central American refugees to receive international protection in the US. To this extent, there are similarities between the situation at the US south-western border and some practices in other jurisdictions discussed in this volume.[65]

A. Dangers in Crossing

Crossing the US–Mexico border has become significantly more dangerous and expensive over the past two decades. Hundreds of people a year die while attempting to cross. Though the number of reported deaths has varied significantly from year to year, the number has been steadily rising over time, with peaks in 2005 and 2012 (albeit a significant drop in 2014).[66] The numbers include only those migrants whose bodies have been found. Because many entrants attempt to cross in remote, isolated areas with harsh desert temperatures, significant numbers of deaths go unnoticed and therefore unreflected in official statistics.[67]

The price to cross—that is, the money paid to smugglers to facilitate the journey—has risen substantially in the past 20 years. This increase reflects a number of factors, including high demand, as well as the difficulty and danger of the journey. In the past, migrants and refugees from Mexico and Central America would often pay several hundred dollars to a courier in a border town who would guide them across to the US.[68] Now, criminal organisations have merged the smuggling routes for both people and drugs and charge up to seven or eight thousand dollars a person; some migrants even carry drugs on their persons to fund their journey.[69]

[65] See for instance border push backs at the Hungarian border (ch 3) and on the high seas in the area surrounding Australia where the borders and interception practices are highly militarised (ch 5).

[66] US Customs and Border Patrol, 'US Border Patrol Fiscal Year Southwest Border Sector Deaths (FY 1998–FY 2014)' (Stats and Summaries, US Department of Homeland Security, 2015) www.cbp.gov/sites/default/files/documents/BP%20Southwest%20Border%20Sector%20Deaths%20FY1998%20-%20FY2015.pdf.

[67] US Government Accountability Office, 'Illegal Immigration: Border-Crossing Deaths Have Doubled Since 1995; Border Patrol's Efforts to Prevent Deaths Have Not Been Fully Evaluated' (Report to the Honourable Bill Frist, Majority Leader US Senate, GAO-06-770, August 2006).

[68] See B Roberts, G Hanson, D Cornwell and S Borger, 'An Analysis of Migrant Smuggling Costs along the Southwest Border' (Office of Immigration Statistics, US Department of Homeland Security, November 2010) www.dhs.gov/xlibrary/assets/statistics/publications/ois-smuggling-wp.pdf.

[69] eg the crossing of the Rio Grande is controlled by the Gulf Cartel of Mexico—average prices in this monopoly run operation average $7,000 a person with $4,000 due up front: D Cave, 'Long Border, Endless Struggle' (New York Times, 2 March 2013); S Stillman, 'Where are the Children? For Extortionists, Undocumented Migrants Have Become Big Business' (The New Yorker, 27 April 2015) www.newyorker.com/magazine/2015/04/27/where-are-the-children.

The rates of sexual and physical assault during these trips are shockingly high.[70]

B. Border Militarisation

The US' increasingly robust policy of border militarisation has substantially increased the risk associated with border crossings. The US expends an extraordinary amount of money in militarising the border, more than $18 billion on immigration enforcement in financial year (FY) 2012, which is greater than the amount spent by all other federal criminal law enforcement efforts combined.[71] After over two decades of an unprecedented militarisation of the border, by 2012, the US had over 21,000 border patrol agents, almost 700 miles of border fence, drones, sophisticated electronic surveillance systems and networks, and numerous facilities to detain migrants.[72]

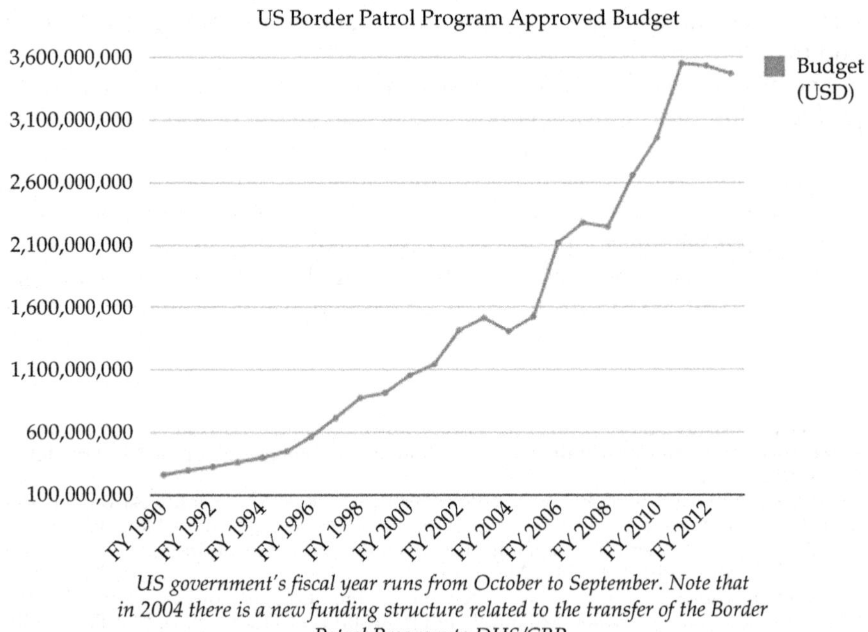

Figure 3: Growth in US Border Patrol Budget, 1990–2012
Source: US Customs and Border Protection 2013

[70] Surveys have estimated that 60–80% of women and girls crossing the US–Mexico border are sexually assaulted—above n 5.

[71] D Meissner, DM Kerwin, M Chishti and C Bergeron, *Immigration Enforcement in the United States: The Rise of a Formidable Machinery* (Washington DC, Migration Policy Institute, January 2013).

[72] ibid.

The US Border Patrol was established in 1924 but for decades, the border remained largely unregulated, with relatively free flows of people travelling between the US and Mexico. However, during the Reagan administration in the 1980s, the Border Patrol began to work much more closely with military agencies on anti-drug enforcement co-ordination within the federal government.[73] The military even provided ground troops to assist civilian police in border duties, including surveillance and patrol.[74] During the 1990s, several different immigration enforcement operations were initiated. The Border Patrol more than doubled its workforce from 1993–2000, from 4,000–9,000 agents. Its budget skyrocketed from $1.5 billion to more than $5 billion over the same time period.[75]

Though significant resources were expended to securitise the border in the 1990s, the effect on migration was inconclusive at best.[76] However, border security efforts continued to increase until 11 September 2001. After the terrorist attack on the World Trade Center and the Pentagon, militarisation on the south-western US border grew substantially. The renamed Customs and Border Patrol (CBP) more than doubled its workforce and budget in the decade after.[77] More and more companies began to develop technologies meant for military operations but marketed for border enforcement use, including drones and attack helicopters.[78]

Beginning in 1993 under the Clinton administration, the US changed its border policy so that regular and familiar crossings like San Diego, California and El Paso, Texas were fortified against entrants.[79] Both the George W Bush and Obama administrations continued this pattern of intensified

[73] While the ostensible purpose of military involvement was to combat drug trafficking, there was also evidence of military involvement in immigration enforcement in certain areas. See TJ Dunn, 'Border Militarization Via Drug and Immigration Enforcement: Human Rights Implications' (2001) 28: 2(84) *Social Justice* 7.

[74] Before 1982, American law had prohibited the military from making arrests or conducting searches and seizures domestically; however, that year, Congress made statutory changes allowing the US military to provide certain types of assistance, including transport of military equipment and training, to the Border Patrol. See ibid.

[75] At this time, government officials focused their rhetoric on the need to reign in the 'chaos' and 'disorder,' which they attributed to the border. President Clinton's 'Border Czar' Alan Bersin stated that the new initiatives were an attempt to 'manage [the border] away from the epic of lawlessness that has characterized that border for the 150 years that the American Southwest has been a part of the United States.' J Ackleson, Constructing Security on the US–Mexico Border (2005) 24(2) *Political Geography* 165, 173.

[76] US General Accounting Office, 'Illegal Immigration: Southwest Border Strategy Results Inconclusive; More Evaluation Needed' (Report to the Committee on the Judiciary and the US Senate, GAO/GGD-98-21, December 1997); see Ackleson, above n 77, 174.

[77] CC Hadal, 'Border Security: The Role of the US Border Patrol' (Congressional Research Service Report RL32562, 11 August 2010) www.fas.org/sgp/crs/homesec/RL32562.pdf.

[78] See AH Michel, 'Customs and Border Protection Drones' (Center for the Study of the Drone at Bard College, 7 January 2015) www.dronecenter.bard.edu/customs-and-border-protection-drones/.

[79] See Cave, above n 70.

enforcement, including the construction of a border wall.[80] Unsurprisingly, the increased difficulty of crossing forced refugees and others in desperate circumstances to cross over unfamiliar and unregulated territory. Crossing points shifted from more travelled areas of California and Texas to dangerous areas near the Arizona desert.[81] The American Civil Liberties Union estimated that the risk of dying while crossing in Arizona was 17 times greater in 2009 than only a decade earlier. From 2009–12, the mortality rate almost doubled, with children constituting roughly 10 per cent of fatalities each year (an estimated 18–25 children annually).[82]

The following table shows that the number of deaths of migrants at the south-western border has remained steady despite a dramatic drop in the number of apprehensions. The increasing ratio of border deaths to apprehensions indicates that the risk to migrants in crossing has substantially increased over the past decade.

Between the fiscal years of 2007 and 2011, apprehensions of migrants crossing illegally at the southwest border plummeted nearly 62 per cent. Deaths decreased less than 8 per cent during the five-year period and have remained steady at an average of about 386 per year.

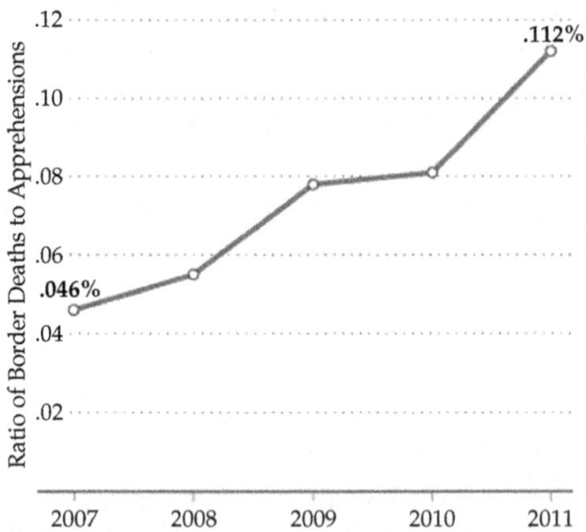

Deaths and Apprehensions on The Southwest Border

	Deaths	Apprehensions
2007	**398**	**858,638**
2008	**385**	**705,005**
2009	**420**	**540,865**
2010	**363**	**447,731**
2011	**368**	**327,577**

Source: US Customs and Border Protection

Figure 4: Ratio of Border Deaths to Apprehensions

[80] In 2006, Congress appropriated $1.5 billion for fencing along the southwest border and installation of roads, physical barriers and lighting that would allow border patrol agents to gain 'operational control'. By 2010, the section of the fence from San Diego, California to Yuma, Arizona was finished and portions of the fence in Texas had been completed. Fences were often constructed in urban areas in order to force people to cross in more rural areas, where it would be harder to escape detection: C Haddal, Y Kim and MJ Garcia, 'Border Security: Barriers Along the US International Border' (Congressional Research Service Report RL33659, 16 March 2009) www.fas.org/sgp/crs/homesec/RL33659.pdf, 9.

[81] See ibid; D Cave, 'Better Lives for Mexicans Cut Allure of Going North' (New York Times, 6 July 2011) www.nytimes.com/interactive/2011/07/06/world/americas/immigration.html.

[82] M Jimenez, 'Humanitarian Crisis: Migrant Deaths at the US–Mexico Border' (American Civil Liberties Union of San Diego and Imperial Counties; Mexico's National Commission of

Recent co-operation between the US and Mexico to curb Central American migration has had a large impact on refugee populations. In the summer of 2014, under apparent pressure from the US, Mexico launched its Plan Frontera Sur (Southern Border Plan), which aimed to reduce the number of immigrants travelling from Central America across Mexico's southern border.[83] Under this programme, Mexico has substantially increased its apprehensions and deportations of Central Americans. In the first eight months of 2015, Mexico apprehended 173,000 Central Americans, compared to 110,000 apprehended in the US; in 2014, Mexico also deported six times more unaccompanied children than the US that same year.[84] The total number of deportations of Central Americans from Mexico in 2015 is expected to be 70 per cent higher than the number from the previous year.[85]

The data suggest that Mexico's enforcement efforts are at least partially responsible for the drop in apprehensions of Central Americans, including unaccompanied children, at the US border in 2015; however, figures from 2016 are showing an increase in the number of unaccompanied children apprehended at the US border when compared to the previous year.[86] Reports from the border also indicate that this increased enforcement has compelled at least some individuals to attempt to cross Mexico through more physically dangerous routes in order to reach the US.[87]

C. Expedited Removal/Credible Fear Screenings

In addition to border militarisation, other immigration policies have eroded the ability of refugees to access international protection. Of particular salience is the 1996 'expedited removal' statute. This statute authorises truncated immigration procedures for people apprehended within 100 miles

Human Rights, 1 October 2009); F Clifford, 'The Border Effect' (The American Prospect, 18 September 2012) www.prospect.org/article/border-effect.

[83] See S Nazario, 'The Refugees at Our Door' (New York Times, 15 October 2015) www.nytimes.com/2015/10/11/opinion/sunday/the-refugees-at-our-door.html?_r=0.

[84] D Bonello, 'Mexico's Deportations of Central American Migrants are Rising' (Los Angeles Times, 4 September 2015) www.latimes.com/world/mexico-americas/la-fg-mexico-migrants-20150905-story.html.

[85] ibid.

[86] See United States Border Patrol Southwest Family Unit Subject and Unaccompanied Alien Children Apprehensions Fiscal Year 2016, https://www.cbp.gov/newsroom/stats/southwest-border-unaccompanied-children/fy-2016; W Eulich, 'As Mexico Tightens Southern Border, Migrants Confront New Threats' (Christian Science Monitor, 16 July 2015) www.csmonitor.com/World/Americas/2015/0716/As-Mexico-tightens-southern-border-migrants-confront-new-threats.

[87] These more dangerous routes include routes farther from well-travelled roads or shelters, located in more rural areas, and areas largely controlled by drug cartels or large gangs. See ibid.

of the US border when apprehended at the border or within 14 days of entry into the US.[88] Many more people are consequently removed from the US than by the prior, more fulsome procedural regime of administrative hearing with appellate rights. By FY 2013, more than 70 per cent of deportees, or about 101,000 people, were removed under these newer summary removal procedures.[89] The use of summary or accelerated procedures and their impact upon the ability of asylum seekers to obtain procedural due process is a theme also addressed in other chapters in this volume.[90]

Under this regime, individuals seeking refugee protection who are apprehended at the border or within 100 miles of it after entry must undergo a screening process, referred to as a 'credible fear' interview, to determine whether they will be allowed to remain in the country to apply for asylum or related relief.[91] If an asylum officer determines that an applicant has a credible fear of being persecuted upon return to his or her home country, he or she will be placed in removal proceedings and have the opportunity to present a full asylum claim before an administrative judge. If, however, the individual receives an adverse credible fear determination, the individual may appeal that ruling to an administrative judge as a final step but if denied there, he or she will have no further recourse.

The standard for passing an initial credible fear interview is, in principle, considerably lower than that needed to prevail on the final asylum claim. To be granted asylum, an applicant need only establish a well-founded fear of persecution, defined under US law as at least a 10 per cent chance of persecution on account of one of five enumerated grounds.[92] This standard of proof is designed especially for refugees with the understanding that they may be victims of trauma and often lack direct proof of their persecution. Because the credible fear interview is a preliminary screening, the burden of proof is lower at this stage. An applicant need only show a *significant possibility* of a well-founded fear: in other words, a significant possibility of establishing a 10 per cent chance of persecution on account of an enumerated ground.[93]

The UNHCR, human rights groups and scholars, among others, have criticised the credible fear screening process for serious procedural deficiencies.[94] NGOs, in particular, Human Rights Watch and the American

[88] INA §235(b)(1)(A)(ii), 8 USCA § 1225(b)(1)(A)(ii); 8 CFR §§ 208.30, 1208.30.

[89] American Immigration Council, 'Removal Without Recourse: The Growth of Summary Deportations from the United States' (Washington DC, Immigration Policy Centre, 28 April 2014) www.immigrationpolicy.org/sites/default/files/docs/expedited_removal_fact_sheet_final.pdf.

[90] See Iván, ch 3 (Hungary) and Kirk, ch 11 (Australia and the UK).

[91] INA §235(b)(1)(A)(ii), 8 USCA § 1225(b)(1)(A)(ii); 8 CFR §§ 208.30, 1208.30.

[92] *INS v Cardoza-Fonseca*, 480 US 421 (1987).

[93] 8 USC § 1225 (b)(1)(B)(v); 8 USC § 1158.

[94] See S Campos and J Friedland, 'Mexican and Central American Asylum and Credible Fear Claims: Background and Context' (American Immigration Council Special Report, May 2014)

Immigration Council, have pointed to such serious problems as insufficient access to legal representation, incorrect or misleading instructions provided to applicants by immigration officials, lack of privacy and confidentiality during the interview process, absence of adequate interpreters, and long delays for interviews, among other issues.[95]

Despite these challenges, many recently arrived Central Americans have been able to access the credible fear process and gain entrance to the US. Indeed, people from Guatemala, Honduras and El Salvador currently constitute the three largest groups receiving credible fear interviews, with positive determinations made in 73.6 per cent, 91.2 per cent and 93.7 per cent of the cases, respectively, from these three countries in the first quarter of 2015.[96]

After passing their credible fear interviews, asylum seekers must appear before an administrative immigration court to present their asylum claims. Though Central Americans have high positive credible fear screening results, they tend to be much less successful in gaining asylum. Immigration courts granted asylum to only 3 per cent of Salvadorans and 4 per cent of Hondurans in FY 2014.[97]

A 2015 nationwide survey found low asylum grant rates in immigration court for Central American and Mexican women who arrived with their children. Legal representation makes a significant difference; 26 per cent of the women represented by attorneys received some form of immigration relief (such as asylum or prosecutorial discretion). In contrast, the success rate for unrepresented women, who constituted three-quarters of the overall study sample, was only 1.5 per cent.[98]

Some recent trends in the administrative jurisprudence, however, demonstrate growing sophistication and new recognition of different rights violations, such as violence against women, which are especially

www.immigrationpolicy.org/sites/default/files/docs/asylum_and_credible_fear_claims_final.pdf.

[95] C Long and A Parker, '"You Don't Have Rights Here": US Border Screening and Returns of Central Americans to Risk of Serious Harm' (Human Rights Watch, 16 October 2014) www.hrw.org/report/2014/10/16/you-dont-have-rights-here/us-border-screening-and-returns-central-americans-risk; see Campos and Friedland, above n 97.

[96] The statistics are based on the number of credible fear interviews conducted at the four family detention facilities in the US: Karnes, Dilley, Berks and Artesia (no longer operating): US Citizenship and Immigration Services, 'USCIS Asylum Division: Family Facilities Credible Fear' (US Citizenship and Immigration Services, 2015) www.uscis.gov/sites/default/files/USCIS/Outreach/PED-CF-RF-familiy-facilities-FY2015Q2.pdf.

[97] US Department of Justice 'Asylum Statistics: FY 2010–2014' (Executive Office of Immigration Review, Immigration Courts, March 2015) www.justice.gov/sites/default/files/eoir/pages/attachments/2015/03/16/fy2010-fy2014-asylum-statistics-by-nationality.pdf.

[98] Transactional Records Access Clearinghouse (TRAC), 'Representation is Key in Immigration Proceedings Involving Women with Children' (TRAC Series on Juveniles and Families in Immigration Court: III Representation for Women with Children, Syracuse University, 18 February 2015) www.trac.syr.edu/immigration/reports/377/.

important for women and children fleeing Central America. Most prominently, in 2014, the highest US administrative decision-making authority, the Board of Immigration Appeals, recognised domestic violence as a basis for asylum.[99] This hard-won victory by legal advocates followed years of increasing recognition of domestic violence claims by lower immigration courts and the US Asylum Office.[100] Several federal courts have also recognised the validity of asylum claims for individuals fleeing the violence of gangs and gang repression in Central America[101] including those forced to join but who are no longer members.[102] These suggest a change of direction, while inadequately framed protection claims[103] and perhaps most importantly, lack of legal representation continue to constitute substantial barriers for Central American asylum seekers and development of the law generally.

D. Detention

In addition to legal and procedural obstacles to accessing protection, refugees at the US south-western border often face long periods of detention that may stretch for months. Following apprehension, immigrants often experience lengthy stays at border stations in harsh conditions such as freezing temperatures, overcrowding, inadequate food, unsanitary spaces lacking privacy,[104] and lack of access to legal counsel.[105] Abusive conditions in 'hieleras' and 'perreras' are well-known to advocacy groups.[106]

[99] Matter of ARCG 26 I & N Dec 388 (BIA 2014) (finding that Guatemalan woman fleeing domestic abuse could potentially qualify for asylum as a member of a particular social group of 'married women in Guatemala who are unable to leave their relationship').

[100] See DE Anker, 'Legal Change from the Bottom Up: The Development of Gender Asylum Jurisprudence in the United States' in E Arbel, C Dauvergne and J Millbank (eds), *Gender in Refugee Law: From the Margins to the Centre* (Oxford and New York, Routledge, 2014).

[101] See *Crespin-Valladares v Holder*, 632 F.3d 117, 124–26 (4th Cir 2011) (finding a potential basis for asylum for Salvadoran citizens who acted as prosecutorial witnesses against gangs); *Garcia v Attorney General of US*, 665 F.3d 496, 504 (3d Cir 2011), as amended 13 January 2012.

[102] See *Benitez Ramos v Holder*, 589 F.3d 426, 429 (7th Cir 2009).

[103] See Anker and Lawrence, above n 5 (whereas most Central American gang jurisprudence engaged the particular social group ground, the political opinion ground could be viable in Central American gang cases).

[104] M Hennessy-Fiske and C Carcamo, 'Overcrowded, Unsanitary Conditions Seen at Immigrant Detention Centers' (Los Angeles Times, 18 June 2014) www.latimes.com/nation/nationnow/la-na-nn-texas-immigrant-children-20140618-story.html#page=1.

[105] Lutheran Immigration and Refugee Service; Women's Refugee Commission, 'Locking Up Family Values—Again' (Family Detention Report, October 2014) www.irs.org/wp-content/uploads/2014/11/LIRSWRC_LockingUpFamilyValuesAgain_Report_141114.pdf, 12.

[106] E Pilkington, '"It Was Cold, Very Cold": Migrant Children Endure Border Patrol "Ice Boxes"' (The Guardian, 26 January 2015) www.theguardian.com/us-news/2015/jan/26/migrant-children-border-patrol-ice-boxes.

Reports of physical or sexual abuse by immigration agents have also been documented.[107]

Even immigrants who have passed a credible fear interview have often been subject to a no-release policy to deter future asylum seekers from seeking refuge in the US. Some of these individuals are being held in detention for over six months.[108]

In 2015, the Government developed an 'alternatives to sentencing' programme. This involves releasing some detainees on the conditions that they wear a bulky GPS monitoring device on their ankles and report to immigration authorities on a regular basis, similar to programmes established for persons subject to probation within the US criminal justice system. However, this programme has also been criticised by advocates on the grounds that it is unnecessary and ineffective, stigmatises the wearer, makes employment difficult, and can lead to discomfort and even health risks.[109]

V. CONCLUSION

This chapter addresses several of the challenges that Central American asylum seekers face when attempting to access international protection. In particular, it focuses on the plight of women and children, whose proportion of the overall flow has increased dramatically over the past several years. Many are fleeing persecution, including physical abuse, rape, death threats and other forms of harm, at the hands of large-scale third-generation gangs as well as domestic abusers. Before they can obtain relief, however, they must overcome several major challenges, among which are exploitative traffickers, dangerous physical terrain, an increasingly militarised south-western border, a truncated expedited removal process and often-sceptical adjudicators applying or misapplying relevant jurisprudence. On a positive note, refugee law has progressed in many respects

[107] D Cave, 'Complaints of Abuse by Border Guards Often Ignored Records Show' (New York Times, 5 May 2014) www.nytimes.com/2014/05/06/us/complaints-of-abuse-by-border-agents-often-ignored-records-show.html.

[108] A Gonzales, S Speed and G Rosas, 'In the Arena: Why We Need to End Family Detention—Again' (*Politico*, 30 March 2015) www.politico.com/magazine/story/2015/03/family-detention-centers-border-crisis-116521#ixzz3vx2hAlAU.

[109] This device is often referred to as a 'grillete' (shackles). Responsibility for monitoring former detainees through this programme has been outsourced by US immigration officials to a private contractor, BI Inc, a subsidiary of the US's second-largest prison company, which also operates an immigration detention facility. This has led many advocates to express concern about a possible conflict of interest. See M Hennessy-Fiske, 'Immigrants Object to Growing Use of Ankle Monitors after Detention' (Los Angeles Times, 2 August 2015) www.latimes.com/nation/immigration/la-na-immigrant-ankle-monitors-20150802-story.html.

including recognition of the particularised violence affecting women and children, especially in countries where non-governmental actors such as gang members and domestic abusers operate with impunity from punishment by the state. Continued advocacy along these lines will further strengthen the ability of Central American refugees to receive the protection to which they are entitled under US domestic law and international treaty obligations.

Part III

Access to Justice and a Refugee Status Determination Procedure

7

Accessing Fair and Efficient Asylum Procedures in the EU

Legal Safeguards and Loopholes in the Common European Asylum System

KRIS POLLET

I. INTRODUCTION

IN THE TIME that the European Union (EU) has developed a Common European Asylum System (CEAS),[1] accessing and finding international protection within the EU has become an obstacle course.[2] Those fleeing human rights abuses, widespread violence or war are in many cases forced to risk their lives if they want to get access to the territory of EU Member States in order to apply for international protection. As discussed and analysed elsewhere in this volume, as there are few or no legal channels available for persons in need of international protection to cross the external borders of the EU safely and legally, many refugees have to resort to irregular ways to enter, often making use of smugglers. The death toll resulting from the absence of legal channels is unacceptably

[1] See the Consolidated Version of the Treaty on the Functioning of the European Union (TFEU) [2008] OJ C115/4 art 78(2) which established an obligation for the European Parliament and the Council to adopt measures for a 'common European asylum system'. This provides the framework for the EU's common policy on asylum, subsidiary protection and temporary protection which must be in accordance with the 1951 United Nations Convention Relating to the Status of Refugees 189 United Nations Treaty Series 150 (Refugee Convention) and other relevant treaties.

[2] The term 'international protection' is employed here reflecting its usage in EU law, eg Council Directive 2011/95/EU of 13 December 2011 on standards for the qualification of third-country nationals or stateless persons as beneficiaries of international protection, for a uniform status for refugees or for persons eligible for subsidiary protection, and for the content of the protection granted (recast) [2011] OJ L337/9. In the EU context, 'international protection' refers to both refugee status and subsidiary protection status.

high. In 2014, 3,279 migrants lost their lives at sea in the Mediterranean.[3] In 2015, the International Organisation for Migration (IOM) reported that 3,770 migrants perished in the Mediterranean Sea in their attempt to reach Italy or Greece.[4] Furthermore, in the first two months of 2016 alone, 425 persons lost their lives crossing the Mediterranean.[5]

Those who make it alive to the EU's borders are confronted with a range of obstacles in accessing the territory or the asylum procedure. Non-governmental organisations (NGOs) have documented, for instance, persistent allegations of push backs at the Greek–Turkish and Bulgarian–Turkish borders,[6] while non entrée policies have been pursued by a number of governments along the so-called 'Western Balkans route' as of March 2016.[7] Moreover, increased levels of co-operation of border authorities of EU Member States with law enforcements authorities and border guards of third countries at land borders may imply a further shift towards preventing the arrival of migrants, including those with protection claims, at the EU's external borders. The construction of a fence along the Hungarian–Serbian border combined with legal amendments barring access to protection inter alia by considering Serbia as a safe third country in response to the sharp increase of refugees arriving in the summer of 2015 is one of the most vivid illustrations of this trend,[8] soon followed by the reintroduction of controls at the internal Schengen borders by many Member States, and condoned by the European Commission under the pretext of saving Schengen. Reaching the EU territory is for many in search of international protection not the end of their ordeal. Today, many asylum seekers

[3] See AIDA, 'Common Asylum System at a Turning Point: Refugees Caught in Europe's Solidarity Crisis' (Annual Report, ECRE 2014–15) 26–27.

[4] IOM, 'Mediterranean Sea: Data of Missing Migrants' (IOM Missing Migrants Project, 2014–16) www.missingmigrants.iom.int/mediterranean.

[5] ibid.

[6] See L Gall, 'Dispatches: Stopping "Pushbacks" at Bulgaria's Border' (Human Rights Watch, 31 March 2015) www.hrw.org/news/2015/03/31/dispatches-stopping-pushbacks-bulgarias-border; Human Rights Watch, 'Bulgaria: New Evidence Syrians Forced Back to Turkey' (18 September 2014) www.hrw.org/news/2014/09/18/bulgaria-new-evidence-syrians-forced-back-turkey; Pro Asyl, 'Pushed Back: Systematic Human Rights Violations Against Refugees in the Aegean Sea and at the Greek–Turkish Land Border' (7 November 2013).

[7] At a meeting of countries along the so-called 'Western Balkan route', Austria, Bulgaria, Croatia, Albania, Bosnia-Herzegovina, Kosovo, Montenegro and Serbia, on 24 February 2016, agreed on a policy whereby only persons from Syria, Iraq and Afghanistan were allowed to enter their territory for the purpose of requesting international protection or onward travel to another (EU) state of destination and those who are not 'in proven need of protection' would be denied entry at the Greek border. See G Gotev, 'Visegrad Countries Call for "Alternative Plan" to Counter Migration Crisis' (Euractive, 16 February 2016) www.euractiv.com/section/central-europe/news/visegrad-countries-call-for-alternative-plan-to-counter-migration-crisis/.

[8] See Hungarian Helsinki Committee, 'Building a Legal Fence: Changes to Hungarian Asylum Law Jeopardise Access to Protection in Hungary' (Information Note, 7 August 2015) discussed in Iván, ch 3.

continue to face additional impediments to a fair examination of their application for international protection. They may face difficulties in some EU Member States to have their asylum application registered and receive proper documentation, be subjected to prolonged periods of detention or be processed in under-resourced and expedited procedures without effective access to quality legal assistance, undermining the right to asylum as laid down in Article 18 of the EU Charter of Fundamental Rights.[9] For many, the application of the Dublin Regulation is another hurdle to swift access to a substantive examination of their need for international protection as it constitutes an additional procedural layer that may also violate their fundamental rights.[10] Moreover, in order to avoid the application of the Dublin Regulation and be stuck in substandard conditions in countries such as Greece and Hungary, refugees and asylum seekers have to resort to smugglers in order to reach the Member State of their preferred destination, which often results in exploitation, serious human rights abuses and death. The 71 refugees who were found dead in an abandoned truck on a motorway in Austria in August 2015 is one of the most gruesome examples of this sad reality.[11]

The Commission's 'asylum package'[12] negotiated and adopted between December 2008 and June 2013 has established a new legal framework for EU Member States' asylum policies consisting of the recast Qualification Directive,[13] the recast Reception Conditions Directive,[14] the recast Asylum

[9] [2000] OJ C364/01, art 18: 'The right to asylum shall be guaranteed with due respect for the rules of the Geneva Convention of 28 July 1951 and the Protocol of 31 January 1967 relating to the status of refugees and in accordance with the Treaty establishing the European Community.' For further discussion of the Charter, see M-T Gil-Bazo, 'The Charter of Fundamental Rights of the European Union and the Right to be Granted Asylum in the Union's Law (2008) 27 *Refugee Survey Quarterly* 3, 33–52; S Peers, T Hervey, J Kenner and A Ward (eds), *The EU Charter of Fundamental Rights—A Commentary* (Oxford, Hart Publishing, 2014) 519–41.

[10] Council Regulation (EU) 604/2013 of 26 June 2013 establishing the criteria and mechanisms for determining the Member State responsible for examining an application for international protection lodged in one of the Member States by third-country national or a stateless person (recast) [2013] OJ L180/13 (hereafter referred to as the Dublin Regulation (recast)).

[11] See K Strohecker, 'Children Among 71 migrants Found Dead in Truck in Austria' (Reuters, 28 August 2015) www.uk.reuters.com/article/2015/08/28/uk-europe-migrants-austria-idUKKCN0QX0H220150828.

[12] The asylum package consisted of the Commission proposals recasting the Reception Conditions Directive, Asylum Procedures Directive, Qualification Directive, Dublin Regulation and EURODAC Regulation.

[13] See Council Directive 2011/95/EU of the European Parliament and of the Council on standards for the qualification of third-country nationals or stateless persons as beneficiaries of international protection, for a uniform status for refugees or for persons eligible for subsidiary protection, and for the content of the protection granted (recast) [2011] OJ L337/13 (hereafter referred to as the Qualification Directive (recast)).

[14] Council Directive 2013/33/EU of 26 June 2013 laying down standards for the reception of applicants for international protection (recast) [2013] OJ L180/96 (hereafter referred to as the Reception Conditions Directive (recast)).

Procedures Directive,[15] the recast Dublin Regulation and the recast Eurodac Regulation.[16] This has resulted, at least on paper, in strengthened procedural guarantees for asylum seekers and additional guarantees with regard to the quality of the asylum procedure and individual decision-making compared to the first generation of asylum instruments adopted between 2000 and 2005. Other features of the recast asylum *acquis*[17] are less promising from a protection perspective, such as the provisions on the detention of asylum seekers which provide for broadly defined grounds for detention of asylum seekers, possibly leading to an increased use of detention. This chapter focuses in particular on two aspects related to the initial stage of the asylum procedure: (1) the moment of registration of the asylum application and the safeguards under EU law to ensure actual access to the procedure at the border and (2) the personal interview and the report of that interview. These issues will be discussed in light of the procedural guarantees laid down in EU asylum law and the practices observed in various EU Member States by NGOs assisting asylum seekers in the different stages of the asylum procedure in those countries on a daily basis. Before doing so, some reflections are made with regard to the protection under EU law and the European Convention on Human Rights (ECHR) of individuals arriving at the EU external borders before they come within the scope of the EU asylum *acquis*.

II. ACCESS TO PROTECTION AT THE EU EXTERNAL BORDERS: SAFEGUARDS AND GAPS IN THE EU LEGAL FRAMEWORK

Obstacles to accessing protection in the EU arise from a range of border control measures making it more difficult for persons in need of international protection to enter the territory of the EU and from push backs at the EU's external borders denying them actual access to the territory in violation of the principle of *non-refoulement*, enshrined in international

[15] Council Directive 2013/32/EU of 26 June 2013 on common procedures for granting and withdrawing international protection (recast) [2013] OJ L180/60 (hereafter referred to as the Asylum Procedures Directive (recast)).

[16] Council Regulation 603/2013 of 26 June 2013 on the establishment of 'Eurodac' for the comparison of fingerprints for the effective application of Regulation (EU) No 604/2013 establishing the criteria and mechanisms for determining the Member State responsible for examining an application for international protection lodged in one of the Member States by a third-country national or a stateless person and on requests for the comparison with Eurodac data by Member States' law enforcement authorities and Europol for law enforcement purposes, and amending Regulation (EU) No 1077/2011 establishing a European Agency for the operational management of large-scale IT systems in the area of freedom, security and justice (recast) [2013] OJ L108/1.

[17] Since 1999 the EU has adopted laws to deal with asylum issues with the aim of establishing a CEAS to harmonise rules, procedures and conditions. These combined laws are known as the asylum *acquis*.

human rights law as well as in EU law and Article 19 of the Charter of Fundamental Rights of the European Union (the Charter of Fundamental Rights).[18] As illustrated below, asylum seekers also increasingly face problems in simply making an asylum application or having their asylum application registered with the competent authorities once they have entered the territory.

In order to enjoy the rights laid down in the EU asylum *acquis* effectively, an individual must be considered as an applicant for international protection under EU law.[19] Before that time, EU asylum law is not applicable and the individual is, from an EU law perspective, still considered a person who is irregularly on the territory. This does not mean that such a person does not derive any protection under EU legislation before making an application for international protection. The Schengen Borders Code explicitly requires EU Member States to act in full compliance with relevant Union law, including the Charter of Fundamental Rights; relevant international law, such as the 1951 United Nations Convention Relating to the Status of Refugees (Refugee Convention);[20] and obligations related to access to international protection, in particular the principle of *non-refoulement*; and fundamental rights.[21] Also, the EU Return Directive requires Member States to respect the principle of *non-refoulement* when implementing the Directive.[22]

The recent EU Regulation on maritime border surveillance in the framework of Frontex-led joint operations at sea has further strengthened the obligations of Member States under EU law to respect the principle of *non-refoulement* before an explicit application for international protection is made.[23] Article 4 of the Maritime Border Surveillance Regulation prohibits Member States from handing over any third country national to

[18] Article 19: 'Protection in the event of removal, expulsion or extradition: (1) Collective expulsions are prohibited. (2) No one may be removed, expelled or extradited to a State where there is a serious risk that he or she would be subjected to the death penalty, torture or other inhuman or degrading treatment or punishment.'

[19] See below for a more detailed discussion on the distinction between making and lodging an application for international protection and the legal implications and time limits for registration of such applications.

[20] Refugee Convention, above n 1.

[21] See art 3(a), Council Regulation 562/2006 of 15 March 2006 establishing a Community Code on the rules governing the movement of persons across borders (Schengen Borders Code) [2006] OJ L105/1 (consolidated version 26/11/2013).

[22] See art 5, Council Directive 2008/115/EC of 16 December 2008 on common standards and procedures in Member States for returning illegally staying third country nationals [2008] OJ L 348/98 (hereafter referred to as the Return Directive).

[23] Council Regulation 656/2014 of 15 May 2014 establishing rules for the surveillance of the external sea borders in the context of operational cooperation coordinated by the European Agency for the Management of Operational Cooperation at the External Borders of the Member States of the European Union [2014] OJ L189/93 (hereafter referred to as the Maritime External Border Surveillance Regulation).

the authorities of a country where there are reasons to believe that he or she may be subjected to persecution or ill-treatment or from where he or she might be handed over to another country where he or she might be subjected to such treatment.[24] This implies an assessment, not only of the general situation in a third country but also of the personal circumstances of the intercepted or rescued third country national before he or she is disembarked in, forced to enter or otherwise handed over to the authorities of a third country. Last but not least, the persons concerned must be informed of the place of disembarkation in a way they understand or may presumably be supposed to understand and they must be given an opportunity 'to express any reasons for believing that disembarkation in the proposed place would be in violation of the principle of *non-refoulement*'.[25] The latter is an important safeguard that effectively imposes an obligation on the Member State authorities hosting or participating in a joint operation at sea co-ordinated by Frontex to establish a procedure allowing the intercepted or rescued third country nationals to submit the reasons why they believe disembarkation in the intended destination would result in *refoulement*. It obviously also implies an obligation on those Member State authorities proactively to inform the third country nationals concerned of the existence of such a possibility.[26] Where interception or search and rescue takes place in the territorial waters of an EU Member State and as soon as the individuals concerned are present and make an application for international protection in the territorial waters of an EU Member State, the persons concerned must be disembarked on land and have their application examined in accordance with the recast Asylum Procedures Directive.[27] This is the logical consequence of the fact that the recast Asylum Procedures Directive now explicitly includes applications for international protection made at the border, in the territorial waters or in the transit zones of the Member States, in its territorial scope.[28] This means that all standards laid down in the recast Asylum Procedures Directive, including those with regard to the registration and/or lodging of the asylum application, information at border crossing points and in detention facilities and the organisation and conduct of the personal interview, must be complied with.

Where third country nationals are rescued or intercepted outside of the territorial waters of the EU Member States, Article 4 of the Maritime External Border Surveillance Regulation must be read and interpreted in

[24] ibid art 4.

[25] See Maritime External Border Surveillance Regulation, art 4(3).

[26] A very different approach is taken in Australia, as discussed in O'Sullivan, ch 5.

[27] 'Where those persons are present in the territorial waters of a Member State, they should be disembarked on land and have their applications examined in accordance with this Directive'. See Asylum Procedures Directive (recast), recital 26.

[28] Asylum Procedures Directive (recast), art 3(1).

light of the judgment of the European Court of Human Rights (ECtHR) in the case of *Hirsi Jamaa and Others v Italy*[29] and the EU Charter of Fundamental Rights, in particular Article 1 (human dignity), Article 18 (right to asylum) and Article 19 (protection in the event of removal, expulsion or extradition). Whilst an in-depth discussion of the *Hirsi* judgment goes beyond the scope of this contribution (but see for further discussion, Iván, Chapter 3) it is important to highlight a key finding of the Court which is relevant in relation to defining the principle of *non-refoulement* and its implications for Member States as regards the level of procedural safeguards that must be offered even before an application for international protection is made. First, in finding a violation of Article 3 in conjunction with Article 13 of the ECHR, the Court pointed in particular to the fact that 'the applicants had no access to a procedure to identify them and to assess their personal circumstances before they were returned to Libya' and that there were 'neither interpreters nor legal advisers among the personnel on board [the Italian military ships]'.[30] Second, the failure to provide the persons intercepted with information about their destination, or with any access to relevant procedures to challenge their forcible return to Libya was highlighted by the Court in the following terms: the Court 'reiterates here the importance of guaranteeing anyone subject to a removal measure, the consequences of which are potentially irreversible, the right to obtain sufficient information to enable them to gain effective access to the relevant procedures and to substantiate their complaints'.[31]

Third, the Court explicitly stated that the obligations of states under Article 3 of the ECHR apply regardless of whether the person intercepted has explicitly applied for asylum. According to the Court, it was for the Italian authorities, faced with a situation in which human rights were being systematically violated, to 'find out about the treatment to which the applicants would be exposed after their return' and to ascertain 'how the Libyan authorities fulfilled their international obligations in relation to the protection of refugees'.[32]

This means that a person does not necessarily need to say the magic word 'asylum' to be protected from *refoulement* under the ECHR and be entitled to the procedural safeguards that Articles 3 and 13 of the ECHR entail, in particular access to information, legal assistance and an appeal with automatic suspensive effect.[33] From this perspective, Articles 3 and

[29] *Hirsi Jamaa and Others v Italy* App no 27765/09 (ECtHR, 23 February 2012).

[30] ibid para 202. The lack of interpreters and legal advisers on board Australian navy ships is also of concern, as discussed in O'Sullivan, ch 5.

[31] *Hirsi Jamaa and Others v Italy*, above n 29, para 204.

[32] ibid paras 133 and 157. See also Iván, ch 3.

[33] Suspensive effect means suspending removal of an applicant from the country in which he or she is situated and to which he or she seeks admission.

13 of the ECHR, the right to asylum laid down in Article 18 of the EU Charter of Fundamental Rights,[34] the above-mentioned Article 13 of the Schengen Borders Code and Article 4 of the Maritime External Border Surveillance Regulation bridge the legal gap that results from the fact that those seeking international protection in EU territory only come within the protection of EU asylum law after having made an application for international protection. As soon as a person comes within the jurisdiction and effective control of an EU Member State, authorities are bound by their obligation to 'proactively' ensure compliance with the principle of *non-refoulement*, which implies the observance of the range of procedural guarantees laid down in the jurisprudence of the ECtHR relating to Article 13 of the ECHR on the right to an effective remedy.[35] This is also reflected in the EU Charter of Fundamental Rights in Article 19, on the principle of *non-refoulement*, and Article 47, which guarantees everyone whose rights and freedoms under EU law are violated the right to an effective remedy before a tribunal. These provisions place an important responsibility on those who are likely to come first into contact with persons seeking international protection, such as police authorities or border guards. Where previously, border guards may have referred persons immediately to return procedures before any assessment of their protection needs on the basis that they had not explicitly stated that they were seeking asylum or international protection but had nevertheless expressed a fear of going back to their country of origin, this is now clearly unlawful under the ECHR and EU legislation. This is not to say that such practices have been eradicated at the EU's external borders. In fact the gap between legal safeguards in the law and the actual practice at the borders could not be greater. Consistent and credible reports by NGOs on Ceuta and Melilla, or the Bulgaria–Turkey or Greece–Turkey borders, show that push backs of migrants, asylum seekers and refugees at the EU's external borders remain a sad reality.[36]

[34] EU Charter of Fundamental Rights, art 18, provides additional legal guarantees for refugees arriving at the border to be granted access to a fair and efficient asylum procedure or even outside the territory as soon as the person concerned comes within the effective control of a Member State authority. Although the content of art 18 establishing the right to asylum has not yet been interpreted by the Court of Justice of the EU (CJEU), it has been convincingly argued on the basis of the drafting history of the EU Charter that it goes beyond protection from *refoulement* and establishes an individual right that can be enforced by individuals vis-a-vis States when they come within the criteria to be granted asylum or international protection as defined in the EU asylum *acquis*. See Maarten den Heijer, 'Article 18—Right to Asylum' in S Peers, T Hervey, J Kenner and A Ward (eds), above n 9.

[35] See *MSS v Belgium and Greece* App no 30696/09 (ECtHR, 21 January 2011) paras 286–93; *IM v France* App no 9152/09 (ECtHR, 2 February 2012) paras 127–35.

[36] See Human Rights Watch, *Containment Plan: Bulgaria's Pushbacks and Detention of Syrian and Other Asylum Seekers and Migrants* (USA, April 2014); Pro Asyl, above n 6; Human Rights Watch, 'Spain: Excessive Force in Melilla—Ensure Accountability, Halt Summary Returns' (21 October 2014) www.hrw.org/news/2014/10/21/spain-excessive-force-melilla.

III. ACCESS TO THE ASYLUM PROCEDURE AND ENSURING QUALITY OF DECISION-MAKING

Enhancing the level of procedural safeguards for asylum seekers in the EU asylum *acquis* and promoting the frontloading of asylum procedures were among the key objectives of the above-mentioned Commission proposals for reforming the first-generation EU asylum legislation. Frontloading is the policy of investing adequate resources in the asylum system to ensure that accurate and well-considered decisions are taken at first instance of the asylum procedure.[37] 'Getting it right the first time around' is obviously in the interest of both asylum seekers and asylum authorities as it avoids unnecessary appeals procedures, while better initial decisions also reduce the length and expense of the system as a whole by refining the issues to be dealt with at the appeal stage. Frontloading is not about the acceleration of asylum procedures for its own sake but about the inclusion of all necessary safeguards—procedural and in terms of resources—from the very start of the procedure.

Five years of intense negotiations between the European institutions have certainly watered down many of the standards the Commission initially envisaged. In particular, with regard to access to free legal assistance, the treatment of those asylum seekers with special procedural and reception needs, and the detention of asylum seekers raises particular concerns.[38] Nevertheless, overall the level of procedural guarantees for asylum seekers in the recast Asylum Procedures Directive has increased significantly when compared to the minimum standards laid down in the 2005 Asylum Procedures Directive. In this regard it is important to note that some of the key improvements relate in particular to the treatment of asylum applications at the first instance of the asylum procedure, namely access to the procedure and information about asylum seekers' rights and obligations during the procedure and the right to a personal interview and the procedural safeguards surrounding it, including asylum authorities' obligations to rigorously record and report applicants' statements during

[37] First instance decisions are decisions made at the first stage of the asylum process in the receiving country.

[38] For a detailed analysis of the new legal framework of the CEAS see AIDA, 'Not There Yet: An NGO Perspective on Challenges to a Fair and Effective Common European Asylum System' (Belgium, Annual Report 2012/2013) 25–50; ECRE, 'Information Note on Directive 2013/32/EU of the European Parliament and of the Council of 26 June 2013 on Common Procedures for Granting and Withdrawing International Protection (Recast)' (Belgium, December 2014); ECRE, 'Comments on Regulation (EU) No 604/2013 of the European Parliament and of the Council of 26 June 2013 Establishing the Criteria and Mechanisms For Determining the Member State Responsible for Examining an Application for International Protection Lodged in One of the Member States by a Third-Country National or a Stateless Person (Recast)' (Belgium, March 2015).

that interview. These provisions will be discussed here in more detail.[39] Although the deadline for transposition of the recast Asylum Procedures Directive only expired on 20 July 2015 for most of its provisions, the Commission had already announced in April 2016 that it would present before the summer a new proposal replacing the Directive by a Regulation as part of a further reform of the CEAS. Aiming at enhancing the level of harmonisation by reducing the discretion still left to Member States in the recast Asylum Procedures Directive, a single common asylum procedure is envisaged. No details of the proposal are available at the time of writing but the Commission's communication indicates it will include proposals for a fully harmonised list of safe countries of origin and a new mechanism for the adoption of an EU list of safe third countries.[40] In the wake of the 'refugee crisis' of 2015 and 2016, both concepts became central to the EU's response. A proposal for a regulation establishing an EU common list of safe countries of origin was tabled by the Commission in September 2015 and is still under negotiation at the time of writing. The safe third country concept—until 2015 not widely used by EU Member States[41]—is an essential part of the infamous and legally questionable EU–Turkey deal. The arrangement with Turkey includes the much contested 'one for one principle', according to which the EU committed to resettle a Syrian refugee for every Syrian returned and readmitted to Turkey from the Greek islands in addition to financial support of up to €6 billion, speeding up of accession talks and lifting of visa requirements for Turkish citizens by June 2016. Although it ensures an individual assessment of protection needs of those arriving in Greece, this is implemented through expedited admissibility procedures in 'hotspots', on the basis of the flawed assumption that Turkey is a safe third country and without effective access to free legal assistance or adequate information being guaranteed. In this regard, the Commission's intention to establish a mechanism for the adoption of a European list of safe third countries as part of a Regulation is particularly worrying from the perspective of access to the asylum procedure.

[39] It should be noted that the UK and Ireland have opted out of the Asylum Procedures Directive (recast), the Reception Conditions Directive (recast) and the Qualification Directive (recast), while Denmark is not bound by these Directives. The UK and Ireland continue to be bound by Council Directive 2005/85/EC, Council Directive 2004/83/EC and Council Directive 2003/9/EC. The Dublin Regulation (recast) applies to all EU Member States and Norway, Iceland, Switzerland and Liechtenstein.

[40] See European Commission, 'Towards a Reform of the Common European Asylum System and Enhancing Legal Avenues to Europe' (Brussels, COM(2016) 197, 6 April 2016).

[41] Hungary introduced a border procedure in the transit zone at the Hungarian–Serbian border in August 2015, which relies heavily on the systematic application of the safe third country concept with regard to Serbia to curb the arrival of increasing numbers of asylum seekers and refugees at its borders. For an analysis see AIDA, 'Crossing Boundaries: The New Asylum Procedure at the Border and Restrictions to Accessing Protection in Hungary' (Brussels, ECRE, 1 October 2015).

Not only would it oblige all EU Member States to apply such a concept (this is currently at Member States' discretion), it may also result in effectively denying asylum seekers access to fair and effective procedures on EU territory and therefore considerably reduce the progress made on this area through the recast Asylum Procedures Directive.

A. Access to Information on How and Where to Apply for International Protection

As emphasised in the *Hirsi* judgment, effective access to the asylum procedure presupposes accurate knowledge on the part of those arriving on the territory about the possibility of applying for international protection. This is somewhat opaquely reflected in Article 8 of the recast Asylum Procedures Directive in relation to third country nationals in detention facilities and at border crossing points. Member States are under an obligation to provide third country nationals with information on the possibility of making an application for international protection 'where there are indications that third country nationals or stateless persons held in detention facilities or present at border crossing points, including transit zones, at external borders, may wish to apply for international protection'. This sets a rather dubious standard as the obligation to provide information is made conditional on the existence of 'indications' that an individual may wish to apply for international protection in a detention facility or at the border. The wording is vague and unclear and leaves room for interpretation, despite the fact that the provision of accurate and timely information with regard to the possibility of applying for international protection, and the ways in which to do so, are crucial to ensure 'effective access to the examination procedure', a key objective of the recast Asylum Procedures Directive.[42] The way in which Article 8(1) is formulated almost suggests that the main objective is to avoid any encouragement of persons at the border or in detention facilities to apply for international protection rather than to inform them accurately of the possibility of doing so. It is entirely unclear what is to be interpreted as an indication of a person's wish to make an application and how this is to be applied in practice. In fact, it is hard to see how staff working in detention facilities or at border crossing points could make such an assessment on an individual basis without being arbitrary or discriminatory.[43] It is therefore deplorable that the EU

[42] See Asylum Procedures Directive (recast), recital 26, emphasising the crucial role of officials who first come into contact with persons seeking international protection, in particular border guards, in ensuring access to the asylum procedure and the importance of training personnel in how to provide persons who make an application for international protection with the relevant information as to where and how to lodge such an application.

[43] See also Iván, ch 3.

legislator did not opt for a straightforward obligation in the recast Asylum Procedures Directive to provide every person at the border or in a detention facility with information on the possibility of applying for international protection and on how this should be done. Moreover, interpretation arrangements must be made 'to the extent necessary to facilitate access to the asylum procedure'.[44] Here too, the Directive seems to set a questionable standard, but Article 8 must, in any case, be interpreted in light of the jurisprudence of the Court of Justice of the EU (CJEU) regarding the principle of effectiveness as a general principle of EU law.[45] This implies that, where necessary, language interpretation must be made available so as to ensure that the persons concerned are able to understand that they can make an application for international protection. Whether this requires interpretation in the mother tongue of the person is not specified in Article 8 and in practice this may not be realistic nor absolutely necessary for the purpose of facilitating access to the asylum procedure.[46] Informing individuals of the possibility of making an asylum application is not an overly complicated task and does not require the use of significant resources; it can be provided by way of brochures or information leaflets or through oral communication, including audio-visual material made freely accessible in detention facilities or border crossing points.[47]

B. Registration of Applications for International Protection

Article 6 of the recast Asylum Procedures Directive distinguishes between making an asylum application, the registration of an asylum application and the lodging of an asylum application. Each of these steps has specific legal consequences for the applicant and the authorities involved.

As mentioned above, once an asylum application is made, the applicant is entitled to a set of rights derived from the EU asylum *acquis*. This

[44] Asylum Procedures Directive (recast), art 8(1).

[45] The principle of effectiveness requires that national rules and procedures should not render the exercise of EU rights impossible in practice: Case C-13/01 *Safalero Srl v Prefetto di Genova* [2003] ECR I-8679, para 49.

[46] With respect to the right to be informed of the procedure to be followed and the rights and obligations during the procedure, the standard set in the Asylum Procedures Directive (recast) is that individuals must be informed of such rights and obligations in a language they understand or *are reasonably supposed to understand*. The latter standard is problematic as there are no guidelines on how to assess whether a person can be reasonably supposed to understand a language other than his or her mother tongue and fully understand the content of the information provided; see the Asylum Procedures Directive (recast), art 12(1).

[47] This obligation must also be observed in the context of joint border operations coordinated by Frontex, which include screening (establishing nationality and identity on a mandatory basis) and debriefing (gathering information on travel routes, use of smuggling networks, etc on a voluntary basis) interviews conducted at the border. See also ECRE, above n 38, 13–14.

is particularly relevant with regard to access to material reception conditions which must be made available to applicants 'when they make their application for international protection',[48] while the assessment of whether an applicant is a person with special reception needs must be initiated 'within a reasonable period of time after the application for international protection is made'.[49] Moreover, the CJEU in the case of *Cimade, Gisti v Ministre de l'Intérieur, de l'Outre-mer, des Collectivités territoriales et de l'Immigration* held that Member States' obligations to provide material reception conditions under the Reception Conditions Directive also apply with regards to asylum seekers awaiting a decision under the Dublin Regulation on which Member State will be held responsible for examining their application until the applicant is actually transferred to that Member State.[50] Moreover, the CJEU also stated that Article 4(1), according to which the Dublin procedure starts as soon as an application for asylum is first lodged with a Member State, must be interpreted as meaning that 'an application for asylum is made before the process of determining the Member State responsible begins'.[51] In this regard it should also be noted that the Court's confirmation that a person is to be considered an asylum seeker before the Dublin procedure starts also questions the legality of detention for the purpose of securing a Dublin transfer under the ECHR and the EU Charter of Fundamental Rights.[52]

The case law of the ECtHR on Article 5 of the ECHR has so far assessed the lawfulness of immigration-related detention exclusively under Article 5(1)(f) of the ECHR and consistently held that such detention is only possible on two exclusive grounds: to prevent unauthorised entry or with a view to deportation or extradition. The lawfulness of the detention of an asylum seeker for the purpose of his or her transfer to another EU Member State is to be assessed under the second limb of Article 5(1)(f). A decision to transfer an asylum seeker to the responsible Member State constitutes removal from the territory and thus deportation, as was confirmed by the ECtHR in the case of *MSS v Belgium and Greece*.[53] However, under the EU asylum and immigration *acquis*, an asylum seeker is authorised to remain on the territory and therefore to reside there at least until a final decision is taken on his or her application.[54] Referring to such explicit authorisation

[48] Reception Conditions Directive (recast), art 17(1).

[49] ibid art 22(1).

[50] Case C-179/11 *Cimade, (GISTI) v Ministre de l'Intérieur, de l'Outre-mer, des Collectivités territoriales et de l'Immigration* [2013] 1 CMLR 11.

[51] ibid para 41.

[52] See AIDA, 'The Legality of Detention of Asylum Seekers Under the Dublin III Regulation' (Brussels, AIDA Legal Briefing No 1, ECRE, June 2015) www.ecre.org/component/downloads/downloads/1024.

[53] *MSS v Belgium and Greece*, above n 35, para 365.

[54] Asylum Procedures Directive (recast), art 9 and Return Directive, recital 9.

of entry or stay under EU law, the ECtHR has held that detaining asylum seekers to prevent unauthorised entry 'may raise an issue as to the lawfulness of detention under Article 5 §1 (f)',[55] while it has clearly confirmed that detention of asylum seekers with a view to deportation under the second limb of Article 5(1)(f) is unlawful, since the Refugee Convention prohibits the expulsion of an asylum seeker before a final decision has been taken on the asylum application.[56]

According to the recast Asylum Procedures Directive, registration of the application for international protection must take place no later than three working days after an application is made, except where such application is made to an authority other than that which is competent under national law for registering asylum applications,[57] or in situations where large numbers of third country nationals are applying simultaneously.[58] In most EU Member States applications for international protection can be made to different authorities from the asylum authorities.[59] At the border, for instance, the first contact between asylum seekers and the authorities is often with border guards and not with the authorities responsible for examining or registering the asylum applications.[60] But also for those already on the territory, national legislation often provides the possibility of making an application for international protection to local authorities, or, for instance, to the director of a detention facility. The possibility of making an application to such authorities is an additional guarantee against *refoulement*, as explained above. In such a case, the Directive allows for an extension of the time for registration, which must then take place no later than six working days after the application is made. However, where the authorities are confronted with 'simultaneous applications for international protection by a large number of third-country nationals', which make it very difficult in practice to respect the above-mentioned time limits, the period for registration of the application may be extended to 10 working days after the application is made.[61]

The fact that police authorities, border guards or immigration authorities are often the first authorities to 'receive' an application for international protection implies a responsibility for those authorities to refer the applicant to the competent authority for the registration of his or her

[55] *Suso Musa v Malta* App no 42337/12 (ECtHR, 23 July 2013) para 97.

[56] *SD v Greece* App no 53541/07 (ECtHR, 11 June 2009) para 62; *RU v Greece* App no 2237/08 (ECtHR, 7 September 2011) para 94.

[57] Asylum Procedures Directive (recast), art 6(1)(2).

[58] ibid art 6(5).

[59] In France, for instance, an application on the territory must be made to the *Préfecture*, whilst the application is registered and examined by OFPRA. See AIDA, 'Country Report: France' (Update, January 2015) 15–18.

[60] See also Iván, ch 3.

[61] Asylum Procedures Directive (recast), art 6(5).

application. The obligation on Member States to ensure that the personnel of those authorities have the relevant information, receive the necessary training and instructions to inform applicants where their application for international protection can be lodged, is an additional guarantee that may contribute to such referrals being carried out swiftly and accurately. Recently, the European Asylum Support Office (EASO)[62] and Frontex have started jointly developing a training module which focuses inter alia on the role of border guards in ensuring effective access to the asylum procedure and respecting the EU Charter of Fundamental Rights in their daily work. This is a most welcome initiative, in particular in light of continuing reports of cases of *refoulement* at the external borders of the EU such as in Ceuta and Melilla or at the Bulgarian–Turkish border as mentioned above.

Finally, Article 6(2) of the recast Asylum Procedures Directive requires Member States to ensure that those who have made an application for international protection have an 'effective opportunity to lodge it as soon as possible'. An application must be deemed to be lodged once a form has been submitted by an applicant or an official report has reached the competent authorities of the Member States.[63] However, except for these formalities, the Directive does not define what 'lodging' consists of and it is therefore unclear what information is to be included in the form or national report referred to in Article 6(4). Moreover, where an applicant does not lodge an application, it may be considered as implicitly withdrawn or abandoned.[64] As the recast Directive does not provide any further guidance on how to assess whether a person has had an 'effective' opportunity to lodge an application as soon as possible, this may in practice result in a protection gap, in particular where asylum systems are under pressure, creating delays in processing the forms submitted for the lodging of the application. Whether or not an applicant has had an effective opportunity to lodge the application as soon as possible is likely to be open to interpretation in practice, with potentially far-reaching consequences for the individual. Where it is considered that the applicant did have such opportunity, the application may be considered to be implicitly withdrawn or abandoned at any point in time, despite the fact that, particularly when an application is made at the border, but must be lodged elsewhere, it may take time before the applicant is able to do so.

It should be noted that the moment when an application is lodged is decisive in triggering certain obligations of Member States under the recast Reception Conditions Directive, such as providing information to applicants on their rights and obligations with regard to reception

[62] The EU's asylum agency established to support the EU Member States in developing their national asylum systems to meet the standards in the EU asylum *acquis*.

[63] Asylum Procedures Directive (recast), art 6(4).

[64] ibid art 28.

conditions,[65] the issuing of a document certifying the status of an asylum seeker or his or her right to stay on the territory,[66] education of minors[67] and access to the labour market.[68]

C. Access to a Quality Personal Interview and Country of Origin Information

Examining whether a person is eligible for international protection is a complex process that goes far beyond the application of a set of legal norms to an individual's situation. A number of conditions must be fulfilled in order for quality of decision-making to be fully ensured. Two aspects of that decision-making process—the use of country of origin information (COI) and the right to a personal interview—are discussed here as they are fundamental to the fairness of the asylum procedure, which is reflected in the recast Asylum Procedures Directive as well as the Regulation establishing the EASO.

Access to up-to-date country information is, of course, fundamental to an asylum application since the person's well-founded fear of persecution or real risk of being subjected to serious harm must be assessed against an analysis of the human rights situation in the country of origin or habitual residence. Notwithstanding its central role in assessing asylum applications, the use and collection of COI is barely regulated in the asylum *acquis*. The recast Asylum Procedures Directive reflects the prominent role of COI by stating the key principles that must be observed. Caseworkers and those taking decisions must have access to information that is precise and up-to-date, is obtained from various sources such as EASO, the UNHCR and 'relevant international human rights organisations' and such information must relate to the general situation prevailing in countries of origin of applicants and transit countries.[69] In addition the recast Asylum Procedures Directive

[65] Reception Conditions Directive (recast), art 5 requires Member States to inform applicants in writing and in a language they understand or may reasonably be supposed to understand, within a reasonable time, not exceeding 15 days after they have lodged their application, of at least any established benefits and of the obligations with which they must comply, relating to reception conditions.

[66] Reception Conditions Directive (recast), art 6 requires Member States to provide asylum seekers with such a document 'within three days of the lodging of an application for international protection', except when they are detained or in the context of a border procedure.

[67] According to the Reception Conditions Directive (recast), art 14(2), access to the education system shall not be postponed for more than 'three months from the date on which the application for international protection was lodged by or on behalf of the minor'.

[68] Access to the labour market must be granted 'no later than 9 months from the date when the application for international protection was lodged': Reception Conditions Directive (recast), art 15.

[69] Asylum Procedures Directive (recast), art 10(3)(b).

imposes a strict prohibition on disclosing the fact that the applicant made an asylum application or on obtaining any information from the alleged actors of persecution or serious harm in a manner that would result in those actors being directly informed of the fact that the applicant has made an asylum application and would endanger the applicants' or his or her dependants' or family members' safety and physical integrity.[70]

EASO has made this a priority activity since its establishment. As it is competent not only to facilitate access to already existing country information in the Member States through the country of origin portal but also to publish its own country of origin reports, EASO is the tool through which a harmonised approach on the collection, interpretation and application of COI in asylum cases is being promoted. While such a harmonised approach is crucial to achieve greater convergence of decision-making across the EU, the role of EASO as a key player in this particular aspect of the decision-making process is not without controversy. The EASO Regulation explicitly prohibits the Agency from taking decisions in individual cases as this remains within the jurisdiction of the national authorities in the CEAS, but its extensive competences in the area of COI nevertheless provide it with important powers to steer the decision-making in individual cases on a country-specific basis. While EASO presents itself as an independent centre of expertise in the field of asylum, its mission is primarily to support the Member States and as EASO's management board consists of representatives of each Member State, its agenda is mainly driven by the needs and interests of Member States. EASO's first COI report on recruitment strategies by the Taliban in Afghanistan was criticised by expert human rights organisations such as Amnesty International, which qualified the EASO report's conclusion that forced recruitment by Taliban military commanders, leaders or fighters has to be considered as exceptional as 'untenable'. Moreover, the UNHCR considered the report used a definition of forced recruitment that was both too narrow and too limited in geographical scope. Similar concerns were raised with regard to an EASO report on the security situation in Afghanistan[71] and an EASO report on South and Central Somalia.[72]

[70] ibid art 30.

[71] See EASO, *Country of Origin Information Report, Afghanistan: Security Situation* (EASO, January 2015). The Dutch Council for Refugees and the UK based Asylum Research Consultancy raised concern that the report at times is inaccurate or on certain points even misleading, see Asylum Research Consultancy and Dutch Council for Refugees, 'Comments on the EASO Country of Origin Information Report Afghanistan: Security Situation, January 2015' (11 March 2015) www.refworld.org/docid/55014e224.html.

[72] See EASO, *Country of Origin Information Report. South and Central Somalia Country Overview* (EASO, August 2014). For a detailed analysis, see Asylum Research Consultancy and Dutch Council for Refugees, 'Comments on the EASO Country of Origin Information Report: South and Central Somalia Country Overview, August 2014 (Published in October 2014)' (21 November 2014) www.refworld.org/pdfid/546f3fd34.pdf.

Given the importance of the individual's statements in the asylum process, the quality of the personal interview and the report of that interview are equally crucial to the outcome of the process. This is reflected in the recast Asylum Procedures Directive, which not only establishes a personal interview as a key feature of any asylum procedure[73] but also imposes an obligation to ensure that the authority responsible for the examination of applications for international protection is provided with appropriate means and, in particular, competent personnel that are properly trained.[74] Here too, EASO has an important role to play. The Agency manages and maintains about 16 e-learning modules for caseworkers in the national asylum authorities dealing with various aspects of refugee law (such as modules on inclusion, exclusion, end of protection) and the CEAS (such as modules on the Dublin Regulation and asylum procedures) as well as specific modules on interviewing techniques, drafting and decision-making and even a module for managers in asylum authorities.[75] The option of transforming EASO into a first instance EU decision-making authority and therefore effectively transferring responsibility for processing asylum applications from the State to EU level in the long run is now also being explicitly considered by the Commission. Whilst it is uncertain whether the current TFEU and TEU provide a legal basis for such a revolutionary move,[76] this option also raises the fundamental questions as to how the independence of the Agency in its individual decision-making capacity can be effectively guaranteed given its current governance structure and whether it would have an actual protection mandate, which it is currently lacking.

The obligation to give every applicant the opportunity of a personal interview applies both with regard to the substance and the admissibility of the application for international protection and is a considerable improvement on the Asylum Procedures Directive 2005.[77] Under this Directive, Member States could omit a personal interview in a broad range of circumstances, such as when the application was considered to be unfounded, and treated in an accelerated procedure on the basis that the

[73] Asylum Procedures Directive (recast), art 14(1): 'Before a decision is taken by the determining authority, the applicant shall be given the opportunity of a personal interview on his or her application for international protection with a person competent under national law to conduct such an interview.'

[74] Asylum Procedures Directive (recast), art 4(1) and (3).

[75] See generally EASO, 'EASO Training Curriculum Brochure' (EU Publications Office, March 2014).

[76] For a discussion see ECRE, 'Enhancing Intra-EU Solidarity Tools to Improve Quality and Fundamental Rights Protection in the Common European Asylum System' (ECRE, January 2013) 41–45.

[77] Council Directive 2005/85/EC of 1 December 2005 on minimum standards on procedures in Member States for granting and withdrawing refugee status [2005] OJ L326/13 (hereafter referred to as the Asylum Procedures Directive 2005).

person was from a safe country of origin or a safe third country, or because the applicant had made inconsistent, contradictory, improbable or insufficient statements making his claim clearly unconvincing.[78] Given the widespread use of accelerated procedures across the EU, and the tendency in many countries to focus on so-called contradictions in the written and/or oral statements of applicants as a reason to reject asylum applications, the Directive provided a potential ground to deny a large proportion of applicants in the EU the opportunity in a personal interview to express their fear of persecution or risk of being subjected to serious harm, often the only way for applicants to substantiate their application in the absence of written proof or documentation on their individual cases.

For those EU Member States bound by the recast Directive this is no longer the case as the possibility of denying applicants a personal interview on the substance of the application is now limited to two situations, namely where a positive decision on the application can be taken without a personal interview; and where the asylum authority is of the opinion that the applicant is unfit or unable to be interviewed and that the reasons making it impossible to interview the applicant are of an enduring nature.[79] Also with regards to the admissibility of an application for international protection, Member States must conduct a personal interview, although they may make an exception in the case of a subsequent asylum application.[80]

The recast Directive adds another ill-defined procedural concept to the EU's tool box in the field of asylum, leaving considerable flexibility to the Member States. This is the notion of 'simultaneous applications for international protection by a large number of third-country nationals or stateless persons [making] it impossible for the determining authority to conduct timely interviews on the substance of each application'. What constitutes a large number of third country nationals applying simultaneously for international protection and the impossibility of conducting timely interviews are impossible to define in abstract and must necessarily be assessed in light of each Member State's capacity. Determining a state's capacity to receive and process asylum applications within a CEAS is not only a complex exercise, which must take into account a variety of factors such as GDP and population size in addition to the number of asylum applications, it is also politically sensitive. Notwithstanding the fact that Article 80 of the Treaty of the Functioning of the EU (TFEU) requires that EU policy in the area of asylum, immigration and border controls is governed by the principles of solidarity and fair sharing of responsibility,[81]

78 Asylum Procedures Directive 2005, art 12(2)(c).

79 Asylum Procedures Directive (recast), art 14(2).

80 ibid art 34(1).

81 See the TFEU, art 80. For an in-depth discussion on the meaning and legal implications of TFEU, art 80, see Directorate-General for Internal Policies, 'The Implementation of

to date, only lip service has been paid in the main to the implementation of these principles in practice between EU Member States. This was illustrated by the initial opposition of a number of EU Member States and, after adoption, the extremely slow pace of implementation of concrete solidarity measures to address the sea-arrivals of just over a million migrants and asylum seekers in 2015 in the EU, the overwhelming majority of them arriving in Greece and Italy.[82] Confronted with the unprecedented rise of arrivals of refugees and migrants as of spring 2015, the Commission submitted in May[83] and September[84] two proposals for a Council Decision on emergency relocation of a total of 160,000 'applicants in clear need of international protection' from Italy, Greece and Hungary and a proposal for a Regulation establishing a crisis relocation mechanism and amending the recast Dublin Regulation.[85] It is beyond the scope of this chapter to discuss these proposals in detail but it should be noted that, in particular, the mandatory nature of the distribution key, determining the relative share of each Member State in the relocation effort on the basis of four criteria—GDP, population size, the average number of asylum applications per one million inhabitants over the period 2010–14 and unemployment rate—was heavily opposed by the so-called Visegrad countries (Hungary, Slovak Republic, Czech Republic and Poland) in particular. After heated discussions, which revealed a deep political and solidarity crisis within the EU, exacerbated by the consecutive introduction of internal border controls within the Schengen area, the two Council Decisions were finally adopted.[86] However, seven months after their entry into force, the number

Article 80 TFEU on the Principle of Solidarity and Fair Sharing of Responsibility, Including its Financial Implications, Between Member States in the Field of Border Checks, Asylum and Immigration' (Study, European Parliament, 2011); ECRE, 'Enhancing Intra-EU Solidarity Tools to Improve Quality and Fundamental Rights Protection in the Common European Asylum System' (ECRE, January 2013) 13–15.

[82] See UNHCR, 'Refugees/Migrants Emergency Response—Mediterranean' (Data on Sea Arrivals, 2015–16) www.data.unhcr.org/mediterranean/regional.php.

[83] European Commission, 'Proposal for a Council Decision Establishing Provisional Measures in the Area of International Protection for the Benefit of Italy and Greece' (Brussels, COM(2015) 286, 27 May 2015).

[84] See European Commission, 'Proposal for a Council Decision Establishing Provisional Measures in the Area of International Protection for the Benefit of Italy, Greece and Hungary' (Brussels, COM(2015) 451, 9 September 2015).

[85] European Commission, 'Proposal for a Regulation of the European Parliament and of the Council Establishing a Crisis Relocation Mechanism and Amending Regulation (EU) No 604/2013 of the European Parliament and of the Council of 26 June 2013 Establishing the Criteria and Mechanisms for Determining the Member State Responsible for Examining an Application for International Protection Lodged in One of the Member States by a Third Country National or a Stateless Person' (Brussels, COM (2015) 450, 9 September 2015).

[86] See Council Decision 2015/1523/EU of 14 September 2015 establishing provisional measures in the area of international protection for the benefit of Italy and of Greece [2015] OJ L 239/146 and Council Decision 2015/1601/EU of 22 September 2015 establishing provisional measures in the area of international protection for the benefit of Italy and Greece [2015] OJ L 248/80.

of asylum seekers effectively relocated from Italy and Greece remains painfully low. As of mid-April 2016, the total number of persons relocated was 1,145 (615 from Greece and 530 from Italy), while only 4,516 pledges were made by Member States of relocation (2.82 per cent of the 160,000 relocation places).[87] Moreover, as part of the aforementioned EU–Turkey deal, it was decided to use 54,000 places under the second Relocation Decision that were not yet allocated, for the resettlement of Syrian refugees from Turkey.[88] Whereas states are under an obligation to receive the number of asylum seekers allocated to them under the second Relocation Decision, their participation in the EU resettlement efforts, including under the EU–Turkey deal, is on a strictly voluntary basis. Although increased commitment to resettlement is certainly necessary, swapping relocation places for resettlement places is of course illustrative of the lack of political support for relocation as a solidarity measure within the EU and raises questions as to the viability of this solidarity tool in the longer term.

Finally, the recast Asylum Procedures Directive further establishes a number of safeguards and requirements that are necessary preconditions to ensure that the personal interview can be conducted properly, such as the use of a same-sex interviewer and interpreter wherever possible, interviews being conducted in a child-friendly manner and taking into account the applicant's cultural origin, gender, sexual orientation, gender identity or vulnerability. The provision of an interpreter is necessary to ensure communication in the language preferred by the applicant unless there is another language which he or she understands or in which he or she is able to communicate clearly.[89] Furthermore, the recast Directive now establishes more detailed rules with regard to the report and recording of personal interviews, which, if applied correctly, could contribute to a more accurate report of the personal interview, which is crucial to ensure that the first instance decision is based on a full and correct understanding of the applicant's statements. A key objective of the new rules laid down in Article 17 of the recast Directive is to provide an opportunity for the asylum seeker to clarify his or her statements during the personal interview before a first instance decision is taken. This is an important principle that can contribute to counter a widespread practice in many countries to focus

[87] See European Commission, 'Second Report on Relocation and Resettlement' (Brussels, COM(2016)222, 12 April 2016).

[88] Those 54,000 relocation places were initially foreseen for relocation of asylum seekers out of Hungary to other EU Member States but as Hungary turned down the offer (it objects to any distribution mechanism that is mandatory for the Member States), it was agreed not to allocate these places at the time of adoption of the Council Decision, but to use them proportionally for Greece or Italy or another Member State should the need arise. See Council Decision 2015/1601/EU of 14 September 2015 establishing provisional measures in the area of international protection for the benefit of Italy and of Greece [2015] OJ L 239/146, recital 20.

[89] Asylum Procedures Directive (recast), art 15, discussed above.

primarily on the (so-called) inconsistencies or contradictions in the applicant's statements in the credibility assessment. This was confirmed in a UNHCR study on credibility assessment in the decision-making practice of asylum authorities in Belgium, the Netherlands and the UK, which found that 'UNHCR's review of case files revealed that minor inconsistencies relating to issues such as dates, duration, and frequency of events, numbers, and verbatim statements were considered to undermine the credibility of the asserted fact'.[90] In addition, Member States must opt for either a thorough and factual report of the personal interview or a transcript of every personal interview and they may provide for audio or audiovisual recording of the interview, which must be available to the applicant and his or her legal counsel or adviser before a decision is taken.[91] However, where a recording and a transcript is made of the personal interview, Member States are no longer obliged to allow the applicant to make comments and/or provide clarification of the transcript,[92] which would undermine the objective of clarifying actual or perceived contradictions, errors in translation or inconsistencies before a first instance decision is being made.

IV. ACCESS TO A FAIR AND EFFICIENT ASYLUM PROCEDURE IN PRACTICE IN SELECTED EU MEMBER STATES

It goes far beyond the scope of this short contribution to this volume to provide a comprehensive overview of the practice in the 28 EU Member States with regard to access to the procedure and the procedural safeguards relating to the personal interview. Rather, the examples of Greece, France, Belgium and Bulgaria will be used to illustrate the challenges asylum seekers may be facing in the EU simply to register their asylum applications while a number of observations will be made relating to the practice in selected EU Member States with regard to some of the safeguards laid down in the recast Asylum Procedures Directive aimed at improving the quality of personal interviews and the reporting and recording of such interviews.

A. Registration of Asylum Applications

In a number of EU Member States it may take a considerable amount of time before individuals are able to register after arriving on the territory.

[90] See UNHCR, 'Beyond Proof—Credibility Assessment in EU Asylum Systems' (May 2013) 164. See also O'Sullivan, ch 5, who discusses the ostensibly sophisticated procedural fairness provisions provided in law in Australia, but which in practice can be evaded for those interdicted on high seas.

[91] See Asylum Procedures Directive (recast), art 12(1) and (2).

[92] See ibid art 17(3)(2).

The delay in the registration of their asylum application or their intention to do so not only delays their access to the rights they have under EU asylum law as soon as an application is made, it also puts them in an uncertain legal situation, since they are not formally considered as applicants for international protection until they have been able to make an application. This means that under EU law they can be considered as staying irregularly on the territory and therefore come within the scope of the Return Directive, and potentially also be subject to *refoulement* in a worst case scenario.

The delay in registering asylum applications is a long-standing problem in Greece, which was exacerbated as a result of the tremendous increase of arrivals of refugees and migrants in 2015. Before the Asylum Service, established as a result of the Greek Action Plan, became operational in June 2013,[93] the Hellenic Police were responsible for the registration and examination of asylum applications. Until 7 June 2013 asylum applications could only be registered with the Hellenic Police in Athens. As Greece has been a major entry point to the EU for a number of years now, and in practice the Hellenic Police only registered a limited number of asylum applicants on Saturday mornings, this resulted in huge delays in the registration of asylum applications and accordingly long queues in front of the police station in Petrou Ralli in Athens, often beginning in the middle of the week. However, since the Asylum Service became operational and five regional asylum offices were established in various regions of Greece, asylum applications have to be registered by the Asylum Service, which initially improved the situation. However, delays in the registration of asylum applications both in Athens and in the regional asylum offices persist. This is partly because the capacity of the Asylum Service to immediately register the number of persons wishing to apply for asylum is insufficient,[94] and also because, at one point, the first priority of the Asylum Service was to ensure that those applying for asylum in Greece received a first instance decision within three months from the registration of their asylum application. A similar approach is being taken in the regional asylum offices in other parts of Greece where capacity to register asylum applications is even lower and is frequently hampered by the lack of interpreters, due to insufficient financial resources to honour the contract with an NGO to provide interpreters, often undertaken by phone.[95] Moreover, those who are not able to register their application

[93] See AIDA, 'Country Report: Greece' (Third Update, April 2015) 20.

[94] eg in December 2014, 150–250 persons presented themselves on a daily basis in Athens, while the Asylum Service was only able to register about 30 applications a day. See ECRE, 'What's In a Name? The Reality of First "Reception" at Evros—AIDA Fact-Finding Visit in Greece' (February 2015) 7.

[95] ibid 11.

are not provided with any written proof of their intention to apply. This is highly problematic as it potentially exposes refugees and other persons in need of international protection to risks of *refoulement*, as they may be arrested by the police as part of identity controls and subsequently detained with a view to return them to their country of origin as irregular migrants.[96] The establishment of the 'hotspots' in 2015 and 2016 contributed to improved registration of asylum applications of those arriving on the Greek islands, but the problems related to the registration of asylum applications on the Greek mainland remain unresolved. A Skype-based system allowing asylum seekers to book an appointment with the Asylum Service did not result in a smoother and more efficient registration of asylum applications. However, at the time of writing, Greek authorities were exploring the possibility of introducing a system of 'pre-registration' of asylum applications in reception centres in Greece, which would confirm the applicant's right to reside on the territory before actual registration of the application as well as access to basic reception conditions, except the right to work. Being a clear breach of international refugee law, the above example of Greece also illustrates the limitations of the EU asylum *acquis* to ensure effective access to the asylum procedure. Notwithstanding the attempt to strengthen the safeguards for those wanting to apply for asylum in the recast Asylum Procedures Directive, inter alia by introducing strict time limits for the registration of asylum applications made, an important gap remains: as long as no application is officially made, the person is outside the scope of the EU asylum *acquis*.[97]

The impact of such delays in the registration of asylum applications on the fundamental rights of asylum seekers in Greece are even more poignant in the case of persons wanting to apply for international protection after arriving in the First Reception Centre in Fylakio, in the Evros region close to the land border with Turkey. The First Reception Centre became operational in March 2013 and was set up to conduct a first screening of those crossing the border of Greece irregularly, including their nationality and specific vulnerabilities within a short period of 15 days, extendable to 25 days for vulnerable persons. After 'first reception procedures' are conducted those wanting to apply for international protection are referred to the Regional Asylum Service, which has an office on the premises of the First Reception Centre, for the registration of their asylum application and they should be subsequently referred to appropriate reception accommodation.

[96] This risk was highlighted by the Greek Refugee Council which reported that it had identified a number of persons in pre-removal detention centres who had tried previously to submit an asylum application but did not manage to have their claim registered. Moreover, during 2014, the organisation recorded regular allegations of Syrians claiming to have been sent back from Greek territory to Turkey before being able to access the asylum procedure in Greece. See AIDA, above n 93, 23–24 and 30.

[97] See above for a more in-depth discussion.

However, in the vast majority of cases, because of understaffing and lack of interpreters, the Asylum Service is not able to register asylum applications within the time limits laid down in law which means that the persons concerned are automatically referred to the adjacent Fylakio Detention Centre as irregular migrants, where conditions are substandard. Referral to the Fylakio Detention Centre also means that the registration of their asylum application is no longer a priority for the Regional Asylum Service as the registration of the applications of those newly arrived in the First Reception Centre is the first priority. Where their asylum application is registered within the 15- or 25-day time limit, asylum applicants are nevertheless almost systematically referred to the Fylakio Detention Centre for the 'speedy completion' of their asylum claim, mainly because of the lack of open reception accommodation for asylum seekers in Greece. In summary, those applying for international protection and those wanting to apply in the First Reception Centre in Evros find themselves in a 'detention carrousel' resulting from the combination of Kafkaesque bureaucratic procedures and the lack of a functional system of reception for applicants of international protection. While efforts have been made by the Greek authorities and the EU institutions, including the provision of financial support to bolster the capacity of the asylum authorities in Greece, asylum seekers still face the shortcomings of a dysfunctional system in Greece.[98]

The tremendous increase of arrivals of refugees and migrants in 2015 and 2016 has further exacerbated the deficiencies of the asylum system in Greece. In view of the economic and financial crisis facing the country, coupled with the lack of a functioning asylum system, the vast majority of the refugees arriving in Greece in the first nine months of 2015 aimed to travel on to other EU Member States, using the Western Balkan route through the Former Yugoslav Republic of Macedonia and Serbia to cross the external border of the EU again in Hungary.[99] Due to the increase in the number of arrivals, the situation on various Greek islands deteriorated rapidly as refugees were forced to stay in makeshift camps with only NGOs and solidarity initiatives set up by volunteers and Greek citizens supporting them for some time.[100] The above-mentioned hotspot approach

[98] Both the Commission and the UNHCR acknowledged in 2014 that some progress has been made in the Greek asylum system in recent years but stressed the continued existence of serious gaps, in particular with regard to the lack of sufficient reception capacity and accommodation for particularly vulnerable groups of asylum seekers, see UNHCR, 'UNHCR Observations on the Current Situation of Asylum in Greece' (December 2014) www.refworld.org/docid/54cb3af34.html; European Commission, 'Commission Staff Working Document on the Assessment of the implementation of the Greek Action Plan on Asylum and Migration Management' (Brussels, SWD(2014) 316, 6 October 2014).

[99] For discussion of the Western Balkans and Hungary see Iván, ch 3 and Porobić and Župarić-Iljić, ch 9, respectively.

[100] See MSF, 'Greece: Authorities Inaction Equal to Abuse of Refugees in Kos' (12 August 2015) www.msf.ie/article/greece-authorities%E2%80%99-inaction-equal-abuse-refugees-kos.

contributed to addressing the humanitarian situation on the Greek islands only to a limited extent as it is primarily aimed at regaining control over the EU external borders. The hotspot concept is strikingly similar to the 'first reception' model as already applied in Fylakio as it aims to ensure quick registration, identification and fingerprinting of newly arriving refugees and migrants with the objective of swiftly channelling them either into an asylum procedure or a return procedure. Such activities are carried out with the support of EU agencies, EASO and Frontex while EU agencies Europol and Eurojust will assist the host Member States with investigations into smuggling and trafficking networks.[101] In particular since the entry into force of the new law amending Greek immigration law at remarkable speed in order to implement the 'EU–Turkey deal', the hotspot approach results in large-scale and systematic detention of all those arriving from Turkey, including those requesting international protection. Based on the (flawed) presumption that Turkey can be considered a safe third country or a first country of asylum, asylum applications of those arriving after 20 March 2016 (starting date agreed between the EU and Turkey for the implementation of their co-operation agreement) are routinely processed in an admissibility procedure in detention, without effective access to quality legal assistance. So far those arriving are detained without any individual assessment of the necessity and proportionality of their detention, while access to sound legal advice on the islands is extremely limited. In this regard, the UNHCR's decision to suspend part of its activities in the hotspot in Lesvos because no guarantees have been given that fundamental rights of asylum seekers will be respected, was of course an important signal of the structural flaws in the hotspot approach from a human rights perspective. Swift registration of persons wishing to apply for international protection is of little use if there is no functioning asylum system in place, including sufficient reception accommodation in the EU Member States concerned.

Delays in the registration of asylum applications may also occur in EU Member States with well-established asylum systems such as France, where asylum seekers, prior to the asylum law reform adopted in July 2015, faced difficulties in lodging their asylum application formally with the *office français de protection des réfugiés et apatrides* (OFPRA), the authority responsible for examining the asylum application. Under the previous law, in order to lodge an asylum application in France, asylum seekers had to present themselves to the local *préfecture* and request a temporary residence permit on asylum grounds during an appointment which should take place within a maximum of 15 days and in which asylum seekers had to provide an address. This requirement created an additional delay for

[101] See European Commission, 'Explanatory Note on the "Hotspot" Approach' (July 2015) www.statewatch.org/news/2015/jul/eu-com-hotsposts.pdf.

asylum seekers as some *préfectures* did not respect the prescribed time limit of 15 days between the filing of the required documents and the appointment at the *prefecture* to deliver the temporary permit. In practice, it could take several weeks or even months before asylum seekers obtained an appointment with the *préfecture* to have their address registered. In particular, this was problematic in the Paris region, where it was reported that for families in 2013 it generally took seven and a half months to lodge their asylum application with the OFPRA.[102] The new law adopted on 15 July 2015 may alleviate this problem as it requires, in line with Article 6 of the recast Asylum Procedures Directive, that every asylum application be registered within three days, with a possible extension to 10 days in case of large numbers of asylum seekers applying simultaneously. Moreover, the applicant is no longer required to provide an address in order to have the application registered, while after registration the person should receive a certificate stating that an asylum claim was registered, except where the Dublin Regulation is being applied. This is certainly an illustration of the positive impact on national legislation of the strengthened guarantees relating to access to the procedure laid down in the recast Asylum Procedures Directive. However, despite these strengthened guarantees in law, cases of asylum seekers, particularly in the Paris region, facing serious obstacles in having their asylum applications registered at the *préfecture* continue to be reported. In some cases, asylum seekers received an appointment for registration of their asylum application at the *préfecture* several months after they made their asylum application. As the registration of their asylum application is required in order to get access to reception conditions, the Administrative Court in Paris handed down over 130 judgments in the first months of 2016 ordering the *préfecture* to register asylum applications and finding that the delays in registration asylum seekers face constitute a clear breach of the relevant provisions in the Administrative Justice Code implementing Article 6 of the recast Asylum Procedures Directive and a violation of the right to asylum guaranteed under Article 18 of the EU Charter of Fundamental Rights.[103]

Recently in Belgium, asylum seekers also faced difficulties in having their asylum applications registered by the Immigration Service. In

[102] This consisted of four months to have an appointment to obtain a 'domiciliation' address, an additional three months to get an appointment at the *préfecture* to request the temporary residence permit and another three weeks to receive the permit and to eventually be given the asylum application form, which must be sent to the OFPRA. From that moment the asylum seeker only has 21 calendar days to fill in the form in French and send it to the OFPRA, which in practice often proves challenging. See AIDA, above n 59, 15–18.

[103] See Administrative Tribunal of Paris, Decision of 22 February 2016, No 1602545/9 www.asylumlawdatabase.eu/en/case-law/france-administrative-tribunal-paris-decision-22-february-2016-no-16025459. In this case the applicant, an Afghan asylum seeker who presented himself on 9 February 2016, received a notice for registration of his asylum application at the *préfecture* on 13 May 2016.

August 2015, due to a significant increase in the number of asylum seekers arriving in Belgium, not all asylum seekers could be registered on the day they presented themselves at the Aliens Office and received appointments for a later date. The State Secretary of Asylum and Migration announced that only a maximum of 250 asylum seekers could be registered per day, referring to the small size of the waiting room at the Aliens Office and the lack of personnel and resources as justification.[104] As registration with the Aliens Office is necessary in order to access reception accommodation, this resulted in a number of asylum seekers having to camp outside in a park near the Aliens Office in Brussels for several days. In 2016 a system of pre-registration was installed to address the delays in actual registration. As part of this system, asylum seekers receive a document allocating a number and a link to a website where asylum seekers would be informed of the date of their appointment to register their asylum application. While their fingerprints are taken as part of the registration, NGOs reported that asylum seekers were explicitly informed that their fingerprints were not registered until their asylum application was actually registered. Combined with the substantial delays between the time of pre-registration and the time of actual registration of their asylum application, this suggests an—at least implicit—incentive for asylum seekers not to pursue their asylum application in Belgium but to apply instead for asylum in another EU Member State.

Asylum seekers in Austria also face serious legal and practical barriers to access to the asylum procedure in Austria, resulting from delays in the first factual registration by the police as well as from the legal impediments to registration of their asylum application in federal reception centres.[105] Asylum seekers often find themselves confronted with a catch 22 situation where they are left homeless because of a lack of capacity in the reception system and in practice they cannot have their asylum application officially registered until they have a registered address. Under a new law, passed in the Australian Parliament in April 2016, further restrictive measures are envisaged. Following the examples of Hungary and Greece, according to the new law, in case of a government-declared state of emergency resulting from a mass refugee influx, applications made at the border would be subject to fast-track admissibility procedures on the basis of the safe third country concept.[106] The new Austrian law, which could effectively result

[104] See Le Soir, 'Nous enrégistrons 4.000 à 5.000 demandeurs d'asile par mois, c'est irréel' (3 September 2015) www.lesoir.be/978298/article/actualite/belgique/2015-09-02/francken-nous-enregistrons-4000-5000-demandeurs-d-asile-par-mois-c-est-irreel.

[105] See AIDA, 'Navigating the Maze: Structural Barriers to Accessing Protection in Austria' (Brussels, ECRE, December 2015) 13.

[106] ECRE, 'Austrian Parliament Approves Law Repudiating Right to Asylum' (ECRE Weekly Bulletin, 29 April 2016) www.ecre.org/component/content/article/70-weekly-bulletin-articles/1468-austrian-parliament-approves-law-repudiating-right-to-asylum.html

in the closure of the Austrian border and denial of effective access to the asylum procedure in Austria, is yet another example of an EU Member State making use of the safe third country concept to effectively shift protection responsibilities to neighbouring non-EU countries and beyond.

B. Conducting, Recording and Reporting of Personal Interviews

The crucial importance of a personal interview in asylum cases has been generally acknowledged. This is now reflected in the law of most EU Member States, where at least one substantial personal interview in the regular procedure is foreseen, although in a number of Member States reasons permitting the omission of the personal interview before implementation of the recast Asylum Procedures Directive went beyond the limited grounds laid down therein.[107] While interpreters appear to be generally available in most countries it remains problematic in some, such as Greece, whilst the quality of interpretation services may be a cause for concern in others, such as Hungary[108] and Bulgaria.[109] Good practice has been identified in countries such as the UK, Malta and Sweden where gender guidelines have been adopted to inform the preparation of the interview and the decision-making in cases of gender-based persecution.[110] However, research in the UK has at the same time revealed that the possibility of choosing same-sex interviewers is not always understood and that, even if asked, women would not take advantage of such an offer for fear of appearing 'difficult'.[111] Audio-recording with the informed consent of the applicant as a back-up to a verbatim transcript offers the best guarantee of precluding lengthy discussions about what has been said during the interview and contributes to a fairer and more efficient process overall. However, audio-recording or audio-visual recording of the personal interview is only rarely used in EU Member States.[112]

[107] For the situation regarding 14 EU Member States as of September 2013, see AIDA, 'Not There Yet: An NGO Perspective on Challenges to a Fair and Effective Common European Asylum System' (Annual Report, 2012–13) 57–58.

[108] AIDA, 'Country Report: Hungary' (Update, February 2015) 15–16.

[109] See AIDA, 'Country Report: Bulgaria' (Update, January 2015) 20.

[110] eg UK Visa and Immigration, 'Gender Issues in the Asylum Claim: Process' (29 September 2010) www.gov.uk/government/publications/gender-issue-in-the-asylum-claim-process.

[111] See Asylum Aid, 'Unstainable: The Quality of Initial Decision-Making in Women's Asylum Claims' (London, January 2011) 35–36.

[112] See for discussions of UK, the Netherlands, Hungary and Germany: AIDA, 'Country Report: United Kingdom' (Update, January 2015) 21; AIDA, 'Country Report: The Netherlands' (Update, January 2015) 16; AIDA, 'Country Report: Hungary' (Update, February 2015) 16–17; AIDA; 'Country Report: Germany' (Update, January 2015) 24.

V. CONCLUSION

The new EU asylum legislation has strengthened the procedural safeguards for asylum seekers considerably, in particular when compared with the first generation of asylum instruments. It includes a number of elements which, if transposed and implemented properly, may contribute to the frontloading of asylum procedures and increasing the quality of decision-making at first instance. In particular, the legal safeguards included in the recast Asylum Procedures Directive regarding the personal interview, the requirements relating to the report of the personal interview and the possibility for applicants to comment on the report and clarify misinterpretations and perceived inconsistencies are a welcome development.

Also, with regard to the very first phase of the process—making an asylum application and having that application registered properly—steps have been taken to clarify the respective responsibilities of national authorities in order to enhance access to the procedure. However, the success of such measures will only be revealed over time and rigorous monitoring of the transposition and implementation of the new standards will be key to evaluate their impact on the quality and fairness of the asylum procedure and of decision-making.

Current practice in EU Member States shows that there is indeed room for much improvement in many aspects of the asylum process. The examples of Greece, France and Austria above illustrate the difficulties asylum seekers may face at times in some countries of the EU in simply making their application and having it registered properly, let alone having their applications examined in a fair manner. Recent developments in Greece and Austria show an extremely worrying trend of outright denial of access to fair and efficient asylum procedures in the EU at the borders, through the systematic use of fast track admissibility procedures in which asylum applications risk being routinely denied on the basis of flawed safe third country concepts. This approach shifts protection responsibilities to other non-EU countries with often poor human rights records and malfunctioning asylum systems and ultimately renders the right to asylum, guaranteed by the EU Charter of Fundamental Rights as well as the safeguards laid down in EU asylum law, meaningless in practice. With the world currently witnessing the movement of the largest number of refugees since the Second World War, the EU is under a legal and moral obligation to reverse these trends and ensure that people fleeing persecution and conflict can have effective access to protection in the EU—that is, to 'asylum justice'.

8

The State of the Asylum System in South Africa

COREY JOHNSON AND SERGIO CARCIOTTO

I. INTRODUCTION

SOUTH AFRICA'S TRANSITION to democracy in 1994 ushered in a new era of human rights protections, including a fundamental reconfiguration of its approach to refugee issues. The previous apartheid Government had rejected international refugee instruments and did not recognise any legal status for refugees. Consequently, forced migrants in need of protection who found themselves in South Africa were generally treated as 'illegal aliens'. The country's position began to change as the apartheid era drew to a close, and the Government signed a series of agreements with the United Nations High Commissioner for Refugees (UNHCR) in the early 1990s,[1] followed by the formal adoption of the Organization of African Unity Convention on the Specific Aspects of Refugee Problems in Africa[2] (OAU Convention) in 1995 and the United Nations Convention relating to the Status of Refugees (Refugee Convention) and its 1967 Protocol[3] in 1996. Critically, most of the provisions of

[1] eg UNHCR, 'Agreement Between the Government of the Republic of South Africa and the United Nations High Commissioner for Refugees (UNHCR) Governing the Legal Status, Privileges and Immunities of the UNHCR Office and its Personnel in South Africa' (2 September 1991); UNHCR, 'Tripartite Agreement Between the Government of the Republic of South Africa, the Government of the Republic of Mozambique and the UNHCR for the Voluntary Repatriation of Mozambican Refugees from the Republic of South Africa' (22 March 1993).

[2] Organization for African Unity, Convention on the Specific Aspects of the Refugee Problems in Africa [1969] United Nations Treaty Series 1000, 46. The OAU became the African Union (AU) in 2002.

[3] 189 United Nations Treaty Series 150, supplemented by the 1967 Protocol relating to the Status of Refugees, 606 United Nations Treaty Series 267 (Refugee Convention). South Africa signed and acceded to the Convention on 12 January 1996.

South Africa's 1996 Constitution's Bill of Rights,[4] modelled on the United Nations Universal Declaration of Human Rights, apply to all people in the Republic, including non-citizens.

South Africa's migration policy framework was developed through a formulation process involving government and civil society, including a Green Paper on International Migration[5] and a White Paper on Refugees[6] before the Refugees Act (No 130) of 1998 (Refugees Act) entered into force in 2000. The Refugees Act establishes an individual status determination system that provides both asylum seekers and refugees with the right to freedom of movement and freedom from detention, and the right to work,[7] and it encourages local integration. The model is unique in Africa for providing an individual status determination system. By contrast, most African states rely heavily on the UNHCR, refugee camp reception settings, and prima facie group refugee status determination methods often resulting in protracted refugee situations.[8] The protection framework was described by the High Commissioner as 'one of the most advanced and progressive systems in the world'.[9]

The Immigration Act (No 13) of 2002[10] establishes the framework for regular immigration options and repealed the Alien Controls Act (No 96) of 1991, one of the final pieces of apartheid legislation that emphasised control and exclusion based on racial criteria and the exploitation of regional migrant labour. The Immigration Act has inherited some of these principles and immigration policy under the new legislation 'remains largely exclusionary'.[11] The Immigration Act prioritises highly skilled migrants but for semi- and unskilled migrants, there are few options available to

[4] Constitution of the Republic of South Africa, Act 108 of 1996, ch 2.

[5] Republic of South Africa 'Green Paper on International Migration' (383 GG 18033, 30 May 1997).

[6] Republic of South Africa, 'Draft Refugee White Paper' (396 GG 18988, 19 June 1998).

[7] The right to work, which initially applied to recognised refugees only or to asylum seekers with discretion, was extended to all asylum seekers in 2004 by the Supreme Court of Appeal, see *Minister of Home Affairs and Others v Watchenuka and Others* (010/2003) [2003] ZASCA 142; [2004] 1 All SA 21 (SCA) (28 November 2003).

[8] eg J Crisp, 'No End in Sight: the Problem of Protracted Refugee Situations in Africa' (Center for Comparative Immigration Studies Working Paper No 68, December 2002).

[9] P Rulashe, 'UNHCR Chief Commends Pretoria's Refugee Policy, Pledges Cooperation' (News Stories, Johannesburg, UNHCR, 24 August 2007) www.unhcr.org/46cf10634.html.

[10] As amended by the Immigration Amendment Act (No 3) of 2007 and the Immigration Amendment Act (No 13) of 2011 (hereafter referred to as the Immigration Act).

[11] S Peberdy, *Selecting Immigrants: National Identity and South Africa's Immigration Policies, 1910–2005* (Johannesburg, Wits University Press, 2009) 148. For a discussion of immigration policy in the immediate post-apartheid era, see J Crush and DA McDonald, 'Introduction to Special Issue: Evaluating South African Immigration Policy after Apartheid' (2001) 48 *Africa Today* 2.

work in the country legally, making it 'next to impossible for residents of other countries to seek work legally in South Africa'.[12]

This imbalance between the restrictive immigration framework and the liberal refugee protection framework, in a region characterised by high rates of mobility and mixed migration flows, has resulted in large numbers of migrants turning to the country's asylum system as a means to temporarily regularise their stay. From 2005–11, South Africa received the highest number of individual asylum applications globally, with a peak of over 200,000 applications in 2009.[13] This resulted in increased pressure on the system and delays in adjudication times, effectively allowing individuals without legitimate asylum claims to reside and work in the country legally while awaiting final adjudication of their claims.

This dynamic has led the Department of Home Affairs (the Department), the government department responsible for administering the asylum system, to view the individuals in the asylum system as illegitimate claimants without protection needs. Accordingly, the Department has implemented increasingly restrictive practices and policies, stemming both physical access at the border and at the refugee reception offices (RROs), as well as access to protection in adjudication procedures. These practices and policies include administrative obstacles, arbitrary limits on the number of applications received, the misapplication of the first and third 'safe' country concepts, and the closure of urban RROs. These restrictions have been implemented to curb the perceived tide of illegal immigrants from accessing legal status in the country under the auspices of national security. The negative view of asylum seekers and refugees within the Department is largely reflected by the citizenry, who also view foreigners as the cause of many social problems and therefore support more restrictive and anti-asylum policies.[14]

This chapter will discuss the access to the South African asylum system, specifically the evolution of practices and policies designed to limit access to the asylum system. The chapter first discusses the legal framework as established in the early 2000s and in force until 2014. It then analyses the implementation of restrictive, often extra-legal, practices employed to

[12] LB Landau, A Segatti, R Amit and Z Jinnah, 'Challenging Presumptions, Changing Process: Towards Progressive, Pro-Poor Migration Policy' (Presentation to Parliamentary Portfolio Committee on the Department of Home Affairs, Cape Town, 12 February 2013).

[13] UNHCR, 'Displacement: The New 21 Century Challenge—UNHCR Global Trends 2012' (Geneva, UNHCR, 19 June 2013).

[14] J Crush, 'Shocking Anti-Migrant Sentiment Exposed' (IOL, Pretoria News, 3 June 2013) www.iol.co.za/pretoria-news/opinion/shocking-anti-migrant-sentiment-exposed-1.1526510#.Vaild_nzook.

deny access to asylum seekers roughly during this period. Lastly, the chapter analyses the Department's purported 'Paradigm Shift' in migration management that was announced in 2011 and fundamentally reconfigures the asylum system through the closure of urban RROs and the codification of restrictive practices through legislative amendments. These issues will be discussed through the lens of the Department's recurring contention that asylum seekers are not genuine and are instead abusing the asylum system. While discussing access to asylum nationally, the chapter will pay particular attention to these practices and policies in relation to the Cape Town Refugee Reception Office (CTRRO) due to the authors' experience with access issues at the facility.

II. LEGAL FRAMEWORK: 1998–2014

A. The Refugees Act 1998

Under the South African framework, the primary point of contact between refugees and the state occurs at the RROs established in urban areas throughout the country; these RROs are a critical component of the framework, as refugees attend to all documentation issues and processes at these offices.

The reception system envisions that asylum seekers will register their intentions to apply for asylum at ports of entry (although irregular entry is not penalised) where they will receive an asylum transit visa allowing them to proceed to an RRO to lodge their application formally in person by filling in a proscribed form.[15] Regulation 2(1) requires applicants to lodge their applications 'without delay', while Regulation 2(2) provides that any individual encountered who wishes to lodge an asylum application, but has not yet done so, shall be issued with an asylum transit visa allowing them to complete an asylum application. After lodging their claim, they then undergo an individual status determination interview to examine the merits of their claim. If the claim is denied in the first instance, the asylum seeker is allowed either an appeal hearing (for unfounded rejections) or to submit written representations before the rejection is reviewed (for manifestly unfounded rejections).

Throughout this process, the individual is to receive documentation, that is, a temporary asylum seeker permit, to legalise his or her sojourn until the claim is finally adjudicated. During the adjudication process, the asylum seeker must continually renew his or her documentation by visiting an RRO. Asylum seeker permits are generally extended anywhere

[15] Refugees Act, s 21(4)(b); Immigration Act, s 23(1).

from one to six months in validity, requiring asylum seekers to make numerous visits to RROs before receiving a final status determination on their application. The Refugees Act stipulates that all applications should be adjudicated within 180 days,[16] but practically, asylum seekers can expect the process to take several years, if not longer.[17] After receiving refugee status, refugees must access the RROs for all further administrative actions related to their status.

In addition to the inclusion of the Refugee Convention refugee definition, the Refugees Act also incorporates the OAU Convention Article 1(2) definition, which recognises individuals who:

> Owing to external aggression, occupation, foreign domination or events seriously disturbing or disrupting public order in either a part or the whole of his or her country of origin or nationality, is compelled to leave his or her place of habitual residence in order to seek refuge elsewhere.[18]

The inclusion of this definition extends protection to those forced to flee conflict situations and not necessarily individual persecution. The Refugees Act also incorporates an expanded definition of *non-refoulement* in section 2, which states:

> Notwithstanding any provision of this Act or any other law to the contrary, no person may be refused entry into the Republic, expelled, extradited or returned to any other country or be subject to any similar measure, if as a result of such refusal, expulsion, extradition, return or other measure, such person is compelled to return to or remain in a country where:
>
> (a) He or she may be subjected to persecution on account of his or her race, religion, nationality, political opinion or membership of a particular social group; or
> (b) His or her life, physical safety or freedom would be threatened on account of external aggression, occupation, foreign domination or other events seriously disturbing or disrupting public order in either part or the whole of that country.

The South African definition is thus comprehensive, clarifying obligations and making clear that otherwise contested issues, such as refusal of entry at the frontier and return to any other country, amount to violations of the *non-refoulement* principle. The Refugees Act thus offers expanded protections for asylum seekers and refugees beyond the Refugee Convention's provisions.

[16] Refugees Act Regulations (Forms and Procedure) R6779 GG21075, 6 April 2000, 3(1) (hereafter referred to as the Refugees Act Regulations).

[17] See MS Gallagher, 'Refugee Status Determination in Southern Africa' (2009) 32 *Forced Migration Review* 55.

[18] Refugees Act, s 3(b).

B. The Immigration Act 2002

Operating in parallel to the Refugees Act is the Immigration Act, which is read with its accompanying Regulations[19] and governs aspects of regular immigration matters (in effect until the 2011 Amendment Act came into force on 26 May 2015, discussed in Section III below). Although these pieces of legislation establish separate frameworks, the immigration and refugee systems do interact at several key points, including the provision of asylum transit visas and in the distinction between asylum seekers and 'illegal foreigners'.

Section 23 of the Immigration Act provides for the provision of the asylum transit visa, stating:

> (1) The Director-General may issue an asylum transit permit to a person who at a port of entry claims to be an asylum seeker, which permit shall be valid for a period of 14 days only.
> (2) Despite anything contained in any other law, when the permit contemplated in subsection (1) expires before the holder reports in person to a Refugee Reception Officer at a Refugee Reception Office in order to apply for asylum in terms of section 21 of the Refugees Act, 1998 (Act No 130 of 1998), the holder of that permit shall become an illegal foreigner and be dealt with in accordance with this Act.

The Immigration Regulations provide that '[a] person claiming to be an asylum seeker contemplated in section 23(1) of the Act shall apply for an asylum transit permit by completing a form'. The form requests basic details about the asylum seeker and states that the asylum seeker acknowledges that they are obligated to report to an RRO within 14 days to lodge an asylum claim. Accordingly, there is no authority for officials to use their discretion on the issuance of the permit nor does the legislation require an asylum transit visa to lodge an asylum application or that the asylum seeker enter through a recognised port of entry.

An illegal foreigner is defined as 'a foreigner who is in the Republic in contravention of this Act', referring to individuals without documentation to prove legal status. This does not include asylum seekers or refugees in possession of a permit or those in possession of an asylum transit permit. Although section 23(2) stipulates that an asylum seeker becomes an illegal foreigner if the asylum transit permit expires before reaching an RRO, the Supreme Court of Appeal (SCA) has found that the lapse of an asylum transit visa by itself does not render an asylum seeker an illegal foreigner.[20] The SCA also found that undocumented asylum seekers not

[19] Immigration Act Regulations R616 GG 27725, 27 June 2005 (hereafter referred to as the Immigration Regulations).

[20] *Erusmo v Minister of Home Affairs* 2012 (4) SA 581 (SCA).

in possession of asylum transit visas cannot be summarily considered as 'illegal foreigners' and that the intent of the Refugees Act as set out in Regulation 2(2) of the Immigration Regulations is to 'ensure that where a foreign national indicates an intention to apply for asylum, the regulatory framework of the RA [Refugees Act] kicks in, ultimately to ensure that genuine asylum seekers are not turned away'.[21]

These rulings narrow the broad definition of an illegal foreigner to protect those who are intending to seek asylum, as well as those who have already lodged applications, and they clearly provide a separate framework for asylum seekers and refugees in light of the potentially harmful consequences of *refoulement*.

III. RESTRICTING ACCESS: POLICIES AND PRACTICE

Since the inception of the Refugees Act, policy-makers in South Africa have repeatedly stated their intention to better manage migration, while fulfilling their international obligations and commitment to the respect of human rights.[22] The Department has attempted to address these problems through a variety of administrative measures designed to restrict access to RROs, territory, and refugee status, and therefore, to alleviate the caseload.

A. Pre-screening Procedures at the RRO

In 2006, the Department introduced pre-screening measures at various RROs designed to deny access to documentation and adjudication procedures for asylum seekers deemed to have illegitimate claims. The measure arose as a response to the inability of the Department to receive all of the asylum applicants presenting at an RRO on a given day; to cut down on the number of applications, officials began to administer an additional form to those waiting in the queue outside of the RRO. The form, not contemplated in the legislation, asked a series of questions regarding the intent of the applicant and their reasons for applying. Officials would then

[21] *Bula v Minister of Home Affairs* 2012 (4) SA 560 (SCA) para 74.

[22] Department of Home Affairs, 'Statement: Addresses by Home Affairs Minister Dr Nkosazana Dlamini Zuma ahead of voting on the Refugee Amendment Bill' (Cape Town, Department of Home Affairs Republic of South Africa, 16 March 2011) www.defenceweb.co.za/index.php?option=com_content&view=article&id=14180:statement-addresss-by-home-affairs-minister-dr-nkosazana-dlamini-zuma-ahead-of-voting-on-the-refugee-amendment-bill&catid=86:government-affairs&Itemid=187.

use the forms to determine which individuals could lodge applications and would refuse access to those who were deemed illegitimate based on the answers provided. Those who were refused would either be arrested as illegal foreigners or be advised of other immigration permit options. The form consisted of basic demographic information and two questions: Why did the person leave his or her country and what would happen if they were returned? The forms were administered to asylum seekers outside of the RROs without access to interpreters, severely prejudicing illiterate asylum seekers; further, the one-page form did not allow for any in-depth answers to be provided and the environment for completion (the car park or crowded queue) was not conducive to full disclosure.

The Department stated that the pre-screening form was a result of their officials becoming aware 'that many of the applicants were not really desirous of wanting asylum or … would not even remotely qualify for asylum'.[23] The pre-screening forms were administered and collected by a refugee reception officer, whose duties are to assist in the completion of asylum applications and submit them to a refugee status determination officer (RSDO) for formal consideration.[24] In court papers, the Department admitted that, in the initial stages of the pre-screening form's introduction, some asylum seekers were refused applications, but that the policy was later revised to only 'advise' individuals of other immigration permit options. The Department stated that no individuals were refused outright in submitting their application based solely on the pre-screening form, but a number of individuals reported receiving a document with the Department's letterhead stating that they did not qualify for asylum and were required to leave the RRO.[25]

The court found that the letter of advice 'effectively precludes an applicant from continuing with his application for asylum' and that 'it would be impossible for an applicant to get an interview … to complete the necessary BI-1590 form without successfully going through the pre-screening process'.[26] Additionally, the court noted that the two questions posed on the form were not sufficient to prompt a relevant response and that the asylum applicant could only supply information within a limited time,

[23] *Tafira and Others v Ngozwane and Others* (12960/06) ZAGPHC 136 (TPD), 12 December 2006, 5–6.

[24] Refugees Act Regulations 4(a)–(e) state that the duties of a refugee reception officer are to ensure that an applicant is provided with interpretation, to issue asylum seeker permits and notice to appear dates, to verbally notify applicants of conditions on the permit and their rights associated therein, and to renew the permit each time the applicant appears during the adjudication process.

[25] *Tafira and Others v Ngozwane and Others*, above n 23, 32–35.

[26] ibid 36.

without any assistance and without any knowledge about the relevant factors that would be considered. The pre-screening process was found to prevent applicants from lodging their claims, and at best, to impede an applicant for asylum in exercising his rights in terms of the Refugees Act, thereby violating the constitutional rights of asylum seekers.[27]

B. 'Quota' Systems and Limits on the Number of Applications Lodged

A similar practice was implemented establishing a quota on the number of asylum applications allowed per day. This practice has been implemented at various RROs with varying conditions; Vigneswaran notes that some RROs set an absolute maximum on the total number of cases, while others set quotas on the number of applicants per nationality.[28] At the CTRRO, this practice was prevalent in 2004–05 and set the maximum number of asylum applications at 20 per day.[29] The result was that asylum applicants were left undocumented for long periods of time, and desperate applicants slept overnight at the RRO to ensure their spots in the queue in hopes of lodging their claims. Their inability to access the RRO resulted in many frustrated asylum seekers, and eventually, a riot causing serious injuries requiring hospital treatment.[30]

The quota system directly contravenes the Department's obligation to receive asylum applications and greatly diminishes access and legal protections for asylum seekers. In court papers, the Department argued that the quota was due to a limited number of staff, backlogs and inadequate facilities, and that the policy was put in place as a measure to cope with demand while the Department attempted to implement long-term solutions and strategies.[31] The court found the practice unlawful and inconsistent with the fundamental rights of asylum seekers to dignity and freedom, and security of the person as set out in sections 10 and 12 of the Constitution.[32]

[27] ibid 38. The court did note that, in principle, a pre-screening procedure is not unlawful 'if it exists genuinely to assist a person to quickly arrive at the correct office' and if the necessary assistance is given to the asylum seeker.

[28] D Vigneswaran, 'A Foot in the Door: Access to Asylum in South Africa' (Forced Migration Studies Working Paper 40, University of Witswatersrand, August 2008) 12.

[29] *Kiliko and Others v Minister of Home Affairs and Others* 2006 (4) SA 114 (C) 2730/05 para 23.

[30] Cape Times, 'Department to Tackle Refugees' Problems' (Reported by South African Migration Project, 3 March 2005) www.queensu.ca/samp/migrationnews/article.php?Mig_News_ID=798&Mig_News_Issue=3&Mig_News_Cat=8.

[31] *Kiliko and Others v Minister of Home Affairs and Others*, above n 29, paras 15–17.

[32] ibid para 31.

C. First and Third 'Safe' Country Concepts

The first and third safe country concepts have been used to remove asylum seekers to subsequent countries and to prevent individuals who have simply transited through other states to apply for refugee status. The first safe country concept involves an expectation that asylum seekers lodge their asylum applications in the first safe country they reach, while the third safe country differs in that a state may return an asylum seeker to a third country through which the individual passed (not necessarily the first safe country). These concepts do not exist in international law, but have been developed in bilateral and multilateral agreements by various states. South Africa had not entered into any such agreements at the time of writing, but the concepts have been implemented at various times since the Refugees Act entered into force as a means of bypassing international protection obligations and denying access to territory and documentation for asylum seekers.

The utility of these concepts as a burden-sharing mechanism was discussed during the migration policy development process prior to the implementation of the Refugees Act; the 1997 draft Green Paper urged South Africa to seek a 'collectivised system of protection' to share the responsibility for refugees with neighbouring countries, stating:

> A transition toward collectivised refugee protection is in the interests of South Africa not only as a means of avoiding regional instability, but also to put in place a rights-regarding alternative to so-called 'first country of arrival' rules applied by some states to allocate responsibility for refugee protection on the basis of mechanism rules that do not adequately take protection concerns into account.[33]

Although mentioned in the draft Green Paper, little progress on any regional system has been made to harmonise migration policies in relation to refugee protection and responsibility, and instead, the 'first country of arrival rules' have been invoked in an ad hoc and arbitrary manner. Individuals have often been denied access to territory or rejected during refugee status determination interviews for having transited 'safe countries', often supported by the misapplication of section 4(d) of the Refugees Act, which provides for the exclusion of refugee status to individuals 'if there is reason to believe that he or she enjoys the protection of any other country in which he or she has taken residence'.[34]

[33] Republic of South Africa, above n 5, s 4.7.5.

[34] eg the Refugee Appeal Board Case 1159/08 as cited in T Polzer, 'Policy Shifts in the South African Asylum System: Evidence and Implications' (2013) *African Centre for Migration & Society and Lawyers for Human Rights Report* 24–25, www.lhr.org.za/publications/policy-shifts-south-african-asylum-system-evidence-and-implications.

As early as 2000, the Department undertook efforts to implement these concepts into policy. In 2000, the Department circulated a memo regarding the 'first country of asylum' that instructed officials to verify the good faith of asylum seekers who arrived in South Africa after transiting through 'safe neighbouring countries', and to return those who had and detain those who entered the country. The practice made it practically impossible for asylum seekers to reach South Africa by land and also heightened the risk of both direct and indirect *refoulement*; the memo was withdrawn after the matter was taken to court and a settlement was reached.[35]

In the following years, the Department has made repeated efforts to introduce the concepts, often referring to them as principles of international law, and, in practice, officials have used the concepts as a means to deny asylum seekers physical access at border posts and RROs, as well as a means to reject asylum seekers' claims to refugee status in status determination hearings.[36] The abuse of this practice, based on the assumption that individuals could have sought international protection in a safe third country on their way to South Africa, is a clear example of the arbitrary implementation of a principle not supported by legislation and demonstrates a lack of knowledge regarding refugee law and international obligations amongst the Department's officials.

The misapplication of these concepts has dire consequences for asylum seekers and refugees, as the lack of any substantive agreements results in the rudimentary application of the concepts, with little regard given to protection concerns or notions of what criteria might be used to define a safe country.

Individuals in South Africa with documentation have also had these concepts applied as demonstrated in the case of *Abdi v Minister of Home Affairs*.[37] This case involved two Somali nationals, a recognised refugee and a documented asylum seeker in South Africa, who travelled to Namibia irregularly and were arrested and detained by the Namibian authorities, who arranged for their deportation to Somalia via South Africa. South African officials argued that the individuals could not be readmitted, as they fell under the jurisdiction of Namibia and they attempted to deport the individuals to Namibia. However, the court found that the individuals were entitled to be readmitted and that the principle of *non-refoulement* is protected under the Constitution. In such cases, the state is obligated

[35] *Lawyers for Human Rights v Minister of Home Affairs* (TPD) unreported case no 10783/2001 (9 May 2001); see generally M–T Gil-Bazo, 'Responses to Secondary Movements of Refugees: A Comparative Preliminary Study of State Practice in South Africa, Spain, and the USA' (Discussion paper for UNCHR Expert Meeting on International Cooperation to Share Burdens and Responsibilities, Amman, Jordan 27–28 June 2011).

[36] Polzer, above n 34, 23–25.

[37] *Abdi v Minister of Home Affairs* (734/10) [2011] ZASCA 2 (15 February 2011).

to assist individuals irrespective of their legal status, as long as the individuals can demonstrate that they 'might qualify as refugees or asylum seekers'.[38] The court also held that the Department's contention that the individuals would not face hardship in Namibia was flawed in that '[i]f returned to Namibia the appellants would simply be deported again—this time perhaps via another country—to Somalia' and that 'deportation to another state that would result in the imposition of a cruel, unusual or degrading punishment is in conflict with the fundamental values of the Constitution.'[39]

D. Safe Country of Origin Principle

Another restrictive practice implemented by the Department is the arbitrary application of the principle of the *safe country of origin*, which, on numerous occasions, has led to the a priori exclusion of certain groups of asylum seekers from access to territory and from refugee status. The safe country of origin principle has been used as a means to bar asylum applications from certain 'safe' countries (often from a compiled list of such countries) and also as means to place certain applications into accelerated procedures.[40]

In South Africa, the Refugees Act does not provide for accelerated procedures, nor does it mention safe countries of origin. In the past, the Department has adopted an unpublished 'white list' of countries deemed 'safe' or 'non-refugee generating countries', and asylum claimants have often been treated on a prima facie basis and divided according to their nationalities.[41] This policy not only represents an arbitrary and unlawful implementation of the Refugees Act, but also introduces a new geographical limitation and discriminates against individuals from a specific country, contravening the spirit of the Convention.[42]

At the RRO, the safe country of origin concept has been used to deny access to documentation as exemplified by the refusal of the Cape Town RRO to allow individuals from Fiji and Nepal to lodge asylum applications,

[38] ibid para 28.

[39] *Abdi v Minister of Home Affairs*, above n 37, paras 31, 26.

[40] UNHCR, 'Asylum Processes (Fair and Efficient Asylum Procedures) Global Consultations on International Protections' (2nd Meeting, EC/GC/01/12 31, May 2001) para 38.

[41] J Handmaker et al, *Perspectives on Refugee Protection in South Africa* (Lawyers for Human Rights, South Africa, 2001) 8.

[42] J van Selm, 'Access to Procedures: "Safe Third Countries", "Safe Countries of Origin" and "Time Limits"' (Background Paper, Third Track Discussions, Global Consultations on International Protection, June 2001) 36.

as they are from 'safe countries'.[43] At the border, the concept has been used to deny entry to asylum seekers due to their country of origin. This practice has most negatively affected Zimbabwean applicants. In 2011, Lawyers for Human Rights noted that officials at the Musina/Beitbridge border post were refusing to allow undocumented Zimbabwean asylum seekers access to the country, as they are 'not genuine asylum seekers'.[44]

The application of the *safe country of origin* concept was invoked in Parliament during the discussion regarding amendments to the Immigration Act. A Parliamentarian from the ruling party, the African National Congress (ANC), suggested that 'people from safe countries such as Botswana should not even be considered asylum seekers'.[45]

E. Asylum Transit Visa Requirements at RROs

Another administrative barrier erected by the Department to bar individuals from lodging asylum applications was the requirement to produce an asylum transit visa in order to lodge an asylum application. This practice was prevalent from approximately 2011–12 and resulted in large numbers of undocumented asylum seekers being refused access to RROs around the country if they were not in possession of an asylum transit visa, despite that no such a requirement is contemplated in the Refugees Act.[46]

In Cape Town, the refusal was challenged in the Western Cape High Court, where the Department went to great lengths to explain that there was no 'practice, policy or procedure' implemented at the CTRRO to exclude asylum applicants from lodging claims.[47] The Department instead attributed the refusals to a managerial meeting that discussed the difficulties arising due to the fact that many 'asylum-seekers simply do not report to a border post and enter the country clandestinely and illegally' and lodge asylum claims without any form of documentation.[48]

[43] TH Schreier, 'An Evaluation of South Africa's Application of the OAU Refugee Definition' (2008) 25 *Refuge* 53, 55.

[44] Lawyers for Human Rights, 'Situation Report: Refoulement of Undocumented Asylum-Seekers at South African Ports of Entry with a Particular Focus on the Situation of Zimbabweans at Beitbridge' (Lawyers for Human Rights, September 2011) 9.

[45] Department of Home Affairs, 'Briefing to Portfolio Committee on Home Affairs' (Cape Town, Department of Home Affairs Republic of South Africa, 29 June 2011).

[46] Integrated Regional Information Networks (IRIN), 'South Africa: Red Tape Ensnares Asylum Seekers' (ks/cb, Johannesburg, IRIN, 20 January 2012) www.irinnews.org/report/94692/south-africa-red-tape-ensnares-asylum-seekers.

[47] *Dennis Ssemakula v Minister of Home Affairs* (4139/11) [2012] ZAWCHC 398 (5 March 2012).

[48] Richard Sikakane Responding Affidavit, ibid, para 6.

The meeting resulted in a 'misunderstanding on the part of some managers' that asylum seekers required asylum transit visas to lodge an asylum application.[49] The practice was halted after litigation during which the Department clarified through the State Attorney's office that no such policy exists.

Ironically, the asylum transit visa requirement was implemented during a period of time in which asylum transit visas were not being administered at border posts, in effect making it impossible to apply for asylum. The result of the policy was that large numbers of undocumented asylum seekers were unable to access documentation at RROs. The abuse resulting from this discriminatory practice was condemned by international organisations such as Doctors Without Borders as an unlawful procedure denying the constitutional right of asylum in breach of international obligations and in contravention of the principle of *non-refoulement*.[50]

IV. POLICY SHIFT: THE 'NEW PARADIGM'

The practices discussed above were implemented by the Department in an ad hoc manner to restrict access to the asylum system without any legal basis. In 2010, the Department moved into the Justice and Crime Prevention cluster from the Governance and Administration cluster, increasing its focus on security measures such that limiting access to the asylum system became intertwined with national security. The increased focus on security led the Department to introduce changes into the refugee and immigration legal and policy framework in 2011 by means of legislative amendments to the Immigration Act, codifying some of the practices discussed above, and by reconfiguring the asylum system by closing urban RROs with the intention of moving all RROs closer to the country's borders. These changes were a part of the Department's 'paradigm shift in the management of immigration' in which policy would be informed by 'national security and development imperatives, international commitments and constitutional prescripts' to counter the prior era's immigration regime, which was 'characterised by weak borders and systems combined with the indiscriminative application of international protocols and constitutional prescripts'.[51] A main outcome of the focus on security has been

[49] *Dennis Ssemakula v Minister of Home Affairs*, above n 47, para 8.

[50] Médecins Sans Frontières, 'No Way in Means No Way Out: South African Immigration Policy Entraps Asylum Seekers in Catch-22 Situation' (Johannesburg/Musina, 31 January 2012) www.msf.org.za/msf-publications/%E2%80%9Cno-way-means-no-way-out%E2%80%9D-south-african-immigration-policy-entraps-asylum-seekers.

[51] Department of Home Affairs, 'Presentation to Joint Committees on Borderline and Border Post Security' (Cape Town, Department of Home Affairs Republic of South Africa, 8 November 2011) 29.

that the restriction of access to the asylum system is an integral part of the Department's security mandate.

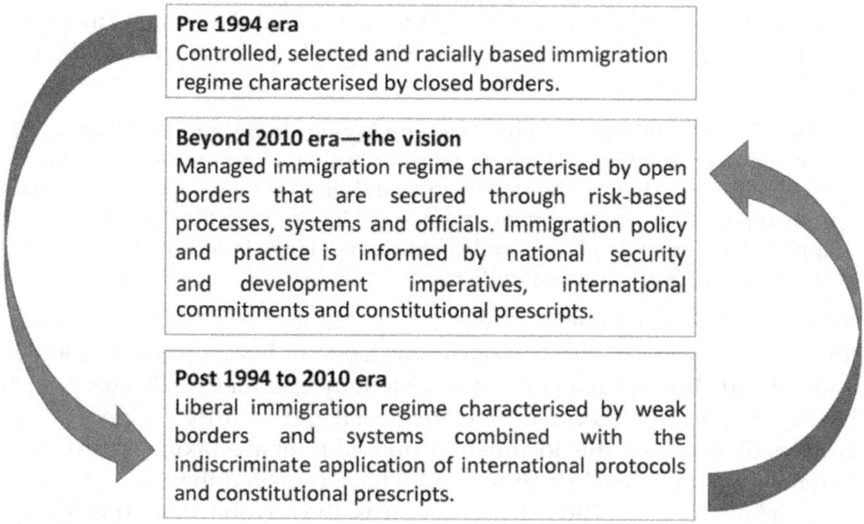

Figure 1: Paradigm Shift in the Management of Immigration

Source: Presentation by Director General of Home Affairs, Mr Mkuseli Apleni, Joint Meeting of the Portfolio Committee on Police, Portfolio Committee on Defence, Portfolio Committee on Home Affairs, Standing Committee on Finance & Joint Standing Committee on Intelligence, (National Assembly and National Council of Provinces) [Joint Meeting with South African Revenue Services (SARS): Assessing Borderline and Border Post Security, 8 November 2011]

A. Security and the 'New Paradigm'

In its rationale for its paradigm shift, the Department noted that a weakness in the immigration policy framework was that refugee and immigration matters were 'not integrated into a national security strategy and system in which all elements focus on just two goals—national security and public safety'.[52]

Shortly thereafter, the ANC released a policy discussion document entitled 'Peace and Stability' prior to the policy conference summarising the ANC's internal discussions on refugee and immigration policy changes.[53]

[52] ibid 30.

[53] ANC, 'Peace and Stability: Policy Discussion Document' (Johannesburg, ANC, May 2012) www.anc.org.za/docs/discus/2012/peacev.pdf.

The document noted that the Department 'plays a decisive role as the backbone of the developmental state and is central to enabling security' and that 'a major reason for the failure to manage immigration securely and effectively was the failure in 1994 to realise that the Home Affairs is a highly strategic security department'.[54] Regarding the asylum system, it stated:

> Over 95% of applicants of those claiming asylum in SA are not genuine asylum seekers but rather looking for work or business opportunities … who are allowed to earn a living while awaiting adjudication of their applications, which with appeals that can take many months. While awaiting the outcome of their applications, many applicants endeavour to regularize their stay through other means … which are often fraudulent.[55]

In summary, it concluded that the 'combination of large numbers of asylum seekers, gaps in the law, weak systems and corruption has led to widespread abuse of an overloaded system by criminal syndicates [which has] led to widespread corruption and social and security problems'.[56] To address these issues, the document proposed inter alia taking robust steps to refuse asylum to asylum seekers who have transited through safe countries, the relocation of RROS to border areas, the possible detention of high risk asylum seekers while awaiting adjudication and the strengthening of by-laws to limit the possibility of asylum seekers operating in the informal sector.[57] The introduction of a limitation to economic activities for asylum seekers has been proposed based on the consideration that, while refugees in South Africa have a right to conduct business, asylum seekers do not have such a right, due to their different legal status.[58]

The resulting policy recommendation document from the ANC National Conference noted that the existence of undocumented migrants poses both an economic and security threat and recommended that the Government consider a policy on centres for asylum seekers during the consideration of their status.[59]

The changes outlined above have been justified by national security imperatives due to the perceived threat that large numbers of illegitimate asylum seekers are posing to the country. While the Department relies heavily on its adjudication figures as a rationale for restricting access,

[54] ibid 3.
[55] ibid 5.
[56] ibid.
[57] ibid 6.
[58] K Magubane, 'Gigaba Not Keen on Asylum Seeker Spazas' (Business Day, 9 February 2015) www.bdlive.co.za/national/2015/02/09/gigaba-not-keen-on-asylum-seeker-spazas.
[59] ANC, 'Recommendations from the 4th National Policy Conference' (Johannesburg, ANC, June 2012) 14.

research has shown systemic problems in the Department's adjudication processes, which result in unlawful rejections and delays in the appeal system.[60] As evidence of the security risks posed by asylum seekers, the Department released a diagram detailing a fictional asylum seeker who accesses citizenship through fraudulent means.

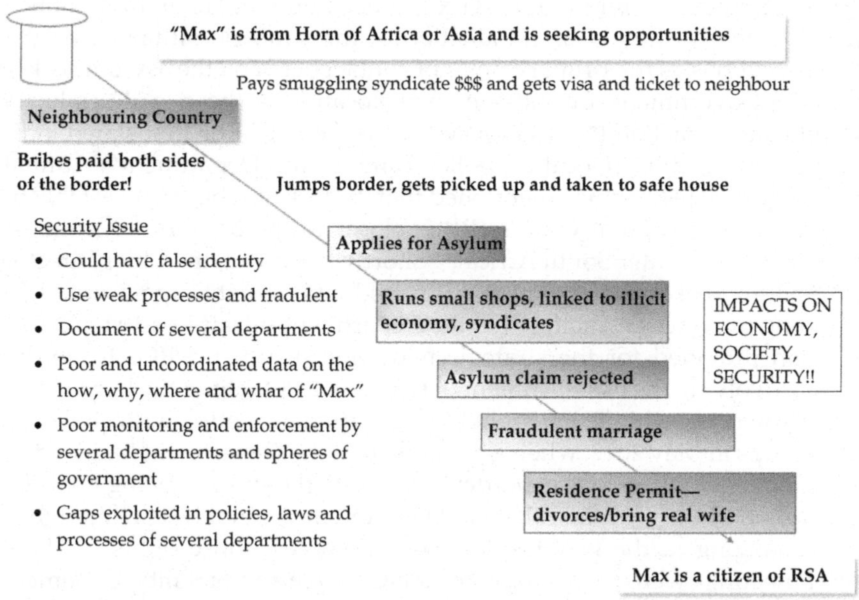

Figure 2: Department of Home Affairs: Asylum Fraud in South Africa

Source: Presentation by Director General of Home Affairs, Mr Mkuseli Apleni, Joint Meeting of the Portfolio Committee on Police, Portfolio Committee on Defence, Portfolio Committee on Home Affairs, Standing Committee on Finance & Joint Standing Committee on Intelligence, (National Assembly and National Council of Provinces) [Joint Meeting with South African Revenue Services (SARS): Assessing Borderline and Border Post Security, 8 November 2011]

B. Urban RRO Closures and Relocation

Prior to 2011, there were six RROs in operation across South Africa—Johannesburg, Pretoria, Port Elizabeth, Cape Town, Durban, and Musina. The Department began closing urban RROs in 2011 with the Johannesburg RRO closed entirely in May 2011, the Port Elizabeth RRO closed to new

[60] See R Amit, 'Protection and Pragmatism: Addressing Administrative Failures in South Africa's Refugee Status Determination Decisions' (Forced Migration Studies Programme Report, Johannesburg, University of the Witswatersrand, April 2010).

applicants in October 2011, and the Cape Town RRO closed to new applicants in July 2012, with the expressed intention to relocate all RROs to the country's northern land borders. The closures of these urban RROs were justified by the Department due to the unsuitability of urban areas for RROs, abuse of urban RROs by economic migrants, and urban areas not being strategically located.

The closures and relocation policy has been undertaken without policy development or any clear explanation of the strategic rationale. As the RRO functions as the primary point of contact between the asylum seeker and the Government, the closure and relocation of these facilities has a significant impact on the asylum system as a whole. The first stated indications of the RRO relocation policy came in the Department's Annual Report for 2011–12, which mentioned that '[w]ork also began on establishing Refugee Reception Offices (RRO) closer to the borders where most asylum seekers enter South Africa'.[61] Shortly thereafter, the Chief Director of Asylum Seeker Management addressed civil society organisations in Gauteng province and stated that the Department's draft Road Map 2012–15 plan provided for the strategic relocation of urban RROs to border areas, involving the establishment of two new RROs along the border.[62] In Cape Town, the Chief Director held an additional meeting with civil society groups in May 2012, where she stated that the Department had made a decision to relocate RROs to border areas (with the strategy being finalised by the end of the year) and that the Department was not restricting rights, but 'changing … the way [asylum seekers] access those rights'.[63] These brief meetings were followed by the ANC 'Peace and Stability' document discussed above.

In the case of unsuitability, the Department argued it had 'historically experienced great difficulties in maintaining and running the CTRRO in the Cape Town metropolitan area' and had 'been faced with expensive litigation resulting in court orders to close the CTRRO as a result of various factors, in particular nuisance factors and the breaching of zoning regulations'.[64] In Cape Town, two locations were found to be operating in contravention of local zoning codes, and area businesses complained about the daily presence of large crowds of asylum seekers (some of whom were

[61] Department of Home Affairs, '2010/2011 Annual Performance Presentation to NCOP Social Services' (Cape Town, Department of Home Affairs Republic of South Africa, 31 October 2011).

[62] Meeting minutes on file with authors, Johannesburg, 21 December 2011.

[63] Meeting minutes on file with authors, Cape Town, 22 May 2012.

[64] Department of Home Affairs, 'Reasons for the Decision of DG of the Department of Home Affairs Made on 31 January 2014 in Respect of the Future of the Cape Town Refugee Reception Office' (Cape Town, Department of Home Affairs Republic of South Africa, 7 February 2014) 7.

sleeping at the RRO overnight), makeshift offices outside the RRO to help RRO users, and the presence of street vendors, traffic, litter and human waste, and criminality.[65]

Second, the Department has argued that the abuse of urban RROs by economic migrants was a factor in the RRO relocation plan. While the separation of economic migrants or fraudulent applicants from genuine refugees has historically been the major challenge of administering and efficient asylum systems globally,[66] in South Africa (as elsewhere), the issue has been compounded by the poor quality of Refugee Status Determination (RSD) decisions,[67] the presence of corruption in the asylum,[68] and the lack of alternative immigration options for low-skilled migrants.[69] In the case of the CTRRO, it argued that 77 per cent of all applications from 2008–12 were rejected and were not 'genuine asylum seekers but economic migrants'; it further argued that these individuals were exploiting the system and 'have been able to move to Cape Town and obtain work in Cape Town while the asylum process has taken its course'.[70]

Third, the Department has argued that urban areas are not strategically located to assist asylum seekers where they enter the country. According to statistics furnished by the Department, roughly 95 per cent of the asylum seekers who lodge asylum applications enter the country along its northern border with Zimbabwe at the Musina border post. In the case of the CTRRO, from 2008–12, fewer than 10 asylum seekers per month enter the country through the Cape Town ports of entry (at the Cape Town harbour and International Airport), demonstrating that the CTRRO location was poorly located.[71]

The reduction in the number of fully functioning RROs has posed more access challenges to asylum seekers, both new applicants and those

[65] See *Intercape Ferreira v Minister of Home Affairs* 2009 (5) SA 367 (WCC) and *410 Voortrekker Road Property Holdings CC v Minister of Home Affairs* 2010 (4) All SA 414 (WCC).

[66] See E Feller, 'Asylum, Migration and Refugee Protection: Realities, Myths and the Promise of Things to Come' (2006) 18 *International Journal of Refugee Law* 509.

[67] See R Amit, 'All Roads Lead to Rejection: Persistent Bias and Incapacity in South African Refugee Status Determination' (African Centre for Migration & Society Research Report, University of the Witswatersrand, Johannesburg, June 2012) www.migration.org.za/uploads/docs/report-35.pdf.

[68] Corrupt officials have been projected to extort as much as R90-million from asylum seekers: M Schmidt, 'Wits Fingers Home Affairs on Corruption' (Independent News Online, 11 December 2004) www.iol.co.za/news/south-africa/wits-fingers-home-affairs-on-corruption-1.229292#.VBKn6fm4VvA.

[69] G Mthembu-Salter, R Amit, C Gould, and LB Landau, 'Counting the Cost of Securitising South Africa's Immigration Regime' (Migrating Out of Poverty Working Paper 20, September 2014) 18.

[70] Department of Home Affairs, above n 64, 9–10.

[71] ibid 10–11.

already in the system. In addition to capacity issues that have been exacerbated by the reduction in RROs, the closures have had serious effects on the ability of asylum seekers, and to some extent, refugees, to exercise their right to freedom of movement and on their ability to integrate locally while they navigate the adjudication process.

Since the Department began closing urban RROS, the Government has received progressively lower numbers of applications: 85,058 asylum seekers in 2012,[72] 70,010 applicants in 2013,[73] and 71,914 in 2014.[74] Speaking about the drop in asylum seekers in 2012, Deputy Director-General Fatima Chohan explained that the Department

> is not making it more difficult to apply for asylum… [but is the result] of more efficiency at our centers, ports of entry, the re-deployment of the South African Defence force on our borderline, and most importantly the relative peace and stability that has been maintained on our Continent during this time.[75]

In addition to the lower overall figures, caseloads have increased at the remaining RROs, with Pretoria registering 70 per cent of new claims, the Musina RRO registering 19 per cent, and the Durban RRO registering 9 per cent.[76] While access at RROs has historically been difficult for asylum seekers, the increased influx at the remaining RROs has made general access issues more acute, particularly at the Pretoria RRO. One news report from June 2012 reported that over a thousand asylum seekers were present at dawn, with many reporting that they had arrived at 4 a.m.[77] More recently, there have been allegations of corruption, and eruptions of violence have occurred at the RRO.[78]

[72] The figure was stated by Deputy Director-General Fatima Chohan in Parliament, but contradicts a previous figure of 61,500 released by the Department in March 2013. To date, the Department has not clarified the discrepancy; see J Boswell, 'Government Contradicts Own Asylum Seeker Figures' (South Africa, eNCA News, 21 June 2013) www.enca.com/south-africa/government-contradicts-own-asylum-seeker-figures.

[73] Department of Home Affairs, '2013 Asylum Statistics: South Africa' (Cape Town, Department of Home Affairs Republic of South Africa, March 2014).

[74] Department of Home Affairs, 'Presentation to the Portfolio Committee on Home Affairs: Regional Migration Trends and Regional Integration' (Cape Town, Department of Home Affairs Republic of South Africa, 5 May 2015).

[75] Department of Home Affairs, 'Chohan Budget speech' (Cape Town, Department of Home Affairs Republic of South Africa, 9 May 2013).

[76] The CTRRO received the remaining 2% of applications through the Refugees Act, s 3(c) for dependants joining principal applicants with CTRRO-based asylum claims lodged prior to the closure.

[77] N Makhubu, 'Foreigners Swamp Offices for Papers' (IOL Pretoria News, 5 June 2012) www.iol.co.za/pretoria-news/foreigners-swamp-offices-for-papers-1.1311909.

[78] D Skelton, 'Treated like Scum' (The Times, 23 June 2014) www.timeslive.co.za/the-times/2014/06/23/treated-like-scum; K Ongmu, 'Home Affairs Corruption Exposed' (The New Age, 29 June 2015) www.samigration.com/blog/home-affairs-corruption-exposed/.

The right to freedom of movement has been a critical component of the asylum system, allowing asylum seekers and refugees the ability to reside where employment opportunities and social networks are available to support them. Individuals who lodged asylum applications at RROs and subsequently moved to another part of the country could have their asylum file transferred from the RRO of application to the RRO in the area of their new residence.

The closure of the aforementioned RROs has now made residence in those areas of the country no longer feasible for individuals with asylum seeker permits. While the Port Elizabeth(PE) and Cape Town (CT) RROs are continuing operations in order to finalise the backlog of asylum applications, the Department is no longer allowing individuals to transfer files, as these RROs are no longer fully operational and exist as 'temporary facilities'. In the case of the CTRRO, the Director-General has implemented a policy by which asylum seekers with permits from other RROs 'will need to present themselves at the RRO at which they applied' and may only receive a one-off extension of their permit in Cape Town valid for a period of not less than six months to enable them to travel to the RRO of application. In exceptional circumstances, such as medical emergencies, file transfers may be allowed to Cape Town.[79] The policy now requires those individuals to travel long distances and invest a considerable amount of resources to reach one of the functioning RROs to lodge an application for asylum or extend their permit. Given the poor quality of RSD decisions and general administrative inefficiency within the asylum system, this policy might require an asylum seeker to make the journey multiple times per year over a several-year period before a final decision on the application is rendered. Individuals would also be unlikely to access the RRO in one day and may be required to stay for an extended period of time. The end result of this policy is that many asylum seekers may find themselves stranded in Cape Town with expired permits, exposing them to the risk of being arrested and deported due to the lack of valid documentation, and to potential *refoulement*.[80]

C. Legislative Amendments

In addition to the urban RRO closures, the Department has introduced legislative amendments to the Immigration Act which are intended to mit-

[79] Department of Home Affairs, above n 63, 13–14.

[80] See IRIN, 'Cape Town's Asylum Seekers Struggle to Get Documented' (ks/rz, Cape Town, IRIN, 16 May 2013) www.irinnews.org/report/98051/cape-town-s-asylum-seekers-struggle-to-get-documented.

igate perceived security threats such as inter alia the abuse of the asylum system and the challenges that high numbers of asylum seekers have posed to the Department's overburdened administrative machinery.[81] The Refugees Act also had amendment bills passed through Parliament (in 2008 and 2011), but those revisions were largely positive, such as recognising gender as a basis for persecution and documentation issues regarding unaccompanied children. In any event, those amendment acts have been scrapped and will not enter into force in their current form. However, in 2014, a draft amendment bill for the Refugees Act Regulations was published which further conflates economic migration with refugee protection.

The 2011 Immigration Amendment Act,[82] which entered into force in May 2014 with the publication of the 2014 Immigration Act Regulations,[83] introduced changes to the asylum transit visa that have codified elements of the pre-screening process discussed above. The issuance of asylum transit visas has been reconfigured to allow discretion on the part of the official at the port of entry on whether the applicant can receive a transit visa. The regulations state that 'a person claiming to be an asylum seeker' will not be issued with a transit visa if they do not complete the requisite form, already have refugee status in another country, or are a fugitive from justice.[84] These changes allow for the formal implementation of pre-screening measures at border posts by unspecified officials to determine whether individuals are eligible to be considered an asylum seeker, a procedure found unlawful in *Tafira and Others v Ngozwane and Others*.[85]

The amendment also reduced the period of validity of the asylum transit permit from 14 to five days. This change is unlikely to have any positive effect on the asylum system. As there are currently only three RROs accepting applications, many applicants would be unable to transit from border posts to RROs, especially in light of the Department's application policy of designating one or two days a week for certain nationalities, meaning that many asylum seekers are required to wait longer than one week before even attempting to lodge their applications. The likely effects are twofold: the continued push of asylum seekers towards illegality and the continued direction of asylum seekers to RROs on the border, namely

[81] Department of Home Affairs 'Deputy Minister of Home Affairs Speech on the Occasion of the Department's Budget Vote' (Cape Town, Department of Home Affairs Republic of South Africa, 25 April 2012.

[82] No 13 of 2011.

[83] Immigration Act Regulations, R413 GG 37679 (22 May 2015) www.gov.za/documents/download.php?f=213489.

[84] ibid s 22(2)a–c.

[85] *Tafira and Others v Ngozwane and Others*, above n 23.

Musina. This legislative change also ignores the precedent set by the SCA in *Erusmo v Minister of Home Affairs* discussed above.[86]

The Department introduced a draft amendment bill in late 2014 that makes significant changes to the written forms an asylum seeker is required to complete when lodging an application. These changes include questions regarding what countries they transited en route, who they travelled with and who assisted them, educational background and salary, and how the applicant intends to support themselves while in the country.[87] The changes appear aimed at restricting access to asylum based on the first and third safe country concepts and based on security concerns around migrant smuggling. The amended forms also place more emphasis on the economic motivations (or status) of the applicant and are likely to result in further exclusion from protection. The changes do little to improve the identification of individuals with protection concerns and are preoccupied with the travel routes and economic status of applicants.

V. CONCLUSION

The rise in the number of asylum applications and the perception of South Africa as a land invaded by a huge influx of undocumented economic migrants has led to a process of reviewing immigration policy and practice that has produced more restrictive measures that control and contain access to the country and to a fair and efficient asylum procedure. In particular, the South African Government is developing a plan gradually to relocate RROs near the borders, far away from urban centres where asylum seekers rely on their social networks to make a living. Despite stating this intention in 2011, no new RROs have since been opened, and each RRO closure has been found unlawful.[88]

Like many European countries that have experienced an increase in the numbers of irregular migrants, South Africa is facing the dilemma of how to provide asylum while maintaining the integrity of border control.[89] Between 2010–11, politicians publicly reiterated the urgent need to separate genuine asylum seekers from those who were 'abusing' the system by

[86] *Erusmo v Minister of Home Affairs*, above n 20.

[87] Department of Home Affairs, Draft First Amendment of the Refugees Regulations (Forms and Procedure), 2000, R878 GG 38186, 7 November 2014.

[88] The most recent case was that of the Port Elizabeth RRO before the SCA—the Department has indicated it will appeal the decision to the Constitutional Court. See *Minister of Home Affairs and Others v Somali Association of South Africa Eastern Cape (SASA EC) and Another* (831/2013) [2015] ZASCA 35 (25 March 2015).

[89] M Gibney, 'Policy Primer: Asylum Policy' (The Migration Observatory, University of Oxford, 26 March 2011) www.migrationobservatory.ox.ac.uk/sites/files/migobs/Asylum%20Policy%20Primer.pdf.

de facto aligning immigration and refugee policies with those of European countries, which demonised perceived fraudulent asylum seekers in the 1990s and beyond. In this regard, South Africa is now following the precedent established in developed countries, such as the United Kingdom (UK), where:

> Public opinion regarded the migrants as a mere pest. The new term 'asylum-seeker' rapidly acquired a sarcastic prefix: 'bogus'. The British public came to believe that all migrants were false: none had a right to be here; all were helping themselves at our expense. There was sharp political pressure on the government to get tough.[90]

Non-arrival measures to control asylum seekers and undocumented migrants and to restrict their access to large metropolitan areas have been applied through the years without a clear policy formulation and in contravention of international obligations for refugee protection. Despite repeated announcements discussing changes to migration policy, neither a Green Paper nor a White Paper with a clearly stated set of policy intentions to reform and review the current immigration and asylum systems has yet been presented for public comment.

Prior to 2011, the Department of Home Affairs implemented ad hoc restrictive measures to halt the entry of foreign nationals, but the passing of the Immigration Amendment Act was intended to turn abusive and unlawful practices into official government policy. This new policy shift and the introduction of arguable practices such as border 'pre-screenings' and time restrictions to lodge an asylum application have raised a number of concerns.

The arbitrary application of deterrent practices to securitise borders and discourage asylum seekers from entering South Africa constitutes a de facto asylum policy of access denial that is often applied in contravention of domestic and international laws. If purely employed to deter undocumented migrants from entering a country, these restrictive measures might, in fact, result in denying genuine asylum seekers the right to an individual determination of their status and exposing them to the risk of *refoulement*.

[90] R Winder, *Bloody Foreigners: The Story of Immigration to Britain* (London, Hachette Digital, 2006) 419.

9

Access to Asylum and Reception Conditions in Western Balkans

Focus on Bosnia and Herzegovina and Croatia

SELMA POROBIĆ AND DRAGO ŽUPARIĆ-ILJIĆ

I. INTRODUCTION

AN IMPORTANT ISSUE in the context of access to asylum is the extent to which emerging asylum host states are developing refugee status determination (RSD) procedures and opening their borders to refugee flows. The ability of states which have in the past been *producers* of refugee flows is of particular interest here. This chapter analyses what special challenges such states face in ensuring access to asylum by discussing the dynamics in the Western Balkan region (hereafter WB).

The countries of the WB have traditionally been labour emigration countries as well as being affected by war-displacement in their recent history. Bosnia and Herzegovina (BiH) and Croatia, in particular were severely affected by war-induced displacement during the 1990s' dissolution of the former Yugoslavia, when around 4 million people[1] were uprooted and/or forced to flee their homes. According to the United Nations High Commissioner for Refugees (UNHCR), in 2014, there are still 366,000 displaced persons in this region in a need of a 'durable solution'.[2] For

[1] That is, every sixth inhabitant.

[2] In BiH there are still 84,500 internally displaced persons (IDPs) of whom 10% live in substandard conditions in collective centres, 6,907 refugees from Croatia and 47,000 minority returnees who are still waiting for sustainable solutions. In Croatia, the population of concern includes around 19,750 persons, mostly minority returnees with outstanding housing, reconstruction and civil-status issues to resolve. See UNHCR, 'Estimates of Refugees and Persons Displaced During 1991–1999 Conflict: Still Seeking Solutions in South-Eastern Europe' (Geneva, UNHCR, 30 September 2014) www.unhcr.hr/media/com_form2content/documents/c2/a56/f9/SEE_EstimateOfRefIDPs_MapA3LC_30-06-2013.pdf; UNHCR, *Global Appeal Update 2015: South-Eastern Europe Subregional Overview* (UNHCR 2015) www.unhcr.org/5461e60d14a.html.

this reason, working towards ending the protracted refugee and internal-displacement situations that followed the break-up of the former Yugoslavia remains an important political and humanitarian endeavour in the WB region. In their work towards this goal, the international community[3] continues to provide assistance to BiH, Croatia, Serbia, Montenegro, Macedonia and Kosovo.

However, in the last decade the WB has transformed into a transit route for migrants attempting to reach Western Europe and asylum seekers fleeing from war-affected areas in the Middle East and Northern and Central Africa.[4] This has changed the WB states from refugee and internally displaced persons (IDPs) *generating* countries to asylum and refugee *receiving* states.[5] The dynamic is being propelled by the progression towards European Union (EU) accession. Croatia recently became a member of the EU (July 2013)[6] and BiH is committed to the same path, although for various administrative and political reasons is lagging behind.[7]

At the same time, this process has heightened the challenges involved with providing full refugee protection and integration to recognised refugees in the Balkans. The EU and a number of international organisations (International Organisation for Migration (IOM), the UNHCR and the International Centre for Migration Policy Development) have acted in building the capacity of the governments of the WB states to manage migration movements and to attain harmonisation with the EU *acquis* standards. Within the broader challenge of mixed migration movements, the UNHCR in particular, is supporting WB states in developing the asylum systems that will comply with EU regulations and the management of mixed migration.

At the same time, there is a shortage of systematic academic cross-country studies in the area of asylum and refugee protection in the countries of the

[3] Including the UNHCR, OSCE, and the EU.

[4] Nevertheless, the latest BiH 2014 Progress Report stated 'Overall, the migration, asylum and international protection system in Bosnia and Herzegovina is functioning and is adequate for current inflows': European Commission, 'Bosnia and Herzegovina Progress Report' (Enlargement, October 2014) 54, www.ec.europa.eu/enlargement/pdf/key_documents/2014/20141008-bosnia-and-herzegovina-progress-report_en.pdf.

[5] However, with 7,995 BiH nationals applying for asylum in 2014, BiH ranks as the 24th country of origin of overall asylum applicants. See UNHCR, 'Asylum Trends 2014: Levels and Trends in Industrialized Countries' (2015) www.unhcr.org/551128679.html.

[6] European Commission, 'Detailed Country Information: Croatia' (13 February 2015) www.ec.europa.eu/enlargement/countries/detailed-country-information/croatia/index_en.htm.

[7] See European Commission, 'Bosnia and Herzegovina Progress Report' (1 October 2014) www.ec.europa.eu/enlargement/pdf/key_documents/2014/20141008-bosnia-and-herzegovina-progress-report_en.pdf; European Commission, 'Stabilisation and Association Agreement with Bosnia and Herzegovina enters into force today' (Press Release, 1 June 2015) http://europa.eu/rapid/press-release_IP-15-5086_en.htm.

WB region. Ridvan Peshkopia[8] examined the logic of assistance provided by the EU and UNHCR, as two main actors in the early development of asylum sector in the region. He argues that the ill-functioning of the WB's policies can be explained by different interests and ideologies of these two actors and maintains that asylum and migration policies are perceived as expensive and politically risky for WB states. Further, he also argues that this external assistance provided is not only insufficient to properly accommodate required policies in these states, but also reflects the clash between the United Nations Convention Relating to the Status of Refugees (Refugee Convention)[9] and EU asylum policy (in which human rights principles are sacrificed for internal security policies, leading to attempts to control and halt the immigration influx into EU territories).[10] Liv Feijen[11] on the other hand, reports that great progress in six WB countries (including BiH and Croatia) has been accomplished in the development of the asylum systems in a short period of time, but points to serious challenges that still face these countries—reception centre capacities; provision of legal assistance to asylum seekers, adequate interpreters and second instance procedures. In conclusion, she points to lack of resources, frequent changes in the *acquis* and the presence of new discourse from Western industrialised states to criminalise and securitise the asylum and refugee issues as the most urgent matters which require attention.[12]

As other researchers have noted, the actual development of asylum systems in each country of the region (especially over a long-term perspective) is diverse, due to different contexts, capacities and position vis-a-vis the EU. Moreover, there is evident interconnection between ongoing reforms in the EU and the asylum institution-building in the Balkans. That is, the efficacy of governments in the region to implement legislative and administrative reforms, absorb projects and financial support and establish institutions, is of key relevance for the success of EU reforms.[13]

[8] R Peshkopia, 'Asylum Capacity Building in the Balkans: A Rational Answer to Leaders' Concerns' (2005a) I(1) *Albanian Journal of Politics* 26; R Peshkopia, 'Asylum in the Balkans: European Union and United Nations High Commissioner for Refugees Assistance to Balkan Countries for Establishing Asylum Systems' (2005b) 5(2) *Southeast European and Black Sea Studies* 213.

[9] 189 United Nations Treaty Series 150, supplemented by the 1967 Protocol relating to the Status of Refugees, 606 United Nations Treaty Series 267 (Refugee Convention).

[10] Peshkopia, above n 8, 44–46.

[11] L Feijen, 'Asylum Conditionality: Development of Asylum Systems in the Western Balkans in the Context of the European Union's External Dimension' (2007) 8 *ERA Forum* 495.

[12] L Feijen 'Facing the Asylum-Enlargement Nexus: the Establishment of Asylum Systems in the Western Balkans' (2008) 20(3) *International Journal of Refugee Law* 413.

[13] While Albania, Bosnia and Herzegovina, Croatia and the Former Yugoslav Republic of Macedonia had fully fledged asylum systems at the time of Liv Feijen's research (ibid), Serbia, Montenegro and Kosovo were only in the initial stages of adopting legislation and establishing institutions responsible in this field. Today all these countries have fully fledged asylum systems differently conditioned by external factors such as EU accession progression and different levels of fulfilment of the EU *acquis* standards, but there are also significant discrepancies between the asylum policies and practices.

For this reason, important differences exist in the development of asylum and migration policies in the WB states and these are subjected to further scrutiny in our study.

In this chapter, we will discuss and compare the asylum systems in BiH and Croatia as two separate case studies before conducting a comparative analysis within the regional context. First, we provide insights into the establishment and development of the asylum systems as related to the external policy actors involved and then we discuss practice and procedural issues related to access to asylum and reception conditions. Our discussion and analysis is based on comparative desk-study research (policy study) and qualitative study that involved 15 semi-structured, in-depth interviews with the asylum seekers, along with the longitudinal (six months) observation and monitoring of the reception conditions in the two countries. Finally, we conclude with discussion of findings focusing on the identified shortcomings of the asylum systems in the two countries and provide recommendations on how to address these and improve the refugees' legal right to asylum in the WB.

II. DEVELOPMENT OF ASYLUM SYSTEMS AND THE ROLE OF EXTERNAL CONDITIONING

The former Yugoslav Republic was a founding signatory of the Refugee Convention but it did not institute any form of international asylum procedure standards before the political changes that occurred at the beginning of the 1990s. Following the 1990s disintegration of Yugoslavia, most newly emerged countries did not inherit the federal institutions, including the asylum system. The UNHCR was among the first international organisations in the region that sought to institutionalise its presence by advocating for recognition of the Refugee Convention. The newly elected governments throughout the region were enthusiastic to establish links with the international community, and Slovenia was first of all ex-Yugoslav states to sign and ratify it, in July 1992. Croatia and BiH followed soon after in 1992 and 1993.[14]

A. Bosnia and Herzegovina

The 1990s dissolution of Yugoslavia, characterised by massive scale war-displacement in the Balkans region, also required urgent relief measures. This caused various complications for BiH as the country's protection system was not yet developed at that time. BiH became a signatory to the

[14] Peshkopia, above n 8.

Refugee Convention and the 1967 Protocol when it became independent on 1 September 1993. The national legal framework for refugee protection became enshrined in the Dayton Peace Accords (DPA), which put an end to the war in the country (1992–95), and was subsequently enshrined in the Constitution of Bosnia and Herzegovina (Article IV of the DPA), which incorporates the Refugee Convention. Specifically, Article III/1 (f) of the BiH Constitution prescribes that issues of 'immigration, refugee, and asylum policy and regulations' are the exclusive responsibility of the institutions of BiH.[15]

There have been gradual steps in developing legislation on refugee law in BiH. In 1999, the Parliament of BiH passed the first Act in this area (the Law on Immigration and Asylum).[16] The Law was drafted with the close assistance of the UNHCR, the Office of the High Representative in BiH (OHR) and the Council of Europe and was therefore in conformity with international and EU standards. At the time, the Law was one of a very limited number of laws adopted by Parliament and the knowledge of the provisions of the Law throughout BiH was extremely limited. This situation caused the authorities at lower levels and the judiciary itself to rely on legislation that was technically outdated.[17] Indeed, in the four years after the approval of the 1999 law, there was no adoption of any by-law to regulate refugees' health care, education, social welfare, housing or employment.

There was further development of BiH asylum law in 2003, when the law of 1999 was replaced by the Movement and Stay of Aliens and Asylum Act (MSAAA). This also followed the shifting of government competences over asylum from the Ministry of Civil Affairs and Communication and the Ministry of Human Rights and Refugees, to the Ministry of Security. Subsequently, the Ministry of Security also adopted a Rule Book on Asylum which sets out details of procedures and their implementation.[18] Further changes to the law and rules were made from 2003 to 2008[19] which mainly involved improvements in the access to entitled freedoms and rights during the RSD procedure.

[15] Constitution of Bosnia and Herzegovina, www.constituteproject.org/constitution/Bosnia_Herzegovina_2009.pdf.

[16] This was adopted by the Parliamentary Assembly on 4 December 1999, and entered into force on 31 December 1999: UNHCR, 'The Interface Between Migration and Asylum in Bosnia and Herzegovina' (New Issues in Refugee Research Working Paper. 44, Geneva, UNHCR Office of the Chief of Mission for Bosnia and Herzegovina, May 2001).

[17] ECRE, 'Country Report 2000: Bosnia and Herzegovina' (ECRE) 21.

[18] Ministry of Security of Bosnia and Herzegovina (MoS), 'Strategy for Migrations and Asylum and Action Plan for the Period 2012–2015' (Sarajevo, June 2012) www.msb.gov.ba/PDF/Strategy%20and%20Action%20Plan%202012-2015,%20engleski.pdf, 32.

[19] Between 2003 and 2008 a new MSAAA came into force followed by adoption of new Rule Book on Immigration and Asylum.

The influence of the EU upon the legal and procedural framework for asylum in BiH is similar to that in Croatia during the accession period, and is highly conditioned by the process of negotiating for EU membership. In terms of international influence, BiH is slightly different to Croatia, in that the UNHCR has had a full mandate during the early development phase of the BiH system (2001–04), when it was conducting all RSD procedures. One could say that the UNHCR has had the leading role in developing and shaping the BiH asylum system from the start and thereafter for a long period of time, and remains an actor of key influence up to the present day. At the time of official mandate over RSD procedures, the UNHCR pointed to many challenges posed by the development of an effective national asylum capacity in BiH.[20] Among the main concerns identified were: undefined actors and functions involved in asylum and migration due to the complex political structure of the country; obstacles pertaining to the transitional character of the legal and structural framework (many lacunae in the legislative framework that should be addressed); and the resource context of building an asylum system in the country given the post-war reconstruction, return of displaced persons and economic recovery. Today, some 14 years later, the majority of these issues still remain a challenge for BiH towards establishing a fully functioning asylum system. In general, the country is facing a turbulent political and socio-economic situation which affects functioning at all levels of governance and services. Despite having improved the national legal framework for refugee protection over the years, the need to cope with a legacy of uprooted persons from the 1990s war takes priority on the political agenda of the country's migration management. The current refugee protection and asylum development goals are mainly focused on meeting the EU accession requirements in improving the legislative framework and implementing the EU externalisation policies by strengthening and controlling the external borders, while addressing the irregular migration to and from the country in co-operation with the neighbouring countries of the region.[21]

B. Croatia

The asylum system in Croatia is characterised by external EU conditioning in the sense that its major characteristics have been developed through the process of harmonising the Croatian legislative and institutional framework for the purpose of EU membership. Today, because Croatia is part of the Common European Asylum System (CEAS), it is obliged

[20] UNHCR, above n 16.
[21] MoS, above n 18.

to share responsibility for the current humanitarian crisis in the Mediterranean, as well as to fulfil other tasks related to ensuring standards of refugee protection. In March 2013, preparations for the implementation of the asylum *acquis* were evaluated as 'almost complete'.[22] In practice, harmonisation has to date more or less implied external EU conditioning via direct adjustment and transposition of the directives' minimal standards. As noted by academics,[23] the Government has generally been unwilling to adopt the higher standards of protection proposed by the UNHCR and certain civil society actors.[24] However, implementation of the obligations in practice has been problematic, as discussed below in Section III.

The Croatian asylum system is founded on a provision from the 1990 Constitution and regulated by the Asylum Act, particular provisions of the Aliens Act, the Administrative Disputes Act, and other related ordinances. Harmonising the system with international principles, the EU asylum *acquis* and the CEAS standards has been a lengthy process. Since 2001, when Croatia signed the Stabilization and Association Agreement, the EU has fostered, influenced, monitored and evaluated the development of the Croatian asylum system with the clear goal of adapting and harmonising the national legislative and institutional framework with EU standards.[25] Therefore, the influence of the EU and Europeanisation upon Croatian asylum law has been crucial. In order to correct aspects of the first law that were inadequate and ambiguous, as well as to adapt the legislation to further developments of the CEAS, the Asylum Act was improved through changes and amendments in 2007, 2010 and 2013.[26]

[22] European Commission, 'Communication from the Commission to the European Parliament and the Council: Monitoring Report on Croatia's Accession Preparations' (COM(2013) 171, Brussels, 26 March 2013) 10.

[23] G Lalić Novak, 'Sustav azila u Republici Hrvatskoj: dosadašnji razvoj i moguće perspektive' in D Župarić-Iljić (ed), *Prvih deset godina razvoja sustava azila u Hrvatskoj (s osvrtom na sustave azila u regiji)* (Zagreb, Institut za migracije i narodnosti, Centar za mirovne studije i Kuća ljudskih prava, 2013) 14–32; V Baričević, 'Europske integracije i usvajanje europskih politika azilne zaštite u Hrvatskoj: prava osoba pod zaštitom i njihova integracija u društvo in Župarić-Iljić (ed), ibid 99–130.

[24] The UNHCR played a key role in establishing the foundations of the Croatian asylum system by sharing its expertise and acting in an advisory capacity. It also provided a few mandatory protections in that period and found durable solutions by resettling persons to third countries: J Barberić, 'Asylum in the Republic of Croatia One Year after Accession to the European Union' (*New Issues in Refugee Research*, Research Paper 273, UNHCR, 2014) www.unhcr.org/54dca6ee9.html.

[25] G Lalić Novak, *Razvoj sustava azila u Hrvatskoj* (Zagreb, Društveno veleučilište u Zagrebu, 2010).

[26] Changes in 2013 harmonised the Asylum Act with the Council Regulation (EU) 604/2013 of 26 June 2013 establishing the criteria and mechanisms for determining the Member State responsible for examining an application for international protection lodged in one of the Member States by a third-country national or a stateless person (recast) OJ[2013] L180/13 (the Dublin Regulation) and the Council Directive 2011/95/EU of the

There is some disagreement amongst academics as to the beneficial impact EU harmonisation has had on the Croatian refugee protection system. On one hand, Gregović argues that the effects of Europeanisation on the Croatian asylum system have been 'overwhelmingly positive'.[27] He states that it has strengthened refugee protection, although he recognises that there are cases where human rights standards were not met.[28] On the other hand, Baričević argues that, while Europeanisation has generally benefitted the Croatian asylum system, the indiscriminate application of European standards has also led to the establishment of an inadequate framework for refugee protection. The premise is that Croatia and BiH, most likely, will continue to follow common EU policy in the areas of asylum and migration.[29] However, the recent humanitarian crisis in the Mediterranean has shown that Member States have different understandings of what 'solidarity' means and thus, exercise rather distinct standards on accepting refugees and enabling access to asylum.

In light of the situation with flows of refugees and other forced migrants over the Eastern Mediterranean and Western Balkan route, over 500,000 people passed through Croatia in the period between mid-September and mid-December 2015.[30] UNHCR data show that, of this number, more than 80 per cent are coming from the war-torn areas such as Syria, Afghanistan, Iraq and Eritrea.[31] In co-operation with Serbian and Slovenian state authorities, the Croatian Government has organised reception and temporary short-term accommodation in the reception and transit centre for refugees (temporary admission centres). Organised transportation, with capacity for 5,000 people, from the Serbian border to the centre, has been

European Parliament and of the Council on standards for the qualification of third-country nationals or stateless persons as beneficiaries of international protection, for a uniform status for refugees or for persons eligible for subsidiary protection, and for the content of the protection granted (recast) [2011] OJ L337/13 (the Qualification Directive (recast)). However, Croatia has introduced new Act on International and Temporary Protection in June 2015, which further aligned Croatian law with the Council Directive 2013/32/EU of 26 June 2013 on common procedures for granting and withdrawing international protection (recast) [2013] OJ L180/60 (the Asylum Procedures Directive (recast)) and the Council Directive 2013/33/EU of 26 June 2013 laying down standards for the reception of applicants for international protection (recast) [2013] OJL180/96 (the Reception Conditions Directive (recast)).

[27] M Gregović, 'A Human Rights Based Evaluation of the Croatian Asylum System in the Context of Europeanisation' (2011) 7(1) *Croatian Yearbook of European Law and Policy* 176.

[28] ibid 135–78.

[29] V Baričević, 'Europeizacija azilnih politika i izbjeglička prava: Razvoj hrvatskog sustava azila i zaštita izbjeglica u Hrvatskoj' in A Milardović (ed), *Stranci pred vratima Europe* (Zagreb, Pan liber, 2014) 111–36.

[30] Ministry of Interior of the Republic of Croatia (MoI), 'Reception and Accommodation of Migrants' (2015) http://stari.mup.hr/219696.aspx.

[31] UNHCR, 'Refugees/Migrants Emergency Response: Mediterranean' (2015) www.data.unhcr.org/mediterranean/regional.php.

facilitated by the ministries' and Croatian Red Cross personnel, together with help from local and international non-governmental organisations (NGOs) and activists. Priority is given to the most vulnerable groups and reuniting separated family groups. Once refugees have been registered at the centre, and given accommodation, food and clothing, their further transfer towards the Slovenian border continues.

BiH has not been faced with the numbers of Syrian and other current refugee flows through other WB states, mainly due its geographical position which does not provide a convenient or efficient route to prominent EU countries of destination (namely Germany and Scandinavian countries). Despite this, public and media coverage in BiH of the refugee situation in the region has been dominated by a 'security threat' discourse which has resulted in a polarisation between government and civil society. Media coverage has been dominated by live reports from the borders of Macedonia, Serbia, Croatia and Slovenia and statements by BiH government officials[32] about the need to be prepared for such flows.[33] The need to improve and ensure reception capacities has also been noted by the Government but only for the purpose of enabling satisfactory transitory reception conditions to refugees on their way to Western Europe.[34]

III. ACCESS TO ASYLUM AND REFUGEE STATUS DETERMINATION

Croatia and BiH are part of the heavily frequented Western Balkan route for mixed migration flows, which runs across South-East Europe from Greece through Macedonia, Serbia, BiH, through Croatia to Slovenia and Italy (or through Serbia to Hungary and further west). This route is used by irregular migrants and asylum seekers trying to reach countries in the Schengen area.[35] As a result, very few apply for asylum in Croatia or BiH. For instance, more than 500,000 people passed through Croatia during

[32] Representing various competent security authorities under the umbrella of Ministry of Security.

[33] See www.dnevnik.hr/vijesti/svijet/u-bih-strahuju-da-ce-i-hrvatska-zatvoriti-granice-ocekuju-tisuce-izbjeglica---408896.html; http://ba.n1info.com/a59539/Vijesti/Vijesti/Sirijske-izbjeglice-dolaze-u-BiH.html; http://faktor.ba/izbjeglice-iz-sirije-ipak-dolaze-nakon-ulaska-u-bih-105-osoba-sa-bliskog-istoka-gubi-se-svaki-trag/; http://www.hayat.ba/vijest.php?id=13281.

[34] See www.bljesak.info/rubrika/vijesti/clanak/u-bih-se-grade-tajna-naselja-za-izbjeglice-iz-sirije/111326.

[35] The numbers of irregular migrants in Croatia decreased by more than 40% from 2005–2009 after more effective means of border control were introduced, resulting in fewer persons migrating along the Balkan route. Following a steep rise in the number of irregular migrants intercepted illegally crossing the border during the pre-accession period (from 2,221 in 2010 to 6,839 in 2012), in the second half of 2013 and in 2014 Croatia registered a decrease in these flows. Although the greatest increase in irregular migrations in 2012 was registered on the

the refugee flows in the early period of 2015.[36] Although access to territory and asylum were provided in Croatia, only 18 people (of Syrian nationality) sought protection, with many cancelling their application and continuing with their journey. This insignificant number suggests that almost all of them wanted to continue their journey further west and reach Germany or Sweden where they perceive they will receive not only protection but better opportunities for integration into the employment market and society of those countries. Secondly, the already existing formation of their national communities, the presence of their families abroad, and other social bonds forged before displacement, are also strong incentives to move on from the territories of BiH, Serbia or Macedonia, with their under-developed and lower quality systems of refugee protection. One study shows that lack of integration opportunities in Croatia may be the main reason for secondary movements and continuation of journeys.[37] The prevalent government response in BiH so far has been to follow the neighbouring countries' transitory policies that were observed as normative prior to Syrian refugee crisis in the WB. To date, there are no any official data on whether the current waves of Syrian refugees have been registered whilst travelling through BiH territory towards the EU via Croatia or if they have been received and accommodated in the refugee reception centre.

A. Bosnia and Herzegovina

In order to qualify as a refugee in BiH, an individual who applies for international protection must meet all the requirements of the refugee definition under BiH law.[38] The procedure for granting international protection is managed by several state agencies: the border police; Service for Foreigners; the Asylum Department of the BiH Ministry of Security and the courts. When a person who expresses his or her intention to apply for international protection has been issued a confirmation by the Service for Foreigners, he or she must submit an application for international

Croatian–Slovenian border (Afghani nationals and a growing number of Syrians, Somalis, Algerians and West Africans), in 2013 the Serbia–Hungary land border was still the main entry point for most migrants who attempt to illegally enter the EU via the (Western) Balkan route. The accession of Croatia to the EU did not affect this trend until the summer of 2015: Frontex, 'Western Balkans Annual Risk Analysis 2014' (Warsaw, Frontex, 2014) www.frontex.europa.eu/assets/Publications/Risk_Analysis/WB_ARA_2014.pdf.

[36] MoI, above n 30.

[37] M Valenta, D Zuparic-Iljic and T Vidovic, 'The Reluctant Asylum-Seekers: Migrants at the Southeastern Frontiers of the European Migration System' (2015) 34(3) *Refugee Survey Quarterly* 95.

[38] Movement and Stay of Aliens and Asylum Act, art 105(2) (BIH Official Gazette 36/08 and 87/12).

protection within a set deadline to the Asylum Department Head Office in Sarajevo. After the application is submitted in person, the asylum seeker is registered and issued with an application registration card for asylum seekers allowing them to stay in BiH until a final and binding decision is made on their asylum applications. The applications for international protection and registration of asylum seekers are processed at the asylum seekers' centre in Delijaš, located on the outskirts of the capital town of Sarajevo.[39] Under the provisions of the Administrative Procedure Act, applicants for asylum are entitled to free legal assistance, without restriction, although the state does not fund this service nor it is set out in any written legal regulations that the state should provide funding for free legal aid.[40] To date, the UNHCR has been providing the necessary funding and training in order for legal representatives to provide legal aid to asylum seekers, recognised refugees and many other categories of displaced persons in BiH.

In BiH, according to the provisions of the MSAAA, an asylum seeker is referred to as an 'applicant for international protection' and is an alien seeking recognition of refugee status or subsidiary protection in BiH until a decision on his or her application is taken under the Act.[41] It clearly from the terms of this provision that a person is considered an asylum seeker from the moment he or she first seeks asylum in BiH, that is, protection from the state of BiH at the state border. However, in reality, there is no single, accepted interpretation of this provision. The interpretation of the Asylum Department is that a person only acquires the status of 'an asylum seeker' from the moment he or she submits an application for international protection to the Asylum Department at the main office of the BiH Ministry of Security, located in Sarajevo.[42]

Following this logic, there is a contradiction between Article 5(1)(g) and Article 109(1) of the MSAAA. This is because a person is no longer under the jurisdiction of the Service for Foreigners as soon as he or she has expressed his or her intention to apply for international protection, when it becomes the responsibility of the Asylum Department. This is a confusing bureaucratic practice and an impediment to accessing the asylum procedure as there is no single interpretation of when a person acquires

[39] MoS, above n 18.

[40] The supplemental provisions of the Administrative Procedure Act apply to the procedures for considering asylum applications unless otherwise provided by the MSAAA and the Rule Book on International Protection—Asylum: see art 12 of the Rule Book on International Protection-Asylum.

[41] MSAAA, art 5(g).

[42] The Movement and Stay of Aliens and Asylum Act Amendments Act added art 109(1) which prescribes that 'an asylum procedure starts with filing an asylum application with the Ministry at its seat'.

the status of an asylum seeker in BiH. It both complicates the institutional jurisdictions and responsibilities of the asylum procedure and status regulation, as well as general information sharing on provisions of protection for the asylum seekers.

The Ministry of Security of BiH is the state authority responsible for making decisions on asylum applications. It thus has a central role in the asylum process and any legal decision on the well-foundness of asylum claims. During the refugee status determination process this determining authority can recognise *refugee status* or *subsidiary protection status*, depending on the defined criteria. While a refugee status has no time restrictions, the status of subsidiary protection is limited to one year with a possibility of extending that period.[43] On the other hand, a person who has been denied international protection (ie refugee status or subsidiary protection), and who meets the requirements from Article 91 of the MSAAA (the principle of *non-refoulement*), may also be granted temporary residence on humanitarian grounds. This kind of protection is currently the dominant one provided to Syrian refugees in Bosnia—many of whom have accessed it after being recognised as *sur place* refugees.[44] Moreover, the principle of 'prohibition of return' becomes relevant in situations in which it is not possible to determine precisely a country of origin of the applicant whose protection claim has been rejected or another country to which he or she should be returned.[45]

So far the practice of rejecting asylum applications on the grounds of not having met the first criteria of a well-founded fear (subjective and objective) has been among the main arguments for refusing to grant asylum.[46] In addition, credibility has been a significant factor. However, decisions of authorities in BiH on credibility as a basis for rejection have been contradictory, particularly in relation to identification documents and an applicant's required knowledge of their country of origin. The Ministry of Security, when assessing the credibility of one asylum seeker, noted the following:

> This authority believes that the applicant failed to present sufficient explanation and proof that he comes from Syria and that he is a Syrian national which, should he be returned to Syria, would entail his exposure to persecution or to one or more acts contained in the definition of subsidiary protection … when an applicant comes from a country and does not have identification documents of

[43] The period can be extended until the state authority finds that the circumstances, which initially made an applicant eligible for subsidiary protection, have changed.

[44] MSAAA, art 54(1)(d). During the period of writing this chapter there was a successful case supported by the UNHCR of granting full refugee status to one Syrian family.

[45] See Judgment of the Court of BiH, S1 3 U 013013 13 U (25 June 2013) 5.

[46] Information obtained via private correspondence with legal aid advisers representing asylum seekers at second instance procedures.

> that country, this authority must be convinced that he or she is a citizen of that country. Otherwise, the asylum procedure and the possible situation in a country that the applicant claims as his country of origin would be abused.[47]

The above-quoted position maintained by the Ministry indicates one of the debatable aspects of the process of determining asylum claims, which is determination of the standard which has to be satisfied if an asylum claim is to be considered well-founded. It is not clear from the case law thus far whether it is 'a sufficient degree of probability', 'a high degree of probability' or another standard which is to be determined each time on an ad hoc basis.

Moreover, major impediments to the procedure have been the lack of translators during the RSD, lengthy administrative procedures and shortage in delivery of reception services. Interestingly, Article 12(2) of the MSAAA states that decisions and all other submissions shall be given in one of the languages in official use in BiH. However, the practice of presenting written submissions in a language which applicant does not understand was found by the Appellate Division of the Court of BiH to be in violation of the right of a party to use his or her own language.[48] This represents an example of the courts finding that the authorities have breached RSD procedural standards, as laid down in the adopted UNHCR guidelines. Such a practice is also similar to situations encountered in Croatia in the early days of its asylum system.

There has been an attempt to implement international standards in domestic BiH law and procedures. For instance, the UNHCR has worked on establishing and developing the professional capacity of the Asylum Department of the Ministry of Security by training its employees in conducting the RSD procedures in compliance with international and relevant national law.[49] Furthermore, the UNHCR also trained the inspectors of the border police, Service for Foreigners and the Immigration Department. Special seminars and training events were organised for the judges of the BiH Court. Besides being the main actor in enhancing the capacity of state institutions involved in handling asylum matters, the UNHCR also trained the NGOs' lawyers, working in the NGOs, Vaša Prava BiH and the Foundation of Local Democracy—two organisations directly funded by the UNHCR to provide pro bono legal aid services to the asylum seekers

[47] Decision of the BiH Ministry of Security, UP-1-07/1-41-1-7-3/13 (12 March 2013).

[48] Administrative Procedure Act, art 18.

[49] Until June 2004, RSD procedures were conducted by the UNHCR, when the Asylum Department of the BiH Ministry of Security took over the authority over RSD procedures, even though informally, 'mandate protections' were provided in the transition period up until 2006. This was due to the above-mentioned lack of state capacity to conduct RSD. The 'Memorandum of Understanding to Hand over Refugee Status Determination Process and Other Responsibilities Relating to Asylum' was signed on 29 December 2004 between UNHCR and the BiH Ministry of Security. It defines in detail the handover under the Act,

(since 2004). In this way the UNHCR has been the key actor in the establishment of asylum procedures in BiH. Its work is supplemented by the EU accession obligations of BiH.

Additionally, the provision of free legal aid by the UNHCR's partner NGOs has clearly contributed to the development of the asylum and refugee system in BiH, with the successful resolution of numerous cases before the Court of BiH, the BiH Constitutional Court, the Court of Human Rights in Strasbourg and the UN Human Rights Committee.[50]

B. Croatia

In order for individuals to gain access to the asylum system, it is important that their intention to seek protection once they arrive on state territory be recognised. Refugees can express their intention to apply for protection at the border crossing, or if they are already on Croatian territory, they can do so at police stations and/or the detention centre for (irregular) migrants.[51] According to the Act on International and Temporary Protection(AITP) (Article8),[52] a third country national or stateless person who has illegally entered 'shall not be punished for his/her illegal entry or stay provided that he/she expresses an intention to apply for international protection without delay and shows good cause for his/her illegal entry or stay'. However, the Act does not specify the exact duration of 'delay'. Regardless of this provision, many asylum seekers who entered the country illegally in the first few years after the Act came into power were sanctioned.[53] Croatia registered the largest number of irregular migrants in transit through the country in the period 1998–2001, and it is reasonable to assume that some of them needed protection. It is difficult to assess the extent to which the state violated the *non-refoulement* principle in that period, but it is certain that the Ministry of Interior (MoI)

Rule Book and Procedural Standards for Refugee Status Determination under the UNHCR's Mandate.

[50] See the following judgments of the Court of Bosnia and Herzegovina relating to violation of asylum seekers rights: U-769/08 (6 April 2009); U-485/09 (17 June 2010); S1 3 U 003543 10 U (25 February 2011). See the decisions of the European Court of Human Rights (ECtHR) in *Al Hanchi v Bosnia and Herzegovina*, App no 48205/09 (ECtHR, 15 November 2011) para 33; *Al Husin v BiH*, App no 3727/08 (ECtHR, 7 February 2012).

[51] The problems asylum seekers face in expressing an intention to apply for asylum are also addressed in Iván, ch 3 (Hungary) and Pollet, ch 7 (EU).

[52] MOI, 'Act on International and Temporary Protection 2015' (2 July 2015) www.refworld.org/docid/4e8044fd2.html.

[53] G Lalić Novak, 'Ograničenje slobode kretanja tražitelja azila: zaštitna mjera ili kazna' (2013b) 29(3–4) *Pravni vjesnik* 139.

relatively frequently detained and expelled irregular migrants (and potential asylum seekers) before the Asylum Act entered into force.[54]

The premise that Croatia might soon join Schengen is leading the state to invest in 'securitisation' policies. Examples of heightened security measures noted so far include the purchase of hi-tech border surveillance equipment, an increase in the number of border guards, and the scheduled 2015 opening of two additional reception (ie detention) centres for irregular migrants.[55] Besides detaining and returning irregular migrants, these transit processing centres, which are located near the border, will predominantly conduct accelerated procedures rejecting 'manifestly unfounded asylum applications' (as enabled by Article 61 of the Asylum Act). Hence, migration management and border control measures for preventing irregular migration not only affect potential asylum seekers' access to Croatian territory, but could also limit their access to a fair asylum procedure.

The fact that there were relatively few asylum seekers in the first years of the Croatian asylum system may be related to the border police's lack of knowledge and experience in recognising possible victims of persecution as persons in need of protection.[56] According to a report on border police practices towards irregular migrants, conducted from 2008–12,[57] border monitoring observers recorded no cases of violations of fundamental human rights of irregular migrants and asylum seekers. This might suggest that over time police officers have become more skilled, and that they are now able to better recognise asylum seekers' intention to request protection.

Today's challenges in terms of access to the asylum system largely relate to fulfilling the obligations of the Dublin Regulation[58] and bilateral readmission agreements by returning or taking irregular migrants and asylum seekers, as well as providing them with access to asylum. These policies could result in renouncing border police responsibility for the admittance of persons to Croatian territory and access to procedure. In a recent ethnographic study, one respondent confirmed that he did not have problems

[54] Novak, above n 23.

[55] Croatian Law Centre, 'Mixed Migration Flows in the Republic of Croatia: State of Play, Trends and Challenges'(2013) www.hpc.hr/download.aspx?f=dokumenti/Razno/Mixed-migrationflowsintheRepublicofCroatia_1.pdf

[56] See discussion of this in context of Hungary in Iván, ch3.

[57] The project examined files on conduct, access to the asylum procedure, and the implementation of bilateral readmission agreements. One of the conclusions was that all migrants who expressed their intention to seek asylum were identified by police officers who conducted informative interviews, and all persons were given access to the Croatian asylum system: Croatian Law Centre, above n 55, 8.

[58] See above n 26.

accessing the asylum system per se, but he was subjected to state disputes over shifting jurisdiction:[59]

> In August 2012, I made [applied for] asylum in Slovenia. Three months later, one investigator from the Slovenian Ministry of Interior told me, 'There is a problem because they [we] want to send you back to Croatia.'… I asked, 'Why are you sending me back to Croatia?', and they said, 'Because they [we] think there is no way to go [to come] to Slovenia, you must pass through Croatia.' … And at the border, the Croatian border, they refused to take me here … And they said, these Croatian border police officers, they said, 'You didn't pass by us, and we will not accept you here, You must go back to Slovenia!' And the police took me back to Slovenia … Maybe one week or 10 days I stayed there and I woke one day in morning, and they told me, 'Now you will go to Croatia.' (male, 40)

Furthermore, Croatia follows minimal standards obligations stemming from the Procedure Directive,[60] but the duration of procedures and medical expertise during the interview phase poses particular problems. Upon registering their intention to seek asylum, persons are transferred to the reception centre for asylum seekers, except in cases where they request protection when intercepted in illegal border-crossing or irregular stay, and/or without documents, in which case they are placed in the detention centre. The asylum procedure begins with the submission of an asylum application, and the MoI conducts an interview with the asylum seeker. While initial medical examinations are carried out as soon as migrants arrive at the centre, doctors do not produce written reports detailing whether asylum seekers were victims of torture or inhumane and degrading treatment, though such information could later be used as supporting evidence in procedure.[61]

Free legal aid to asylum seekers includes information, legal counselling, and free legal assistance which 'shall be provided by organisations working to protect the rights of refugees or by attorneys with whom the Ministry shall conclude an agreement on the provision of legal counselling' (AITP, Article 59). Legal assistance means preparation of a complaint and representation before the Administrative Court. In practice, legal information and legal aid are provided by a national implementing partner of the UNHCR (similar to the situation in BiH, described above), primarily by the NGO, Croatian Law Centre. Though the first instance decision should be made within six months, there have been cases where applicants had to wait for more than two years for the final—most often

[59] The data provided here are part of the ongoing research project, 'Why Croatia? Reasons for Choosing Croatia as the Country of Asylum' by the Norwegian University of Science and Technology, Trondheim, together with the Institute for Migration and Ethnic Studies, Zagreb, and the Centre for Peace Studies, Zagreb, above n 37.

[60] See above n 26.

[61] Croatian Law Centre, above n 55, 14.

negative—decision.[62] This occurred regardless of the fact that the asylum system was not burdened with many applications in the early years following the enactment of the Asylum Act, and the Department for Asylum recruited additional decision-makers in 2011. This problem was also emphasised by one respondent:

> And one most important thing is the time they take to make decisions over people. They should have to try to make decisions in very short time. Not to [make us] wait this long. If you have someone who you keep waiting for two years for decision and then got negative… This is how you destroy [someone's] life. (male, 32)

There have been a number of institutional changes to RSD in Croatia. The MoI Department of Asylum decides on asylum applications at first instance. The second Asylum Act entered into force in January 2008, and it introduced subsidiary protection and the Commission for Asylum, a more independent appellate body. However, the Commission for Asylum was abolished at the beginning of 2012 (due to European Commission demand).[63] Thus, the Administrative Court became the only independent second instance appellate body in the asylum procedure. This is despite the fact that it lacked the requisite experience and specialisation in asylum case law—a matter reflected in the level of protection recognition rates, which we will now discuss.

IV. ENABLING PROTECTION: REFUGEES' RECOGNITION RATES

This section addresses the low refugee recognition rates which characterise the WB region.

A. Bosnia and Herzegovina

BiH is characterised by low refugee application rates. For instance, there were only 3,614 asylum applications lodged in BiH in the 13-year period

[62] E Bužinkić, J Kranjec and D Županić-Iljić, *Usklađenost zakonodavstva i prakse hrvatskih institucija s europskom pravnom stečevinom u području azila i neregularnih migracija* (Zagreb, Centar za mirovne studije, 2010).

[63] '[A]ccording to the EU Common Position in Chapter 24: Justice, Freedom and Security of September 2009, one of the benchmarks for the provisional closing of pre-accession negotiations in this chapter was also related to the area of asylum, and included ensuring access to fully functioning asylum procedures for all third country applicants wishing to apply for international protection. Since, in order to meet this benchmark, it was necessary to establish a completely independent appellate body and an effective legal remedy': Croatian

between 2001 and 2014.[64] Despite the massive inflows of refugees from Syria to Europe, in 2014, only 45 individuals sought international protection in BiH.

Refugee recognition statistical data indicate worrying and restrictive RSD practice in BiH. Between 2001 and 2006, when all applications received were decided by the UNHCR, 390 applicants were recognised as refugees.[65] Recognition rates have dropped since the competent authorities of Bosnia and Herzegovina[66] took over authority for RSD in 2006: from 1 January 2005–31 December 2014, of the 1,270 individuals who sought asylum in BiH, less than 1 per cent of those were granted international protection.[67] In addition, the rejection rate is quite high (51 per cent), as is the rate of interrupted, that is, cancelled procedures (40 per cent).[68] So far children in the procedure were mainly minors seeking asylum from the territory of WB (Kosovo and Republic of Serbia). However, the number of asylum seekers from Syria and Afghanistan has increased since 2012[69] among them also minor school age asylum seekers. This increase is a result of a greater inflow of nationals from the Syrian Arab Republic.

The reasons given for rejecting applications for international protection include lack of legal reasons and abuse of process. For instance, in 2013, the main reason given for rejecting applications for international protection[70] was lack of grounds under Article 110, Paragraph 1 of the Law on Movement and Stay of Aliens and Asylum (insufficient legal basis for grant of international protection).[71] The next most common reason for rejecting the

Law Centre, 'National Report on the Asylum System from 2010 to 2012' (2013) www.hpc.hr/download.aspx?f=dokumenti/Razno/Nationalreportonasylumsystem.pdf.

[64] MoS, above n 18, 44–45.

[65] From 2004–06, the UNHCR recognised the refugee status of 211 persons (2004: 41 persons, 2005: 163 persons, 2006: seven persons) as noted in Ministry of Security Immigration Department (MoSID), 'Migration Profile of Bosnia and Herzegovina for the Year 2009' (Sarajevo, March 2010) www.mhrr.gov.ba/iseljenistvo/Publikacije/MigrationProfile2010ENGLISHFINAL.pdf, 44.

[66] The Ministry of Security Sector for Asylum.

[67] Refugee status was granted to only 15 individuals, and subsidiary protection to 66 persons. Of the total number of recognised refugees, five persons were from Palestine, four from the Syrian Arab Republic, and one person each from Serbia, Montenegro, Saudi Arabia, Sri Lanka, Cameroon and Myanmar: MoSID, above n 65, 41–42, and MoSID, 'Migration Profile of Bosnia and Herzegovina for the Year 2014' (Sarajevo, May 2015) www.msb.gov.ba/PDF/MIGRATIONI_PROFILE_2014_E.pdf, 44.

[68] In 2013, 27 applications from 36 persons were ceased for the following reasons: the applicants left or attempted to leave BiH (19 applications for 19 persons), reasons prescribed by the Law on Administrative Procedure (seven applications for 16 persons) and the application submitted by the BiH national (one application for one person): MoSID, above n 65, 45.

[69] From 40 to 73 applications in 2013.

[70] Sixteen applications on behalf of 16 persons.

[71] This ground was cited in relation to 11 of the applications (68.75%) rejected in 2013.

applications was 'an obvious deception or abuse of process'.[72] Other reasons for rejecting applications for international protection are as follows: the request is based on economic reasons (one application); the request is contradictory, unbelievable and inconsistent (one application) and for exclusion from international protection status (one request).

In BiH, asylum seekers have no right to appeal from an asylum decision made by the Ministry of Security (MoS), although they may file an administrative lawsuit with the Court of BiH within 60 days to review the decision of this authority.[73] Under Article 109(9) of the MSAAA, filing a lawsuit postpones the enforcement of a binding decision, which also affects the deportation of the applicant. In legal matters relating to accessing other rights of asylum seekers and persons granted international protection, the applicants may appeal. The appellate body in such cases is the Appeals Council under the BiH Council of Ministers. In practice, there was a question of whether this body had appellate jurisdiction over matters other than the subject-matter of the cases in asylum proceedings (international protection claims). However, this dilemma was clarified when the Appeals Council under the Council of Ministers handed down a decision on the first appeal filed in the proceedings on the rights of the applicants seeking international protection.[74]

It is evident that the asylum system in BiH was developed in a context in which the state authorities were ill-prepared to take over RSD from the UNHCR in 2004. As a result, there were a number of unresolved issues regarding the content of asylum law and the institutional authority of the Appeals Council. Consequently, procedures were prolonged and there have been low rates of recognition of refugee status and complementary protection until the present day.[75]

B. Croatia

In Croatia, still burdened with its own IDPs, Bosnian refugees and returnees during and after the 1990s war, the MoI and misdemeanour courts were unwilling and ill-equipped to grant the individual protections guaranteed by the 1991 Aliens Act. The external pressure to do so came only

[72] This ground was cited in relation to a total of two asylum seekers (12.5%) of applicants in 2013.

[73] In the case of 'manifestly unfounded claims', the deadline for filing an appeal with the Court of BiH is eight days.

[74] Decision on the Appeals Council under the BiH Council of Ministers, 01-07-13/09 (29 May 2009).

[75] MoS, above n 18.

after the beginning of Croatia's negotiation process with the EU. From 1997, when the first (individual) claim for asylum was registered, to 1 July 2004, when the first Asylum Act entered into force, 362 asylum requests were registered, yet there were no cases of protection granted.[76]

Regardless of the legal and institutional framework that was established, Croatia began to offer protection to a significant and gradually increasing number of applicants more recently.[77] In the last decade (July 2004–July 2015), 4,885 asylum seekers from more than 80 countries have applied for protection.[78] After a number of years with low application rates (100–200), there has been a steep increase in the number of asylum seekers in Croatia in the years prior to joining the EU: in 2011 there were only 807 asylum seekers, rising to 1,089 in 2013.[79] Whilst this is significantly lower than in other EU countries, it is higher than historical rates for Croatia. However, in 2014 there were only 453 asylum seekers (representing a 60 per cent decrease compared to 2013). This suggests that by entering the EU, Croatia has not become a 'more preferred' destination to others in the region. Instead, more pressure is being put on Hungary as the closest point of entering the Schengen zone over the Balkan route, as has been evidenced in the mass influx of 2015, before the country closed its borders. This does not appear to have changed in 2015: from January–September 2015 there were only 152 asylum applicants in Croatia, which suggests a continuing trend towards falling numbers of asylum applications in that country.[80] According to the UNHCR report, Croatia is 30th out of 44 'industrialized countries' in terms of the number of registered asylum requests (BiH is 41st).[81]

There has also been some change in the refugee cohort. While initially most asylum seekers were nationals of Serbia, Kosovo and Turkey,

[76] S Božić, 'Strengthening Cross Border Cooperation in the Western Balkans Regarding Migration Management' in V Petronijević (ed), *Migration flows in Southeastern Europe: A Compendium of National Perspectives* (Belgrade, Sinag, 2007) 13–42.

[77] This process included two CARDS twinning projects with colleges from Slovenia and Germany, and later programmes co-ordinated by Hungarian and Dutch immigration authorities. These programmes fostered direct institutional learning through a series of training sessions, consultations, co-operation and experience sharing with the Croatian MoI in the area of visa policy, asylum, migration and border control.

[78] UNHCR, 'Statistical Summary on Asylum Seekers in Republic of Croatia 2004–2015' (2015) www.unhcr.hr/media/com_form2content/documents/c2/a54/f9/Asylum%20Total.xls.

[79] UNHCR, above n 78.

[80] MoI, 'Statistički pokazatelji tražitelja međunarodne zaštite za treće tromjesečje 2015' (2015) www.mup.hr/UserDocsImages/Dokumenti/stranci/2015/trazitelji_medunarodne_zastite_12_10_15.pdf.

[81] UNHCR, 'Asylum Trends 2014: Levels and Trends in Industrialized Countries' (2015) www.unhcr.org/551128679.html, 20.

nowadays they are mostly from Afghanistan, Syria, Somalia, Algeria, Pakistan, Palestine, Iran and Tunisia. Over 80 per cent of registered applicants were young adult males.[82] The number of unaccompanied minor irregular migrants is increasing, as well as the number of minors seeking asylum (391 in the period 2009–14).[83] This reflects broader trends in the cohort of individuals seeking protection in the EU/worldwide.

Like BiH, refugee recognition rates are low. For instance, from July 2004–December 2014, only 133 persons were granted protection: 73 recognised as refugees, and 60 granted subsidiary protection status.[84] Non-state actors (the UNHCR, NGOs) have criticised the fact that only one person was granted asylum in the first four years of the asylum system (2004–07), and have interpreted this as sign that governmental policies for granting protection were restrictive and rigid.[85] However, the official (governmental) position of the MoI remains that 'our [Croatian] practices in asylum procedures characterizes [migrants'] abuse of the institute of asylum'.[86] This attitude is a reaction to the fact that most asylum seekers express their intention to apply for protection after being intercepted illegally crossing the border, during an unregulated stay in the country, or while waiting for the decision on expulsion in the reception (detention) centre for foreigners.

On the other hand, an average 80 per cent of applicants leave the country during the procedure and before a final decision has been made, which results in the suspension of procedures.[87] These facts serve to support the Government's argument that Croatia is still primarily a transit country for mixed flows of migrants and asylum seekers on their way to Western European countries, which was demonstrated by the mass influx of refugees in 2015. However, this alone cannot justify the relatively low number of recognised cases (2.5 per cent in 2013, compared to 34 per cent

[82] MoI, 'Statistički podaci o tražiteljima azila za 2014. godinu' (2015) www.mup.hr/UserDocsImages/Dokumenti/stranci/2015/azil2014.pdf.

[83] The majority came from Afghanistan, Pakistan, Somalia and Algeria: R Kraljević, L Marinović and B Živković Žigante, 'Unaccompanied Migrant Children in Croatia' (Zagreb, UNHCR, 2011) www.refworld.org/docid/4f86a0e82.html; MoI, above n 82.

[84] The first refugee was recognised in 2006, but the rate of protections granted only began to rise from 2008 onwards, with two-thirds of all positive decisions (before the end of 2011) being made by the second instance (appeal) Commission for Asylum. From 2012–July 2014, the Administrative Court overruled negative MoI decisions in only two cases. Almost half of overall positive decisions were made in 2012 and 2013, right before entering the EU (UNHCR, above n 78).

[85] Bužinkić et al, above n 62.

[86] Government of the Republic of Croatia/Ministry of Interior, 'Dokumenti: Migracijska politika Republike Hrvatske' in A Milardović, *Stranci pred vratima Europe* (Zagreb, Pan liber, 2014) 199 [authors' translation].

[87] Croatian Law Centre, above n 55.

recognised in the EU as a whole),[88] neither in Croatia nor in BiH. According to the new European Agenda on Migration from May 2015, in the next 24 months Croatia is preparing its facilities in order to accept and accommodate 1,564 asylum seekers and refugees, through European schemes for relocation and resettlement.[89] This would pose further challenges for the inadequate integration system in Croatia.

V. RECEPTION CONDITIONS IN BOSNIA AND HERZEGOVINA AND CROATIA

A. Bosnia and Herzegovina

In addition to access to a well-functioning RSD procedure, the reception conditions for asylum seekers are an important element of access to asylum. In BiH, the Department for Refugees, Displaced Persons and Housing Policy[90] is responsible for ensuring important reception conditions including the exercise of the right to work, access to health care, social care and education, as well as other rights guaranteed by the MSAAA. These rights enable integration during the length of refugee or subsidiary protection status. Hence, the role of this Ministry in the asylum process becomes important from the moment the asylum application is accepted and refugee status or subsidiary protection granted.

The bureaucracy which handles reception conditions have issued rulebooks for this purpose. The Ministry of Security and the Ministry of Civil Affairs have issued rulebooks under which the persons with international protection are entitled to a travel document and an emergency travel document. On the other hand the Ministry of Human Rights and Refugees (MHRR) has produced rulebooks allowing persons recognised as protected in BiH to exercise other rights provided for in the Asylum

[88] According to Eurostat: A Bitoulas, 'Asylum Applicants and First Instance Decisions on Asylum Applications: 2013' (Data in Focus, Eurostat, 3/2014, 24 March 2014) www.ec.europa.eu/eurostat/en/web/products-data-in-focus/-/KS-QA-14-003.

[89] In July 2015 the EU Commissioners suggested a number of 40,000 Syrian refugees who would be relocated from Turkey to the EU countries. In September 2015, the European Commission adopted the EU Council's proposal for further relocation of a total of 120,000 applicants who could be assumed to have a clear need for international protection (nationals of Syria, Iraq and Eritrea) from Hungary, Greece and Italy: European Commission, 'Managing the Refugee Crisis: Immediate Operational, Budgetary and Legal Measures Under the European Agenda on Migration' (COM(2015) 490, Brussels, 29 September 2015). However, some states disapproved the proposed quota system and that throws doubt on its main purpose—sharing solidarity and responsibility for refugees' reception, fair RSD procedure and further integration in society.

[90] Operating within the Ministry of Human Rights and Refugees.

Act: the right to an identification document; the right to work; the right to education; the right to health and social care; and the right to register their civil status, including the birth of a child, marriage, etc.[91] Within this Ministry, the Department for Refugees, Displaced Persons and Housing Policy is to provide professional assistance to refugees in exercising and protecting their rights in BiH, and carry out duties related to the proper work of refugee centres, that is, it receives refugees and ensures conditions necessary for their accommodation and care in the centres. In practice, the MHRR is overburdened tackling the domestic displacement and returnee issues and provides very little and inadequate assistance to persons under international protection status.

The first reception centres providing accommodation to refugees and asylum seekers in BiH opened in 1998. Until recently the temporary asylum reception centre was located in a small village called Brnjaci, and it was there for over a year without having informed, let alone prepared, the local villagers of the presence of asylum seekers. The new centre, funded by the EU, although meeting European standards and other national legal regulations, is isolated, located 40km from Sarajevo (in Delijaš). The MHRR and the Ministry of Security are responsible for the management of the centres, while the UNHCR is co-financing and providing assistance for management and maintenance purposes. From observation undertaken in the immigration (detention) centre and the asylum reception centre (Brnjaci) and interviews with the asylum seekers, the following is noted regarding the reception services in BiH, and access to, or violation of, asylum seekers' rights:[92]

— two asylum seekers reported violation of their access to primary health. One of these was denied access to a doctor during a weekend, the second was denied access to a dentist in an emergency situation during his stay at the detention centre;
— ten asylum seekers interviewed mentioned a severe shortage of nutritious food, and noted that supplies meant for one week per person are made to last for a month;

[91] UNHCR and the Ministry of Human Rights and Refugees, 'Handbook on the Rights of Persons under International Protection in BiH' (Sarajevo, 2010) 17.

[92] The data provided here are part of the research conducted by Lucie Bacon, from the University of Poitiers, who was in February–March 2014 on an internship at Centre for Refugee and IDP studies (CESI) in Sarajevo. As part of her MA thesis research she conducted 22 interviews with different actors dealing with the irregular migrants, asylum seekers and refugee issues in BiH, including the state ministries, the UNHCR, the operating legal aid NGO and migration scholars in BiH. The purpose was to obtain first-hand information from the migrants, ie to meet with asylum seekers and refugees and to assess their needs and access to entitled rights.

— monthly financial allowances of €15 were not regularly distributed to asylum seekers, and all complained of not receiving their allowance for two or three months referring to corrupted management of the centre and even mobbing;
— all reported being deprived of social contact, meeting only other asylum seekers, migrants and very few local residents, most of whom were smugglers;
— there is no telephone inside the centre and no way of contacting other family members (though they use free internet in the local café);
— two reported lack of a prayer room and a disrespectful attitude to their religious duties/commitments from those in the asylum centre;
— all reported lack of information on the asylum procedure and access to free legal aid (except a brochure published in several languages). They meet with their lawyers very rarely (some asylum seekers saw their lawyers twice during a period of more than a year) and rarely knew the names of their lawyers. It was rare to meet anyone who had benefitted from the services of a translator;
— all informed us that upon being detected and arrested by BiH's border police or other police in the country, they were detained in the local police stations in very bad conditions (one testimony reveals sleeping on the floor and receiving no sustenance for three days, other than a cup of tea) before transfer to the immigration centre near Sarajevo, in Lukavica (Republika Srpska).

In addition, when an asylum seeker is found in BiH with no identification documents, temporary restrictions to his or her freedom of movement have been applied, a measure that is taken because of suspicion that asylum seekers are abusing the asylum process with fraudulent claims.[93] The freedom of movement of asylum seekers has most often been restricted by prohibiting their movement outside a reception facility which, as a rule, is the immigration centre (detention centre).

Between its opening in 2008, and 2012 there were 1,372 migrants detained in the immigration centre, and in 2012 the majority of those detained came from Kosovo, Afghanistan, Somalia, Turkey, Syria, Algeria and Pakistan. The majority of the asylum seekers interviewed in our study mentioned grim conditions, such as being stripped of rights, being given no information about basic rights, referring to harsh conditions of 'prison': 'right to go outside ten minutes each day; isolation cell; right to call family three minutes each week when police or security men agree'.

An interesting notion is that when compared to the asylum reception centre, the detention centre is perceived as being a better option. One

93 MSAAA, art 114(1)(c) and (e).

young informant from Algeria noted: 'In that prison we had everything but freedom, now we have freedom but there is nothing else for us, no food, no people to meet, nothing to do, no hope and home for us in Bosnia.'

In most cases the asylum seekers whose freedom of movement was restricted complained of violations of Article 5 of the European Convention on Human Rights (ECHR) and of Article II/3(d) of the BiH Constitution. The Court assessed the reasons for restricting applicants' freedom of movement but also how long this measure was imposed for, and the characteristics of the centre in which they were housed, and in most cases concluded that 'the restriction on the appellant's freedom of movement does not constitute deprivation of liberty under Article 5 of the European Convention.'[94]

The UNHCR points out that their key work in Bosnia is to 'strengthen asylum reception services and legal counselling' and work on 'full implementation of the law and the inclusion of reception services in State budget allocations in preparation for EU accession'[95] with the aim of 'reducing the use of detention for asylum-seekers'.[96] Given that the agency also continues working on provision and overseeing of the basic services to asylum seekers and recognised refugees so as to support their local integration, it is clear that RSD, reception and integration services in BiH are not yet fully developed and depend on continuous and systematic external capacity building and conditioning (EU requirements) in order to meet the protection and integration needs of asylum seekers and recognised refugees. We will now turn to discuss reception conditions in Croatia, which shares some of the challenges faced in BiH especially concerning the detention practices applied to asylum seekers.

B. Croatia

As well as deciding on applications at first instance, the MoI is also responsible for substantial procedural measures and requirements and for the management of reception conditions, as well as for further accommodation and housing of recognised refugees. Other ministries are responsible for other integration policies and the overall facilitation of the successful inclusion of refugees into society. Under the Asylum Act (Articles 40–51),

[94] Decision on Admissibility and the Merits of the BiH Constitutional Court, AP-4680/10 (22 March 2013) para 33. The conditions in the reception centre are considered by the Court to be substantially different from those in the immigration centre.

[95] UNHCR, 'Global Appeal 2013 Update—South-Eastern Europe' (2013) www.unhcr.org/50a9f82f3.pdf, 255.

[96] UNHCR, above n 2.

beneficiaries are entitled to rights on residence, accommodation (paid by the state for up to two years), work (without a work or business permit), health care (equivalent to the primary health care available for nationals), education (access to all levels of education under the same conditions as nationals), freedom of religion (including private religious upbringing of children), free legal aid, social welfare, maintenance of family unity and integration assistance.[97] In the context of the current adverse economic climate and state austerity policies, the state lacks sufficient financial means to properly implement these policies and measures.[98]

Regarding reception standards, a worrisome practice has been observed in the restriction of movement and detainment of asylum seekers. The first (temporary) reception centre for asylum seekers opened in 2006 and had a capacity of about 100 beds. Due to an increasing number of asylum seekers, this centre was overcrowded so the MoI opened a second (permanent) centre with a capacity of 600 beds in Zagreb in 2011. This new centre also serves as the registration centre and accommodates only single male and female asylum seekers, while the first centre (which was renovated) now accommodates families, minors and other vulnerable groups.[99] The reception centres provide accommodation, food, financial assistance, health care and basic living supplies. Both centres contain sports facilities and offer educational and integration activities. If asylum seekers have their own financial means, they are allowed to stay wherever they like in Croatia, though this must first be approved by the MoI.

However, like most countries, Croatia may choose to restrict asylum seekers' movement for a period of up to three months, which, if there are justified reasons, can then be extended for another three months. Asylum seekers may lodge complaints to the Administrative Court in order to contest the MoI's decision on restriction of movement. Placement in the detention centre should not be an obstacle to applying for asylum. However,

[97] Amendments to the Asylum Act in 2010, which provide persons under subsidiary protection with the same rights asylum grantees are guaranteed, including health care, state-funded housing and integration assistance.

[98] Aside from the lack of political will to tackle challenges in the area of refugees' integration, the general public tends to approach this issue with social distance towards refugees and ignorance of integration problems, fear of 'burdening the state-budget' or with latent hostility (Baričević, above n 23).

[99] Up until July 2014, unaccompanied minors were placed in a residential home for children and young people (intended for the re-socialisation of children with behavioural difficulties). This was unsuitable accommodation that did not take into account the special needs and vulnerability of these children (Kraljević et al, above n 83; Croatian Law Centre, above n 55). Moreover, the scheduled opening of a separate facility for minors and other vulnerable groups of irregular migrants within the existing detention centre in 2015 begs the question of whether putting children in a facility with the primary purpose of detaining and deporting irregular migrants is an adequate solution for their situation and condition, regarding the 'best interest of a child'.

persons applying for asylum sometimes spend the entire duration of the asylum determination procedure in detention, and this constitutes a breach of European standards.[100] Lalić Novak's research shows that 30 per cent of the total number of asylum seekers registered in 2012 spent time at the detention centre at some point of (or during the entire) procedure.[101]

In some cases when irregular migrants tried with misdemeanours for illegally entering or staying in the country were convicted and faced deportation, proceedings were conducted without the presence of a court interpreter, and the decisions were made in Croatian, pointing to a lack of qualified interpreters at many parts of procedure.[102] Since the irregular migrants could not understand the language used, this can be seen as an instance of hindering their access to the asylum system.[103] Although restraint should be a protective measure used only in exceptional cases,[104] the Asylum Act (Article 74) allows for it to be used for a variety of reasons, including determination of the asylum seeker's identity, and suspicion that the submitted asylum application constitutes fraud and misuse of the asylum procedure. These provisions mean that restriction of movement is in practice often used as a form of punishment for seekers whom authorities believe are abusing the asylum procedure to avoid deportation to their country of origin.[105] This interpretation of abuse on the part of the authorities is mostly because applicants submitted their asylum applications after being placed in the reception centre for aliens, while awaiting deportation.

The manner in which the state deals with rejected asylum seekers is an issue of particular concern. Once procedures are completed, asylum seekers who have been refused protection are issued with a decision that requires them to leave Croatia. They are most often unable to legally travel to a third country (in most cases, they do not have documents), and they cannot be deported either because of *non-refoulement* or because the state lacks the financial means to deport them. As concluded in the Croatian Law Centre report:

> [A]t the same time, Croatia does not have a system of assistance for refused asylum seekers nor can they regulate their status. Therefore, such persons are

[100] Croatian Law Centre, above n 55.

[101] Lalić Novak, above n 53, 149.

[102] UNHCR and IOM, 'Roundtable on Refugee Protection and International Migration in the Western Balkans: Suggestions for a Comprehensive Regional Approach (10–11 December 2013, Vienna, Austria)' (Summary Report, revised March 2014) 5, www.unhcr.org/531d8ad29.html.

[103] Croatian Law Centre, above n 55, 9.

[104] O Field, 'Alternatives to Detention of Asylum Seekers and Refugees' (UNHCR Legal and Protection Policy Research Series, POLAS/2006/03, April 2006) www.refworld.org/pdfid/4472e8b84.pdf.

[105] Lalić Novak, above n 23.

> often placed in the Reception [Detention] Centre for Aliens, or they are forced to illegally reside in Croatia or illegally migrate from Croatia.[106]

There is no legal remedy, legal aid or institutional solution for this problem, which leads to further secondary movements, so-called 'orbiting' of 'failed' asylum seekers, and other EU states' suspicions of 'asylum shopping'.

VI. DISCUSSION AND CONCLUSION

As security and the political situation gradually stabilised after the 1990s' dissolution of Yugoslavia and subsequent wars in the WB, the countries of the region transformed from refugee-producing countries into transit countries for refugees and, increasingly, a destination for refugees from other parts of the world. During the last two decades there has been a notable increase in the number of asylum applications in the region. However, inadequate asylum regimes mean that refugees move on before having their protection needs determined.[107] Today, despite the extensive capacity building efforts of international actors such as the UNHCR, most countries in the region do not have an effective administrative apparatus to grant refugees protection nor integration models in place to address the needs of newly arriving refugees and other groups with specific needs from outside the region.

This chapter analysed the main characteristics of the BiH and Croatian asylum systems as two of the countries in the region with different positions regarding the EU. First, we examined the development of the asylum systems in relation to the process of BiH and Croatia's accession to the EU. Here we found that both countries have adopted legislation in line with international norms, but implementation is often lacking or is inadequate and unsystematic. Many basic protection obligations are outsourced to the NGO sector and are highly dependent on the funding and support provided by the UNHCR. This cannot be a long-term solution for the asylum and integration capacities of the two countries.

As is evidenced by data presented, these states—whether they have recently joined the EU, as is the case with Croatia, or are candidate countries, such as BiH—still lack some of the legal prerequisites and many of institutional capacities that would allow for efficient means of refugee

[106] Croatian Law Centre, above n 55, 17.

[107] According to the UNHCR, of particular concern is the growing number of unaccompanied and/or separated children travelling irregularly: UNHCR, 'Subregional Operations Profile: South-Eastern Europe 2015' (2015) www.unhcr.org/pages/49e45b906.html.

protection and integration. The difficulties in applying for asylum at borders, inadequate reception conditions and the lack of procedural safeguards in the RSD process all pose serious challenges. In addition, exceptionally low rates of refugee recognition and asylum granted discourage those in need of protection. Asylum systems of the two countries thus remain unprepared for the potential rise in the number of new asylum seekers or mass influx situations.

We can anticipate even more challenges related to the implementation of the Dublin Regulation, concerning the irregular migrants who transit Croatian territory and travel further into the Schengen area in order to seek asylum in another Member State but who are returned (readmitted) to Croatia for further processing of asylum applications. The same will apply to asylum seekers who leave Croatia before the completion of the procedure and are later intercepted in the EU. These measures put pressure on migrants to apply for protection in Croatia instead of applying for asylum in countries with fully developed asylum systems. Furthermore, given that there are no systematic and coherent integration programmes and a lack of sufficient support services in both BiH and Croatia, living conditions are poor. It is also very clear from our findings that in the context of reduced economic conditions (with budget cuts and savings currently taking place), the two, as yet insufficiently developed, asylum systems have very limited capacity to ensure adequate protection and thus fail to follow minimum reception, procedural and quality standards. It is therefore not surprising that we have witnessed a trend of asylum seekers and asylum grantees voluntarily leaving the two countries and venturing further west to other EU countries.

In the period 1997–2010, Croatia registered only a small number of asylum applications per year. Any predictions that the number of asylum seekers would increase after Croatia's accession to the EU have also not been realised. Mixed migration flows of irregular migrants and asylum seekers increased significantly in 2011 and 2012, in both countries, but both actually *decreased* after Croatia joined the EU. An explanation for this may be the fact that asylum seekers are aware of the detention policies in BiH and the provisions of the Dublin System, which means that (in the case of Croatia) they must now rely on being granted protection in the country which may not be their preferred destination, but is the first point of entry into the EU.[108]

Furthermore, asylum seekers may also be reluctant to seek protection in BiH and Croatia based on information from compatriots about relatively

[108] In the same way, it may be predicted that the numbers of asylum seekers in Croatia, as well as in BiH, will rise again when Croatia applies for membership of the Schengen system.

restrictive status determination practices (which are reflected in relatively low recognition rates) and the lack of integration opportunities (reflected in deficiencies of protection quality standards in practice). A long detention period for asylum seekers who entered BiH illegally, as well as the construction of new transit centres in Croatia to carry out accelerated procedures, may further impede their access to territory and protection.

On the other hand, the situation in BiH is completely in compliance with the EU Directives. According to the state ministry,[109] there are two long-term goals for the asylum sector in BiH: (a) to develop a high-quality system in the area at a national level, with EU standards and the incorporation of international refugee law to enable the integration of BiH into the EU; and (b) active participation of BiH in defining policy and development of immigration and asylum at a regional level, based on defined standards of the EU.

However, it cannot be the case that the only factor encouraging the development of a fully efficient, fair and humane asylum system is external EU conditioning. As signatory states to the Refugee Convention, both states need to fulfil their obligations of international protection to persons seeking security from persecution. Therefore, based on the comparative analysis of the two asylum systems, the following recommendations for resolving the current inadequacies (and applicable to the wider WB countries) are put forward:

1. An effective mechanism of civil monitoring and supervising potential asylum seekers' access to territory and to the asylum system should be established, particularly on borders and as part of the detention centres' activities on deterrence, accelerated procedures and readmission/expulsion.
2. More work is needed on finding proper legal remedies and practical solutions for the problem of restriction of movement and detention of asylum seekers (during a part or the entirety of their application procedure) by using alternatives to detention, as proposed by Field.[110]
3. Proper reception conditions and accommodation standards should provide a safe and nurturing environment, especially for unaccompanied children, victims of torture and other vulnerable groups. Access to full medical and psychosocial care and rehabilitation programmes should also be available.
4. More comprehensive implementation and state-assisted integration measures are needed in order to facilitate refugees' inclusion in society. As a key prerequisite for the effectiveness of other integration measures, language courses should be provided for new persons

[109] MoS, above n 18.
[110] Field, above n 104.

under protection, as well as for those who previously had no access to language courses.

5. A model of assistance and fair treatment for refused asylum seekers should be devised, which either enables them to stay legally under some sort of temporary provision, or finds more durable solutions with help of the UNHCR and/or the European Asylum Support Office.
6. Although experience with 1990s refugees has not significantly influenced the development of integration policies in BiH or Croatia, since that experience was related to a culturally similar population, WB countries should 'capitalize on the experience accumulated over almost two decades of protecting and assisting persons forcibly displaced within the region',[111] but also experiences of refugees from the region successfully integrated in the EU and other asylum reception countries (over 50 per cent of BiH's total population resides abroad).[112]
7. A sustainable regional network of qualified interpreters should be established, especially to provide services remotely via Skype and other media in less common foreign languages, in order to avoid the current problems of inadequate access to interpreters during the asylum procedure.

Importantly, as a long-term investment in the improvement of the asylum system and the work of actors involved, it is crucial to conduct more research in this area so that evidence-based data may be produced, both to support government policies and programmes, but also the ways in which society delivers these services. Data are urgently required on:

— the social and legal situation of refugees and other vulnerable migrants in BiH and Croatia;
— the treatment of refugees and migrants by the BiH and Croatian authorities, NGOs and external actors;
— the conditions of BiH and Croatian detention centres and other holding places for refugees and other migrants in the country;
— the implementation of asylum and refugee rights in the two countries;
— access to protection, notably RSD procedures in BiH and Croatia;
— the legal, social, cultural and political needs of the client group in the areas of housing, health care, education, legal advice and public awareness (and all of these should be supported by testimonies from asylum seekers themselves).

[111] UNHCR and IOM, above n 102, 4.
[112] Ibid.

10

Access to Justice for Syrian Refugees in Lebanon

DALLAL STEVENS

I. INTRODUCTION

THIS COLLECTION IS concerned with access to asylum justice in the sense outlined in chapter one; that is, it focuses on the ability of protection seekers to overcome the physical obstacles to reaching territory as well as the legal, policy or political barriers to a quality asylum procedure. The majority of chapters have explored the interplay between law and asylum, largely focusing on restrictive interpretations of the law or the inability of asylum seekers and refugees to benefit from rights and entitlements provided by the law. The countries considered are all party to the 1951 UN Convention Relating to the Status of Refugees/1967 Protocol (Refugee Convention)[1] and they are therefore bound under international law to meet their obligations to refugees as set out in the Convention. Some, of course, have gone further and have established sophisticated refugee determination systems or constructed an architecture of asylum, ostensibly to provide asylum seekers and refugees with minimum standards of treatment.[2] Lebanon is different and the position of Syrian refugees in Lebanon is arguably unique. Alongside many of its Middle Eastern neighbours, it is not a signatory to the Refugee Convention or to the Protocol. It does not have a national asylum process and it has a very regional view towards the idea of the 'refugee' or those seeking protection within its borders. It is also an example of a developing, low income economy that has been obliged to handle enormous numbers of displaced people over a considerable period of time with limited and shrinking resources,

[1] 189 United Nations Treaty Series 150, supplemented by the 1967 Protocol relating to the Status of Refugees, 606 United Nations Treaty Series 267 (Refugee Convention).

[2] The EU is, of course, at the forefront of such an enterprise with its establishment of a Common European Asylum System (CEAS); see Pollet, ch 7 for discussion of the CEAS.

a public debt (as a ratio of Gross Domestic Product (GDP)) continuing to rise,[3] and enduring political instability.[4] The consequences have been extreme. This chapter will examine the Lebanese refugee context by outlining the legal background in relation to migration and border controls and exploring the handling of refugee arrivals with special reference to the recent Syrian conflict.

II. LEGAL BACKGROUND

Lebanon is not a party to the Refugee Convention and does not regard itself as a final destination for refugees. In 2003, the General Security Office in the Ministry of Interior agreed a Memorandum of Understanding (MOU) with the UNHCR in which this position was acknowledged.[5] Similar to arrangements with other countries in the region, the Memorandum also accorded the UNHCR the responsibility for conducting refugee status determination (RSD) with the specific obligation that it resettle any refugees within six months, extendable to nine months.[6] This is seldom achieved.[7] The MOU acknowledges that 'Lebanon is not an asylum country' and that 'the only viable durable solution for refugees recognized under the mandate of UNHCR is the resettlement in a third country'.[8] Furthermore, there is no specific recognition of the principle of *non-refoulement* in the MOU.[9] The UNHCR is of the view that the Memorandum 'was not designed to respond to a situation of such a large number of refugees and asylum-seekers, as were generated by the conflict in Iraq'.[10] Equally,

[3] At end of 2015, it stood at 148.7%: The World Bank, 'Countries: Lebanon, Overview' (Beirut, 1 April 2016) www.worldbank.org/en/country/lebanon/overview#1.

[4] Y Trofimov, 'Political Deadlock Leaves Lebanon to Unravel' (The Wall Street Journal, 5 May 2016).

[5] See UNHCR, 'Submission by the UNHCR for the Office of the High Commissioner for Human Rights' Compilation Report—Universal Periodic Review: The Republic of Lebanon' (Human Rights Liaison Unit, Division of International Protection, April 2010) lib.ohchr.org/HRBodies/UPR/Documents/Session9/LB/UNHCR_HighCommissionerforRefugees.pdf, para 1; See also UNHCR and General Security Office, 'The Memorandum of Understanding between the Directorate of the General Security (Republic of Lebanon) and the Regional Office of the UN High Commissioner for Refugees, Concerning the Processing of Cases of Asylum-Seekers Applying for Refugee Status with the UNHCR Office' (9 September 2003). There is no available copy of the MOU in English but a summary of the MOU exists: Frontiers Center, 'Lebanon–UNHCR Memorandum of Understanding' (Beirut, November 2003).

[6] UNHCR, above n 5, 1. Note that an alternative analysis of the MOU states that the UNHCR has up to 12 months to resettle: Frontiers, 'Legality vs Legitimacy: Detention of Refugees and Asylum Seekers in Lebanon—Legal Study' (Beirut, Frontiers Association, May 2006) 9.

[7] eg in 2009 the UNHCR resettled 2900 people: ibid.

[8] Frontiers Center, above n 5, 2.

[9] ibid.

[10] UNHCR, above n 5, 1.

and importantly, it has not been applied to the Syrian influx on the request of the Government of Lebanon. Consequently, there were discussions in 2013 to agree a new and more appropriate Memorandum but none materialised, and the will for reform on the part of the Government has now dissipated.[11]

Palestinian refugees are dealt with under a separate regime from non-Palestinians, with the creation in 1959 of the Department of Palestinian Refugee Affairs in the Ministry of Interior (changed to the Department of Political and Refugee Affairs in 2000), which was to work closely with the UN Relief and Works Agency for Palestine Refugees in the Near East (UNRWA).[12] Their objectives were to provide assistance to refugees; examine passport requests and deliver necessary documents relating to personal status; authorise marriages between a Palestinian refugee and Lebanese citizen; and authorise the movement or resettlement between camps.[13] The legal status of Palestinians in Lebanon has remained problematic since their arrival from the 1940s onwards and they are regarded as foreigners for the purposes of domestic law (see below).

Lebanon has signed a number of international human rights law instruments. Of particular relevance in the context of asylum are the 1966 International Covenant on Civil and Political Rights (ICCPR) and 1966 International Covenant on Economic, Social and Cultural Rights, the 1979 Convention on the Elimination of all Forms of Discrimination Against Women, the 1990 Convention on the Rights of the Child, the 1984 Convention Against Torture and Other Cruel, Inhuman or Degrading Treatment or Punishment (CAT), the 1965 International Convention on the Elimination of All Forms of Racial Discrimination; the 1994 Arab Charter on Human Rights;[14] and the 1965 Casablanca Protocol for the Treatment of Palestinians in Arab States. The Lebanese Constitution of 1926 (as amended) is particularly interesting in its explicit commitment to human rights principles. The preamble states: 'Lebanon … abides by its covenants and by the Universal Declaration of Human Rights. The Government shall embody these principles in all fields and without exception.'[15] Thus, there

[11] UNHCR, 'Global Appeal 2013 Update: Lebanon' (UNHCR, 2013).

[12] Decree Nos 927 of 1959 and 4082 of 2000. See S Shafie, 'Palestinian Refugees in Lebanon' (Expert Guides, Forced Migration Online, July 2007) www.forcedmigration.org/research-resources/expert-guides/palestinian-refugees-in-lebanon/fmo018.pdf; International Federation for Human Rights, 'Report of the Investigative International Mission: Lebanon—Palestinian Refugees: Systematic Discrimination and Complete Lack of Interest on the Part of the International Community' (Paris, FIDH, No 356/2, March 2003) www.refworld.org/publisher,IFHR,LBN,46f1467f0,0.html.

[13] International Federation for Human Rights, above n 12, 10.

[14] The League of Arab States adopted the Charter in 1994 but it has never come into force.

[15] Preamble, para (B). For a copy of the Constitution see www.presidency.gov.lb/English/LebaneseSystem/Documents/Lebanese%20Constitution.pdf.

is implicit acceptance of 'the right to seek and to enjoy asylum in other countries asylum from persecution' as provided by Article 14(1) of the 1948 Universal Declaration of Human Rights. However, it should be noted that, despite international law taking precedence over domestic law in accordance with the Lebanese Constitution, this is seldom adhered to by the Lebanese courts,[16] and as will become clear in the discussion in this chapter, the fundamental 'right to seek asylum' in Lebanon is now arguably under threat.

Lebanon has no asylum-specific law. Again, mirroring its Levantine neighbours—Jordan and Syria—, it does have immigration law with asylum provisions. These are: the Law Regulating the Entry and Stay of Foreigners in Lebanon and their Exit from the Country 1962 and the Minister of the Interior's Decision No 320 of 2 August 1962 on the control of entry and exit from Lebanese border posts.[17] The 1963 Law contains a Chapter (VIII) on political asylum (*Le droit d'asile politique*), with Article 26 stating specifically that 'Every foreigner who is persecuted or sentenced for a political crime outside Lebanon, or whose life or liberty is threatened on account of political activity, may apply for asylum in Lebanon'.[18] *Non-refoulement* of a 'former political refugee' is prohibited.[19] Interestingly, the Law includes a very basic asylum process according to which a Committee, comprising the Minister of the Interior and the Directors of the Ministries of Justice, Foreign Affairs and General Security, is empowered to grant asylum.[20] The Committee's decision is final and there is no right of appeal, even where there has been an abuse of power.[21] It appears that the grant of asylum through this mechanism has only been used once.[22]

Finally, insofar as Syria is concerned, there is a Treaty of Brotherhood, Cooperation and Coordination between the Syrian Arab Republic and the Lebanese Republic[23] and a number of bilateral agreements agreed between

[16] UNHCR, above n 11.

[17] Liban: Loi du 1962 réglementant l'entrée et le séjour des étrangers au Liban ainsi que leur sortie de ce pays, Bulletin de Législation Libanaise (Journal Officiel) No 28-1962, 10 July 1962 www.refworld.org/docid/3ae6b4f30.html.

[18] 'Tout étranger faisant l'objet d'une poursuite ou d'une condamnation de la part d'une autorité non libanaise pour cause d'un crime politique, ou dont la vie ou la liberté est menacée, également pour des causes politiques, peut demander le droit d'asile politique au Liban.'

[19] Article 31: 'En cas d'expulsion d'un ancien réfugié politique, celui-ci ne pourra être conduit sur le territoire d'un pays où sa vie ou sa liberté est menacée.'

[20] Article 27.

[21] Article 27.

[22] Frontiers, above n 6, 15; Lebanese Centre for Human Rights, 'Asylum Seekers and Refugees in Lebanon: Languishing in Injustice' (Beirut, CLDH, 31 March 2011) 6.

[23] 22 May 1991, UN Treaty Series, www.peacemaker.un.org/sites/peacemaker.un.org/files/LB-SY_910522_TreatyBrotherhoodCooperationCoordination.pdf.

Syria and Lebanon that privileged the movement of peoples between the two countries, until recently. For example, Article 1 of the 1993 Agreement for Economic and Social Cooperation and Coordination between Lebanon and Syria enshrines the 'Freedom of persons' movement between both countries' and the 'Freedom to stay, work, employ and practise economic activity in conformity with the laws and regulations in force in each country'.[24] The 1994 Agreement in the Field of Labour between the Governments of Lebanon and Syria supplements these commitments by guaranteeing that 'Workers of each of the two States shall enjoy in the other State the same treatment, privileges, rights and obligations, according to the laws, regulation and directives applied in both states'.[25] The practical effect of these arrangements was that Syrians, including Palestinians based in Syria,[26] could enter Lebanon with their identity cards and movement across the border was for many years regular and generally unproblematic.

While favouring migration for work, these legal structures have not provided a strong framework for the protection of refugees and their rights. Rather, as will be shown, formal and informal policy plays a primary and significant role in approaches to foreigners and refugees in Lebanon.

III. REFUGEE PRESENCE, POLICY AND ACCESS TO PROCESS

Like many countries in the region, Lebanon has a long history of refugee arrivals, the major groups being Palestinians in 1948, 1967 and in the 1990s, Iraqis in the 1980s and 2000s, and Syrians from 2011 onwards.[27] On 31 March 2016, there were 1,048,275 registered Syrian refugees in Lebanon.[28] In addition to this, there were an estimated 450,000 Palestine refugees, 42,000 Palestine refugees from Syria (PRS), and about 6,000 Iraqi refugees.[29] In a population of 5.98 million, based on the latest United Nations (UN)

[24] For an informal English version of the agreement, see www.syrleb.org/docs/agreements/03SOCIAL_ECONOMICeng.pdf.

[25] Article 4. For an informal English version of the agreement, see www.syrleb.org/docs/agreements/11LABOR_AGREEMENTeng.pdf.

[26] Under Syrian Arab Republic Law No 260 of 1957, Palestinians living in Syria have the same duties and responsibilities as Syrian nationals, excluding nationality and political rights: Shafie, above n 12.

[27] S Herbert, 'Responding to the Syrian Refugee Crisis in Lebanon: Lessons Learned' (Helpdesk Research Report, GSDRC, 14 August 2013) 3.

[28] Inter-agency Information Sharing Portal, 'Syrian Regional Refugee Response' (UNHCR, 2016) www.data.unhcr.org/syrianrefugees/country.php?id=122.

[29] European Commission Humanitarian Aid and Civil Protection, 'Lebanon: Syria Crisis' (Echo Factsheet, Brussels, May 2016) www.ec.europa.eu/echo/files/aid/countries/factsheets/lebanon_syrian_crisis_en.pdf.

estimates, this equates to 25.8 per cent. Lebanon is therefore currently experiencing the highest per-capita concentration of refugees in the world.[30] However, caution about refugee statistics should be exercised, particularly in relation to the numbers of Palestinians. As Sulieman notes,

> There are no accurate or reliable figures for the actual numbers of Palestinians in Lebanon. Because of the country's delicate sectarian structure, any one figure has political implications for its potential impact on Lebanon's 'demographic balance'.[31]

What these statistics do show, however, is that Lebanon has largely adopted what is termed an 'open-door policy' to those forced to flee across the border into the country. Indeed, even the Shiite Muslim party, Hezbollah, urged the Lebanese in 2013 'to welcome refugees regardless of sect or politics'.[32] Considering that Syrians are mainly Sunni Muslims, this was certainly a bold statement.

A. Palestinians

The history of Palestinians in Lebanon is long and complex and has been through periods of welcome, dialogue, discrimination and restriction. The Government of Lebanon is accused of applying both a policy of 'containment' of Palestinians[33] and 'discriminatory measures against the refugees, some of which verge on collective punishment'.[34] At present, about 53 per cent of Palestinians live in the country's 12 authorised refugee camps, but also in many unofficial areas of the country.[35] While the UNRWA is charged with providing assistance and protection to registered Palestine refugees, conditions and access to rights and services have long been very poor.[36] For example, Palestinians are restricted from working in the public

[30] ibid.

[31] J Suleiman, 'Marginalised Community: The Case of Palestinian Refugees in Lebanon' (Development Research Centre of Migration, Globalisation and Poverty, University of Sussex, April 2006). An example is the difference in the numbers of PRS—the figure provided by the European Commission is 42,000 while UNRWA provides a figure of 53,070 in April 2014: UNRWA, 'PRS in Lebanon' (April 2014) www.unrwa.org/prs-lebanon.

[32] A Barnard, 'Swollen with Syrian Refugees, Lebanon Feels its Stitching Fray' (The New York Times, 23 February 2013).

[33] Herbert, above n 27, 3.

[34] N Saghieh, 'Manufacturing Vulnerability in Lebanon: Legal Policies as Efficient Tools of Discrimination' (*The Legal Agenda*, 19 March 2015).

[35] For further information see UNRWA, 'Where We Work' (1 July 2014) www.unrwa.org/where-we-work/lebanon; J Suleiman, 'Marginalised Community: The Case of Palestinian Refugees in Lebanon; Lebanon Crisis Response Plan 2015–16' (15 December 2015).

[36] For a recent report on the situation see J Chaaban, N Salti, H Ghattas, A Irani, T Ismail and L Batlouni, 'Survey on the Socioeconomic Status of Palestine Refugees in Lebanon 2015' (American University of Beirut/ UNRWA, 3 June 2016).

sector and in certain professions, such as medicine, law or engineering, and are not treated on the same basis as other foreigners living and working in Lebanon; they do not have access to the public school system in Lebanon and, instead, must attend one of the 67 UNRWA schools (though 50 per cent of schools have reportedly been impacted by armed conflict and violence over the past five years).[37] This contributes to a situation in which, according to the UNRWA, 'Lebanon has the highest percentage of Palestine refugees living in abject poverty'.[38]

Such a challenging context was always going to prove difficult for PRS seeking to gain entry to Lebanon and, indeed, this has proved to be the case. While they were admitted early on in the Syrian conflict on the same basis as other Syrians, the policy soon altered, and by 2013, the Government was reviewing its stance. In August 2013, the border authorities started to enforce new practices of entry for PRS. They were only permitted to enter Lebanon in certain circumstances if they had one of the following: a valid pre-approved visa that required a guarantor in Lebanon to apply; a valid visa and ticket to a third country; a scheduled medical or embassy appointment; or if it could be proved that a family member was already legally resident in Lebanon.[39] According to a study undertaken on Syrian refugees in the Levant, '[t]he practice was plagued by arbitrary delays and refusals of entry by the General Security Office. UNRWA sought to monitor and intervene to prevent arbitrary denials of entry by placing observers at the border crossing with the highest traffic.'[40] The border was effectively closed to most PRS by April 2014, thereby revoking the so-called 'open-door' policy. In a show of intent, the authorities acted on the new policy immediately. Amnesty International reported that on 4 May 2014, 40 PRS, who 'had been arrested and detained at Beirut airport on 3 May 2014, along with several other people, for allegedly holding forged identity documents' were forcibly returned to Syria.[41] Following an international outcry, the Lebanese Minister of Interior, Machnouk, issued a statement on 8 May in which he stated that that 'there is no decision preventing Palestinian refugees in Syria from entering Lebanon and passing through the country'.[42] Machnouk also announced new regulations for the

[37] OCHA, 'Humanitarian Bulletin—Lebanon' (Issue 19, 1–31 May 2016).

[38] UNRWA, above n 35.

[39] Amnesty International, 'Denied Refuge: Palestinians from Syria Seeking Safety in Lebanon' (Amnesty International Publications, 1 July 2014) 11; see also Boston University Law Students, 'Protecting Syrian Refugees: Laws, Policies, and Global Responsibility Sharing' (Boston MA, Boston University School of Law, 2014) 37.

[40] Boston University Law Students, above n 39, 37.

[41] Amnesty International, above n 39, 13.

[42] V Rainey, 'Machnouk: New Entry Rule for Palestinians from Syria' (The Daily Star, 9 May 2014) www.dailystar.com.lb/News/Lebanon-News/2014/May-09/255811-machnouk-new-entry-rulesfor-palestinians-from-syria.ashx#ixzz350oAkLbP.

entry of PRS, which were similar to the exceptions applied in 2013, namely that entry would be granted for those with: an entry permit approved by the General Security Office; a one-year or three-year residency visa; an exit and return permit; or a valid ticket and visa to a third country.[43]

The reason for this uncompromising attitude is very clear: the Government of Lebanon has long wished to reduce numbers of Palestinians in Lebanon and has always been nervous of the potential implications of a sizeable Palestinian population in its territory.[44]

B. Non-Palestinians

While UNRWA in Lebanon assumes responsibility for the needs of the displaced PRS, the UNHCR deals with non-Palestinian Syrians. The UNHCR is charged with registering non-Palestinian Syrians and identifying unaccompanied minors and the vulnerable. With no MOU specifically focused on Syrians, the process concentrates on registration rather than detailed refugee status determination, but does address some RSD issues. All family members are interviewed and information is obtained on personal data, religion, ethnicity, circumstances of departure from Syria, military history, the reasons why they should not be returned and any particular needs they might have.[45] The UNHCR is required under arrangements with the Government to share certain information, such as names and addresses. There is the option for more detailed interviews for undocumented individuals and for possible combatants.[46]

Once registered, Syrians are provided with a UNHCR certificate, valid for two years in the first instance. This provides an element of protection for those registered, including acceptance by the Government of Lebanon that registered Syrians would not be returned to Syria. The UNHCR sees its protection strategy as addressing the following key challenges and priority concerns of refugees, including:

— Ensuring access to territory and reducing the risk of *refoulement*,
— Ensuring timely registration and adequate reception conditions,[47]
— Preventing, monitoring and addressing protection violations,

[43] Amnesty International, above n 39, 14.

[44] See M Dumper, 'Palestinian Refugees' in G Loescher, J Milner, E Newman and GG Troeller, *Protracted Refugee Situations—Political, Human Rights and Security Implications* (Tokyo, UN University Press, 2008) 189–213.

[45] Lebanon Humanitarian INGO Forum, 'Background Paper on Unregistered Syrian Refugees in Lebanon' (LHIF, 15 July 2014) 5.

[46] ibid 6.

[47] Note that the Government of Lebanon has instructed the UNHCR to cease registrations.

— Providing access to legal services and civil status documentation to ensure the rights of refugees are respected, and
— Ensuring durable and humanitarian solutions are made available.[48]

Access to territory is obviously key to accessing protection and further rights; yet, the UNHCR is restricted in terms of providing refugee status or helping to differentiate Syrians from other non-Syrians. As described above, no asylum-specific law is applied to Syrians (or other possible refugees); all are subject to the 1962 Law Regulating the Entry and Stay of Foreigners, with its limited and largely non-functioning political asylum provisions. Furthermore, the Government of Lebanon has frequently avoided using the politically loaded term 'refugees', in view of its association with Palestinians, and due to concerns about legal obligations that might arise from refugee status.[49] Alternatives have been employed, such as *nazihoun*,[50] guests, Syrians or Palestinians, and there has been some disagreement over terminology.[51] As a senior advisor in the Ministry of Social Affairs explained, the preferred term is 'displaced', meaning someone forced out of his or her normal place of residence, since it does not accord legal status under international law.[52] This view was confirmed in a live debate on forced displacement hosted by the World Bank in April 2016 when the Lebanese Minister of Education said:

> We have to differentiate between refugees and displaced groups. People leaving a country because of a war or any other reason—these are displaced people and we must call them displaced because refugees is a big word that scares everyone because they have different rights, and they will be remaining in the country.[53]

The picture is further complicated by the different language employed internationally and by non-governmental organisations (NGOs). There is a presumption that post-March 2011 Syrians are refugees. For example, the Inter-Agency Information Sharing Portal, which provides a wealth of information on the Syrian Regional Refugee Response, states that in Lebanon there are 1,048,275 'persons of concern' as at 31 March 2016 but also records the same number of 'registered Syrian refugees'.[54] This despite no

[48] UNHCR, 'UNHCR Lebanon: Protection Update' (UNHCR, December 2014).

[49] See, for similar issues in Jordan in relation to Iraqi refugees, D Stevens, 'Legal Status, Labelling, and Protection: the Case of Iraqi "Refugees" in Jordan' (2013) 25(1) *International Journal of Refugee Law* 1.

[50] The word means 'displaced'.

[51] Act for Human Rights (ALEF) 'Two Years On: Syrian Refugees in Lebanon' (ALEF/ IKV PAX Christi, September 2013) archive.paxchristi.net/2013/2013-0397-en-me-HS.pdf, 14.

[52] F Dionigi, 'The Syrian Refugee Crisis in Lebanon—State Fragility and Social Resilience' (Middle East Centre Paper Series, 15 February 2016) 24.

[53] World Bank Live, 'Forced Displacement: A Global Development Challenge' (World Bank Group HQ & Online, 15 April 2016) www.live.worldbank.org/forced-displacement-a-global-development-challenge.

[54] Inter-agency Information Sharing Portal, above n 28.

clear statement from the UNHCR that they are applying prima facie refugee status to Syrians in Lebanon.[55] Commentators, too, seem confused: some claim that '[t]he UNHCR has granted *prima facie* recognition of refugee status to Syrians and this has allowed them to benefit from the services and protection that the UNHCR can provide with the collaboration of its subsidiary agencies';[56] others maintain '[t]here is … no *prima facie* refugee status for Syrians in Lebanon'.[57] The coyness of the UNHCR on this matter is understandable. Its usage of the term '*prima facie* refugee' in relation to Iraqis from central and southern Iraq in Jordan in 2007 created difficulties with members of the Jordanian Government, who demanded compliance with the UNHCR–Jordan MOU according to which those registered with the UNHCR were asylum seekers so long as individual RSD had not been conducted.[58]

As with PRS, there has long been anecdotal evidence of refusals of entry to Syrians at the border due to damaged documentation or the individuals being male and single.[59] In 2014, the attitude of the Government started to alter. Prior to June 2014, Syrians who crossed into Lebanon through an official border crossing, and who possessed either a Syrian passport or identity card, were able to obtain a temporary six-month residence visa, renewable for a further six months, without charge. Further renewals incurred a fee of $200, a significant amount for many of the impoverished Syrians. The first sign of change occurred in May when it was announced that Syrians who crossed back over the border to Syria and returned to Lebanon were no longer to be regarded as 'displaced'. Then, in June 2014, the Lebanese authorities declared that entry of displaced Syrians would be restricted to those coming from areas close to the Lebanese border where there was fighting; and that anyone returning to Syria from Lebanon would risk losing their refugee status.[60] The Ministry of the Interior was reported as saying: 'All Syrian refugees registered with the UNHCR are asked to refrain from entering Syria starting June 1, or else they might be stripped of their refugee status.'[61] Such returns were undertaken for many

[55] cf the approach adopted towards Iraqi refugees in Lebanon after 2007: A Harper, 'Iraq's Refugees: Ignored and Unwanted' (2008) 90 (869) *International Review of the Red Cross* 175.

[56] F Dionigi, 'The Syrian Refugee Crisis in Lebanon: State Fragility and Social Resilience' (London School of Economics Middle East Centre Paper Series No 15, Middle East Centre, London, LSE, February 2016) 26.

[57] M Janmyr, 'The Legal Status of Syrian Refugees in Lebanon—Working Paper' (AUB Policy Institute, Issam Fares Institute for Public Policy and International Affairs, American University of Beirut, March 2016).

[58] Stevens, above n 49, 11.

[59] ALEF, above n 51, 21.

[60] Amnesty International, above n 39, 7.

[61] P Sykes, 'Lebanon Claims Right to Strip Syrians of Refugee Status' (MEMO Middle East Monitor, 3 June 2014).

reasons, often financial, as those in Lebanon exhausted their resources and were often unable to work. On this occasion, though, the timing of the decision was clear, coming as it did just before 3 June 2014, the date of the presidential elections in Syria and by which time many Syrians had hoped to return to vote. In August, the border controls were tightened and further refusals of entry were reported.

By October 2014, the Social Affairs Minister, Rashid Derbas, was reported in Lebanon's Al-Akhbar newspaper to have stated that 'Lebanon is no longer officially receiving any Syrian refugees, except those with urgent humanitarian reasons'.[62] Such a policy had come directly from the Council of Ministers.[63] The objective was plain: to stop the influx of refugees.[64] In an unprecedented move, the Government went further and called upon the UNHCR to deregister refugees who had returned to Syria, seemingly with Article 1C(1) as the basis for such a request.[65] This can be seen as a somewhat odd request from a Government that has refused to be party to the Refugee Convention and does not regard Syrians as refugees. Notwithstanding, the UNHCR was more compliant than might have been expected. Ninette Kelley, the UNHCR Representative to Lebanon, stated:

> We have looked at those names and tried to determine what number of those names, because there are a lot of names, also matches our database, and then we have called people in … to interview them and find out the reasons for their going back. And we have deregistered people for whom their going back to Syria has shown that they aren't in need of international protection or assistance, and that's something that we have done willingly with the government, recognizing that refugee status is for persons who have a well-founded fear of persecution and are fleeing civil unrest inside Syria.[66]

This practice of the UNHCR can certainly be questioned. According to its own Handbook, there are five conditions under which an asylum seeker or refugee is no longer of concern to the organisation and can be deregistered. These are: (a) final rejection of the asylum claim; (b) cessation of refugee status; (c) cancellation of refugee status; (d) revocation of refugee

[62] Al-Akhbar, AFP, 'Lebanon Will Stop Receiving New Syrian Refugees: Derbas' (Al-Akhbar English, 20 October 2014) www.english.al-akhbar.com/node/22106.

[63] The Council includes the Prime Minister, the Minister of Interior and Municipalities, Minister of Social Affairs, and the Minister of Foreign Affairs and Immigrants: Amnesty International, 'Pushed to the Edge: Syrian Refugees Face Increased Restrictions in Lebanon' (Amnesty international Publications, 2015) 9.

[64] ibid.

[65] Article 1C(1): 'This Convention shall cease to apply to [a refugee] if … [h]e has voluntarily re-availed himself of the protection of the country of his nationality'.

[66] S Kullab, 'Lebanon Borders Still Open to Syrian Refugees: UN' (Albawaba News, 23 October 2014).

status; and (e) death.[67] Clearly, from Kelley's statement, the presumption is that refugee status has ceased under Article 1C because they have returned to Syria and 'aren't in need of international protection'. However, the UNHCR's Handbook makes it very clear that deregistration due to cessation of refugee status 'is a protection issue', that the application of Article 1C(1) 'is relatively rare' and that the refugee must act voluntarily, must intend to re-avail himself or herself of the protection of the country of nationality, and, finally, must actually obtain such protection.[68] Returning to vote or to obtain more financial resources does not immediately fulfil these criteria, particularly re-availment of the protection of the country of nationality. Despite these concerns, the Government of Lebanon has encouraged increased deregistrations of Syrian refugees. Finally, in May 2015, the UNHCR was instructed to suspend registrations of Syrians. This is still active policy.[69]

Apparently dissatisfied with the impact of the June 2014 amendments to inward flows, new regulations were issued on 31 December 2014, which came into effect on 5 January 2015. Lebanon now decided that its best course of action to address the seemingly never ending movement of people across the Syrian border to its territory was to implement a visa requirement for entry, reversing what had hitherto been very fluid and flexible border controls. The regulations provided for seven categories of prospective entrant:

(i) tourism, shopping, business, landlords and tenants;
(ii) studying;
(iii) transiting to a third country;
(iv) the displaced;
(v) medical treatment;
(vi) embassy appointment; and
(vii) those entering with a pledge of responsibility (a Lebanese sponsor).[70]

Not only are Syrians expected to prove they fall within one of these categories before temporary residence of between 24 hours and one month is granted (with extension in exceptional cases), but they must also provide valid identity documents.[71] One might assume that category (iv)—those who have been displaced—must include Syrians but this is, in fact, not the

[67] UNHCR, 'UNHCR Handbook for Registration: Procedures and Standards for Registration, Population Data Management and Documentation' (Provisional Release, September 2013) 193.
[68] ibid 197.
[69] As at July 2016.
[70] Amnesty International, above n 63, 10.
[71] ibid.

case. Syrians are explicitly excluded unless they fall within a discretionary, humanitarian exception, subsequently defined by the Ministry of Social Affairs as including:

> [u]naccompanied and/or separated children with a parent already registered in Lebanon; persons living with disabilities with a relative already registered in Lebanon; persons with urgent medical needs for whom treatment in Syria is unavailable; persons who will be resettled to third countries.[72]

Thus, a clearly pressurised Government has elected to ignore both its political and legal obligations under the bilateral agreement and its moral obligations to admit desperate people in search of some form of sanctuary.

These amendments were accompanied by further new regulations relating to residency permits. As noted above, residency permits were free of charge for six months, renewable for a further six months, before a fee of $200 was imposed. The regime has now become significantly more stringent. The UNHCR has described it thus:

> Syrians who are registered with UNHCR must pay a fee of US $200 and in addition provide: a housing commitment (certified copies of a lease agreement or real-estate deed); certified attestation from a mukhtar (village leader) that the landlord owns the property; and a notarized pledge not to work; and proof of their financial means or of the support they receive. Some refugees are also asked to sign a notarized pledge that they will return to Syria when their permit expires or when requested by the Government. Most refugees are not able to pay the US $200 fee, nor can they produce the documents required since most do not have formal lease agreements or ways of demonstrating that they have financial means to live in Lebanon. As a result of these measures, there is a growing sense of insecurity and unease in refugee communities. Many are fearful of arrest or detention because of lapsed residency visas or are feeling increasingly vulnerable to abuse given their irregular status in the country.[73]

The pledge not to work was replaced in July 2016 with a 'pledge to abide by Lebanon's laws and regulations'.[74] Those who are not registered with the UNHCR have similar requirements with a 'pledge of responsibility', which is a form of sponsorship by a Lebanese national who offers to obtain a work permit for an individual Syrian or a group of Syrian nationals, or offers to host and assume responsibility for a Syrian family.[75] Amnesty International has reported that '[i]n many cases even when refugees

[72] UNHCR, Protection Sector—Monthly Dashboard: Inter-agency Coordination Lebanon April 2015' (UNHCR, 30 April 2015) www.data.unhcr.org/syrianrefugees/working_group.php?Page=Country&LocationId=122&Id=25; Amnesty International, above n 63, 11.

[73] UNHCR, 'Syrian Refugees in Lebanon—Quarterly Snapshot January–March 2015' (UNHCR 2015) 1.

[74] My thanks to Maja Janmyr for this information.

[75] Amnesty International, above n 63, 14–15.

provide all the necessary documents and pay the required fees their request to renew their residency permits are denied, for reasons that are often unclear'.[76] Obtaining documentation is expensive; the UNHCR and protection partners have estimated that an average family of five will have to spend $1,375 to regularise their stay for one year.[77]

IV. CONDITIONS AND CONSEQUENCES

It is evident that Syrians have suffered from Lebanon's approach towards the plight of the displaced. But this is not purely the fault of Lebanon. From the outset of the crisis, study after study has warned of dire consequences, calling for a concerted effort by both Lebanon and the 'international community' to seek durable resolutions to the problems. This has sadly been absent.

A. Deteriorating Conditions

From the perspective of law, there are a number of issues that need to be highlighted. The reluctance to sign the Refugee Convention and the lack of domestic asylum law and refugee determination procedures have reinforced the shift in responsibility from state to the UNHCR and its partner organisations. During an emergency phase of mass influx, this shift can be effective, and the best course of action where a state's own capacity to handle such a crisis is limited, but the passage of time has seriously impaired the ability to deliver protection and basic needs of the many organisations working alongside the UNHCR and UNRWA. Conditions for all Syrians in Lebanon have deteriorated as the displacement becomes protracted. In almost all cases, those delivering humanitarian aid have been forced to cut assistance to Syrians, with obvious negative consequences. For example, in a recent survey of the economic status of Palestine refugees in Lebanon, the authors concluded that:

> UNRWA has been struggling to ensure adequate shelter, education, health care and other services to PRS, who now represent an approximate 20 per cent increase of beneficiaries in need of assistance in Lebanon. As the primary provider of assistance to PRS, UNRWA instituted in February 2014 programs of monthly cash assistance for food (US$ 30 per person) and housing (US$ 100 per family). In April 2015 food assistance was reduced from US$ 30 to US$ 27, and

[76] ibid 15.

[77] UNHCR, 'Lebanon Crisis Response Plan—Monthly Dashboard: Inter-Agency Coordination Lebanon February 2015' (UNHCR 2015).

in May 2015, due to financial constraints, UNRWA announced a suspension of cash for housing assistance to PRS, effective in July 2015. This suspension in aid comes at a time when PRS are becoming increasingly vulnerable, with UNRWA cash assistance representing the main source of income for 92.6 per cent of the population, according to the survey.[78]

The situation is further complicated for NGOs by the fact that Syrian refugees are spread around the country in more than 1,700 locations due to the 'no camp' policy of the Government (PRS are residing in one of the 12 refugee camps or outside the camps). According to a 2016 European Commission briefing, 'they live in apartments, collective shelters, tented settlements, unfinished houses, garages, warehouses or worksites' and '[a]lmost 9 out of 10 refugees live in 251 locations, which are some of the poorest and most vulnerable neighbourhoods in Lebanon.'[79] Children appear to be suffering the most. Under half of the Syrian refugee children aged between three and 17 years are currently in formal education (200,000 of 460,000), raising the very real prospect of a 'lost generation'.[80] Many are forced to work and are 'sustaining households' survival as partial or sole breadwinners' (see below).[81]

There are also broader implications of uncertain legal status for both PRS and non-Palestine Syrians, which have been exacerbated by deliberate policy-making. Numbers arriving have diminished since the Government's effective closing of borders in May 2014, with its target of Palestinians from Syria, and since January 2015 for others. Both PRS and Syrian refugees have been failing to renew their residency permits due to the renewal cost. They face arrest, detention and even deportation as a result, though it appears that few have been removed.[82] More usual, however, is the impact on freedom of movement and the increased likelihood of harassment.[83] Syrians want to work if possible to help support themselves and their families but the current requirement of employer sponsorship and the need for valid work permits has pushed many into illegal activities or negative coping strategies. Exploitation and abuse is on the rise, particularly of children. A recent report by the Freedom Fund has linked the legal constraints with a significant rise in child labour (estimated at 60–70% of Syrian refugee children), early marriage for Syrian girls, a rise in 'survival sex' and sexual exploitation and forced labour possibly becoming the 'new

[78] ibid 8.

[79] European Commission, Humanitarian Aid and Civil Protection, above n 29.

[80] UNHCR, 'UNHCR Lebanon Operational Update January–March 2016' (UNHCR, 2016) 3.

[81] UNOCHA, 'Humanitarian Bulletin—Lebanon' (Issue 18, 1–30 April 2016).

[82] Chaaban et al, above n 36, 25.

[83] European Commission Humanitarian Aid and Civil Protection, above n 29.

norm'.[84] There have been calls on Lebanon by the European Union (EU) amongst others to open up its domestic labour market, but it has resisted, the Government suspicious that the real concern of the EU is to prevent onward travel to EU countries.[85]

B. *Refoulement* and Rejection

As mentioned above, the MOU makes no mention of *non-refoulement*, though there is an assumption that anyone falling under its provisions will be protected from return or removal during the time in which the UNHCR processes applications for asylum and seeks a durable solution—that is, resettlement under the MOU. Since there are notoriously few offers of resettlement places globally, and the time taken to action resettlement is often lengthy and uncertain, many of those identified by the UNHCR as refugees will continue to remain in-country well beyond the 9–12 months outlined in the MOU. In theory, therefore, they are vulnerable to removal or *refoulement*. It can be argued, of course, that Lebanon has committed to *non-refoulement* obligations in its ratification of various international treaties, such as the CAT and ICCPR,[86] and through its own Constitution. Furthermore, domestic case law on the CAT appears to have endorsed the *non-refoulement* obligation of Article 3. In a study conducted in 2006 on detention in Lebanon, the authors reported two cases in which both the Court of First Instance and the Court of Appeal overturned expulsion orders imposed on refugees on account of Article 3.[87]

Concrete examples of repatriations of Syrians have occurred. As early as 2012, there were reports in the Lebanese media of the return of 14 Syrians to the Syrian authorities by the General Security Office tasked with border control, a move that was denounced by, inter alia, the EU, the US Embassy

[84] K Jones and L Ksaifi, 'Struggling to Survive: Slavery and Exploitation of Syrian Refugees in Lebanon' (The Freedom Fund, 2016) 3; see also for discussion of the position of refugee women from Syria, Amnesty International, '"I Want a Safe Place"—Refugee Women from Syria Uprooted and Unprotected in Lebanon' (London, Amnesty International, February 2016).

[85] M Armstrong, 'Lebanon Resists Granting Work Permits to Syrian Refugees' (Middle East Eye, 4 February 2016) www.middleeasteye.net/news/lebanon-syria-refugees-jobs-554259285.

[86] eg Art 3(1) of the CAT makes specific reference to *non-refoulement*: 'No State Party shall expel, return ("*refouler*") or extradite a person to another State where there are substantial grounds for believing that he would be in danger of being subjected to torture.' The CAT came into force in Lebanon in 2000.

[87] Court of First Instance, Beirut, Decision No 2003/1119; Court of Appel, Beirut, Decision No 2001/580, President Tanious al Khoury, 20 June 2001, discussed in Frontiers, above n 6, 19–20.

in Beirut and Human Rights Watch.[88] In May 2014, in contravention of its apparent assurance that refugees would not be returned to Syria, the General Security Office forcibly removed 43 Palestinians to Syria from Beirut International Airport.[89] Then, in January 2016, it was again reported that over 100 Syrian refugees had been forcibly removed to Syria from Lebanon, and that a further 150 were being held at the airport and were at risk of removal.[90] Amnesty International has argued powerfully that by refusing entry at the border and excluding the vast majority of people fleeing the conflict in Syria with its associated human rights infringements, the Government of Lebanon is acting in contravention of Lebanon's *non-refoulement* obligations, whether under Treaty law (CAT; ICCPR) or customary international law.[91]

While forcible removals are clearly of great concern and likely to be in breach of international law, the 2015 regulations have much greater implications in terms of numbers and consequences. Under current interpretations of the development of the *non-refoulement* principle, which have progressed beyond the concerns of the drafters of the Refugee Convention not to create a duty to grant asylum, rejection at the frontier constitutes *refoulement*. As Goodwin-Gill and McAdam argue:

> By and large, States in their practice and their recorded views, have recognized that *non-refoulement* applies to the moment at which asylum seekers present themselves for entry, either within a State or at its border. Certain factual elements may be necessary before the principle is triggered, but the concept now encompasses both non-return and non-rejection.[92]

The implications for countries such as Lebanon, which have received vast numbers of Syrians, are extremely serious and raise the question

[88] G Frangieh, 'Forced Departure: How Lebanon Evades the International Principle of Non-Refoulement' (The Legal Agenda, 29 December 2014); EU, 'Statement by the Spokesperson of High Representative Catherine Ashton on Expulsions by the Lebanese Authorities of Syrian Nationals to Syria' (4 August 2012); US Embassy Beirut, 'US Ambassador Meets with MP Michel Anon' (2 August 2012); Human Rights Watch, 'Letter to Lebanese Officials Regarding Deportation of Syrians' (4 August 2012) www.hrw.org/news/2012/08/04/letter-lebanese-officials-regarding-deportation-syrians.

[89] MA Nayel, 'Lebanon Deports Palestinians Back to Syria' (Aljazeera, 9 May 2014); Human Rights Watch, 'Lebanon: Palestinians Barred, Sent to Syria: Reverse Blanket Rejection of Refugees' (News Release, Beirut, 5 May 2014).

[90] Amnesty International, 'Lebanon: Forcible Return of More Than 100 Refugees to Syria a Shocking Setback' (News Release, 8 January 2016) www.refworld.org/docid/569756cd4.html.

[91] Amnesty International, above n 63, 11. The general consensus amongst academic commentators and practitioners is that *non-refoulement* constitutes a principle of customary international law. This is disputed by JC Hathaway, see JC Hathaway and M Foster, *The Law of Refugee Status* (Cambridge, Cambridge University Press, 2014) 27, fn 64; JC Hathaway, 'Leveraging Asylum' (2010) 45 *Texas International Law Journal* 503.

[92] GS Goodwin-Gill and J McAdam, *The Refugee in International Law* (Oxford, Oxford University Press, 2007) 208.

of whether mass influx justifies derogation from the principle of *non-refoulement*. Goodwin Gill and McAdam, amongst others, respond with a resounding 'no'! 'As a matter of international law', they argue, '*refoulement* is not justifiable no matter how debilitating a sudden influx of refugees might be on a State's resources, economy or political situation.'[93] This applies whether or not the state in question is party to the Convention. So, according to such a reading, Lebanon is in breach by refusing entry to refugees, displaced or those at risk of human rights breaches in their home or other countries. Lebanon would counter such an argument by pointing to the fact that it is not party to the Refugee Convention, has a right to control its borders, has not undertaken a blanket refusal of entry but is requiring Syrians to comply with new visa requirements, as do many countries, and is confronting enormous economic and social challenges with inadequate external support or willingness to share responsibility by other, wealthier countries.[94] And in relation to the economic strain, it is certainly correct. The World Bank has estimated that, since 2012, the country has incurred losses of $13.1 billion, of which $5.6 billion arose in 2015 alone.[95] Even prior to the Syrian crisis, all public services, including education, health, energy, water, waste collection and treatment, were under immense pressure.[96] The failure of the international community to seek early solutions for the problem of protracted displacement in Lebanon has now created an environment in which access to territory, access to protection and access to an opportunity to live a life of dignity is becoming increasingly remote. It has also helped contribute to instability in Lebanon and the region, and led, in part, to the recent migration of Syrians to Europe as they abandon hope of a future in Lebanon, Jordan, Turkey or Syria.[97] In such circumstances, to argue for the complete adherence to the principle of *non-refoulement*, however correct legally, is unrealistic and unhelpful without further action and considerable international support for Lebanon. New financial initiatives, announced in February 2016 at the

[93] ibid 335. See also J-F Durieux and J McAdam, '*Non-refoulement* through Time: The Case for a Derogation Clause to the Refugee Convention in Mass Influx Emergencies' (2004) 16(1) *International Journal of Refugee Law* 4.

[94] The annual GDP growth rate is said to have dropped from 8.5% to 1.4% in Lebanon between 2009 and 2012: O Dahi, 'The Refugee Crisis in Lebanon and Jordan: The Need for Economic Development Spending' (September 2014) *Forced Migration Review* 47.

[95] Republic of Lebanon, 'London Conference—Lebanon Statement of Intent' (Supporting Syria & the Region, London, 4 February 2016) www.gov.uk/government/uploads/system/uploads/attachment_data/file/498026/Supporting_Syria__the_Region_London_2016_-_Lebanon_Statement.pdf.

[96] ibid.

[97] See research undertaken by the author as part of ESRC research funder project, 'Crossing the Mediterranean Sea By Boat: Mapping and Documenting Migratory Journeys and Experiences': www2.warwick.ac.uk/fac/soc/pais/research/researchcentres/irs/crossingthemed/.

London Conference, which are expected to invest $20 billion in Jordan and Lebanon in the next five years, is a sign that the scale of the problem has finally been appreciated.[98] Whether it alone is sufficient to solve the many issues is unlikely.

V. CONCLUSION

Many of the countries considered in this collection have accepted the application and obligations of international refugee law as outlined in the Refugee Convention and have developed asylum procedures with which to process applicants in a seemingly fair and just manner. However, as evidenced in this collection, in spite of the apparent commitment to international principles, much effort is expended in avoiding legal obligations whether it be through limitations on access to territory or questionable interpretations of due process. We are sadly becoming very familiar with—and despairing of—proclamations by the 'international community' of their commitments to protect asylum seekers and refugees and the reality of increasing exclusion and failures of protection. The Lebanese Government, for its part, does not engage in the same rhetoric, makes no pretence of the fact that it considers Syrians as a form of temporary visitor or migrant worker, has no intention of assuming more international law obligations towards refugees than it considers necessary and is not interested in adopting formal asylum procedures. This chapter has identified some of the costs of this approach for livelihoods, hope and dignity, but one question does remain, and it reflects the focus of this book: what difference, if any, would unrestricted access to territory and due process make for the individual seeking asylum in Lebanon? At present, this is incredibly difficult to answer. Territorial protection—that is, a generous entry policy—is clearly fundamental, but without a commitment to rights and tolerance, or simply the value of the individual, without planning and resources, and without collective responsibility and 'burden-sharing', the prospects are not overwhelmingly positive. What is becoming very evident both in Lebanon and across the world is that law alone cannot provide the solution (and, at times, it is part of the problem when it supports exclusion and deterrence over inclusion and integration). There is a real need for a multi-faceted, comprehensive reimagining of asylum if any advances are to be made. Lebanon exemplifies the risks and consequences of failure, which reach far beyond the lives of the individual refugee and the borders of the state. It is a warning to us all.

[98] The World Bank, 'Statement by World Bank Group President Jim Yong Kim at the Syria Conference' (London, Syria Conference, 4 February 2016) www.worldbank.org/en/news/speech/2016/02/04/statement-world-bank-group-jim-yong-kim-syria-conference.

11

Accelerated Asylum Procedures in the United Kingdom and Australia

'Fast Track' to *Refoulement*?

LINDA KIRK

I. INTRODUCTION

DURING THE CURRENT global 'migration crisis', many receiving states have introduced a range of measures to regulate and restrict the movement and entry of asylum seekers to their territory and limit their access to asylum status determination procedures. Amongst these measures are 'accelerated' or 'fast track' asylum procedures designed to expedite the asylum status determination process. This chapter examines the accelerated asylum determination procedures that have been implemented in two jurisdictions, the United Kingdom (UK) and Australia. It considers how these states have sought to limit the access of certain categories of asylum seekers to 'regular' procedures on the basis of a perception that their claims are less 'well-founded' than those of applicants who are processed via regular channels. It assesses these procedures against internationally recognised standards for the circumstances in which it is acceptable to accelerate the assessment of asylum claims, specifically those detailed by the United Nations High Commissioner for Refugees (UNHCR).

It is widely accepted that it is in the interests of both applicants and the state that asylum processes are concluded quickly.[1] From the perspective

[1] See M Reneman, 'Speedy Asylum Procedures in the EU: Striking a Fair Balance between the Need to Process Asylum Cases Efficiently and the Asylum Applicant's EU Right to an Effective Remedy' (2013) 25(4) *International Journal of Refugee Law* 717, 718. This chapter only

of the state, accelerated procedures have the benefit of efficiency in that 'unfounded' asylum claims can be refused rapidly thereby freeing up time and resources to determine 'well-founded' applications. Lengthy asylum procedures result in a long period of uncertainty for applicants as to their legal status.[2] When an asylum seeker is detained during the processing of their asylum application it is particularly important that the asylum process be concluded as quickly as possible.[3]

However, the desirability of expeditiously deciding asylum applications must be balanced against states' obligations under international human rights and refugee law, particularly the prohibition of *refoulement*. The UNHCR has consistently argued that accelerated procedures are only appropriate for 'manifestly unfounded' and 'clearly abusive' claims,[4] and effective procedural safeguards must be included in such procedures to ensure that asylum claims are fully examined and properly assessed.[5] The UNHCR has also emphasised that following a decision to refuse to grant asylum status, an applicant must have the right to an effective remedy, and the review by the court or tribunal must examine both facts and law based on current information.[6]

This chapter examines the 'fast track' procedures in the UK and Australia. It shows that neither procedure selects for the 'fast track' only those applicants whose claims are 'manifestly unfounded' or 'clearly abusive'. The time frames for both the primary and appeal stages of the UK Detained Fast Track System (DFT) are truncated to the extent that necessary procedural safeguards are sacrificed and, as the courts have

uses UNHCR standards to assess the UK and Australian accelerated asylum procedures. It does not assess these accelerated procedures against other relevant international standards such as the International Covenant on Civil and Political Rights [1976] United Nations Treaty Series 999, 171 (ICCPR), Convention Against Torture and Other Cruel, Inhuman or Degrading Treatment of Punishment [1984] United Nations Treaty Series 1465, 85 (Convention Against Torture) and Council Directive 2013/32/EU of the 26 June 2013 on common procedures for granting and withdrawing international protection [2013] OJ L180/60 (Recast Asylum Procedures Directive).

[2] Reneman, above n 1, 718.

[3] ibid.

[4] UNHCR, 'The Problem of Manifestly Unfounded or Abusive Applications for Refugee Status or Asylum' (ExCom Conclusions No 30 (XXXIV)—1983, 20 October 1983); UNHCR, 'Global Consultations on International Protection/Third Track: Asylum Processes (Fair and Efficient Asylum Procedures)' (2nd Meeting, EC/GC/01/12, 31 May 2001) paras 25–26; UNHCR, 'Statement on the Right to an Effective Remedy in Relation to Accelerated Asylum Procedures' (21 May 2010) paras 5–7.

[5] UNHCR (1983), above n 4, para (e); UNHCR, 'Improving Asylum Procedures: Comparative Analysis and Recommendations for Law and Practice' (UNHCR, Brussels, March 2010) 239.

[6] UNHCR (2010), above n 4, para 21. The UNHCR, 'Handbook on Procedures and Criteria for Determining Refugee Status' (Reissued, Geneva, December 2011) states, at para 192(vi), that the applicant: 'should be given a reasonable time to appeal for a formal reconsideration of the decision, either to the same or a different authority, whether administrative or judicial, according to the prevailing system.'

recognised, the system is 'structurally unfair and unjust'.[7] While the time frames for decision-making under the Australian Fast Track Procedure (FTP) are longer, it denies applicants a full de novo merits review of a refusal decision by an independent tribunal, and thereby does not provide access to an effective remedy. Neither 'fast track' procedure adequately meets the intended purpose of an asylum status determination system, which is to identify individuals with international protection needs and protect them from *refoulement*.

II. UNITED KINGDOM

A. Introduction and Development of the DFT

Accelerated procedures for the determination of asylum claims were first introduced in the UK in the 1990s following a gradual increase in the number of asylum applications from approximately 4,000 in 1988 to almost 45,000 in 1991.[8] During this decade, procedures were introduced for the 'fast tracking' of both first instance asylum decisions and asylum appeals[9] and a DFT process existed in various forms from the 1990s until its suspension in July 2015. The DFT was implemented by the Secretary of State for the Home Department (SSHD) pursuant to policy, the most recent being contained in *Detained Fast Track Processes*.[10]

In 2000, in response to an increasing volume of asylum applications,[11] Oakington Immigration Removal Centre began to be used to facilitate a

[7] *R (Detention Action) v FTT (Immigration and Asylum Chamber)* [2015] EWCA Civ 840; [2015] 1 WLR 5341, para 45.

[8] Independent Chief Inspector, UK Border Agency, 'Asylum: A Thematic Inspection of the Detained Fast Track' (ICI Report, February 2012) 8, Figure 1.

[9] An accelerated or 'fast track' *appeals* process was first introduced in the Asylum and Immigration Appeals Act 1993 for 'without foundation' cases. Further measures were introduced in the Asylum and Immigration Act 1996, which extended the category of cases for the 'fast track' appeals process to 'white listed' cases, that is those claims by applicants from countries where it was considered there was no general risk of persecution, ie designated safe countries of origin. The Immigration and Asylum Act 1999 removed the distinction between the 'fast track' and 'standard' streams so that all applicants had 10 days to appeal a first instance decision. The Nationality, Immigration and Asylum Act 2002 reinstated the fast track procedure to five days if the applicant was in detention and 10 days for non-detention cases.

[10] Home Office, UK Border Agency, 'Detained Fast Track Processes' (Formerly Titled DFT & DNSA Intake Selection (AIU Instruction), first published June 2013, revised October 2014) www.gov.uk/government/uploads/system/uploads/attachment_data/file/370322/Detained_Fast_Track_Processes_v6_0.pdf. This policy has now been suspended.

[11] Between July and September 1999, the average monthly number of asylum applications was approximately 7,000, 60% higher than the previous year: *R (Saadi and Ors) v SSHD* [2001] EWCA Civ 1512; [2002] 1 WLR 356) para 3.

DFT process. The initial decision was made within seven days, after which asylum seekers were released with the opportunity to pursue an appeal against a negative decision. The aim of the policy was to deal with asylum applications 'quickly' on the grounds that many of the claims were 'unfounded'.[12] The rationale for holding applicants in detention while claims were processed was to ensure that applicants were available for an early interview, and to facilitate their access to lawyers and the making of further representations where necessary. This policy of 'detention for administrative convenience' was the subject of widespread criticism and a number of unsuccessful legal challenges.[13]

In 2003 a 'super fast track process' was introduced following a peak in asylum applications in 2002 of 84,132.[14] This DFT process was based at Harmondsworth Immigration Removal Centre and extended the detention period of asylum applicants beyond the initial decision to include the appeals process, and if the appeal were unsuccessful, until the removal of the applicant from the UK. In *R (Refugee Legal Centre) v SSHD*[15] it was argued that the DFT carried an unacceptable risk of unfairness and was therefore unlawful. Sedley LJ, who gave the judgment of the Court, noted that the question was: 'did the system provide a fair opportunity to asylum applicants to put their case?'[16] He continued:

> The choice of an acceptable system is in the first instance a matter for the executive, and in making its choice it is entitled to take into account the perceived

[12] This was primarily on the grounds that the applicant was from a safe country of nationality.

[13] The lawfulness of the detention of asylum applicants for 'administrative convenience' was considered in 2001 in *R (Saadi and Ors) v SSHD* [2001] EWHC Admin 670. The High Court found that the Immigration Act 1971 permitted the SSHD to detain asylum claimants where necessary to deal with their claims expeditiously, at para 46. However, Collins J found that there was a breach of ECHR art 5(1)(f). On appeal, both the Court of Appeal [2001] EWCA Civ 1512, para 69 and the House of Lords in *R (Saadi and Ors) v SSHD* [2002] UKHL 41; [2002] 1 WLR 3131, para 47 held that the detention was lawful under domestic law and did not amount to a violation of the ECHR. The ECtHR Grand Chamber in *Saadi v UK* (2008) 47 EHRR 17 found that the detention of applicants for seven days 'was within the limits of what could be regarded as acceptable'; however, any period of detention 'significantly in excess of this period' would be incompatible with ECHR art 5(1)(f). In *R (Detention Action) v SSHD* [2014] EWHC 2245 (Admin), Ouseley J found that none of the changes introduced since *Saadi* were disproportionate (ECHR), contradicted art 18 of Council Directive 2005/85/EC of 1 December 2005 on minimum standards on procedures in Member States for granting and withdrawing refugee status [2005] OJ L326/13 (Procedures Directive), the Council Directive 2003/9/EC of 27 January 2003 laying down minimum standards for the reception of asylum applicants [2003] OJ L31/18 (Reception Directive), nor resulted in a finding of unlawfulness of the DFT system, para 219.

[14] Home Office UK, 'Immigration Statistics: January to March 2013' (ONS, 23 May 2013) para 1.5.

[15] *R (Refugee Legal Centre) v SSHD* [2004] EWCA Civ 1481; [2005] 1 WLR 2219.

[16] ibid para 6.l.

> political and other imperatives for a speedy turn-round of asylum applications. But it is not entitled to sacrifice fairness on the altar of speed and convenience, much less of expediency; and whether it has done so is a question of law for the courts[17]

His Lordship referred to Professor Craig's summary of the three factors that the court must weigh in determining the content of procedural fairness in administrative decision-making, namely individual interest, benefits of additional procedure and cost,[18] and noted that these are not of equal weight.[19] Referring to Bingham LJ's judgment in *SSHD v Thirukumar*,[20] and Lord Woolf MR's judgment in *R v SSHD ex parte Al-Fayed*,[21] Sedley LJ concluded: 'There has to be in asylum procedures, as in many other procedures, an irreducible minimum of due process.'[22]

Sedley LJ rejected the argument that unfairness in the initial decision-making process was capable of correction through the appeal process as 'an applicant is entitled not only to a fair appeal but to a fair initial hearing and a fair-minded decision'.[23] However, he concluded that the system itself is not '*inherently* unfair and therefore unlawful' (emphasis in original)[24] and it can 'operate without an unacceptable risk of unfairness'.[25] The Court qualified this by recommending that 'flexibility' in the application of the DFT time frames to the circumstances of an individual applicant should be contained in a written policy document,[26] which at the time did not exist. Following this decision, the Flexibility Guidelines (discussed below) were introduced as part of the DFT.

By 2005 asylum applications had reduced from a peak of 9,000 per month in 2002 to consistently below 3,000.[27] Despite the drop in the number of asylum applications, the DFT remained a central element of the Government's policy, which included a projection that up to 30 per cent of asylum claims would be determined by way of a 'fast track' procedure while applicants were held in detention.[28]

[17] *R (Refugee Legal Centre) v SSHD*, above n 15, para 8.

[18] ibid, citing P Craig, *Administrative Law*, 5th edn (London, Sweet & Maxwell, 2003) ch 13.

[19] *R (Refugee Legal Centre) v SSHD*, above n 15, para 8.

[20] *R (Refugee Legal Centre) v SSHD*, above n 15, citing *SSHD v Thirukumar* [1989] Imm AR 402, 414.

[21] *R (Refugee Legal Centre) v SSHD*, above n 15, citing *R v SSHD ex parte Al-Fayed* [1998] 1 WLR 763, 777.

[22] ibid.

[23] *R (Refugee Legal Centre) v SSHD*, above n 15.

[24] ibid para 25.

[25] ibid.

[26] ibid para 23.

[27] Home Office, 'Controlling our Borders: Making Migration Work for Britain—Five Year Strategy on Asylum and Immigration Policy' (Cm 6472, HMSO, February 2005) para 27.

[28] ibid.

B. Selection of Applicants for the DFT

(i) Screening Interview

All new applications for asylum are referred to the National Asylum Allocation Unit (NAAU)[29] and applicants are interviewed by a NAAU screening officer. Legal representatives may attend the interview with the applicant; however, if the applicant does not already have a representative, the presence of a lawyer is not facilitated.[30] The interview is conducted on the basis of a pro forma questionnaire and any supplementary questions the interviewer considers appropriate to ask the applicant.[31] The purpose of the screening interview is to gather personal information.[32] It is not for the purpose of considering the asylum claims in detail or the substantive merits of the claims.[33] During the screening interview a decision is made as to whether the applicant's claims are suitable for the DFT.[34]

The DFT suitability exclusion criteria[35] provide that certain individuals and groups may be excluded from the DFT process. These include women who are 24 or more weeks' pregnant, family cases, children, people with a disability, physical or mental medical condition, potential victims of trafficking or torture, and persons who lack the mental capacity to understand the asylum process.[36]

Applicants are allocated by the NAAU into one of five asylum procedures, which include the DFT and detained non-suspensive appeals (DNSA). In 2012, 2,482 asylum applications were subject to the DFT and 2,278 to the DNSA at first instance representing 17 per cent of the total number of asylum applications in the UK (28,260).[37]

The screening interview is a critical first stage of determining whether a claim will be assessed within the DFT. However there are serious

[29] The task of the NAAU is to consider the suitability of every referral against policy and operational considerations 'based on all information and evidence held on file and otherwise known about the applicant and his claim'—see Home Office, UK Border Agency, above n 10, para 4.4.1.

[30] The screening process is detailed in Ouseley J's judgment in *R (Detention Action) v SSHD*, above n 13, paras 94–112.

[31] ibid para 95.

[32] This involves an interview of the applicant during which biometric data is taken, health and family information collected, details of their route of travel obtained, and the broad outline of their claims ascertained: see ibid paras 95–98.

[33] ibid para 95.

[34] ibid para 98.

[35] Home Office, UK Border Agency, above n 10, para 2.3.

[36] ibid.

[37] Asylum Information Data Base (AIDA), 'National Country Report: The United Kingdom' (ECRE, April, 2014) 7, Table 4.

shortcomings in the screening process and it has been the subject of considerable criticism.[38] The major flaw is that it assumes that the applicant is willing and able to present important information about their claims and their personal circumstances to the screening officer.[39] Vulnerable applicants in particular may not be willing to reveal the details of their vulnerability at this early stage of the process, particularly if they are not represented.

In *R (Detention Action) v SSHD*,[40] the High Court rejected a wide-ranging legal challenge mounted by Detention Action to the DFT. One of the grounds of challenge was the selection process of applicants for inclusion in the DFT. Ouseley J stated that 'the lawful operation of the DFT depends on the selection of cases which are suitable for it, and the removal of those initially placed in it which turn out not to be suitable, whether through error of judgment in the first place or because of further information'.[41] He found that evidence of large numbers of applicants being wrongly allocated to the DFT did not indicate the unlawfulness of the process. In his view, the screening process does 'largely address the issues relevant to suitability for proper, reasonable, and non-arbitrary decisions to be made on suitability of the claim for allocation to the DFT'.[42] However, he found that there was room for improvement in the screening process to ensure that only those applicants who are suitable are allocated to the DFT.[43] He suggested that applicants should be specifically asked whether there are any reasons why their application would be unsuitable for fast-tracking as this may 'elicit more sensitive aspects' of the applicant's circumstances.[44] In his view, the pro forma questionnaire should be reviewed so that the focus is on 'whether the claim as then revealed can fairly be determined on the DFT timetable'.[45] While the screening interview need not amount to a 'detailed preliminary investigation',[46] it is necessary for relevant information to be elicited from the applicant; a task that is made more difficult when an applicant does not have the benefit of legal advice.[47]

[38] The Independent Chief Inspector expressed concern that the screening process was inadequately focused on ascertaining the suitability of a claim for fair determination in the DFT: Independent Chief Inspector, UK Border Agency, above n 8, para 5.38.

[39] Discussed in T Last, 'Selected. Detained. Accelerated. Refused' (Undergraduate Law Dissertation, University of Warwick, April 2011) 11.

[40] *R (Detention Action) v SSHD*, above n 13.

[41] ibid para 94.

[42] ibid para 104.

[43] ibid para 106.

[44] ibid para 108.

[45] ibid para 109.

[46] ibid para 111.

[47] ibid paras 110–12.

Detention Action also argued that certain categories of vulnerable applicants should be automatically excluded from the DFT. Ouseley J rejected this argument, noting that an automatic exclusion of vulnerable applicants would assume that applicant claims in relation to vulnerability are true, without the need for independent substantiation.[48] He held that the SSHD is entitled to follow a policy that does not automatically exclude vulnerable applicants at the screening stage.[49]

(ii) 'Quick Decision'

The policy on suitability of cases for the DFT provides that an applicant may be allocated into or remain in the DFT if there is power to detain them under immigration law, it appears that a 'quick decision' is possible, and they are not excluded from the DFT.[50] Whether a 'quick decision' is possible must be assessed in each individual case.[51] Cases in which a 'quick decision' is possible may include where 'it appears that no further inquiries are necessary in order to obtain clarification, complex legal advice or corroborative evidence'; 'it appears likely that any such inquiries can be concluded to allow a decision to be made within normal indicative timescales'; 'it appears likely that it will be possible to fully and properly consider the claim within normal indicative timescales'; 'it appears likely that no translations of documents' will be required or that these can be obtained within a period which will allow a decision to be made within the prescribed timeframes'.[52]

Other 'relevant factors' in determining whether a claim should be routed to the DFT include whether the application was made 'merely in order to delay or frustrate the enforcement of a [removal] decision'; if the applicant '[h]as failed without reasonable cause' to make an application at an earlier stage; or where the applicant '[i]s seeking to enter or has entered the UK unlawfully' or if the applicant's stay had become unlawful and there was no good reason for an asylum application not to have been made.[53]

The criteria for the inclusion of a claim in the DFT are considerably broader than the claims that UNHCR has recognised as suitable for an accelerated procedure.[54] The UNHCR has made clear that only 'manifestly unfounded' and 'clearly abusive' claims should be made subject to an expedited process, and 'these terms must be defined and interpreted

[48] ibid para 114.
[49] ibid para 116.
[50] Home Office, UK Border Agency, above n 10, para 2.1: 'DFT Processes Suitability Policy'.
[51] ibid para 2.2: 'Quick Decisions'.
[52] Home Office, UK Border Agency, above n 10.
[53] ibid para 2.2.1.
[54] UNHCR (2010), above n 4, paras 5–7.

restrictively'.[55] Kees Wouters notes that accelerated procedures should be limited to:

> claims made by applicants who are without a shadow of a doubt not in need of refugee protection (no substantive issue under the Refugee Convention is raised) or claims which are abusive and involve deception or the intention to mislead the country of refuge in order to claim protection.[56]

In *R (Detention Action) v SSHD* one of the grounds of challenge was the lack of clear criteria for the inclusion of claims in the DFT and the resultant inclusion of a large number of complex claims. Ouseley J did not accept that 'the need for clarity and the avoidance of arbitrariness requires the entire set of circumstances' warranting inclusion in the DFT to be fully detailed or exhaustive,[57] and found that the DFT was not unlawful for want of clarity and openness in the selection criteria.'[58]

(iii) Flexibility Guidelines

Once an applicant is allocated to the DFT their claim is assessed in the same way as applicants in the 'regular' asylum process. Applicants are entitled to free legal advice and representation through a duty solicitor rota system. Approximately 65 per cent of DFT applicants are publicly funded; 30 per cent are privately funded; and a very small number are unrepresented.[59]

The Flexibility Guidelines[60] recognise that the DFT process is 'built on an overriding principle of fairness' and that 'timetable flexibility or removal from the DFT … must be considered in all situations where fairness demands it.'[61] An application may be made for an applicant to be removed from the DFT if it becomes apparent that the applicant is not suitable for detention, or the claim raises complex issues and cannot therefore be decided quickly, or further evidence is required.[62] A request for the removal of an applicant from the DFT is made to the Home Office case manager who makes the decision whether to exclude an applicant from

[55] UNHCR (2010), above n 5, 224. Accelerated procedures may also be used where claims are 'well founded', that is where a positive decision is expected: UNHCR (2001), above n 4, 7 para 30.

[56] K Wouters, *International Legal Standards for the Protection from Refoulement* (Antwerpen, Intersentia, 2009) 168.

[57] *R (Detention Action) v SSHD*, above n 13, para 88.

[58] ibid para 92.

[59] ibid para 159.

[60] Home Office, UK Border Agency, 'Detained Fast Track Process: Timetable Flexibility' (UK Visas and Immigration, 11 November 2012).

[61] ibid para 2.1.

[62] ibid ch 9.

the DFT.[63] The Guidelines also provide that the DFT time frames can be extended (usually by 24 hours) in circumstances of illness, interpretation problems or lack of legal representation. The UNHCR UK Representative noted in August 2010 that there is a tendency to grant time frame extensions rather than to approve the removal of the applicant from the DFT.[64]

(iv) Detained Non-suspensive Appeal (DNSA)

The second accelerated procedure is the DNSA process, which is used where an asylum claim is certified to be 'clearly unfounded'.[65] The effect of a claim being designated for processing through the DNSA procedure is that there is no in-country appeal available following a negative decision.[66] In practice it is very difficult to appeal from outside the UK and as a consequence very few appeals are successful.[67]

The majority of cases certified as 'clearly unfounded' are claims by applicants from a deemed safe country of origin.[68] The applicant may be detained during the process.[69] Not all asylum claimants from designated countries have their claim considered for certification as 'unfounded'. A claim may also be certified 'clearly unfounded' and routed through the DNSA on an assessment of the individual merits of the case.[70] Policy states that this should only occur where the caseworker considers that the claim is incapable of succeeding before an independent tribunal.[71]

[63] UNHCR, 'Quality Initiative Project: Fifth Report to the Minister' (UNHCR Representation to the UK in London, March 2008) noted that in a number of cases inappropriate or inadequate reasons were given for refusing a request to remove an applicant from the DFT, see paras 2.3.68 and 2.3.70.

[64] UNHCR UK Representative, 'Quality Integration Project: First Report Key Observations and Recommendations' (UNHCR Representation to the UK in London, August 2010) 5.

[65] Home Office, UK Border Agency, 'Non Suspensive Appeals (NSA): Certification under Section 94 of the NIA Act 2002' (UK Visas and Immigration, 29 May 2013) para 2.1 (DNSA Policy).

[66] Under the Nationality, Immigration and Asylum Act 2002 (NIA), s 94 the right to an in-country appeal on asylum claims is removed where cases are 'clearly unfounded'.

[67] J Vine, 'An Inspection of the Non-Suspensive Appeals Process for "Clearly Unfounded" Asylum and Human Rights Claims: October 2013–February 2014' (Independent Chief Inspector of Borders and Immigration, July 2014). Of 114 NSA appeals lodged since 2007 only one appeal succeeded, see para 4.11.

[68] The applicant may reside in the list of designated states in NIA, s 94(4) or, if outside of one of the designated states, their claim must be clearly unfounded under NIA, s 94(2). Countries contained in the list of designated states must meet NIA, s 94(5). The UNHCR accepts that an accelerated procedure may be adopted in cases involving safe country or origin or a safe third country however it insists that appeals should have suspensive effect.

[69] Not all asylum claims from designated countries are certified as unfounded: see Vine, above n 67, para 4.5.

[70] About 10% of claims were certified clearly unfounded in 2013: Home Office Research and Statistics Directorate, 'Immigration Statistics: Asylum Table 13' (Q4, 2013).

[71] Home Office, UK Border Agency, above n 10, para 2.3. See also *NA (Iran) v SSHD* [2011] EWCA Civ 1172.

The DNSA was challenged in *R (L) v SSHD*.[72] The applicants argued that the procedures were unfair as a number of safeguards essential for fairness were absent.[73] The Court of Appeal noted that the process may be the applicant's sole chance to establish their refugee claim, without a further opportunity to appeal before their removal.[74] Lord Phillips considered how long an applicant requires 'if they are to be given a fair opportunity to demonstrate that they have an arguable claim to asylum'.[75] Having regard to the time allocated and the assistance made available to them, was this sufficient to enable the applicant to adequately present their case to the interviewer? This, he said, was a question of 'the nature of the material that is likely to be required to demonstrate that the applicant has, or may have, an arguable case.'[76] He concluded that the DNSA did not prevent the applicant from demonstrating that their case is arguable, and therefore that the process was not unfair.[77]

(v) DFT Time Frames and Access to Legal Representation

In his 2012 report, the Independent Chief Inspector of Borders and Immigration found that the average period between entry into the DFT and the substantive interview is 11 days and a further 13 days elapsed before a decision was made on the claim.[78] Applicants are frequently not allocated a lawyer for more than a week following their detention, and often the allocation occurs only one or two days prior to the applicant's asylum interview.[79]

In *R (Detention Action) v SSHD*, the High Court accepted that although the practice and policy of the DFT was not unlawful, various shortcomings of the process meant that access to timely legal representation was essential. Ouseley J found that the system for allocation of lawyers was a crucial failing which was 'sufficiently significant that the DFT ... carries with it too high a risk of unfair determinations for those who may be vulnerable applicants.'[80] Ouseley J noted that access to a lawyer is a 'crucial ingredient' to a fair hearing.[81] Allocation of a lawyer should occur immediately

[72] *R (L) v SSHD* [2003] EWCA Civ 25; [2003] 1 WLR 1230.
[73] ibid para 2.
[74] ibid para 27.
[75] ibid para 39.
[76] *R (L) v SSHD*, above n 72.
[77] ibid paras 48–54.
[78] Independent Chief Inspector, UK Border Agency, above n 8, cited by Ouseley J in *R (Detention Action) v SSHD* above n 13, para 161.
[79] *R (Detention Action) v SSHD*, above n 13, para 166.
[80] ibid para 221.
[81] ibid para 195.

following detention to allow adequate time for applicants to communicate instructions, taking into account potential delays. The delayed allocation of lawyers inherent in the DFT system created an 'unacceptably high risk of unfairness' and this could not be remedied by a hearing before the First Tier of the Tribunal.[82]

(vi) Decision Outcomes in the DFT

Almost *all* asylum claims channelled into the DFT are refused.[83] The refusal rate in 2012 of 95–99 per cent in the DFT compared to 74 per cent in the regular procedure is said by SSHD to show that suitable cases are being selected for the DFT, with a higher proportion lacking merit than those assessed through the regular procedure.[84] The very low approval rate of claims processed through the DFT has fuelled the widespread belief shared by lawyers, non-governmental organisations (NGOs) and refugees that claims routed into the DFT are effectively treated as 'unfounded'.[85]

C. Appeal Process

Appeals against refusal decisions made in the DFT are made to the Immigration and Asylum Chamber of the First Tier Tribunal (FTT). An asylum appeal involves a full adversarial hearing in which the FTT hears oral evidence from the SSHD and the appellant on all issues of fact and law. It can consider evidence that was not before the primary decision-maker, including evidence about matters arising after the decision is made, and it makes fresh findings of fact.[86]

The UNHCR has made clear that the right to an effective remedy in asylum cases, including those determined by way of an accelerated procedure, includes the right to appeal a negative decision.[87] In addition, the UNHCR has said it is essential for the appellate authority to be able to obtain a personal impression of the applicant,[88] and for the proceedings to involve

[82] ibid para 198.

[83] See Home Office Research and Statistics Directorate, Immigration Statistics: Outcomes of Main Applicants Accepted onto the Detained Fast Track Process, Vol 4 Table 12 Q4 2012 cited in AIDA, above n 37, fn 113, 34.

[84] *R (Detention Action) v SSHD*, above n 13, para 181.

[85] AIDA, above n 37, 35 citing Detention Action, 'Briefing: The Detained Fast Track' (London, Detention Action, February 2013).

[86] See discussion of the appeals process in *R (Detention Action) v FTT (Immigration and Asylum Chamber)*, above n 7, para 19.

[87] UNHCR (2010), above n 4, para 21.

[88] UNHCR (2001), above n 4, para 43.

a consideration of both the relevant facts and law.[89] The appeal process for the DFT meets these requirements as it provides for a full de novo appeal by the FTT of a refusal decision in asylum cases. The UNHCR does however emphasise that an essential safeguard for an effective remedy is that any appeal should have suspensive effect,[90] and that the applicant be permitted to remain until such time as their application is determined by a final judgment.[91] Whereas applicants in the DFT are permitted to remain until their appeal is concluded, those in the DNSA procedure do not have a right to an in-country appeal following a refusal decision.

The Executive Committee of the UNHCR (ExCom) has stated that an applicant who is found not to be a refugee, and any applicant whose claim for refugee status is declared manifestly unfounded or abusive, must be given the right to appeal such a decision within a *reasonable* time.[92] The Asylum and Immigration Tribunal (Fast Track Procedure Rules) 2005 (FTR) detail the basis for applicants to appeal against asylum decisions made in the DFT. The process for appeal of a DFT decision is accelerated in accordance with a statutory timetable. Appeals must be lodged within two working days of the refusal decision being received.[93] Extensions of time are permitted under the Rules. The hearing is required to occur two days after the appeal is lodged,[94] however an application for an adjournment of a maximum of 10 days may be granted. The FTT can remove an applicant from the DFT.[95] A decision should be made two days after the hearing.[96] In the regular procedure an applicant has five days to lodge an appeal; there is usually at least 35 days before the hearing; adjournments of up to 28 days may be granted;[97] and a decision is made after 10 days.[98] Asylum seekers are not guaranteed legal representation before the Tribunal.[99] However, in 2013 approximately 70 per cent of applicants were represented.[100] In 2013, 93 per cent of refusal decisions were upheld on

[89] ibid para 41.

[90] UNHCR, 'Determination of Refugee Status' (ExCom Conclusions No 8 (XXVIII)–1977, 12 October 1977) para (e)(vii); UNHCR (2001), above n 4, 10 para 43. Discussed in Wouters, above n 56, 175–76.

[91] Wouters, above n 56, 176.

[92] UNHCR (1977), above n 90, para (e)(vi).

[93] FTR, r 8.

[94] ibid r 11.

[95] FTR, r 30. 6% of cases are removed from DFT: *R (Detention Action) v SSHD*, above n 13, para 187.

[96] NB that in practice the average time taken for the appeal to be heard is nine days after lodgment of the appeal: AIDA, above n 37, 37 citing Vine, above n 67.

[97] *R (Detention Action) v SSHD*, above n 13, para 183.

[98] ibid para 191.

[99] AIDA, above n 37, 37.

[100] *R (Detention Action) v SSHD*, above n 13, para 190.

appeal.[101] The Secretary of State has argued that this evidences 'the quality or at least correctness' of the first instance decisions.[102]

In *R (Detention Action) v SSHD*,[103] Ouseley J refused to rule on the legality of detention in the DFT after the initial refusal decision and pending appeal against that decision. In *R (Detention Action) v SSHD*[104] the Court of Appeal held that whereas the application of the 'quick processing criteria' to post-decision DFT detention pending appeal is not objectionable in principle, and did not breach the Home Office's guidance, it does not satisfy the required standards of clarity and transparency.[105] There had been no clear statement made by the Government or the Home Office that there had been a change of policy from the former requirement that detention post-decision would require satisfaction of the general detention criteria, to the existing application of the detained fast track 'quick processing criteria' at the appeal stage.[106]

In *R (Detention Action) v FTT (Immigration and Asylum Chamber)*,[107] Detention Action mounted another challenge to the appellate stage of the DFT process by attacking the legality of the FTR.[108] Nicol J held that the FTR were ultra vires the powers of the Tribunal Procedure Committee (TPC), which has the power to make procedural rules ensuring that justice be done and that the tribunal system is fair. He found that the FTR incorporated 'structural unfairness'[109] as they put the appellant at a 'serious procedural disadvantage' which comes from 'the abbreviated timetable and curtailed case management powers together with the imposition of this disadvantage on the appellant by the respondent to the appeal.'[110] He found that as the rules did not secure these statutory objectives, the TPC thereby acted outside its powers.[111] The TPC 'could not impinge on the minimum level of fairness or the irreducible minimum of due process bearing in mind the appropriate degree of fairness that asylum appeals require.'[112]

[101] ibid para 73. There are in excess of 2,000 appeals per year in the DFT.

[102] ibid para 181.

[103] ibid.

[104] *R (Detention Action) v SSHD* [2014] EWCA Civ 1634; [2015] INLR 372.

[105] ibid para 70.

[106] ibid.

[107] *R (Detention Action) v FTT (Immigration and Asylum Chamber)* [2015] EWHC 1689 (Admin); [2015] EWHC 1689 (Admin).

[108] Contained in a schedule to the Tribunal Procedure (First-tier Tribunal) (Immigration and Asylum Chamber) Rules 2014 (SI 2014/2604).

[109] *R (Detention Action) v FTT (Immigration and Asylum Chamber)*, above n 107, para 57.

[110] ibid para 60.

[111] ibid para 71.

[112] ibid.

In *R (Detention Action) v FTT (Immigration and Asylum Chamber)*[113] the Court of Appeal upheld the judgment of Nicol J. Delivering the judgment of the Court, the Master of the Rolls, Lord Dyson noted that '[t]hese asylum appeals are often factually complex and difficult [and] sometimes raise difficult issues of law'.[114] He emphasised that 'the requirements of fairness and justice include that the appeal process in the DFT provides a fair opportunity for appellants to present their cases properly.'[115] However 'the time limits [of the FTR] are so tight as to make it impossible for there to be a fair hearing of appeals in a significant number of cases … The system is therefore structurally unfair and unjust.'[116] Lord Dyson noted that whereas cases are placed in the DFT so that they can be decided 'quickly and efficiently … the consequences for an asylum seeker of mistakes in the process are potentially disastrous.'[117] It is for this reason that the legislation recognises 'that justice and fairness should not be sacrificed on the altar of speed and efficiency'.[118] He concluded that '[t]he FTR do not strike the correct balance between … speed and efficiency and … fairness and justice' being 'too heavily weighted in favour of the former.'[119]

On 2 July 2015 the Minister for Immigration and Security, the Rt Hon James Brokenshire MP, announced the suspension of the DFT.[120] While confirming the Government's ongoing commitment to the underlying principles of the DFT, he stated that '[r]isks surrounding the safeguards within the system for particularly vulnerable applicants have … been identified to the extent that we cannot be certain of the level of risk of unfairness to certain vulnerable applicants who may enter DFT.'[121]

Whereas the 'fast track' processes in the UK have been declared lawful by the courts, it has been recognised that the efficiencies associated with accelerated procedures must not be at the expense of fairness to asylum applicants for whom an erroneous decision will have disastrous consequences. The courts have not required satisfaction of all the standards prescribed by the UNHCR for accelerated procedures, particularly that these are suitable only for 'manifestly unfounded' or 'clearly abusive' claims nor, in the case of DNSA, that appeals be suspensive. However, the

[113] *R (Detention Action) v FTT (Immigration and Asylum Chamber)*, above n 7.
[114] ibid para 37.
[115] ibid para 24.
[116] ibid para 45.
[117] ibid para 49.
[118] ibid.
[119] ibid para 49.
[120] House of Commons: Written Statement, 'Written Statement made by: The Minister of State for Immigration (James Brokenshire) on 02 Jul 2015' (HCWS83, 2 July 2015).
[121] ibid. On 12 November 2015 the UK Supreme Court refused the Government permission to appeal against the Court of Appeal's judgment.

requirement that an applicant be afforded a 'reasonable time' to appeal a refusal decision has been found by the courts to be an essential element of a just and fair asylum process.[122]

III. AUSTRALIA

A. Background to the 'Fast Track' Procedures

Australia has a long and controversial history of restrictive immigration policies. The arrival of asylum seekers, particularly those who come by boat and subsequently make claims for Australia's protection, are the subject of an intense, often hysterical debate, in political circles and the community. The debate has been fuelled by a significant increase in asylum seekers arriving by boat in the past decade. In 2008–09 the number of boat arrivals was 985; however, in 2012–13, it peaked at 25,173.[123]

By mid-2013, a consensus had emerged between the two major political parties (Labor and the Coalition) that asylum seekers who arrive by boat, termed 'illegals' or 'unlawful maritime arrivals' (UMAs) would no longer have their claims for refugee status processed in Australia. The Rudd Labor Government had re-established a system of offshore processing for UMAs, known as the 'Pacific Solution'. Pursuant to this policy, UMAs are intercepted by Australian authorities and sent to either Manus Island (Papua New Guinea) or Nauru for processing and subsequent resettlement in these countries if found to be owed protection obligations.[124]

The re-introduction of the 'Pacific Solution' did not quell the fear that the flow of asylum seekers to Australia would continue. As a consequence, preventing 'illegals' from coming to Australia and 'breaking the business model of the people smugglers' assumed central significance in the

[122] The *Shaw Review* made a number of recommendations in relation to the detention of asylum seekers, including the strengthening of legal safeguards against 'excessive length of detention' and urging that greater attention be given to exploring alternatives to detention: see S Shaw, *Review into the Welfare in Detention of Vulnerable Persons A Report to the Home Office* (Cm 9186, HMSO, January 2016) (*Shaw Review*) www.gov.uk/government/uploads/system/uploads/attachment_data/file/490782/52532_Shaw_Review_Accessible.pdf. The Minister of State for Immigration, James Brokenshire accepted 'the broad thrust' of the recommendations: '*Immigration Detention: Response to Stephen Shaw's Report into the Welfare in Detention of Vulnerable Persons: Written Statement*—HCWS470' (Home Office Written Statement, 14 January 2016) www.parliament.uk/business/publications/written-questions-answers-statements/written-statement/Commons/2016-01-14/HCWS470/.

[123] J Phillips and H Spinks, 'Background Note: Boat Arrivals in Australia Since 1976' (Parliamentary Library Research Paper, Parliament of Australia, July 2013) Appendix B.

[124] Australian Labor Party, 'National Platform' (46th National Conference, George Wright, 2011) 171–75.

Federal election campaign in September 2013. During the six-week election campaign, the then Opposition Leader, Tony Abbott, repeatedly made the bold claim that, if elected, the Coalition would 'Stop the Boats'.[125]

The other limb to the Opposition's immigration policy during the 2013 election campaign was a pledge to remove the right of approximately 30,000 asylum seekers who had already arrived in Australia[126] to an independent review of a decision of the Department of Immigration and Border Protection (DIBP) to refuse to grant them a protection visa. The Opposition declared that it would introduce expedited processing of these asylum seekers, and that this new process would be modelled on the DFT in the UK.[127]

The Coalition was elected to Government in September 2013. In December 2014 the amendments to the Migration Act contained in the Migration and Maritime Powers Legislation (Resolving the Asylum Legacy Caseload) Act 2014 (Cth) passed both Houses of the Commonwealth Parliament. The amendments introduced a 'fast track' procedure for a group of UMAs known as the 'asylum legacy caseload'. However, as the next section explains, despite the Coalition's claim during the election campaign that it would introduce expedited processing modelled on the UK DFT, the FTP that now forms part of the Australian protection status determination process is markedly different from its British counterpart.

B. Brief Overview of Australia's Protection Status Determination System

(i) Primary Decision

Onshore applicants for a protection visa make their claims in writing to DIBP.[128] Applicants are interviewed by a DIBP officer who makes a decision on the application. If the application is refused, applicants have a right to review of the decision by the Migration and Refugee Division (MRD) of the Administrative Appeals Tribunal (AAT). Reviews of primary protection visa decisions were conducted by the Refugee Review Tribunal

[125] Liberal Party of Australia and National Party of Australia, 'The Coalition's Operation Sovereign Borders Policy' (Brian Loughnane, July 2013).

[126] As of 31 August 2013, 32,835 applicants were awaiting determination of the claims, either in detention or in the community.

[127] Liberal Party of Australia and National Party of Australia, 'The Coalition's Policy to Clear Labor's 30,000 Border Failure Backlog' (Brian Loughnane, August 2013) 8–9.

[128] Applicants may make claims under the refugee or the complementary protection criterion under the Migration Act 1958 (Cth) (MA), s 36. Applicants must state their claims in full at the time of application: MA, s 5AAA.

(RRT) until 1 July 2015 when the RRT and its sister tribunal, the Migration Review Tribunal (MRT), were incorporated into the AAT.[129]

(ii) Review by the Administrative Appeals Tribunal

Applicants *must* be invited to a hearing of the AAT unless a favourable decision can be made 'on the papers'.[130] Hearings are held in almost all cases, as it is rare that a favourable decision can be made without a hearing.[131] Face-to-face hearings are held with the applicant, unless the applicant is in a remote location, in which case the hearing is conducted by video-conference.[132] Hearings are often more than three hours in duration and more than one hearing is sometimes held.[133]

The AAT is bound by a strict code of procedure, which incorporates the common law principles of procedural fairness.[134] It is required to conduct its review in a manner that is 'fair, just, economical, informal and quick' and act according to the substantial justice of the case.[135] It is not bound by the rules of evidence and reviews are conducted in an informal, inquisitorial manner.[136]

Applicants do not have a right to be represented, but they may obtain assistance from a lawyer or registered migration agent (RMA) who may accompany them to a hearing and make written and oral submissions on their behalf at any time during the course of the review. Applicants are able to present additional and new evidence to the AAT, which conducts a full de novo review of the decision.[137] The AAT has the power to affirm the DIBP decision or remit it for reconsideration to DIBP with a direction that the applicant is owed protection obligations. The time taken to finalise a review varies according to the complexity of the case. In 2014–15, it took

[129] Tribunals Amalgamation Act 2015 (Cth).

[130] MA, s 425.

[131] In 2014–15 favourable decisions without a hearing were made in 1% of RRT cases, see Migration Review Tribunal and Refugee Review Tribunal, 'Migration Review Tribunal and Refugee Review Tribunal Annual Report 2014–15' (Sydney, Administrative Appeals Tribunal, 2015) 20.

[132] In 2014–15 video hearings were used in 18% of cases: ibid 20.

[133] In 2014–15 the average duration of hearings was 144 minutes. Two or more hearings were held in 6% of cases, see Migration Review Tribunal and Refugee Review Tribunal, above n 131, 20.

[134] MA, Pt 7, Div 4.

[135] Administrative Appeals Tribunal Act 1975 (Cth) (AATA), s 2A(b); MA, s 420.

[136] AATA s 2A(b); MA, s 420.

[137] MA, s 424. Under MA, s 423A if an applicant seeks to present new claims or evidence that was not presented to the primary decision-maker, the Tribunal is to draw an inference adverse to the credibility of the applicant unless the applicant has a 'reasonable explanation' for not raising the claim or presenting the evidence at the primary stage.

on average 264 days (approximately nine months) from the date of the lodgement of the application for review to the date of decision.[138]

A large number of primary DIBP decisions are 'set aside' on review.[139] In 2014–15, the RRT set aside 21 per cent of the total primary decisions reviewed.[140] The set aside rate of decisions for UMAs has been consistently higher than that for non-UMAs. For example, in 2012–13, the set-aside rate of decisions in relation to nationals from Afghanistan was 84 per cent and in 2013–14 it was 72 per cent.[141] These high set-aside rates cast doubt on the quality of primary DIBP decisions and highlight the critical role of independent review of refusal decisions.

(iii) Judicial Review

Where the decision of DIBP is affirmed by the AAT, an applicant may seek judicial review of the AAT's decision by the Federal Circuit Court (FCC). The FCC is limited to review of the AAT decision on the grounds of jurisdictional error. Applicants may appeal to the Federal Court against an adverse FCC decision and then, with leave, to the High Court. A very small number of Tribunal decisions are overturned by the courts. In 2014–15, only 0.7 per cent of RRT decisions were set aside or quashed by the courts.[142]

C. The 'Fast Track' Procedure for 'Asylum Legacy Caseload' Applicants

The 2014 amendments to the Migration Act inserted a new Part 7AA to provide for a 'fast track' process (FTP) for a defined group of applicants.[143] These are UMAs, that entered Australia on or after 13 August 2012 and 1 January 2014 for whom the Minister has 'lifted the bar' preventing the UMA from making a valid visa application under subsection 46A(1), and who have subsequently been invited to and have made a valid application for a protection visa.[144] These applicants form the 'asylum legacy caseload', which consists of approximately 30,000 asylum seekers currently

[138] Migration Review Tribunal and Refugee Review Tribunal, above n 131, 23.

[139] In 2014–15 the RRT made 4,893 decisions; in 790 of these, the primary Department decision was set-aside (overturned) or remitted to the Department with a direction that the applicant meets the criteria for the grant of a protection visa, see ibid 21.

[140] ibid.

[141] ibid Table 19.

[142] Migration Review Tribunal and Refugee Review Tribunal, above n 131, 24.

[143] The amendments to MA contained in the Migration and Maritime Powers Legislation (Resolving the Asylum Legacy Caseload) Act 2014 (Cth) came into effect on 18 April 2015.

[144] The Minister can extend the definition to other classes of asylum seekers by a legislative instrument: MA, s 5(1AA).

living in the community on a bridging visa.[145] Applicants who form part of the 'asylum legacy caseload' are termed 'fast track applicants.'[146] The FTP commenced on 18 April 2015 and the first 'asylum legacy' applicants were invited by the Minister to lodge protection visa applications in late May 2015.[147]

(i) Selection for Inclusion in the FTP

The only 'selection criteria' for entry of an applicant into the FTP is the date and mode of their arrival. All 'asylum legacy caseload' applicants, including children, are automatically subject to the FTP,[148] irrespective of the factual or legal complexity of their claims, and regardless of their age or other characteristics, including where there is evidence that the applicant is the victim of trafficking, sexual abuse or torture.[149]

Although currently only 'asylum legacy' applicants are subject to the FTP, the legislation gives the Minister power to make other applicants subject to the FTP.[150] This provision opens the way for the Minister to make *all* onshore protection visa applicants subject to the FTP and remove entirely the right of access by onshore protection visa applicants to a full de novo merits review by the AAT.

[145] As of 30 June 2015 there were 28,588 asylum seekers who had arrived by boat (including 3,579 children) who had been permitted to live in the community on bridging visas while waiting for their claims for protection to be processed: Australian Border Force, 'Illegal Maritime Arrivals on Bridging E Visas' (Department of Immigration and Border Protection, June 2015).

[146] MA, s 5(1).

[147] In October 2015 DIBP was processing claims for applicants who arrived in Australia between 13 August–13 November 2012. In late 2015 applicants who arrived between 14–28 November 2012 were to be invited to make an application for a protection visa.

[148] Applicants subject to the FTP are 'fast track applicants': MA, s 5(1).

[149] Vulnerable asylum seekers who, for reasons outside their control, fall within the category of 'excluded' applicants may be specified by the Minister (in a legislative instrument) to have access to review by the IAA: see Department of Immigration and Border Protection, 'Migration and Maritime Powers Legislation Amendment (Resolving the Asylum Legacy Caseload) Bill 2014 Submission 171' (4 November 2014) 15.

[150] The legislative instrument can be disallowed by Parliament. There are currently three legislative instruments in force that expand the Class of Persons Defined as Fast Track Applicants: IMMI 16/049 (7 May 2016); IMMI 16/008 (1 April 2016) and IMMI 16/010 (24 March 2016). The effect of these legislative instruments is extend those subject to the fast track process to include an UMA who was taken to a regional processing country between 13 August 2012 and 19 July 2013 and who has returned from that country to Australia; and also a person who was born in the migration zone or a regional processing country and is a child of an UMA referred to in the instrument who is currently in the migration zone and has made a valid application for a protection visa (IMMI 16/008). IMMI 16/010 extends the fast track process to include a person who was born in the migration zone between 6 November 2013 and 5 December 2014 and who is a child of an UMA who entered the migration zone between 6 November 2013 and 5 December 2014 and was taken to Nauru. This instrument also includes similar provisions that extend the class of fast track applicants to include parents and siblings of UMAs who entered the migration zone during the same period.

(ii) Access to Legal Assistance

Since March 2014, protection visa applicants are not entitled to public funded legal assistance.[151] Applicants who are unable to afford legal advice or representation by a RMA must represent themselves at all stages of the assessment of their claims. The DIBP website contains *Protection Application Information and Guides* (PAIG) which provide information about the protection visa application and decision-making process.

The lack of public funding for legal assistance significantly disadvantages protection visa applicants who cannot afford to pay for legal advice. This is confirmed by recent RRT statistics which show that the set-aside rate of decisions when applicants were represented is considerably higher (27 per cent) than for those who were unrepresented (9 per cent).[152]

D. The Stages of the FTP

(i) Primary Decision

'Asylum legacy caseload' applicants who are invited to apply for a protection visa must complete in English a three-part application form and lodge it with DIBP.[153] Primary decisions are made by DIBP following an interview conducted by a DIBP officer with the applicant.[154] Refusal decisions[155] are referred automatically by DIBP for review by the Immigration Assessment Authority (IAA).

(ii) 'Excluded Fast Track Review Applicants'

Certain applicants, termed 'excluded fast track review applicants' ('excluded' applicants),[156] do not have access to review by the IAA.[157] It is the DIBP decision-maker who decides whether an applicant is 'excluded'. Excluded' applicants are those who:

[151] From March 2014 asylum seekers who arrive in Australia without a valid visa are not entitled to access public funded legal advice. Previously the Immigration Advice and Application Assistance Scheme (IAAAS) was available to applicants for assistance in preparing their protection visa applications to DIBP and for merits review of refusal decisions.

[152] Migration Review Tribunal and Refugee Review Tribunal, above n 131, 22.

[153] Form 866. Applications that are not completed in English are invalid.

[154] Where a positive decision is made, an applicant is entitled only to the grant of a temporary protection visa: Temporary Protection (Class XD), subclass 785 visa; Safe Haven Enterprise (Class XE), subclass 790 visa.

[155] Termed 'fast track reviewable decisions': MA, s 5(1).

[156] MA, s 5(1): definition of 'excluded fast-track review applicant'.

[157] The Minister may allow specified 'excluded fast track applicants' to access the same review process as fast track applicants by means of a legislative instrument: MA, s 473DC(3).

- provided a 'bogus' document 'without reasonable explanation';[158]
- made, in the opinion of the Minister, a 'manifestly unfounded' claim';[159]
- made an unsuccessful claim for protection in another country or with the UNHCR;[160]
- previously entered Australia and made a protection visa application which was refused or withdrawn;[161]
- came from a 'safe third country' or has access to 'effective protection' in another country.[162]

The Minister can expand the grounds on which an applicant may be designated an 'excluded' applicant by way of a legislative instrument.[163]

A 'manifestly unfounded' claim is defined to include claims that 'are without any substance', or have no 'plausible or credible basis'; those based on country information that cannot be substantiated by any objective evidence; or are based on a deliberate attempt to mislead or abuse Australia's asylum process in an attempt to delay or frustrate removal.[164] The Supplementary Explanatory Memorandum (EM) notes that the reference to 'manifestly unfounded' claims 'reflects an interpretation … that is commensurate with [the UNHCR's] position on responding to manifestly unfounded claims.'[165] However, the UNHCR has emphasised that 'manifestly unfounded' claims must be interpreted narrowly and should be restricted to claims that are 'clearly fraudulent' or which are not related to the criteria for granting asylum status. Asylum claims that are supported by 'insufficient or false information or documentation … cannot for that reason alone be declared abusive.'[166] Even in circumstances where documentation has been wilfully destroyed by an applicant the claim may not necessarily be abusive, as they 'may have acted out of fear, exhaustion or distress.'[167]

Excluded applicants in the FTP only have access to an *internal* Departmental review of the decision. The EM provides the rationale for excluding

[158] MA, s 5(1)(a)(vi).
[159] MA, s 5(1)(aa).
[160] MA, s 5(1)(a)(iii) and (iv).
[161] MA, s 5(1)(a)(ii).
[162] MA, s 5(1)(a)(i) under ss 91C, 91N.
[163] MA, s 5(1)(b); s 5(1AA)–(1AD). The legislative instrument can be disallowed by Parliament.
[164] MA, s 5(1)(aa).
[165] Minister for Immigration and Border Protection, 'Supplementary Explanatory Memorandum: Amendments to the Migration and Maritime Powers Legislation Amendment (Resolving the Asylum Legacy Caseload) Bill 2014 [GH118]' (Parliament of the Commonwealth of Australia, 2013–14, 10 February 2015) 14.
[166] UNHCR (2011), above n 6, para 196; UNHCR (2001), above n 4, 8 para 35 cited in Wouters, above n 56, 169.
[167] Wouters, above n 56, 169.

these applicants from access to independent review, '[i]t is the Government's position that such persons should not have access to merits review because the nature of their claims is so lacking in substance that further review would waste resources and unnecessarily delay their finalisation'.[168]

The UNHCR's ExCom has stated that an applicant who is found not to be a refugee, and any applicant whose claim for refugee status is declared manifestly unfounded or abusive, must be given the right to appeal such a decision within a reasonable time.[169] The UNHCR emphasises that for a remedy to be effective, it is essential that the appeal be to an authority *different* from and *independent* of the primary decision-maker.[170] The internal review of refusal decisions of 'excluded' applicants clearly does not meet this requirement. This was recognised by the Parliamentary Joint Committee on Human Rights (PJCHR) in its report examining the Bill:

> By its nature [the review] lacks the requisite degree of independence required under international human rights law to provide a sufficient safeguard ... such internal reviews by the department would be performed by the department itself, which, being the executive arm of government, would amount to executive review of executive decision-making.[171]

Applicants may also be denied access to review of a refusal decision if the Minister issues a 'conclusive certificate' preventing the decision from being changed or reviewed on the basis that to do so would be 'contrary to the national interest'.[172]

(iii) *Review by the Immigration Assessment Authority for Non-excluded Fast Track Procedure Applicants*

Refusal decisions[173] in relation to FTP applicants who are not 'excluded' are reviewable by the IAA. An applicant cannot make an application for review directly to the IAA.[174] Decisions must be referred to the IAA by

[168] Minister for Immigration and Border Protection, 'Explanatory Memorandum: Migration and Maritime Powers Legislation Amendment (Resolving The Asylum Legacy Caseload) Bill 2014' (Parliament of the Commonwealth of Australia, 2013–14) para 722.

[169] UNHCR (1977), above n 90, para (e)(vi); UNHCR (1983), above n 4.

[170] UNHCR (2001), above n 4, para 43. See UNHCR, 'Submission to the Senate Legal and Constitutional Affairs Legislation Committee: Migration and Maritime Powers Legislation Amendment (Resolving the Asylum Legacy Caseload) Bill 2014' (31 October 2014) 18.

[171] Parliamentary Joint Committee on Human Rights, *Examination of Legislation in Accordance with the Human Rights (Parliamentary Scrutiny) Act 201: Bills introduced 30 September—2 October 2014—Fourteenth Report of the 44th Parliament* (Commonwealth of Australia, October 2014) 88 para 1.411.

[172] MA, s 473BD. This excludes access to both merits review and judicial review.

[173] Termed 'fast track reviewable decisions': MA, s 473BB.

[174] Established by Division 8: MA, s 473JA.

DIBP 'as soon as reasonably practicable after the decision is made'.[175] The IAA is required to advise the applicant within two working days that an application for review has been referred to it by DIBP.[176]

The IAA is a separate office within the MRD of the AAT.[177] It consists of the President of the AAT, the MRD Division Head, a Senior Reviewer and other Reviewers who exercise the powers and functions of the IAA.[178] There are no statutory qualifications for appointment as a Senior Reviewer or Reviewer of the IAA, and appointees are public servants[179] appointed by the Minister on a non-ongoing basis for up to three years.[180] By contrast, appointments to the AAT are made for a fixed term by the Governor-General,[181] and Members are required to have legal qualifications or relevant experience that qualifies them for appointment.[182]

As the ongoing appointment of IAA Reviewers is subject to executive approval, there is a considerable risk that IAA decisions will be little more than a 'rubber stamp' of the primary DIBP decision. This risk is heightened by the statutory objectives, limited review function and reduced procedural fairness obligations of the IAA.

(iv) The Powers of the Immigration Assessment Authority (IAA)

Whereas the AAT is required to provide a review that is 'fair, just, economical, informal and quick',[183] the review provided by the IAA need only be 'efficient, quick, free of bias and consistent with Division 3.'[184] The absence of 'fair' and 'just' as stated objectives of the review process is

[175] MA, s 473CA. The Department must provide information to the IAA: MA, s 473CB.

[176] MA, s 473CC.

[177] MA, s 473JA(1). The IAA commenced operations on 1 July 2015.

[178] MA, s 473JA(2) and (3). The President and the Division Head are responsible for the overall operation and administration of the IAA and may issue directions and determine policies for this purpose: MA, ss 473JB(1) and 473FB. The Senior Reviewer manages the IAA subject to the direction of and policies determined by the Division Head and President: MA, s 473JB(2). The Senior Reviewer is appointed by the President, who must consult with the Minister before making an appointment: MA, s 473JC.

[179] The Reviewers and the Senior Reviewer are engaged under the Public Service Act 1999 (Cth): MA, s 473JE(1).

[180] A recent advertisement for Reviewers stated that 'relevant tertiary qualifications will be highly regarded'. Reviewers are required to 'have very good analytical skills, interpersonal and communication skills, possess a strong sense of fairness, have sound knowledge of administrative law, exercise good judgement and be able to make and write high quality decisions.'

[181] Senior Members and Members are appointed for a fixed term of up to seven years: AATA, s 8.

[182] Senior Members and Members must have been enrolled as a legal practitioner for five years or have relevant special knowledge or skills: AATA, s 7.

[183] AATA, s 2A(b).

[184] MA, s 473FA.

indicative of the fact that review by the IAA is an inferior form of review. Unlike the AAT, which can only make a favourable decision without inviting the applicant to a hearing,[185] the IAA reviews decisions 'on the papers'.[186] While the IAA does not have a duty to obtain, request or accept new information, it may invite a person to provide new information in writing or at an interview.[187] An applicant has 21 days to make a written submission not exceeding five pages outlining why they disagree with the decision of the Department or 'on any claim or matter presented … to the Department that was overlooked'.[188]

In contrast to the full de novo review of the decision undertaken by the AAT, the IAA does not 'conduct a full rehearing of the evidence or information that was before the Department.'[189] The IAA is not permitted to take into account 'new information'[190] unless the applicant can demonstrate that the information was not and could not have been provided to DIBP *and* there are 'exceptional circumstances'[191] to justify the consideration of the information.[192] An applicant who wishes to provide new information to the IAA must:

> provide an explanation as to why the information could not have been given to the Department before the decision was made, or the information is credible personal information which was not previously known and may have affected consideration of [the] claims, had it been known.[193]

Applicants are prevented from making new claims at the review stage.[194]

The IAA need not give the applicant any material that was before the primary decision-maker,[195] and an applicant has no right to comment on any information before the IAA, unless it would be the reason, or part of the reason for affirming the primary decision.[196] The IAA has the discretion

[185] MA, s 425.

[186] MA, s 473DB(1).

[187] Interviews may be conducted in person, by telephone, or in any other way: MA, s 473DC(3); if held, interviews are generally conducted by telephone: President AAT, 'Practice Direction for Applications, Representatives and Authorised Recipients' (Practice Direction 1, Australian Government Immigration Assessment Authority, 21 September 2015) para 33.

[188] ibid paras 20–21.

[189] ibid para 32.

[190] MA, s 473DC.

[191] MA, s 473DD.

[192] The term 'exceptional circumstances' is not defined in the Act. The EM indicates that the term is intended to give a broad discretion to the IAA.

[193] President AAT, above n 187, para 23. The explanation must be no more than five pages and provided within 21 days.

[194] Amendments to the Migration Act effected by the Migration Amendment (Protection and Other Measures) Act 2015 (Cth) require applicants to specify the particulars of their claims at the primary decision stage: MA, ss 5AAA and 423A.

[195] MA, s 473DA(2).

[196] MA, s 473DE.

to seek additional information, but it is under no obligation to do so.[197] The Act provides that the provisions are an 'exhaustive statement' of the procedural fairness requirements.[198]

The review function of the IAA is vastly inferior to that of the AAT and falls well short of the requirement that an applicant be given access to an effective remedy for refusal decisions. The UNHCR has emphasised that to be effective, the remedy must provide for a review of the claim by a court or tribunal, and the review must examine both facts and law based on up-to-date information.[199] The UNHCR recognises that given the potential consequences for an asylum seeker of an erroneous decision, the appeal authority must have the power to conduct a rigorous scrutiny of the case.[200] In addition, the UNHCR has said it is essential for the appellate authority to be able to obtain a personal impression of the applicant,[201] and for the proceedings to involve a consideration of both the relevant facts and law.[202] An 'on the papers' review does not allow the IAA to assess the credibility of the applicant in circumstances where it is an issue,[203] does not allow it to make an assessment based on the applicant's current circumstances, and gives it the discretion to take into account (or disregard) relevant and new evidence, including country of origin information, which may be critical to an accurate assessment of the applicant's protection needs.

The limited review function of the IAA does not provide an adequate mechanism for the identification of inaccurate primary decisions and thereby does not ensure that refugees will not be *refouled* to danger. The PJCHR noted that the process appears to be directed at ensuring that the assessment and review processes be 'as brief as possible' and that, while:

> administratively efficient processes are generally desirable, it is unclear whether the proposed fast track process will ensure that genuine claims for protection are identified and, in the case of the fast-track review process, that is capable of ensuring that the true and correct decision is arrived at.[204]

[197] MA, s 473DC. The Department has stated that '[g]iven the short period of time elapsing between a refused decision being referred … and a review being completed (expected to take two weeks) and the resultant limited period in which an applicant's circumstances could change during that time, it is anticipated the IAA will very rarely exercise its power to seek new information of its own volition while reviewing a case': Department of Immigration and Border Protection, above 149, 13–14.

[198] MA, s 473D.

[199] UNHCR (2010), above n 4, para 21.

[200] UNHCR, 'Submission by the United Nations High Commissioner for Refugees in the Case Between Mir Isfahani and Netherlands—Application 31252/03' (Geneva, UNHCR, May 2005) paras 38 and 40. Discussed in Wouters, above n 56, 175.

[201] UNHCR (2001), above n 4, 10 para 43; UNHCR (2014), above n 170, 18.

[202] UNHCR (2001), above n 4, 9 para 41; UNHCR (2014), above n 170, 18.

[203] ibid.

[204] Parliamentary Joint Committee on Human Rights, above n 171, para 1.406.

(v) Time Frames for Decision-making

Neither the Act nor the Regulations prescribe time frames for the making of 'fast track' decisions by either DIBP or the IAA. The time frames for the primary assessment will therefore be unlikely to be significantly different to those under the regular procedure.[205] The IAA review process is generally completed within six weeks.[206] This is in stark contrast to the average of nine months taken for the RRT to finalise a review in 2014–15.

(vi) Challenges to IAA Decisions

All 'fast track' applicants have access to judicial review.[207] However, applications for judicial review by 'excluded' applicants may only be made to the High Court.[208] The IAA provides the applicant with a 'written statement of decision' that sets out the decision and the reasons for decision.[209] The IAA (unlike the AAT) is not required to set out in its written statement any findings of fact or refer to the evidence on which the findings were based.[210] The absence of this requirement will make it difficult for the Court to identify jurisdictional error in IAA decisions. Furthermore, the limited procedural fairness obligations imposed on the IAA significantly limits the grounds on which an applicant might make a successful application for judicial review. For example, there would be no denial of procedural fairness in circumstances where the IAA failed to consider new information or claims, whether sought and obtained by the IAA, or received from an applicant without request.

IV. CONCLUSION

The Australian FTP, while purportedly modelled on the UK DFT, establishes a process for the assessment of asylum claims that is quite different to

[205] Regulations provide the time frames for applicants to comment on adverse or new material considered by decision-makers: Migration Amendment (Resolving the Asylum Legacy Caseload) Regulation 2015—Select Legislative Instrument 48/2015.

[206] President AAT, above n 187, para 28.

[207] Unless a conclusive certificate is issued under MA, s 473BD. As at 16 April 2016, the IAA had finalised 38 reviews of fast track decisions, and the first judicial review application in relation to a negative IAA decision was before the Federal Circuit Court in Sydney: www.abc.net.au/news/2016-04-16/fast-track-process-asylumseekers-lengthy-delays-court-challenge/7331296—accessed 20 May 2016.

[208] The High Court is the only court with jurisdiction to review the decision to designate an applicant as 'excluded' as a primary migration decision under MA, ss 476–477.

[209] MA, s 473EA(1). The IAA may affirm the fast track reviewable decision or remit it for reconsideration in accordance with its directions or recommendations, MA, s 473CC(2).

[210] MA, s 430.

its British counterpart. Whereas applicants are detained for the duration of the assessment of their claims in the UK, they are routed into the DFT only if a 'quick decision' is considered likely. Applicants have access to public funded legal representation to assist them in presenting their claims. Vulnerable applicants are able to be excluded from the DFT, and there is provision for flexibility in the time frames and removal of a case to the regular procedure if the matter is found to be complex or otherwise unsuitable for the DFT. Refusal decisions are appealable to the FTT which conducts a full de novo review of the facts and law. The courts in the UK have subjected the DFT to close scrutiny and have criticised the applicable time frames, suggested improvements to the screening process to protect vulnerable applicants, and insisted on meaningful access by applicants to legal representation. The UK Government was finally forced to recognise the considerable shortcomings of the DFT process and suspended its operation.

The criterion for selection for the Australian FTP is the mode and date of arrival of the asylum seeker without regard to the complexity of the claims or the age, characteristics or vulnerabilities of the applicant. Applicants do not have access to public funded legal representation and must present their claims in full to the DIBP decision-maker. Refusal decisions are reviewable by executive authorities (DIBP and IAA) that fall short of internationally recognised standards of independence, and the review is effectively restricted to the information available at the time of the primary decision. Whereas applicants have access to judicial review, the IAA's limited procedural fairness obligations restrict the potential for decisions to be declared invalid on the grounds of jurisdictional error.

Neither process is limited to the assessment of claims that are 'manifestly unfounded' or 'clearly abusive' as recommended by the UNHCR. The Australian FTP denies applicants access to an effective remedy for a refusal decision, and appeals in the DNSA process in the UK are non-suspensive thereby reducing the likelihood of a successful appeal. The 'fast track' processes in both countries are examples of governments implementing accelerated asylum procedures that 'sacrifice fairness on the altar of speed and convenience' and which fail to meet the intended purpose of an asylum status determination system. Both of these accelerated procedures heighten the risk of inaccurate decisions being made and the consequential *refoulement* to danger of individuals with international protection needs.

12

Access to Asylum for Victims of Trafficking under a Human Rights-based Approach

NULA FREI AND CONSTANTIN HRUSCHKA

I. INTRODUCTION

IT IS WIDELY accepted that persons belonging to so-called 'vulnerable groups' may face particular challenges to access to asylum procedures at large and more specifically to refugee protection or other forms of humanitarian protection. For instance, persons who have been or are at risk of being trafficked may have a well-founded fear of persecution but are not identified properly by the state authorities who are in contact with them. Often even specialised asylum authorities have significant difficulties in identifying and properly assessing cases of victims of trafficking. The shortcomings comprise specifically the non-identification of potential victims of trafficking, the denial of procedural rights, the denial of adequate protection and even *refoulement*.

The following cases illustrate these difficulties:

> Dede, 15 years old, from Nigeria, landed at Geneva Airport and immediately asked for asylum. She was assigned to accommodation for minor asylum applicants in the region of Geneva and provided with a train ticket to reach this accommodation. However, she never arrived there. Six months later, Dede was seized by the Austrian police during a brothel raid and identified on the basis of her fingerprints.

> Marie, 21 years old, from Cameroon, applied for asylum in Germany. At her asylum interview, she claimed that she had been lured to France by relatives under false promises. An aunt had promised her that she would be able to work as a waitress in Europe. However, when she arrived there she was forced to work as a domestic servant in a private household, could not leave the house and was regularly mistreated. Since her escape, her relatives had been threatening her as

well as her family back in Cameroon. Therefore, she did not want to return to France, nor to Cameroon.[1]

In addition to cases like Dede's and Marie's, there are various reasons why victims of human trafficking[2] find themselves in asylum procedures. As reflected in seminal UN High Commissioner for Refugees (UCHCR) Guidelines on International Protection dealing with trafficking,[3] the situations are manifold.[4] In the European context, the 'Dublin' admissibility system adds even more complexity: a victim may have been exploited in several countries of the Dublin area or have been granted entry based on a protection claim (like Dede) and then disappeared from the procedure or escaped and fled to another European country before seeking protection (like Marie).

Although international legal instruments concerning human trafficking recognise the right to reside for victims of trafficking,[5] this obligation has mostly been implemented by states in a manner focusing primarily on the needs of their law enforcement entities. For instance, residence permits are often subject to strict conditions, such as the co-operativeness and/or the 'utility' of the victim in criminal procedures.[6] In many national immigration systems, residence permits for victims of trafficking are of short duration. Expiry or revocation is often foreseen following the closure/conclusion of (related) criminal proceedings or if the victim resumes contact with the traffickers.[7] Frequently, these permits do not include the right

[1] Both cases cited here are fictitious. Any resemblance to real persons is coincidental.

[2] Human Trafficking is defined by the Trafficking Protocol, art 3 as: 'the recruitment, transportation, transfer, harbouring or receipt of persons, by means of the threat or use of force or other forms of coercion, of abduction, of fraud, of deception, of the abuse of power or of a position of vulnerability, or of the giving or receiving of payments or benefits to achieve the consent of a person having control over another person, for the purpose of exploitation. Exploitation shall include, at a minimum, the exploitation of the prostitution of others or other forms of sexual exploitation, forced labour or services, slavery or practices similar to slavery, servitude or the removal of organs': Protocol to Prevent, Suppress and Punish Trafficking in Persons, Especially Women and Children [2000] United Nations Treaty Series 2237 (39574) 319 (Trafficking Protocol).

[3] UNHCR, 'Guidelines on International Protection No 7: The Application of Article 1A(2) of the 1951 Convention and/or 1967 Protocol Relating to the Status of Refugees to Victims of Trafficking and Persons at Risk of Being trafficked' (HRC/GIP/06/07, 7 April 2006) (UNHCR Trafficking Guidelines).

[4] UNHCR Trafficking Guidelines, above n 3, para 13.

[5] Trafficking Protocol, above n 2, art 7; Council of Europe Convention on Action against Trafficking in Human Beings [2005] Council of Europe Treaty Series 197 (CoE Convention), above n 5, art 14.

[6] eg art 36 of the Swiss Federal Decree on Admission, Residence and Employment (Verordnung über Zulassung, Aufenthalt und Erwerbstätigkeit) of 24 October 2007 (SR 142.201) allows for the issuing of a short-term residence permit for victims of trafficking only if the presence of the victim is necessary for police investigations or court proceedings.

[7] eg ibid art 36(3).

to family reunification or come with very restricted access to the national labour market or to social security.

Compared to the limitations of these trafficking-specific residence options, asylum and international protection are powerful, but still very much under-utilised protection tools for victims of human trafficking.[8] In many legal systems, asylum leads to a residence permit, a longer-term status, unrestricted access to the labour market and to integration measures. According to the United Nations Convention Relating to the Status of Refugees (Refugee Convention),[9] refugees are, inter alia, entitled to 'the same treatment as is accorded to nationals' with regard to access to health care, social security and other assistance.[10] International legal instruments on human trafficking explicitly recognise the right of victims of trafficking to seek asylum: Both Article 14(1) of the Trafficking Protocol and Article 40(4) of the CoE Convention state that:

> Nothing … shall affect the rights, obligations and responsibilities of States and individuals under international law, including international humanitarian law and international human rights law and, in particular, where applicable, the 1951 Convention and the 1967 Protocol relating to the Status of Refugees and the principle of non-refoulement as contained therein.[11]

In practice, however, access to an asylum procedure by a victim of human trafficking is often limited. This is mainly due to two reasons: first, victims are often not identified as such in the asylum procedure. This is a general challenge, which is addressed in Section III below. This problem of access to the procedure for victims of trafficking is further accentuated in admissibility procedures, such as the Dublin Regulation in Europe (Section IV). Secondly, victims of trafficking are often denied international protection based on—from our perspective—an improper interpretation of the requirements for granting refugee status or complementary forms of protection which is not reflective of victim's experiences or vulnerabilities (Section V). Consequently, the two main areas of concern regarding the access to asylum are: (1) access to the refugee status determination (RSD) *procedure* and (2) access to substantial (refugee) *protection.* This

[8] J Bhabha and C Alfirev, 'The Identification and Referral of Trafficked Persons to Procedures for Determining International Protection Needs' (PPLAS/2009/03, UNHCR, 2009) 9. See also A Dorevitch and M Foster, 'Obstacles on the Road to Protection: Assessing the Treatment of Sex-Trafficking Victims under Australia's Migration and Refugee Law' (2008) 9(1) *Melbourne Journal of International Law* 18.

[9] 189 United Nations Treaty Series 150, supplemented by the 1967 Protocol relating to the Status of Refugees, 606 United Nations Treaty Series 267 (Refugee Convention).

[10] Refugee Convention, above n 9, arts 23–24.

[11] Trafficking Protocol, above n 2; CoE Convention, above n 5.

chapter illustrates why and how these challenges need to be addressed by employing a human rights-based approach.[12] The contribution is mainly based on the research of the authors on European case law and practice with a particular focus[13] on Swiss cases.[14] Section II of this chapter will address the human rights framework for victims of human trafficking. Section III will treat the difficult identification of victims of trafficking in asylum procedures, followed by Section IV where we will examine the challenges victims face in accessing the asylum procedure, before we go on to discuss the access of victims to international protection (refugee status and complementary forms of protection) in Section V. We will conclude the chapter with some possible solutions in Section VI.

II. THE HUMAN RIGHTS FRAMEWORK FOR VICTIMS OF HUMAN TRAFFICKING

There are a number of ways in which international and European Union (EU) law deal with protection of victims of trafficking in asylum procedures. Indeed, the international legal instruments on trafficking set out a broad range of states' obligations towards persons who are or are suspected to be victims of trafficking. The positive obligations of states are to be found both in the trafficking conventions and in human rights treaties: the Trafficking Protocol (which is international) and the

[12] According to the OHCHR, 'Recommended Principles and Guidelines on Human Rights and Human Trafficking' (text presented to the Economic and Social Council as an addendum to the report of the UNHCHR, E/2002/68/Add 1) principle 1, a human-rights based approach consists mainly of the following two principles: 'The *human rights of trafficked persons shall be at the centre of all efforts to prevent and combat trafficking* and to protect, assist and provide redress to victims. Furthermore, anti-*trafficking measures shall not adversely affect the human rights and dignity of persons*, in particular the rights of those who have been trafficked, and of migrants, internally displaced persons, refugees and asylum-seekers' (emphasis added).

[13] The focus on Swiss cases was chosen because of the areas of research of the authors. Nevertheless, it seems from exchanges with other researchers that the difficulties are basically the same in many other national protection systems in Europe. See for Germany: IOM/UNHCR/BAMF, 'Identifizierung und Schutz von Opfern des Menschenhandels im Asylsystem' (Nuremberg 2012) www.bamf.de/SharedDocs/Anlagen/DE/Publikationen/Broschueren/iom-projektbericht-menschenhandel-asylverfahren.pdf?__blob=publicationFile.

[14] The chapter is mainly based on an analysis conducted by Constantin Hruschka of 30 first instance asylum case files concerning (presumed) victims of trafficking at the Swiss State Secretariat for Migration and an analysis of 59 second instance decisions of the Swiss Federal Administrative Court by Nula Frei. While the first instance files are not accessible to the public, all Court decisions are accessible at www.bvger.ch/publiws/. The analysis of the cases was accompanied by discussions with practitioners and other asylum and anti-trafficking specialists in Switzerland. For our results we focused on the main trends that we deducted from this analysis and research.

CoE Convention (regional). Both of these contain duties regarding the protection and assistance of victims of trafficking. The EU has issued two directives dealing with residence permits for victims[15] and protection of victims[16] respectively. Two of the universal human rights treaties also contain specific obligations relating to the protection of victims of trafficking: Article 6 of the Convention on the Elimination of all Forms of Discrimination Against Women (CEDAW);[17] and Articles 32, 34 and 35 of the Convention on the Rights of the Child (CRC),[18] as well as the Optional Protocol to the Convention on the Rights of the Child on the Sale of Children, Child Prostitution and Child Pornography.[19] Moreover, the jurisprudence and practice of international human rights treaty bodies interpreting the 'traditional' prohibitions of slavery, servitude and forced labour contained in Article 8 of the International Covenant on Civil and Political Rights (ICCPR)[20] and Article 4 of the European Convention on Human Rights (ECHR),[21] have also proven to be inclusive with regards to human trafficking.[22]

In the following sections, we will briefly outline the human rights obligations of states towards victims of human trafficking.[23]

[15] Council Directive 2004/81/EC of 29 April 2004 on the residence permit issued to third-country nationals who are victims of trafficking in human beings or who have been the subject of an action to facilitate illegal immigration, who cooperate with the competent authorities [2004] OJ L261/19 (referred to hereafter as Directive 2004/81).

[16] Council Directive 2011/36/EU of 5 April 2011 on preventing and combating trafficking in human beings and protecting its victims, and replacing Council Framework Decision 2002/629/JHA [2011] OJ L101/1 (referred to hereafter as Directive 2011/36).

[17] Convention on the Elimination of All Forms of Discrimination Against Women 1979 [1981] United Nations Treaty Series 1249, 13 (referred to hereafter as CEDAW).

[18] Convention on the Rights of the Child [1990] United Nations Treaty Series 1577, 3.

[19] Optional Protocol to the Convention on the Rights of the Child on the Sale of Children, Child Prostitution and Child Pornography 2000, United Nations Treaty Series 2171, 227.

[20] International Covenant on Civil and Political Rights [1976] United Nations Treaty Series 999, 171.

[21] European Convention for the Protection of Human Rights and Fundamental Freedoms 1950, Council of Europe Treaty Series 5.

[22] See *Rantsev v Cyprus and Russia* App no 25965/04 (ECtHR, 7 January 2010) and *Siliadin v France* App no 73316/01 (ECtHR, 26 July 2005). In *Rantsev*, the Court explicitly included human trafficking within art 4 ECHR. However, the Court refused to determine whether trafficking constituted slavery, servitude or forced labour or whether it constituted an additional, unwritten element of art 4.

[23] It is not intended to provide a comprehensive treatise on the human rights framework. For that, see V Stoyanova, 'Human Trafficking and Slavery Reconsidered. Conceptual Limits and States' Positive Obligations' (PhD Thesis, Lund University, 2015, Cambridge University Press, forthcoming 2017). See also J Planitzer, *Trafficking in Human Beings and Human Rights. The Role of the Council of Europe Convention on Action Against Trafficking in Human Beings* (Vienna, NWV Verlag, 2014).

A. Protection from Further Harm

The basic and most important human rights obligation of states relating to the prohibition of trafficking is to protect persons from such acts.[24] According to jurisprudence of the European Court of Human Rights (ECtHR), wherever there is a credible suspicion that a person has become victim of human trafficking or that there is a real risk she or he may become a victim, states are obliged to take measures to protect that person.[25] The 'credible suspicion' standard used by the ECtHR essentially means that there is no need for actual proof or elevated substantiation of the trafficking to activate this obligation. The Trafficking Protocol and the CoE Convention require states first and foremost to protect the physical safety of the (potential) victims.[26] Furthermore, states also have a duty to protect a victim from trafficking-related harm in case of return to his or her home country.[27] However, these protection measures must be carried out whilst fully respecting the victim's human rights.

B. Identification

Identification of potential victims of trafficking is of fundamental importance and a key element of any adequate protection measure. As victims rarely self-identify or self-report[28] their situation, states are required to take proactive measures. In the European context, Article 10(1) of the CoE Convention, Article 11(4) of Directive 2011/36, and relevant international

[24] M Nowak, *UN Covenant on Civil and Political Rights*, 2nd edn (Kehl, NP Engel, 2005) art 8, para 6. See also, inter alia, Human Rights Committee (HRC), 'Consideration of Reports Submitted by States Parties Under Article 40 of the Covenant: Concluding Observations of the Human Rights Committee—Australia' (HRC 95th Session, CCPR/C/AUS/CO/52, Geneva, 2 April 2009) para 22; Committee on the Rights of the Child (CRC), 'Consideration of Reports submitted by States Parties Under Article 12, paragraph 1, of the Optional Protocol to the Convention on the Rights of the Child on the Sale of Children, Child Prostitution and Child Pornography: Concluding Observations—Sweden' (CRC 58th Session, CRC/C/OPSC/SWE/CO/1, 23 January 2012) para 23(d).

[25] *Rantsev v Cyprus and Russia*, above n 22, para 286. Interestingly, the 'credible suspicion' standard seems to be used by the ECtHR only in cases concerning (alleged) human trafficking, see *M and Others v Italy and Bulgaria* App no 40020/03 (ECtHR, 31 July 2012) para 156 and *CN v The United Kingdom* App no 4239/08 (ECtHR, 13 November 2012) para 69.

[26] CoE Convention, above n 5, art 12(2); Trafficking Protocol, above n 2, art 6(5).

[27] See Section II below.

[28] 'Self-identification' means that the victims identify themselves as a victim of the crime of trafficking. 'Self-reporting' means that the victims will describe the exploitation they have been subjected to, which will be recognised as a situation of trafficking in human beings by a person with the necessary qualifications. See European Migration Network (EMN), 'Identification of Victims of Trafficking in Human Beings in International Protection and Forced Return Procedures' (EMN Study, March 2014) 20.

human rights practice[29] explicitly require states to sensitise and train their personnel who may come into contact with victims of trafficking. The CoE Convention (Article 10(1)) and international human rights bodies[30] furthermore oblige states to ensure that the different authorities collaborate with each other as well as with relevant support organisations. Article 10(2) of the CoE Convention prohibits the expulsion from the territory of a respective Member State as long as the identification process is not completed. This obligation also helps from a refugee protection perspective to safeguard the principle of *non-refoulement* contained in Article 33(1) of the Refugee Convention, as it is normally impossible to determine whether a potential victim of trafficking is a refugee before a proper identification process has been carried out. We will examine the process of identification in more detail in Section III.

C. Residence Permit

The residency rights given to victims of trafficking are addressed in different ways in international and EU provisions. Both the Trafficking Protocol and the CoE Convention invite states to adopt measures to permit victims of trafficking in persons to remain in their territory. While Article 7(1) of the Trafficking Protocol is formulated in vague terms, the drafters of the CoE Convention chose a clearer language, and established a more sophisticated protection mechanism by distinguishing between a recovery and reflection period (Article 13 of the CoE Convention) and a residence permit (Article 14 of the CoE Convention).

The so-called recovery and reflection period is a time frame of at least 30 days, during which the state needs to abstain from any enforcement of an expulsion order. The purpose of this period is to enable the victim to recover physically and psychologically and to take an informed decision as to whether to co-operate with the law enforcement authorities. This period is contained in the CoE Convention and in EU law (Article 6

[29] See, inter alia, HRC, 'Concluding Observations on the Sixth Periodic Report of Finland' (CCPR/C/FIN/CO/6, 22 August 2013) para 9; Committee on the Elimination of Discrimination against Women (CEDAW), 'Concluding Observations on the Seventh and Eighth Periodic Reports of Austria Adopted by the Committee at its Fifty Fourth Session (11 February–1 March 2013)' (CEDAW/C/AUT/CO7-8, 1 March 2013) para 47; CRC, 'Consideration of Reports Submitted by States Parties Under Article 44 of the Convention—Concluding Observations of the Committee on the Rights of the Child: Denmark' (CRC/C/DNK/CO/4, 4 February 2011) para 62(d). This obligation to identify victims is, however, not contained in the Trafficking Protocol.

[30] See CRC, 'Consideration of Reports Submitted by States Parties Under Article 44 of the Convention—Concluding Observations: Bangladesh' (51st Session, CRC CRC/C/BGD/CO/4, 12 June 2009) para 89(d).

of Directive 2004/81). It applies as soon as there are reasonable grounds to believe that the person concerned is a victim (Article 13(1) of the CoE Convention). During this period the person shall be entitled to basic assistance and protection measures.[31] These provisions also apply if the victim is identified in the asylum procedure. The wording of both the CoE Convention and the Directive 2004/81 ('shall') clearly obliges states to grant a recovery and reflection period in any case.[32]

Furthermore, states may issue renewable residence permits for victims of trafficking (Article 7 of the Trafficking Protocol, Article 14 of the CoE Convention and Article 8 of Directive 2004/81). Granting residence permits is also seen as an important protection tool by the international human rights treaty bodies.[33] The conditions for the granting of a residence permit differ considerably between these three sources, but remain in essence related to the participation in criminal proceedings. This means that victims who are not giving evidence against their traffickers or victims in whose cases no criminal proceedings were started (eg due to lack of evidence or because the trafficker could not be found) might not benefit from this kind of residence permit.

D. Assistance

Both international and EU provisions on trafficking provide that states shall assist victims in their physical, psychological and social recovery by providing a standard of living that ensures their subsistence. The Trafficking Protocol (Article 6(3)), the CoE Convention (Article 12) and EU Directive 2004/81 (Article 11) set forth similar measures, namely: appropriate (and secure) housing or accommodation, psychological, material and medical assistance, counselling and information and, where necessary, translation or interpretation services. These same instruments also provide that children shall enjoy access to at least primary education.[34]

[31] Such as the guaranteeing of physical safety, standards of living capable of ensuring their subsistence, access to emergency medical treatment, translation and interpretation services, counselling and information, access to education for children (CoE Convention, above n 5, art 12(1)–(2)).

[32] Despite the clear wording of the provisions Stoyanova, above n 23, 177 sees no clear manifestation of a binding obligation in either the CoE Convention or the Directive.

[33] CEDAW, 'Concluding Observations of the Committee on the Elimination of Discrimination Against Women: The Netherlands' (45th Session, CEDAW/C/NLD/CO/5, 5 February 2010) para 29; CEDAW, 'Concluding observations of the Committee on the Elimination of Discrimination Against Women: Belgium' (42nd Session, CEDAW/C/BEL/CO/6, 7 November 2008) para 42.

[34] CoE Convention, above n 5, art 12(1)(f); EU Directive 2004/81, above n 15, art 10(b).

The international human rights treaty bodies also recommend the same scope of assistance to victims.[35] For instance, several committees have recommended that assistance should not be subject to the ability and/or willingness of the victim to collaborate in investigation or criminal proceedings, nor to the issuance of a residence permit.[36]

E. Repatriation and Prohibition of *Refoulement*

Finally, the international legal framework concerning victims of trafficking also contains basic guarantees in case the victim is returned to his or her home country or any other third state. Both the CoE Convention (Article 16) and the Trafficking Protocol (Article 8) oblige states to pay due regard to the safety of the returned person. The CoE Convention furthermore prescribes that the human rights and the dignity of that victim shall be respected.[37] While these provisions are rather vague, the jurisprudence of the ECtHR indicates that returning a person to a place where there is a real risk that she or he will be re-trafficked or will face other serious harm, such as reprisals, would violate Article 4[38] of the ECHR. For instance, in an admissibility decision regarding a woman from Nigeria who had been trafficked to France, the Court stated that due to the 'intangible and absolute character' of Article 4, the question of extraterritorial application of Article 4 could arise.[39] In other cases involving similar circumstances, the Court has ordered interim measures.[40] As the Court usually equates the

[35] See HRC, above n 29, para 9; HRC, 'Concluding Observations on the Sixth Periodic Report of Germany, Adopted by the Committee at its 106th Session (15 October–2 November 2012)' (CCPR/C/DEU/CO/6, 12 November 2012) para 13; CRC, 'Consideration of Reports Submitted by States Parties Under Article 12, Paragraph 1, of the Optional Protocol to the Convention on the Rights of the Child on the Sale of Children, Child Prostitution and Child Pornography—Concluding Observations: Canada' (61st Session, CRC/C/OPSC/CAN/CO/1, 5 October 2012) para 35(d); CEDAW, Concluding Observations of the Committee on the Elimination of Discrimination Against Women: Norway (51st Session, CEDAW/C/NOR/CO/8, 9 March 2012) para 26(d)).

[36] In HRC, 'Consideration of Reports Submitted by States Parties Under Article 40 of the Covenant—Concluding Observations of the Human Rights Committee: Poland' (100th Session, CCPR/C/POL/CO/6, 27 October 2010) para 14, the HRC recommended that Poland should take measures 'to ensure that a trafficked victim's protection is not made conditional upon the person's cooperation in legal proceedings'. See also CEDAW, above n 35, para 26(d); CEDAW, 'Concluding Observations of the Committee on the Elimination of Discrimination Against Women: Czech Republic' (47th Session, CEDAW/C/CZE/CO/5, 22 October 2010) para 25.

[37] CoE Convention, above n 5, art 16(1).

[38] According to the Court, the prohibition of slavery and servitude also includes trafficking (above n 22).

[39] *VF v France* App no 7196/10 (ECtHR, 29 October 2011).

[40] See *Joy Idemugia v France* App No 4125/11 (ECtHR, 27 March 2012); *M v UK* App No 16081/08 (ECtHR, 1 December 2009); *BL v France* App No 25037/09 (ECtHR, 17 May 2011);

prohibition of trafficking with the right to life (Article 2) and the prohibition of torture (Article 3), we conclude that Article 4 also includes protection from *refoulement*.[41]

However, the 'transfer' of these principles of international trafficking law to national asylum systems started only recently and would need to be further developed in law and practice.[42] This is true for the substantial asylum procedure and even more so for admissibility regimes like the Dublin system in Europe.

III. IDENTIFICATION OF VICTIMS OF TRAFFICKING IN ASYLUM PROCEDURES

In addition to trafficking provisions, the obligation to identify victims of trafficking also applies to asylum procedures.[43] For a number of reasons, identification of victims in asylum procedures is, in principle, easier and should therefore be more likely to occur than under other procedures. For example, where victims come into direct contact with a relevant caseworkers, a favourable practical setting for identification is created, whereas in other circumstances, the detection of victims of trafficking often requires pro-active investigation by police officers or labour inspectors, possibly in a prostitution environment or other (illegal) business sectors. The asylum system can therefore significantly contribute to the fight against trafficking. That notwithstanding, only recently have states and international and regional organisations begun to address the topic of identification of

LR v UK App No 49113/09 (ECtHR, 14 June 2011); *XD v France* App No 48189/08 (ECtHR, 22 February 2011); *FA v UK* App No 20658/11 (ECtHR, 10 September 2013); *LO v France* App No 4455/14 (ECtHR 26 May 2015); *OGO v UK* App No 13950/12 (ECtHR, 18 February 2014).

[41] See also R Piotrowicz and C van Eck, 'Subsidiary Protection and Primary Rights' (2004) 53(1) *International and Comparative Law Quarterly* 125; J McAdam, *Complementary Protection in International Refugee Law* (Oxford, Oxford University Press, 2007) 149; V Stoyanova, 'Complementary Protection for Victims of Human Trafficking under the European Convention on Human Rights' (2011) 3(2) *Goettingen Journal of International Law* 777.

[42] See V Stoyanova, 'Victims of Human Trafficking: A Legal Analysis of the Guarantees for "Vulnerable Persons" under the Second Phase of the EU Asylum Legislation' in C Bauloz, M Ciger, S Singer and V Stoyanova (eds), *Seeking Asylum in the European Union: Selected Protection Issues Raised by the Second Phase of the Common European Asylum System* (The Hague, Brill/Martinus Nijhoff, 2015). From the German-speaking doctrine see H Janetzek and C Lindner, 'Opfer von Menschenhandel im Asylverfahren' [2014] *Asylmagazin* 105; N Frei, 'Der Schutz von Menschenhandelsopfern im Asylsystem' [2013] *ASYL* 14; N Frei, 'Menschenhandelsopfer im Asylverfahren' in A Achermann, C Amarelle, M Caroni, A Epiney, W Kälin and Peter Uebersax (eds), *Jahrbuch für Migrationsrecht 2014/2015* (Bern, Stämpfli, 2015).

[43] For Member States of the European Union (EU), this obligation is implicitly recognised in the Council Directive 2013/33/EU of 26 June 2013 laying down standards for the reception of applicants for international protection (recast), [2013] OJ L180/96 (referred to hereafter as Reception Conditions Directive), art 21.

trafficking victims in the context of asylum procedures, and serious obstacles to identification remain, as we will show in the following paragraphs.

A. The Identification Process in Asylum Procedures

Identification usually consists of two stages: *detection* and *ascertainment*.[44] During the *detection stage*, measures must be taken to guarantee that persons who may be victims actually trigger the necessary attention of the authorities. The goal is to establish, with a reasonable grounds standard, whether the concerned person is a victim or not. Two detection mechanisms are typically used in asylum procedures:[45]

- Self-reporting, either by the victim or through her or his counsel. Strictly speaking, this is not a detection mechanism. While a system that only relies on self-reporting for identification will certainly miss many opportunities to identify victims and is therefore not recommendable,[46] it is clear that asylum systems should be open to self-reporting of victims.
- Proactive screening of all applicants or of at least all applicants with certain risk profiles (such as women from Western Africa, Southeast Asia or Eastern Europe, unaccompanied children, pregnant girls or teenage mothers). This is considered by the European Migration Network to be good practice.[47] In this context, screening means that applicants from such risk profiles are more or less thoroughly examined on whether their claim, behaviour or other factors indicate potential trafficking. This usually involves asking specific questions about the reasons why the person left her or his home country, if she or he had been promised a 'better future', etc. One important aspect to ask questions about is the 'recruiting strategy', since the strategies are often the same in one specific country of origin. Indicators lists, such as the ones developed by the UN Office on Drugs and Crime (UNODC),[48] International Labour Office (ILO),[49] or many

[44] The terminology used may differ depending on the author, eg Stoyanova, above n 23, 171 uses 'reasonable grounds to believe stage' and 'conclusive decision stage'.

[45] See also European Migration Network, above n 27, 19ff.

[46] ibid.

[47] ibid. This view expressed in the study of the EMN reflects a common European understanding that specific screening constitutes good practice.

[48] United Nations Office on Drugs and Crime, 'Human Trafficking Indicators' www.unodc.org/pdf/HT_indicators_E_LOWRES.pdf.

[49] International Labour Office, 'Operational Indicators of Trafficking in Human Beings' www.ilo.org/global/topics/forced-labour/publications/WCMS_105023/lang--en/index.htm.

non-governmental organisations (NGOs) and national authorities can be useful at this stage too, since they contain practical information on the most common signs of trafficking.

Once detection occurs, the standard of proof for referring the person to the second ('ascertainment') stage is the one of reasonable grounds: if there are reasonable grounds that a person might be a victim, positive obligations of states towards victims of trafficking apply, such as the ones outlined in Section II.

The *ascertainment stage* constitutes the core identification process. It serves the purpose of establishing certainty about the initial suspicion in order to determine whether the person is or is not a victim of trafficking. During this stage, victims already enjoy certain rights and are protected from *refoulement*.[50] International law, especially the CoE Convention, provides the State Parties with considerable discretion as to how to organise their identification procedures.[51] Consequently, national asylum systems deal differently with this ascertainment stage. In some countries, asylum authorities are under an obligation to immediately refer a suspected victim of trafficking to the competent authority for official identification, in other countries, asylum authorities are themselves competent to officially identify a victim.[52]

B. The Status Quo: Self-identification, Credibility and Biases

At present, in many national asylum systems self-identification seems to be implicitly expected, even though convincing evidence suggests that self-identification or self-reporting are generally very rare.[53] The reasons why victims actually do not self-identify or self-report themselves are multifaceted: the person might not want to reveal her or his situation to the authorities due to fear (often for the family left behind), embarrassment or traumatisation. Also, the person might not perceive herself or

[50] See above Section II.

[51] Stoyanova, above n 23, 158.

[52] eg according to the research conducted by the EMN, above n 28, 21f, in 12 EU (Member) States (Cyprus, Estonia, Greece, Ireland, Italy, Lithuania, Luxembourg, Malta, Netherlands, Poland, Spain, United Kingdom (UK)), the authority concerned is required to refer the indications of trafficking to the competent authority without undertaking any further investigation. In contrast, in Finland, the Slovak Republic, Norway and the UK, asylum authorities are themselves competent to officially identify a victim, see EMN, above n 28, 22.

[53] See generally EMN, above n 28, 20.

himself as a victim either because of pride ('I am just in a difficult situation, nothing more') or normality ('I knew it would be tough') or because the exploitation and/or abuse has not yet started.[54] Moreover, the person might not trust the authorities, for example because she or he has had unpleasant experiences with authorities in the past or because the traffickers told her or him to stay away from authorities ('they will send you back'). Additionally, if the purpose of the asylum procedure is not made clear to the person, this might also prevent her or him from revealing the 'real' story.

The expectation of self-identification coupled with the shared duty of fact-finding[55] in the asylum procedure, which in many asylum systems includes a quasi-obligation to bring forward the real facts from the onset, often results in a negative outcome of the asylum procedure and a failure to even initiate (or conclude) the identification process. In many cases credibility issues are paramount: if the victim does not tell her or his real story, or only provides it at a later stage of the asylum procedure (which, together with trauma-related difficulties, is a common feature in trafficking cases), asylum caseworkers tend to classify the victims account as not credible and do not enter into a substantive assessment of the claim.[56]

Even if the person shares the actual facts from the onset, the result of the caseworker's assessment of the claim might lead to negative credibility finding since she or he does not believe that such atrocities are actually happening in the relevant country. This is what we call the 'Heidi bias'—meaning that the persons responsible for deciding on the asylum claim have difficulties believing that atrocities against, and exploitation of, victims of trafficking actually happen in his own 'beautiful, peaceful and humanitarian country' (ie Switzerland). In combination with this 'Heidi bias', caseworkers often seem to consider human trafficking as a purely criminal issue that does not need to be addressed in the asylum system, but by law-enforcement authorities. The opposite is correct as refugee law and international protection are—used properly—actually powerful

[54] According to the definition of trafficking, this stage already constitutes trafficking, since in order to fulfil the definition the 'purpose' element exploitation does not yet have to have realised itself (Trafficking Protocol, art 3).

[55] JC Hathaway and M Foster, *The Law of Refugee Status*, 2nd edn (Cambridge, Cambridge University Press, 2014) 118ff.

[56] See the Swiss Federal Administrative Court (BVGer E-3600/2014). See also the report on Switzerland by the CoE Convention monitoring body: Group of Experts on Action Against Trafficking in Human Beings (GRETA), 'Report Concerning the Implementation of the Council of Europe Convention on Action against Trafficking in Human Beings by Switzerland' (COE, GRETA(2015)18, 14 October 2015) para 123.

tools to both fight human trafficking and protect its victims. The 'Heidi bias' and the 'criminality bias' may also be coupled with a general lack of sensitisation for human trafficking among asylum authorities and, in particular, caseworkers and adjudicators. This challenge is multiplied in accelerated and/or admissibility procedures, where time limits are usually a dominant feature of the procedure and where often no in-depth interview with the applicant takes place.

In our view, it is therefore of fundamental importance that where there are reasonable grounds to believe that the person concerned might be a victim of trafficking, the asylum case is transferred to a trained and specialised caseworker. Furthermore, the case should be signalled to an NGO specialised in identifying, assisting and protecting victims of trafficking to ensure that the person receives adequate legal and material support during her or his asylum procedure. The assessment by such an NGO of whether the person might actually be a victim of trafficking should have a certain weight in the asylum procedure (eg on the question of credibility of the victim's account and his or her protection needs).

IV. ACCESS TO THE ASYLUM PROCEDURE

The use of admissibility procedures (such as the Dublin system in Europe), before a substantive examination of an asylum application is carried out, has been described as leading to serious protection concerns in general.[57] So-called 'third country agreements' and related provisions had a further negative impact on the processing of asylum applications in national legal systems. In this context, a 'fair and efficient' asylum procedure often seemed to mean the efficient organisation of an asylum procedure, where only minimum of fairness was required.[58] The focus was mainly on adherence to fundamental human rights principles such as *non-refoulement* and not on the best interests of (potential) refugees.

In this section we will elaborate on the legal relationship between the different legal frameworks that apply ('Dublin' law, anti-trafficking law, human rights law) and will attempt to reconcile the requirements and perceived contradictions of these frameworks.

[57] See Hathaway and Foster, above n 54, 30ff who describe the protection adverse effects of admissibility procedures and provide examples of relevant practice and jurisprudence.

[58] See UNHCR, 'Problem of Refugees and Asylum-Seekers Who Move in an Irregular Manner From a Country in Which They Had Already Found Protection' (ExCom Conclusions No 58 (XL), 1989, 13 October 1989).

A. Access to the Asylum Procedure in Europe: The Dublin Regulation

The recast Dublin III Regulation of 2013[59] aims to improve the human rights protection and to enhance efficiency[60] while confirming the underlying principles for the allocation of responsibilities when examining asylum claims as they have been in place since the creation of the Dublin mechanism in 1990.[61] The criteria for establishing responsibilities under the Dublin system are based—with the exception of the rarely applicable prior-ranking family criteria[62]—on the costs-by-cause principle: the state that granted (or did not effectively hinder) access to the territory and accepted the subsequent stay of the asylum seeking person is responsible for dealing with his or her asylum application and all matters related to the stay of this person. Consequently, the first criterion is the granting of a residence permit (Article 12(1) of the Dublin III Regulation), followed by the issuance of a visa (Article 12(2)) and the irregular crossing of an external border (Article 13(1)).[63]

The Dublin system is based on the 'presumption of safety' of all Dublin Member States (meaning that all Member States adhere to the protection obligations flowing from international and European refugee and asylum law) which derives from the principle of mutual trust between the Member States.[64] Therefore, most of the participating states hold that the Dublin system does not aim at identifying individual needs as it only establishes criteria for the allocation of responsibilities like the necessary 'distribution' of asylum seekers between local entities, for example, in a federal state. Looking at the discrepancies between the protection systems in the Dublin area this presumption of safety is a legal one and is contradicted by empirical evidence.[65]

[59] Council Regulation 604/2013 of 26 June 2013 establishing the criteria and mechanisms for determining the Member State responsible for examining an application for international protection lodged in one of the Member States by a third-country national or a stateless person (recast) [2013] OJ L180/31 (referred to hereafter as the Dublin III Regulation). All articles and recitals cited in Section IV refer to the Dublin III Regulation unless otherwise stated.

[60] See C Hruschka, 'The (Reformed) Dublin III Regulation—A Tool for Enhanced Effectiveness and Higher Standards of Protection?' (2014) 15 *ERA Forum* 469.

[61] See Dublin III Regulation, recital 9.

[62] Articles 8–11.

[63] The other criteria are acceptance of an illegal stay on its territory by a Member State for more than five months (art 13(2)), visa-free entry (art 14) and entry into the international zone of an airport (art 15). If no responsible state is found under these criteria the state where the asylum application was lodged is responsible for dealing with the claim (art 3(2)).

[64] See in particular recital 5. In this context, 'mutual trust' means that Member States trust each other that every Member State will rigorously adhere to its obligations regarding the treatment and the protection of asylum seekers.

[65] UNHCR, 'UNHCR Comments on the European Commission's Proposal for a Recast of the Regulation of the European Parliament and of the Council Establishing the Criteria and

In practice, the result is a system that is only partly sensitive to human rights concerns. For example, even though the non-functioning of the Greek asylum system was apparent since 2007 and manifestly documented since April 2009, it took until January 2011 before the ECtHR stopped transfers to Greece, leading to a situation where Greece was and is factually exempted from the Dublin system since then.[66] Within the Dublin system there is also a lack of binding positive legal obligations, triggering a legal obligation to act, outside the strict application of the criteria. Human rights-related provisions like the 'dependency clause' (Article 16) only apply as a general rule ('shall normally') or are in principle discretionary like the 'sovereignty clause' and the 'humanitarian clause' (Article 17(1)–(2) of the Dublin III Regulation). Moreover, and of critical importance for the practical implementation of the system, the Court of Justice of the European Union (CJEU) argued in *Bundesrepublik Deutschland v Kaveh Puid* that an obligation to use the sovereignty clause is not foreseen within the Dublin system.[67]

These findings are not applicable to unaccompanied children with no family members within the Dublin area (in general) as the CJEU has found in *MA and Others v Secretary of State for the Home Department*:[68] that for unaccompanied children the reference point for the assessment of responsibility is not the first asylum application pursuant to Article 7(2) of the Dublin III Regulation that determines the responsibility, but the last application according to Article 8(4) of the Dublin III Regulation. The Court found that transfers of unaccompanied minors are generally

Mechanisms for Determining the Member State Responsible for Examining an Application for International Protection Lodged in one of the Member States by a Third Country National or a Stateless Person ("Dublin II") (COM (2008) 820, 3 December 2008) and the European Commission's Proposal for a Recast of the Regulation of the European Parliament and of the Council Concerning the Establishment of "Eurodac" for the Comparison of Fingerprints for the Effective Application of [the Dublin II Regulation] (COM(2008) 825, 3 December 2008)' (18 March 2009), 1. www.refworld.org/docid/49c0ca922.html. This UNHCR statement raises concerns regarding the impact of the system 'on the legal rights and personal welfare of asylum seekers'.

[66] *MSS v Belgium and Greece* App no 30696/09 (ECtHR, 21 January 2011).

[67] Case C-4/11 *Bundesrepublik Deutschland v Kaveh Puid* [2014] OJ C9/2 at 35. The only exception to this principle is a Dublin procedure where the allocation of responsibility would take 'an unreasonable length of time.' In this case the Member State where the person resides 'must itself examine' the application according to the sovereignty clause. This was already the wording of the CJEU in the seminal Greek case: Case C-411/10 and C-493/10 *NS v Secretary of State for the Home Department and ME and Others v Refugee Applications Commissioner and Minister for Justice, Equality and Law Reform* [2011] ECR I-13905. In practice, certain Member States do regularly use the sovereignty clause for humanitarian reasons, but the overall practice is inconsistent.

[68] Case C-648/11 *MA and Others v Secretary of State for the Home Department* [2013] OJ C225/1838. One of the applicants in this case was actually a victim of trafficking.

to be considered as being at variance with the rights of the child. In *Tarakhel v Switzerland*, the ECtHR established the principle that also in family cases where children are involved the compliance with basic human rights standards must be guaranteed prior to a transfer.[69] The Court's reasoning was mainly based on the double vulnerability of the applicants as asylum seekers and children.

B. Challenges for Victims of Trafficking Under the Dublin System

It is apparent that the access of victims of trafficking to the rights enshrined in the international and European framework for their protection is at least not secured from the outset. The only provision in the Dublin III Regulation that explicitly refers to trafficking is Article 6(3)(c), stating that in assessing the best interest of a minor, states shall take due account of safety and security considerations, in particular where there is a risk of the minor being a victim of trafficking.

During our research, we have come across several symptomatic case scenarios of victims of trafficking in Dublin procedures. Without any claim to comprehensiveness, the following case scenarios illustrate the current practice in Dublin Europe.

The most frequent cases seem to be women from Western African countries, mostly Nigeria, who are trafficked to Europe to engage in prostitution. The destination countries are often Italy, Spain or France. If they manage to escape and turn to another European country in search for protection, this usually triggers the application of the Dublin Regulation since the person has been residing in another Dublin Member State. This, however, is problematic because the responsible Dublin State is often also the country where exploitation occurred and where the person may actually be at (greater) risk. The case of 'Joye',[70] an under-age girl from Nigeria who had been trafficked to France, illustrates the dilemma. After her escape, she applied for asylum in Switzerland where she directly turned to the personnel of a reception centre, asking for help against her trafficker, who had been following her and was waiting outside (this is one of the very few cases of self-reporting). The Swiss asylum authorities made enquiries of the French police, but since the trafficker was not known to them, Switzerland started a normal Dublin procedure. As Joye was a minor, a so-called person of trust (a quasi-guardian) was assigned. It was

[69] *Tarakhel v Switzerland* App No 29217/12 (ECtHR, 4 November 2014) (selected for case reports).

[70] Name altered.

only because of the commitment of this person of trust, who made enquiries personally of the French authorities and filed several legal petitions at various levels, that Joye was eventually admitted to the substantial asylum procedure in Switzerland.

A strategy of traffickers to gain access to European territory for their victims is—apart from the use of forged visas—to let them ask for asylum at an airport, instructing them to tell a fake story. After the victims gain access to the territory for the duration of the asylum procedures, they are contacted again by their traffickers and taken to their places of exploitation. These cases are often not identified in time by the respective authorities, even though an accumulation of such cases (persons from the same country of origin, same age and same sex telling the same story) is actually a strong indicator of human trafficking. Such cases usually show in asylum statistics as 'implicitly withdrawn asylum applications' and are to some extent also connected to cases of unaccompanied minors who disappear from reception centres. Some of these persons are later detected during brothel raids or in detention pending removal, often in countries other than that of initial entry.

If another state is responsible for the processing of the asylum claim according to the Dublin criteria, practice between European countries varies. While some countries generally abstain from transferring victims of trafficking to the country of exploitation, even within the Dublin area,[71] other countries still adhere to the 'responsibility logic' of the Dublin system and insist on such transferring the victim to the actually responsible state. We have come across many cases where the only 'protection measure' consisted in handing an information leaflet to the victim with addresses of NGOs in the responsible state.[72]

These case scenarios led us to identify several deficiencies in the practical implementation of the protection framework for victims of trafficking. Some of the factors that contribute to these problems have already been mentioned above in Section II: the prosecution focus ('criminality bias'), the lack of qualified assistance especially at the beginning of the asylum procedure and even more so in its admissibility stages, coupled with the general referral logic in Dublin trafficking cases. Subjective and objective obstacles to identification as detailed in Section III; the factually and legally heightened standards of proof; the unclear role of the burden of proof in Dublin procedures and the recurrent credibility issues around

[71] See EMN, above n 28, 23f.

[72] Most of these cases are not publicly available. In BVGer E-6323/2010 para 6.3.1, the Swiss Federal Administrative Court explicitly stated that the referral to the possibility of asking for assistance of an NGO after the transfer is not sufficient to secure the necessary protection.

victims of trafficking significantly lower the chances of a potential victim being effectively identified and protected in the Dublin system.

To sum up, the chances of effectively challenging a transfer decision at an appeals level are severely lowered for a variety of reasons. These reasons include the focus on self-identification due to the 'asylum logic' (the asylum seeking person is often practically obliged to prove the risk); the use of the unclear notion of 'systemic deficiencies of the asylum system,' which does not seem to comprise serious individual risks such as the ones incurred by trafficking victims; the over-reliance on the partner state and a frequently non-rebuttable presumption of safety of the responsible Member State; a lack of individual assessment of the case in question in line with the administrative or procedural approaches of inadmissibility procedures and the lack of expertise at all levels, including the court level, which is often coupled with the 'Heidi bias.'

C. Reconciling the Frameworks

Starting from the cases that constituted the basis of our analysis,[73] we identified some factors that enhance actual identification and protection of trafficking victims in Dublin procedures. Identification works best if the victim is a woman and/or underage (probably because the stereotypical 'trafficking victim' is female and young), if a guardian is assigned to the applicant and if the procedures are carried out by sensitised personnel. Furthermore, the credibility of the victim is much less questioned by the authorities if a criminal investigation has been opened. Protection of the victim furthermore works best where, in addition to the abovementioned factors, a lawyer or legal advisor is assigned to the victim to help the victim claim her or his rights under the trafficking framework, such as the granting of a recovery and reflection period, rigorous compliance with the *non-refoulement* principle and the effective implementation of the guarantees for trafficking victims in cases of return.

How could—on a practical level—the application of trafficking victim's rights in the Dublin context work? Currently, the access-averse and efficiency-distorted manner in which the Dublin Regulation is applied by many Dublin Member States hinders the incorporation of human rights obligations or best interests oriented approaches for victims of trafficking.

Apart from sensitisation and other measures like training and coaching and the incorporation of expert analysis (see above Section II), there are three legal ways to deal with the issue, which could provide for effective

[73] See above n 13.

victim protection. A reconciliation of the frameworks along the lines of recital 17 of the Dublin III Regulation reminding the Member States of the possibility to derogate from the criteria on compassionate grounds has not worked well so far. It is probably necessary to use binding human rights standards and standards of EU law as an argument.

The first approach would address the level of the asylum authorities of the Member States. It needs to be emphasised in line with the EU directives and the CoE Convention that the positive obligations apply irrespective of the country where the crime was committed and that the main responsibility lies with the state of sojourn. This would actually provide for an entry point for the use the discretionary clauses (sovereignty clause and humanitarian clause) contained in Article 17 of the Dublin III Regulation to prevent transfers. This is currently practised by some Member States and may have the potential to be more widely used.

The second approach draws an analogy to the protection of the rights of children and the *Tarakhel* judgment of the ECtHR.[74] It could be argued that the vulnerability as used in the *Tarakhel* case is a 'legal vulnerability' and therefore refers to enhanced protection under the international human rights regime. This enhanced protection is also provided for victims looking at the standards developed at the international level (see especially Section II above). Therefore, in case of transfers of a potential victim an individual assessment of the best protection is necessary prior to the start of a Dublin procedure.

The third approach argues on the basis of the Dublin III Regulation itself: As the recovery and reflection period for victims of trafficking provides for a legal stay during this period, it contains an authorisation of stay in the respective Member State in the sense of Article 2(l) of the Dublin III Regulation. Any such authorisation results in the transfer of responsibility to the Member State where the applicant currently stays in accordance with Article 19(1) of the Regulation. As the recovery and reflection period is mandatory and must be provided immediately by the detecting Member State,[75] the human rights obligations provide for an automatic responsibility of this state.[76] If this is not in the best interests of the victim, a transfer may be envisaged under the humanitarian clause of Article 17(2) of the Regulation.

It is therefore possible to find legal and practical ways to ensure better victim protection in admissibility procedures in general and in the Dublin

[74] *Tarakhel v Switzerland*, above n 68.

[75] See above Section II.

[76] See Frei, above n 42, 45; F Maiani and C Hruschka, 'Dublin III Regulation' in K Hailbronner and D Thym (eds), *EU Immigration and Asylum Law: Commentary on EU Regulations and Directive* s, 2nd edn (Munich, CH Beck, 2015) art 2(1).

system in particular. The need to establish and to understand the existing human rights framework for the protection of victims of trafficking is especially apparent in these admissibility procedures. Any form of discretion in its application works to the detriment of the protection of the victims.

V. ACCESS TO INTERNATIONAL PROTECTION

Gaining access to the substantial asylum procedure is just one part of gaining access to protection. The human rights framework for victims of trafficking outlined in Section II above shows that victim protection is also relevant with a view to international refugee law. Furthermore, human rights arguments play an essential role in interpreting the refugee definition as well as the conditions for complementary protection in a victim-sensitive way.

A. Refugee Law

Certainly victims of human trafficking may fulfil the criteria for being a refugee, but being a victim of trafficking does not make a person a refugee ipso facto. However, the fact that many victims of trafficking who have escaped their traffickers face a real risk of retaliation or re-trafficking indicates that these persons prima facie have strong grounds to apply for refugee status.[77]

Given the focus of this chapter, our aim is not to provide a comprehensive analysis of refugee status for victims of trafficking, but to mention the most important points. Other authors have already treated this subject in a much broader way.[78] Instead, we will focus on selected topics, namely the definition of 'being persecuted', the Convention ground 'membership of a particular social group', the nexus requirement, and the assessment of state protection upon return to the country of origin. Our point is that

[77] See also Dorevitch and Foster, above n 8, 19.

[78] UNHCR, above n 3; Dorevitch and Foster, above n 8; S Kneebone, 'The Refugee-Trafficking Nexus: Making Good (The) Connections' (2010) 29(1) *Refugee Survey Quarterly* 137; S Kneebone, 'Human Trafficking and Refugee Women' in E Arbel et al (eds), *Gender in Refugee Law* (London, Routledge, 2014) 197; K Saito, 'International Protection for Trafficked Persons and Those Who Fear Being Trafficked' New Issues In Refugee Research, Paper 149, UNHCR, December 2007; TM Christensen, 'Trafficking For Sexual Exploitation: Victim Protection in International and Domestic Asylum Law' New Issues In Refugee Research, Paper 206, UNHCR April 2011; S Juss, 'Human Trafficking, Asylum and the Problem of Protection' in S Juss (ed), *The Ashgate Research Companion to Migration Law, Theory and Policy* (Farnham, Ashgate, 2013) 281; R Piotrowicz, 'Victims of People Trafficking and Entitlement to International Protection' (2005) 24 *Australian Year Book of International* Law 159. From Germany, see Lindner and Janetzek, above n 42. From Switzerland, see Frei (2013) and (2015), above n 42.

the potential of the Refugee Convention in the protection of victims of trafficking is currently not fully developed in state practice.

In order to meet the refugee definition, all the elements of the definition must be fulfilled. Article 1A(2) of the Refugee Convention defines a refugee as a person who, 'owing to well-founded fear of being persecuted for reasons of race, religion, nationality, membership of a particular social group or political opinion, is outside the country of his nationality and is unable or, owing to such fear, is unwilling to avail himself of the protection of that country; or who, not having a nationality and being outside the country of his former habitual residence as a result of such events, is unable or, owing to such fear, is unwilling to return to it.'

Due to the severity of the human rights violation of human trafficking it is rarely disputed that trafficking meets the definition of 'being persecuted'. It is not only the forms of severe exploitation that are inherent in the trafficking experience such as abduction, incarceration, rape, sexual enslavement, enforced prostitution, forced labour, removal of organs, physical beatings, starvation and the deprivation of medical treatment that will generally amount to persecution,[79] but also other types of harm that go along with retaliation, for example (such as physical abuse or destruction of property) or with social exclusion, ostracism or punishment by family that will generally also amount to persecution in the sense of Article 1A of the Refugee Convention.

Persecution needs to be linked to one of the five Convention grounds: race, religion, membership of a particular social group, nationality or political opinion. While victims of trafficking might fulfil any of the five Convention grounds,[80] the most important one is 'membership of a particular social group'. Much has been written about this Convention ground already, also in relation to trafficking.[81] We do not intend to examine in detail the theoretical question of how 'membership' is to be defined. As has been shown elsewhere, victims of trafficking can actually fall under both of these definitions.[82]

In continental European cases, a victim's membership of a particular social group has been accepted, for example, by the Austrian Higher Administrative Court in a case involving a young woman from Nigeria

[79] UNHCR, above n 3, para 15.

[80] ibid paras 33ff.

[81] See S Juss, 'Recognizing Refugee Status for Victims of Trafficking and the Myth of Progress' (2015) 34(2) *Refugee Survey Quarterly* 107.

[82] See Dorevitch and Foster, above n 8; UNHCR, above n 3, paras 37ff. See also most recently CEDAW, 'General Recommendation No 32 on the Gender-related Dimensions of Refugee Status, Asylum, Nationality and Statelessness of Women' (CEDAW/C/GC/32, 14 November 2014) para 45: 'States parties are encouraged to classify victims of trafficking under the 'social group' ground in the refugee definition.'

who had been forced into prostitution in Austria.[83] In a more recent case from France,[84] which also concerned a young woman from Nigeria, the French Asylum Court ruled that she belonged to the social group of 'young female victims of human trafficking originating from Edo State in Nigeria who have tried to escape their condition.'[85] However, these examples do not represent common European practice. Quite on the contrary, jurisprudence varies between different countries as well as sometimes between courts of the same country. In Germany, for example, different courts have either affirmed or denied particular social groups in trafficking cases.[86]

In many cases however, asylum decision-makers do not even assess the membership of a particular social group, because the nexus to a Convention ground is denied beforehand. In fact, since trafficking is often viewed as a purely criminal issue that has no connection to 'real refugees', this is the main obstacle in trafficking cases.[87] For example, in a Swiss case concerning a woman from Nigeria who had been exploited in prostitution in Italy,[88] the Swiss Federal Administrative Court held that 'the allegations of the complainant (forced prostitution, economic exploitation under massive threats) do—regardless of their credibility—not satisfy the requirements of the refugee definition, because they lack a relevant Convention ground. In fact, they are ordinary criminal offences which do not constitute persecution in the sense of refugee law.'[89] In our view, this constitutes a misinterpretation of the nexus requirement, which could be avoided by applying the 'contributing cause' test.[90] This test requires the Convention ground to be a meaningful factor in persecution while also allowing other causal factors (such as greed or revenge) to co-exist. As has been shown above, membership to a particular social group may in many trafficking cases be one determining factor of why victims are targeted and selected for trafficking in the first place.[91]

[83] Austrian Higher Administrative Court (Asylgerichtshof) (C15 263.728-0/2008/25E, 14 May 2009).

[84] French National Asylum Court (Cour Nationale du Droit d'Asile) (No 10012810, 14 March 2015).

[85] ibid para 9. The original wording in French is: 'son appartenance au groupe social constitué des jeunes femmes victimes de la traite des êtres humains originaires de l'Etat d'Edo qui ont tenté de s'extraire de leur condition.'

[86] eg Administrative Court (Verwaltungsgericht) Wiesbaden (3 K 1465/09.WI.A, 14 March 2011) 12 (affirmed); Administrative Court (Verwaltungsgericht) Gelsenkirchen (9a K 3963/11.A, 15 March 2013) para 25ff (denied).

[87] See also above Section III on the 'criminality bias'.

[88] Swiss Federal Administrative Court (Bundesverwaltungsgericht) (D-5071/2011, 20 September 2011).

[89] ibid 7.

[90] See JC Hathaway, 'International Refugee Law: The Michigan Guidelines on Nexus to a Convention Ground' (2002) 23(2) *Michigan Journal of International Law* 210, para 13.

[91] See UNHCR, above n 3, para 31; Dorevitch and Foster, above n 8, 37ff.

The final obstacle to refugee protection for victims of trafficking that will be highlighted here is the requirement of absence of state protection. In most cases, the perpetrators of trafficking are private individuals like criminal networks or family members. In this case, we need to assess whether state protection would be available, that is, would the state be willing or able to grant protection to the victim upon return. The availability and quality of state protection is one of the most difficult elements to assess in trafficking asylum claims, basically because no state is able to completely eradicate trafficking—even in countries with a good human rights record the numbers of trafficked persons are high.

The UNHCR suggests that the Trafficking Protocol, which requires states to take steps with regard to protection of victims, could be of guidance when assessing the adequacy of state protection for victims of trafficking.[92] However, the Trafficking Protocol's protection provisions are formulated in a non-binding language, leaving discretion to states as to whether they want to implement the provisions and, if so, in what way, and does not therefore constitute the basis for a binding protection standard. Furthermore, the Trafficking Protocol appears fragmentary when compared to human rights jurisprudence relating to victims of trafficking or even to the CoE Convention. In our view, state protection in a given home country has to be measured against the human rights framework for victims of trafficking outlined above.[93] As a second step, it is necessary to assess whether the identified state protection is also available to the individual concerned. An individual assessment of the availability and accessibility of the state protection concludes the assessment of the state protection.[94]

B. Complementary Protection

Victims of trafficking who do not fall under the definition of refugee within the Refugee Convention might benefit from *refoulement* protection based on human rights grounds. In assessing the harm victims of trafficking might face upon return, it also needs to be taken in account that victims of trafficking prima facie have strong grounds to apply for human rights protection.

The most important and universally accepted human rights ground against *refoulement* is the prohibition of torture, inhuman or degrading treatment or punishment which is laid down in Article 7 of the ICCPR,[95]

92 UNHCR, above n 3, para 22.

93 See Section II.

94 Hathaway and Foster, above n 54, 330.

95 HRC, 'General Comment No 20: Article 7 (Prohibition of Torture, or Other Cruel, Inhuman or Degrading Treatment or Punishment)' (44th Session, 10 March 1992) para 9.

Article 3 of CAT[96] and (on the European level) Article 3 of the ECHR.[97] It has been noted elsewhere that trafficking and the harm that goes with it upon return of a victim, such as re-trafficking, retaliation or punishment and stigmatisation or social exclusion will in many cases amount to torture or at least inhuman or degrading treatment.[98] Returning a person to a place where the person faces a real risk of being subjected to such treatment would therefore constitute a violation of the *non-refoulement* principle. As discussed above in Section II, recent jurisprudence of the ECtHR indicates furthermore that Article 4 of the ECHR, the prohibition of slavery, servitude and forced labour, including trafficking, may also be a ground for *refoulement* protection.

VI. SOLUTIONS

The analysis of the challenges in the three areas, namely 'identification of victims of trafficking in asylum procedures', 'admissibility procedures' and 'substantial asylum procedure', has shown that access of victims of trafficking to asylum—both to the procedure and to substantial protection—remains a challenge for multiple reasons. Given all these shortcomings, we will go on to consider potential solutions to ensure effective victim protection in asylum systems under a human rights-based approach.

First and foremost, it is important to establish a two-fold protection logic: asylum *and* victim of trafficking protection, where the two frameworks are not seen as isolated, separated procedures. Quite on the contrary, both frameworks influence each other. On the one hand, asylum and the asylum procedure are important identification and protection tools in the fight against human trafficking. On the other hand, the anti-trafficking framework is also applicable in the asylum procedure and leads to favourable treatment of victims who have applied for asylum.

Some prerequisites for a functioning system of victim protection have been identified in the course of our analysis. They include:

- the incorporation of sensitisation measures;
- targeted training and expert knowledge into the work of the asylum authorities in general and in particular the availability of these measures for decision-makers and frontline staff;

[96] Convention against Torture and Other Cruel, Inhuman or Degrading Treatment or Punishment [1987] United Nations Treaty Series 1465, 85.

[97] See *Soering v UK* App no 14038/88 (ECtHR, 7 July 1989).

[98] Stoyanova, above n 41, 791ff; U Jayasinghe and S Baglay, 'Protecting Victims of Human Trafficking Within a "Non-Refoulement" Framework: is Complementary Protection an Effective Alternative in Canada and Australia?' (2011) 23 (3) *International Journal of Refugee Law* 489; Piotrowicz, above n 78, 177; AL Seaman, 'Permanent Residency for Human Trafficking Victims in Europe: The Potential Use of Article 3 of the European Convention as a Means of Protection' (2009) 48 *Columbia Journal of Transnational Law* 287, 316.

- the emphasis on establishing physical and psychological safety by mandatorily applying the recovery and reflection period foreseen in the European protection framework;
- the assessment of the best protection solution for the victim, inter alia by taking into account the views of the person concerned;
- the refraining—as a rule—from transferring victims of trafficking to another state under responsibility-sharing agreements, for example, by using the legal provisions of the Dublin III Regulation in a protection sensitive way;
- taking a human-rights sensitive and protection-oriented interpretation of the Refugee Convention in its application to trafficking cases and the use of a similar approach to complementary forms of protection.

We believe that the best way to protect victims of trafficking in asylum procedures is a 'clearing procedure' similar to procedures already in place for unaccompanied minor applicants. This system would aim to assess whether an international protection procedure meets the individual protection and other needs of the victim. The model would be characterised by a multidisciplinary approach, meaning that it would include different actors, such as the asylum authorities, victim support organisations, lawyers or legal advisors and of course the victim herself or himself. Importantly, this model should also involve legal advice for the victim, as soon as she or he is detected (not necessarily identified conclusively) as such.

As a first step in such a clearing procedure, the person concerned should be provided with the necessary information on the potential options (procedures, housing, etc), legal assistance for his or her procedure and counselling to assess immediate physical and psychological protection needs. Subsequently, the recovery and reflection should be granted and conducted in a way that serves its purposes. At the end of the recovery and reflection period, the law enforcement agency, asylum and other migration authorities and legal and social counsel of the victim should then exchange views on the best possible solution for victim protection. This analysis would particularly include a pre-assessment of the outcome of a potential protection procedure, the necessity and willingness of the victim to act as a witness in potential criminal proceedings (including the question of whether the person would need to be placed in a witness protection programme) and other options, including a potential return to another state. Such a clearing procedure should ideally be concluded before any decisive steps on the right to stay on the territory are carried out.

13

States, the Law and Access to Refugee Protection

Concluding Reflections

DALLAL STEVENS AND MARIA O'SULLIVAN

I. INTRODUCTION

AS HAS BEEN evident for many years, and was brought into particularly strong focus in 2015, there is a paradox at the heart of refugee law and policy.[1] On the one hand, many states are party to international human rights law treaties and to the Refugee Convention/Protocol and ostensibly commit to upholding high standards; on the other, they have long sought to restrict entry, limit the number of asylum seekers and refugees, reduce the cost and time of refugee status determination (RSD), and minimise their obligations to protection seekers. With the worldwide need for refugee protection far outstripping the protection places offered by states, and, with the quality of protection often seriously wanting, the aim of this collection was to explore a particular aspect of refugee protection: access to justice. An important objective of the collection was to provide comparative, as well as academic and practitioner, perspectives and the contributions have consequently focused on a range of concerns in several jurisdictions, including Australia, Bosnia and Herzegovina and Croatia, the European Union (EU), Lebanon, South Africa, Turkey and the United States (US).

In Chapter 1, we defined access to justice broadly as access to territory and access to a quality asylum procedure. With this is mind, a number of chapters considered the ongoing concern of physical access to asylum,

[1] See for a recent discussion of some of the paradoxes of refugee law and policy, S Kneebone, D Stevens and L Baldassar, *Refugee Protection and the Role of Law: Conflicting Identities* (Abingdon, Routledge, 2014) especially chs 1 and 14.

while others focused on questions of access to process that, to date, have not been sufficiently discussed in the literature—for example, the components of a quality asylum procedure; the significance of good legal advice for access to asylum justice; the consequences of accelerated 'screening' procedures; and the use of fast tracking of asylum applications. As the analysis reveals, many countries are restricting access to both territory and to due process with increasingly brutal consequences.

In these concluding reflections, we highlight some of the key findings in relation to access to justice.

II. ACCESS TO TERRITORY

Access to territory has been restricted in two key ways—physically and legally. Physical impediments—such as fences and interdiction at sea—are usually easy to identify and have been on the rise in recent years. The most striking example is that of Australia, where the authorities have employed interdiction at sea for 15 years, with growing force and harmful consequences. The use of this practice and the conduct of truncated screening at sea has the clear aim of ensuring that 'irregular migrants', be they refugees or 'economic migrants', who seek entry to Australia by boat will be prevented from succeeding. The 'significant due process concerns',[2] namely the inability of a refugee to gain access to a robust, fair and effective determination process, is extremely worrying. Yet, the status quo has been upheld in the High Court of Australia, which found that procedural fairness did not apply to interdicted asylum seekers on the high seas (O'Sullivan, Chapter 5).[3] Effectively, asylum seekers trying to reach Australia are not only at the mercy of the sea but also of a process and approach to natural justice that consigns them to a form of legal exceptionalism.

In contrast to Australia, the principle of *non-refoulement* is theoretically extremely strong in the EU, either through its place in legislation or on account of case law, especially that of the European Court of Human Rights (ECtHR). Pollet (Chapter 7) discusses the introduction of the EU Regulation on Maritime External Border Surveillance and the deployment of Frontex and Member States' naval assistance to search and rescue. At least as far as interdiction in the Central Mediterranean is concerned, it appears to be preventing whole-scale removal of vessels from European

[2] O'Sullivan, ch 5, Section IV.

[3] *CPCF v Minister for Immigration and Border Protection & Anor* [2015] HCA 1, 28 January 2015, www.refworld.org/docid/54c8be3c4.html.

or extra-European waters, and rescues are taking place, with a seeming opportunity to apply for asylum. What is not being realised is an end to the death-toll at sea. The association of the border with death is not new, but the rhetoric surrounding such deaths has altered over time. While Australia has been at the forefront of a 'stop the boats' policy, which claims to be focused on 'saving lives', the EU's drive to adopt search and rescue practices has met with variable success. More worryingly, deaths at sea continue to occur, with 3,171 reported dead or missing in the Mediterranean between 1 January 2016 and 1 September 2016.[4] The danger and knowledge of the risk of dying do not appear to act as the deterrent that states might envisage.

With Australia's use of Nauru or Papua New Guinea (PNG) to process unauthorised maritime arrivals (O'Sullivan, Chapter 5), and the EU's recent EU–Turkey 'deal', which allows for returns of any nationality crossing without permission from Turkey to Greece,[5] there are serious questions about the failures of protection and compliance with human rights standards (Pollet, Chapter 7; Soykan, Chapter 4). The externalisation of refugee determination and asylum, while meeting the politically motivated migration restriction objectives of the Global North, are failing both protection seekers and the (often less developed) states to where they are sent. The conditions in Nauru and PNG are extremely controversial, with reports of abuse, attempted suicide and depression in detention centres.[6] Medical staff assigned to the island of Nauru have resigned in protest.[7] Children are reported as being severely traumatised but the Australian Government remains unmoved. The presumption of safety of Turkey, which is at the heart of the EU agreement, is equally contentious. The Greek Appeals Committee has ruled in over 55 cases that Syrians could not be returned to Turkey; in only two cases was return agreed and these

[4] www.missingmigrants.iom.int/Mediterranean.

[5] Syrians arriving are subject to a 'one in, one out' policy where for every Syrian returned to Turkey, another will be accepted by the EU. The 'deal' was agreed on 18 March 2016 and came into effect on 20 March: www.consilium.europa.eu/en/press/press-releases/2016/03/18-eu-turkey-statement/. On 4 April 2016, the first group comprising Pakistanis and Afghans was returned to Turkey.

[6] See, eg, C Fleay and S Hoffman, 'Despair as a Governing Strategy: Australia and the Offshore Processing of Asylum Seekers' (2014) 33 *Refugee Survey Quarterly* 2, 1–19; M Grewcock, 'Australian Border Policing and the Production of State Harm' in G Barak (ed), *The Routledge International Handbook of the Crimes of the Powerful* (Abingdon, Routledge, 2015) ch 23; A Dastyari and M O'Sullivan, 'Not for Export: The Failure of Australia's Extraterritorial Processing Regime in Papua New Guinea and the Decision of the PNG Supreme Court in Namah' (2016) 42 (2) *Monash University Law Review* (forthcoming); M O'Sullivan, 'What's Next for Asylum Seekers Under a Re-elected Turnbull Government?', *The Conversation*, 16 July 2016, www.theconversation.com/whats-next-for-asylum-seekers-under-a-re-elected-turnbull-government-62357.

[7] B Doherty and D Marr, 'The Worst I've Seen—Trauma Expert Lifts Lid on "Atrocity" of Australia's Detention Regime', The Guardian, 19 June 2016.

are now subject to further appeal. The cynical response of the EU has been to demand the establishment of new appeals committees with a different judicial composition.[8] In addition, Greece is feeling the strain of 57,000 persons of concern effectively trapped in the country following border closures. Reception centres on the islands are overflowing; there is desperate understaffing, a barely functioning registration system, lack of suitable trained lawyers, and unacceptable living conditions on the mainland. The victims are, inevitably, asylum seekers and refugees.

While Australia is a stark reminder of a state's power to exclude and shift responsibility for access to protection to others that are often less well-resourced or able to meet human rights standards, other countries have many more visible barriers to entry than interdiction at sea. The US, for example, has militarised its border with Mexico placing at further risk vulnerable individuals from Central America who are fleeing violence and persecution. Like those travelling across open waters, Central Americans face many dangers in trying to cross the border, including death and deportation (Morgan and Anker, Chapter 6). Referring to her empirical research, Soykan critiques the Turkish approach in Chapter 4, an aspect of which is the long-term practice of forced return of Afghans to Iran. The EU land borders have, too, become sites of confrontation and potential push backs, as Pollet describes in Chapter 7 in his assessment of EU policy and as noted by Soykan in Chapter 4 in the context of Turkey. Access has been prevented by both the rapid construction of fences, an example of which is evident on the Hungarian–Serbian border, and by the behaviour of border guards, who appear, at times, to ignore the obligations on states to identify protection seekers and provide access to fair and individual refugee determination procedures, as required by the ECtHR judgment, *Hirsi Jamaa and Others v Italy* (Pollet, Chapter 7; Iván, Chapter 3).[9] Research on South Africa also provides evidence that potential asylum applicants from Zimbabwe are being refused entry at the South Africa–Zimbabwe border on the basis of a questionable interpretation of the so-called 'safe country of origin' concept; one possible consequence is *refoulement* (Johnson and Carciotto, Chapter 8). Finally, Lebanon has used a change in the immigration rules to all but close its borders to Syrians in the face of overwhelming numbers and is also ostensibly in breach of the *non-refoulement* principle (Stevens, Chapter 10).

[8] See, eg, E Zalan, 'EU Pushes Greece to Set up New Asylum Committees', *EU Observer*, 15 June 2016: www.euobserver.com/migration/133841; P Kingsley and A Fotiadis, 'Greece Sidelines Officials who Blocked Expulsion of Refugees to Turkey' The Guardian, 17 June 2016: www.theguardian.com/world/2016/jun/17/greece-sidelines-officials-blocked-expulsion-refugees-turkey.

[9] *Hirsi Jamaa and Others v Italy* App no 27765/09 (ECtHR, 23 February 2012).

The case-studies considered in this book reveal very clearly that states are often aware of their domestic and international law obligations but choose nonetheless to ignore or side-step such obligations. This manifests in the construction of physical impediments, such as walls and fences, but also through legal measures or the interpretation of law.

III. ACCESS TO ASYLUM PROCEDURES

Despite decades of thinly disguised *non-entrée* policies, which seek to deter protection seekers from embarking on their journeys or to bar their entry at the border, these actions have been deemed insufficient in affecting motivations to migrate or controlling numbers. States have therefore resorted to law and internal measures as a means by which to restrict entry and limit claimants. They have been assisted in these aims by the media, which has portrayed those on the move in pejorative and vindictive terms, and with little appreciation of important legal distinctions, such as that between 'migrant' and 'refugee' (El-Enany, Chapter 2). The issue for El-Enany is that the language of migration can have a dehumanising effect and may be part of the state's exercise of power. States themselves are apt to ignore legal terminology for political purposes, as in the case of Lebanon, which has resisted the politically loaded term 'refugee' and its association with Palestinians, preferring the regional and cultural nomenclature of 'guest' (Stevens, Chapter 10).

Porobić and Župarić-Iljić (Chapter 9) provide a compelling account of two countries in the Western Balkans—Croatia and Bosnia and Herzegovina—that are relatively new to asylum seeking, both in terms of quantity of asylum applications and the existence/quality of RSD procedures. Despite the best efforts of the EU to encourage harmonisation of asylum law and policy, we find problematic design and implementation of a fair and effective asylum regime and, in this case, a shift in responsibility for protection from the state to civil society and the UNHCR. Rejection rates are high as is the use of detention. Applicants have experienced 'stripping of rights', poor conditions and isolation and in this sense mirror, to a lesser or greater degree, the circumstances of asylum seekers and refugees in many countries explored in this collection. Hungary, too—though it has opted into the recast Common European Asylum System (CEAS) legislation, which seeks to incorporate additional protections for claimants (Pollet, Chapter 7)—is also able to use the law to support a very hard line. Thus, Hungary has elected to apply extremely accelerated processes, which raise concerns that the claims are not being examined appropriately (Iván, Chapter 3; Pollet, Chapter 7). Further, since the summer of 2015, there have been large-scale returns to Serbia, which the authorities regard as 'safe'. New restrictions came into force in July 2016 that 'extend border controls to an eight-kilometre area inside Hungarian territory and authorize the police to intercept people within this area and send them to the other side of the fence, often to remote areas without adequate services'[10]—hardly a good example of permitting access to a fair in-country status determination procedure. Another relatively young asylum system outside the EU territory—that of South Africa—has also clearly endorsed the rhetoric of 'asylum abuse' to limit access to asylum (Johnson and Carciotto, Chapter 8). The authors quote directly from the ANC's 2012 policy document that makes no attempt to disguise its viewpoint:

> Over 95% of applicants of those claiming asylum in SA are not genuine asylum seekers but rather looking for work or business opportunities ... who are allowed to earn a living while awaiting adjudication of their applications, ... with appeals that can take many months. While awaiting the outcome of their applications, many applicants endeavour to regularize their stay through other means ... which are often fraudulent.[11]

The response, similar to that of EU countries, is to turn to 'first country of asylum' and 'safe third country' 'rules'. Parallels with legal developments and policy-making in the 1990s in the United Kingdom (UK) are startling.[12]

Nascent systems are not alone in their flaws and restrictions to access. Many well-established asylum procedures, such as those of the UK, continue to be subject to widespread criticism. Asylum claimants who reach the territory of an EU country such as the UK often find themselves forced into a process that stretches considerably the notion of fairness and justice. The drive for detailed common standards of the CEAS has not prevented the simultaneous drive by states to restrict asylum (see Pollet, Chapter 7). For example, the UK's use of detention in certain asylum cases has recently fallen foul of the courts. While detention of asylum claimants and accelerated procedures are countenanced by the CEAS directives, national implementation can render their usage harmful. This has proved to be the case of the UK. Following an interesting litany of legal challenges, the UK Government has been forced to suspend the so-called Detained Fast Track system (DFT), used where authorities believe an asylum claim can be decided 'quickly'. This was due to the DFT's considerable failings and the courts' disapproving assessment that fairness and justice were being sacrificed in favour of speed and efficiency (Kirk, Chapter 11). That the UK has long employed the DFT, despite the misgivings of academics and

[10] UNHCR, 'UNHCR Concerned Hungary Pushing Asylum Seekers Back to Serbia', 15 July 2016.

[11] ibid 5.

[12] See for discussion of UK policy of the 1990s and early 2000s, D Stevens, *UK Asylum Law and Policy: Historical and Contemporary Perspectives* (London, Sweet & Maxwell, 2004).

practitioners, is testament to the power of law and the authority of government to override basic principles of justice.

Frei and Hruschka (Chapter 12) poignantly describe the impact of procedures on the individual and the significant impediments to access to justice that can arise. They detail the many challenges confronting victims of trafficking in the EU and Switzerland, focusing in particular on identification of potential victims of trafficking, their residency rights and treatment, and the risks of *refoulement*. They also raise concerns regarding the Dublin Regulation and the difficulties of preventing a Dublin transfer in relation to trafficking cases, even where the transfer is to the country of exploitation. Elsewhere—for example in Turkey and Lebanon (Chapters 4 and 10), the suffering can be extreme. The lack of law on asylum, in the case of Lebanon, and the use of special arrangements under law, in the adoption of a temporary protection framework for Syrians in Turkey,[13] both create a situation of extreme vulnerability to poverty, despair, abuse and exploitation. The fact that these countries are all party to a range of human rights instruments and, in most cases, to the Refugee Convention does not minimise the harm suffered.

IV. CONCLUSION

The global sharing of practices is very evident from the jurisdictions discussed in this collection. From closure or militarisation of borders, safe country of origin, first country of asylum and safe third country 'principles' (Hungary, Chapter 3; South Africa, Chapter 8; EU Member States, Chapter 7; Bosnia and Herzegovina and Croatia, Chapter 9; Lebanon, Chapter 10, the US, Chapter 6) to fast tracking processes and increased obsession with securitisation (Hungary, Chapter 3; Turkey, Chapter 4; the US, Chapter 6; Australia and the UK, Chapter 11), the outcome is rarely enhanced protection for vulnerable individuals. Many of the chapters have shown that the conditions confronted by people on the move are dire. In a landmark case on procedural protections for asylum seekers, the English and Welsh Court of Appeal stated that it is not entitled to 'sacrifice fairness on the altar of speed and convenience'.[14] Whilst this was a damning indictment of asylum practices, it is some way removed from the widespread failure to treat people in a humane and rights-compliant

[13] Turkey is party to the Refugee Convention but exercises the geographical limitation to Europe under art 1B. See Soykan, ch 4.

[14] *R (Refugee Legal Centre) v SSHD* [2004] EWCA Civ 1481, para 8, quoted in Kirk, ch 11.

manner to which they are entitled.[15] Indeed, it is not too extreme to suggest that many states appear to be intentionally reinforcing the vulnerability of protection seekers and constructing *refoulement* with specific aims in mind: deterrence and to encourage 'voluntary return'.[16] Considerable evidence points to this conclusion: the fact that Lebanese authorities issue deportation orders to Syrians who have failed to renew their residence permits, but rarely carry out deportation; the reports of Syrians trapped on Lesbos and other islands so desperate that some have attempted to swim back to Greece;[17] the 'reverse smuggling' and voluntary returns of disillusioned and despondent Syrian and Iraqi asylum applicants in Germany and Finland;[18] the traumatic conditions in detention/reception in Greece, Nauru and Manus Island; the abandonment of people in border areas, such as between Hungary and Serbia, Jordan and Syria, Turkey and Syria; and the exploitation and impoverishment of refugees in Lebanon and Turkey, forcing many to undertake further dangerous migrations, in search of an opportunity to live a peaceful, safe and fulfilled life—that is, to live a life of dignity. There is much work to be done globally if these trends are to be reversed and faith restored in asylum and refugee protection, but this will require considerable political courage and will.

[15] See for further discussion, D Stevens, The Humaneness of EU Asylum Law and Policy' in D Kostakopoulou and N Ferreira (eds), *The Human Face of the European Union: Is EU Law and Policy Humane Enough?* (Cambridge, Cambridge University Press, 2016).

[16] See Stevens, ch 10 and, in relation to Lebanon, N Saghieh, 'Manufacturing Vulnerability in Lebanon: Legal Policies as Efficient Tools of Discrimination', *The Legal Agenda*, 19 March 2015.

[17] Information provided by Efi Latsoudi, Social Worker on Lesbos, at conference *Europa an der Grenze: Die Krise unde die Zukunft des Flüchtlingsschutzes*, Berlin, 20–21 June 2016.

[18] Data from interviews undertaken by D Stevens and co-investigators as part of ESRC-funded research project *Crossing the Mediterranean Sea by Boat: Mapping and Documenting Migratory Journeys and Experiences*: www2.warwick.ac.uk/fac/soc/pais/research/researchcentres/irs/crossingthemed/; 'Many Iraqis Abandon Finnish Asylum Process to Return Home', *Al Arabiya English*, 22 January 2016.

Index